Teachers in the Movies

ALSO BY ANN C. PAIETTA

Saints, Clergy and Other Religious Figures on Film and Television, 1895–2003 (2005, McFarland)

Access Services: A Handbook (1991, McFarland)

Teachers in the Movies

A Filmography of Depictions of Grade School, Preschool and Day Care Educators, 1890s to the Present

ANN C. PAIETTA

McFarland & Company, Inc., Publishers
Jefferson, North Carolina, and London

LIBRARY OF CONGRESS CATALOGUING-IN-PUBLICATION DATA

Paietta, Ann Catherine, 1956–
　　Teachers in the movies : a filmography of depictions of grade school, preschool and day care educators, 1890s to the present / Ann C. Paietta.
　　　　p.　　cm.
　　Includes bibliographical references and index.

　　ISBN-13: 978-0-7864-2938-7
　　softcover : 50# alkaline paper ∞

　　1. Teachers in motion pictures.　2. Education in motion pictures. 3. Motion pictures — Catalogs.　I. Title.
PN1995.9.T4P35　　2007
791.43'6557 — dc22   2007028488

British Library cataloguing data are available

©2007 Ann C. Paietta. All rights reserved

No part of this book may be reproduced or transmitted in any form or by any means, electronic or mechanical, including photocopying or recording, or by any information storage and retrieval system, without permission in writing from the publisher.

On the cover: Gérard Jugnot (center) and Jean-Baptiste Maunier (right) in the 2004 film *The Chorus* (Miramax/Photofest)

Manufactured in the United States of America

McFarland & Company, Inc., Publishers
　Box 611, Jefferson, North Carolina 28640
　　www.mcfarlandpub.com

TABLE OF CONTENTS

Introduction 1

Abbreviations 5

THE FILMOGRAPHY 7

Bibliography 225

Subject Index 229

Introduction

The on-screen depictions of educators of young children — teachers, tutors, day care workers, nannies, governesses, and others — date back to the very beginnings of motion pictures. Films drew on everyday life as well as history, drama, and literature for their story ideas.

Cinema is a powerful medium in the world today. Sometimes it is difficult to judge when a film reflects its society and when a film affects its society. Watching a movie can have more of an impact than reading a book, especially in this digital age when people claim they do not have enough time for reading. Many believe that the ways in which educators are portrayed in popular culture contribute to the shaping of the public's image of educators.

This filmography takes an international look at educators of the young in the cinematic world. Today, thanks to DVDs, satellite dishes, and other technologies, such as internet downloading, it is possible to view films from around the world in your own living room.

Films about the teaching occupation differ from those about the legal profession and the health care profession in that we rarely see the teacher in the classroom. We may only know that the character is a teacher, whereas with we frequently see lawyers in the courtroom and doctors in the operating room. Often teachers feel that their profession does not get the respect from filmmakers that other professions do.

Teachers in the Movies includes films in which all we know about the teacher professionally is that he or she *is* a teacher. Even this basic knowledge can give the viewer some insight on how the teacher is or was perceived by society.

Another observation about educators in films is that despite the probability that there are more elementary school teachers than secondary school teachers, most films with a teacher are set in high schools. Typically when teachers in films are discussed, the focus is on high school teachers, with a few exceptions. This book predominantly includes films where the educator deals with younger children. Scriptwriters probably have an easier job writing about violent behavior, sexual tensions, or family crises than about teaching younger children, which removes sexual tension from the classroom — and sex and violence sell movie tickets.

Two recent films, *Half Nelson* (294) and *Akeelah and the Bee* (9), focus on the relationships between students and teachers and both were praised. Ryan Gosling, the lead actor in *Half Nelson* (294), was nominated for an Academy Award for his role in the film in 2007. Two other actors playing cinematic teachers, Robert Donat as Mr. Chips (278) and Maggie Smith as Miss Jean Brodie (582), won Oscars.

The teaching profession has a long history in motion pictures. Educators have been the subject of films since the 1890s. For example, students terrorized their teachers in 1898 in *The Katzenjammer Kids in School* (379) and *The Teacher's Unexpected Bath* (722). In the cinematic classroom, an educator may perform any number of roles for a student — mentor, friend, social worker, spiritual guide, substitute parent, adversary or butt of a joke. The educator as a character is at home in all types of films, in all types of genres — westerns, mysteries, comedies or horror. One recurring female teacher-detective was Hildegarde Withers, a character who solved many murders such as in *The Plot Thickens* (577).

One common theme is the teacher as a catalyst for change in people or environment. Teachers may prompt others to question authority, change their lives for the better, or switch professions. For example, in many westerns, the female teacher encourages the man in her life to become a better man. In many foreign films, the teacher makes positive changes in the lives of her students or neighbors. Sometimes a false accusation or questionable circumstances related to a perceived sexual encounter or misunderstanding is enough to end a teacher's career. For example, in *The Man Without a Face* (446), a male student fixates on the male teacher, leading to an automobile accident in which the student is killed and the teacher is disfigured and disgraced. Two other examples are *These Three* (727) and its remake *The Children's Hour* (139).

Teachers in film have been portrayed positively and negatively. The good teacher is loving, compassionate, knowledgeable, and is cast in a favorable, almost superhuman light. She is inspiring, a self-sacrificing person who gives all of herself to her students, and is found in movies like *The Miracle Worker* (476), *The Corn Is Green* (155), *Feng Huang Qin* (241), and *Chen Yi-Shin lao shi* (131). The good teacher may not always be loved by her students. Good teachers also realize that they can learn as much from their students as their students can from them. In some films, teachers are portrayed as very real human beings who must work hard to teach their students.

Other films depict teachers negatively. The hapless, useless, or meek teacher may be plotted against by his students in movies such as *Child's Play* (140). A teacher may be powerless or play an adversarial role toward the student. Then there is the evil teacher, not uncommon in films; we see, for instance, the particularly sadistic Mr. Jonas in *How Green Was My Valley* (333). Sometimes we see good versus evil: One good teacher is challenged or threatened by evil or incompetent teachers or administrators.

The female teacher in films really does mirror society's perception of her. For years, teaching was among the few professions accepted as careers for women in life and film. In older films, the spinster schoolmarm seemed to be looking for a man; if she hadn't found her match, she became a mother to her students and adjusted herself to this noble cause. Often the female teacher is widowed and has children, as in *The King and I* (385). Even though other occupations opened up for women, films still stereotyped female teachers as unable to balance a successful career and private life, and forced them to choose one over the over. For example, in *Looking for Mr. Goodbar* (419), Theresa searches for love in very dangerous places at night while she is an excellent teacher during the day.

The schoolmaster is also shown as a timid, disorderly dreamer who is tied to his mother's apron strings, yet he proves, in a moment of crisis, that he has the courage to do the right thing. Examples include *This Land Is Mine* (732) and *Zbabelec* (829). One film that differs from this trend is *Dark Command* (176), in which a male teacher despises being just a teacher. Eventually his bitterness leads to his corruption and death. Typically, female teachers are more likely to be seen teaching younger or disabled children, but you do see male teachers take on that challenge in *Ça Commence Aujourd' hui* (116) and *Chiedo asito* (135). Imposters appear quite regularly, and are usually males impersonating teachers as in *Kindergarten Cop* (384). Sometimes the imposter does a better job than the real teacher, as in *Things Are Looking Up* (729). Films like these may lead to the misconception that anyone can teach.

Films also feature other educators besides the traditional schoolteacher; nannies, governesses, tutors, and day care workers all perform the educator role for the young child. We see quite a few evil nannies, as in *The Nanny* (507) with Bette Davis.

This book focuses on films where the educator works in a day care center, preschool, orphanage, public or private school with elementary and middle school age children, or a boarding school or one-room school with mixed ages. High schools have been excluded.

More than 800 films from around the world are described in this book. With this sampling, you will become more informed about the long history of preschool, elementary and middle school educator in the movies.

The Organization of the Book

The selected films fall into one of these three categories:

1. An educator plays a prominent role in the film.
2. A character poses as an educator.
3. The educator works or has worked with preschool, elementary, and middle school age children. High school teachers are not generally included.

Included in this book are theatrical films (both U.S. and foreign releases) from the 1890s through 2006, and made-for-television films. U.S. government films and documentaries are excluded.

The entries provide credits, annotations, and a brief description of the plot and the educator(s). The titles are arranged alphabetically. Foreign-language releases are alphabetized under their original title; translated English titles appear as cross-references. The films are serially numbered from 1 to 831.

The annotated bibliography lists relevant articles and books on educators in films and on television.

Abbreviations

AA	Allied Artists
AB	Associated British
ABC	American Broadcasting Corporation
ABPC	Associated British Picture Corporation
AIP	American International Pictures
B&D	British and Dominions Film Corporation
BBC	British Broadcasting Corporation
BFI	British Film Institute
BIP	British International Pictures
BL	British Lion Film Corporation
B&W	Black and White
C	Color
CBS	Columbia Broadcasting System
EMI	Electrical and Musical Industries
FBO	Film Booking Offices
FN	First National Pictures
GFD	General Film Distributors
HBO	Home Box Office
HMO	Health Maintenance Organization
IFD	Independent Film Distributors
m	Minutes
MGM	Metro-Goldwyn-Mayer
NBC	National Broadcasting Corporation
PBS	Public Broadcasting System
RFD	Rank Film Distributors
RKO	Radio-Keith-Orpheum
TCF	20th Century-Fox
TV	Television
UA	United Artists Film Corporation
UFA	Universum Film Aktiengesellschaft
UI	Universal International Pictures
US	United States

THE FILMOGRAPHY

Abandoned see *Torzók*

1. *Absolution*

Father Goddard (Richard Burton) is a stern, devout priest-teacher at a Catholic boarding school for boys. Two resentful and malicious students use the secrecy of the confessional to drive him to an unwitting killing. The film was completed in 1979 but shelved until 1981.

Enterprise Pictures. Great Britain. 1979. 95m. C. *Producers:* Elliott Kastner, Danny O'Donovan *Director:* Anthony Page *Writer:* Anthony Shaffer *Cast:* Richard Burton, Dominic Guard, David Bradley, Billy Connolly, Andrew Keir, Willoughby Gray, Preston Lockwood, James Ottaway, Brook Williams, Jon Plowman

2. *According to Mrs. Hoyle*

Retired schoolteacher Mrs. Hoyle (Spring Byington) lives in a hotel run by criminals, and becomes involved by spreading her own sweetness.

Monogram. US. 1951. 59m. B&W. *Director:* Jean Yarbrough *Writers:* W. Scott Darling, Barney Gerard *Cast:* Spring Byington, Anthony Caruso, Brett King, Tanis Chandler, Stephen Chase, Robert Karnes, Tristram Coffin

3. *The Acorn People*

An unemployed English teacher takes a job as a counselor at a summer camp for severely disabled children.

NBC. US. 1981. 100m. C. *Producer:* Peter Katz *Writer-Director:* Joan Tewkesbury *Cast:* Ted Bessell, Cloris Leachman, Dolph Sweet, Cheryl Anderson, LeVar Burton, Shawn Timothy Kennedy, Mark Gear, Tim Stone

4. *Adam Had Four Sons*

Emilie is hired as governess for the sons of wealthy Adam and Molly Stoppard. After Molly dies, the boys need Emilie even more. Emilie falls in love with

Adam, who insists that Emilie stay on as part of the family.
Columbia. US. 1941. 81m. B&W. *Producer:* Robert Sherwood *Director:* Gregory Ratoff *Writers:* Michael Blankfort, William Hurlbut, Charles Bonner (novel) *Cast:* Warner Baxter, Ingrid Bergman, Susan Hayward, Richard Denning, Fay Wray

5. *Addams Family Values*

Pubert is the newest addition to the Addams family. Wednesday is unhappy with the newest member, so she and Pugsley are sent to summer camp and nanny Debby Jellinsky (Joan Cusack) is hired. Does she have other plans?
Universal-Paramount. US. 1993. 94m. C. *Producer:* Scott Rudin *Director:* Barry Sonnenfeld *Writer:* Paul Rudnick *Cast:* Angelica Huston, Raul Julia, Christopher Lloyd, Joan Cusack, Christina Ricci, Carol Kane, Jimmy Workman, Carel Struycken, David Krumholtz, Christopher Hart

6. *The Adventures of Sharkboy and Lavagirl in 3-D*

Ten-year-old Max (Cayden Boyd) is a lonely student in Texas. His fellow classmates look for reasons to beat him up. Max's rigid teacher, Mr. Electricidad (George Lopez), discourages him from writing about his imaginary superheroes Sharkboy and Lavagirl. Soon Sharkboy and Lavagirl beg for help from Max.
Columbia Dimension. US. 2005. 93m. C. *Director:* Robert Rodriguez *Writer:* Robert Rodriguez, Marcel Rodriguez *Cast:* Taylor Lautner, Taylor Dooley, Cayden Boyd, George Lopez, David Arquette, Kristin Davis, Jacob Davich, Sasha Pieterse, Rico Torres, Marc Musso, Shane Graham, Tiger Darow, Rocket Rodriguez, Racer Rodriguez, Rebel Rodriguez

7. *Age of Innocence (Ragtime Summer)*

In 1919 Canada, pacifist schoolteacher Henry Buchanan (David Warner) becomes a conscientious objector and stirs up feelings of resentment.
Rank. Great Britain/Canada. 1977. 101m. C. *Producers:* Deanne Judson, George Willoughby *Director:* Alan Bridges *Writer:* Ratch Wallace *Cast:* David Warner, Honor Blackman, Trudy Young, Cec Linder, Tim Henry, Robert Hawkins, Joey Davidson, Jon Granik, Lois Maxwell, Michael Tait, John Swindells, John Bayliss, John Frieson, Vincent Dale, Spencer Harrison

8. *Aire Libre (Out in the Open)*

In the 1880s, two explorers and a young Venezuelan schoolteacher set off into uncharted jungle in search of the mythical river Casiquare.
Venezuela. 1996. 96m. *Producers:* Lidia Córdova, Henrique Vera-Villanueva *Director:* Luis Armando Roche *Cast:* Roy Dupuis, Christian Vadim, Carlos Cruz, Wolfgang Preiss, Dora Mazzone, Dimas González, Orlando Urdaneta

9. *Akeelah and the Bee*

Eleven-year-old Akeelah Anderson (Keke Palmer) lives in a repressed environment with her overworked single mother Tanya (Angela Bassett) and gang member brother and attends a South Los Angeles middle school. To avoid detention for her absences, she enters a spelling bee and wins. Her principal Mr. Welch (Curtis Armstrong) has her seek coaching from English professor Dr. Joshua Larabee (Laurence Fishburne) to prepare for the regional spelling bee. The possibility of going to the Scripps National Spelling Bee and being someone her community can rally around is overwhelming. She must also face the obstacles in her home life.

Lionsgate. US. 2006. 112m. C. *Producers:* Laurence Fishburne, Sidney Ganic, Nancy Hult, Daniel Llewelyn, Michael Romersa *Writer-Director:* Doug Atchison *Cast:* Keke Palmer, Laurence Fishburne, Angela Bassett, Curtis Armstrong, J.R. Villarreal, Sean Michael, Sahara Garey, Lee Thompson Young, Julito McCullum, Erica Hubbard, Eddie Steeples, Dalia Phillips, Tzi Ma, Jeris Poindexter, Sara Niemietz

10. *Akhareen abadeh (The Last Village)*

A teacher from the Ministry of Education is bringing books for the children of a remote mountain village in northern Iran. En route, he is attacked by a pack of hungry wolves. A village boy convinces the people of the village to rescue the teacher.

Iran. 1993. 45m. C. *Director:* Majid Majidi *Writers:* Majid Majidi, Mehdi Shojai *Cast:* Majid Majidi

11. *Aliki — My Love*

An American of Greek ancestry, Barry Wilson (Jess Conrad) believes he inherited a hamburger sauce empire, but he ends up with a Greek island. The secret to the hamburger sauce died with his uncle. Barry travels to the island intending to sell it to a hotel millionaire. Local schoolteacher Aliki (Aliki Vouyouklaki) schemes to keep the island from being sold. It seems that Aliki's mother has the recipe for the special hamburger sauce.

Lionex Film. Great Britain/Greece. 1963. 90m. B&W. *Producers:* Rudolph Maté, George St. George *Director:* Rudolph Maté *Writer:* George St. George *Cast:* Aliki Vouyouklaki, Jess Conrad, Wilfrid Hyde-White, Katherine Kath, Paris Alexander, John Pardos

12. *All for Mary*

In a Swiss Alpine resort, Miss Cartwright, the old nanny of an upper-class man, turns up to tend him when he contracts chicken pox, and gets in the way of his pursuit of Mary, the landlord's daughter. He and an army officer unite against her tyranny in their rivalry for Mary.

Rank. Great Britain. 1955. 79m. C. *Producer:* Paul Soskin *Director:* Wendy Toye *Writers:* Paul Soskin, Peter Blackmore *Cast:* Alan Melville, Kathleen Harrison, David Tomlinson, Jill Day, David Hurst, Leo McKern, Nicholas Phipps, Joan Young, Lionel Jeffries, Parl Hardtmuth, Fabia Drake, Tommy Farr

13. *All Is Fair in Love and War*

A mischievous little girl plays a prank on her schoolmistress.
General Film Company. US. 1911. B&W. *Cast:* Zena Keefe

14. *All Over the Guys*

Tom (Richard Ruccolo), a handsome special education teacher, teaches by day and drinks and sleeps around at night. Eli (Dan Bucatinsky) edits the police blotter for a neighborhood newspaper. Tom and Eli have been set up by their two best friends. Theirs is an on-and-off relationship.

Lions Gate Films. US. 2001. 92m. C. *Producers:* Susan Dietz, Donnie Land, Juan Mas, Dan Bucatinsky *Director:* Julie Davis *Writer:* Dan Bucatinsky *Cast:* Dan Bucatinsky, Richard Ruccolo, Adam Goldberg, Sasha Alexander, Joanna Kerns, Nicolas Surovy, Andrea Martin, Tony Abatemarco, Doris Roberts

15. *All This and Heaven Too*

Governess Henriette Deluzy-Desportes (Bette Davis) works for the family of the Duc de Praslin (Charles Boyer). A love grows between the governess and the frustrated duke. Unfortunately, the duke has an insanely jealous wife (Barbara O'Neil).

Warner. US. 1940. 143m. B&W. *Producer-Director:* Anatole Litvak *Writers:* Casey Robinson, Rachel Field (novel) *Cast:* Charles Boyer, Bette Davis, Barbara O'Neil, Virginia Weidler, Jeffrey Lynn, Helen Westley, Henry Daniell, Harry Davenport, Walter Hampden, George Coulouris, Janet Beecher, Montagu Love, June Lockhart, Ann Todd, Richard Nichols, Fritz Leiber, Ian Keith, Ann Gillis

16. *Almost a Husband*

New England schoolteacher Sam Lyman (Will Rogers) finds himself in a small Southern town. He is drawn into many town events and problems, including a fake marriage to a young girl to help her get rid of an unwanted suitor. The marriage turns out to be legal.

Goldwyn Pictures. US. 1919. B&W. *Director:* Clarence G. Badger *Writers:* Opie Read, Will Rogers *Cast:* Will Rogers, Peggy Wood, Herbert Standing, Cullen Landis, Clara Horton, Edward Brady, Sidney De Gray, Gus Saville

Alone see **Odna**

17. *The Amazing Mrs. Holliday*

Young schoolteacher Ruth Kirke (Deanna Durbin) is traveling with a group of war orphans from China to San Francisco, when their cargo ship is torpedoed and sunk. Ruth and the surviving children arrive in San Francisco and learn that the undocumented children will be held until someone posts $500 bond for each. Ruth and Timothy Blake, another survivor, go to the home of the commodore who owned the ship (and is thought to have died when it was sunk). Timothy states that the commodore and Ruth were married aboard the ship. For the good of the children, Ruth goes along with the deception. When the commodore's grandson Tom shows up, Ruth explains that her father's mission was destroyed in a bombing raid and she escaped with the children. Along the way they discovered a dying Chinese woman and Ruth took her children as well. Ruth smuggled the children aboard and the commodore promised to help her. The deception continues until suddenly the commodore and one of the children, who were presumed dead, turn up. Tom and Ruth fall in love and will marry.

Universal. US. 1943. 98m. B&W. *Producers:* Bruce Manning, Frank Shaw *Director:* Bruce Manning *Writers:* Frank Ryan, John Jacoby *Cast:* Deanna Durbin, Edmond O'Brien, Frieda Inescort, Barry Fitzgerald, Arthur Treacher, Harry Davenport, Grant Mitchell

18. *America for Me*

A vacationing schoolteacher (Ellen Drew) and her friend (Meg Randall) meet cowboy (John Archer) on his way to the rodeo. The teacher and cowboy soon fall in love.

Warner. US. 1953. 20m. C. *Cast:* Ellen Drew, John Archer, Meg Randall, Robert Nichols

19. *An American Haunting*

A present-day woman stumbles across a manuscript written by a schoolteacher about the Bell Witch in Tennessee in the late 1800s. The schoolteacher tells of the curse in the Bell family and their daughter Betsy, who loves him.

Freestyle Releasing. Great Britain/Canada/Romania. 2005. 91m. C. *Producers:* Christopher Milburn, André Rouleau, Courtney Solomon *Director:* Courtney Solomon *Writers:* Brent Monahan, Courtney Solomon *Cast:* Donald Sutherland, Sissy Spacek, Dames D'Arcy, Rachel Hurd-Wood, Matthew Marsh, Thom Fell, Zoe Thorne, Gaye Brown, Sam Alexander, Miquel Brown, Vernon Dobtcheff, Shauna Shim, Madalina Stan, Philip Hurdwood, Vlad Cruceru

20. *Les Amitiés Particulières (This Special Friendship)*

Youthful relationships are explored in the setting of a strict French-Roman Catholic Jesuit boarding school in the 1920s. The faculty is on the alert for any improper relationship and they ensure that the boys are deprived of all privacy. A serious boy from a religious family turns in a boy when he intercepts an innocent letter. The boy who wrote the letter is expelled. The boy becomes enamored of a younger boy and a relationship starts. They are caught playing by a priest-teacher. The older boy gives in and promises not to see the young boy again. The young one feels betrayed and commits suicide. The schoolteachers are ignorant of youthful needs and demand selflessness and dedication to higher values.

Lux. France. 1964. 99m. B&W. *Director:* Jean Delannoy *Writers:* Jean Aurenche, Pierre Bost, Roger Peyrefitte *Cast:* Francis Lacombrade, Didier Haudepin, Louis Seigner, Michel Bouquet, Lucien Nat, François Lecccia, Dominique Maurin

21. Amy

Leaving her husband after the death of their child, Amy (Jenny Agutter) teaches speech at a rural school for the blind and deaf. Her own child was deaf and she wants to help other disabled children. She doesn't sign and most of the other teachers don't believe the deaf can lip-read or speak.

Walt Disney. US. 1981. 100m. C. *Director:* Vincent McEveety *Writer:* Noreen Stone *Cast:* Jenny Agutter, Barry Newman, Kathleen Nolan, Chris Robinson, Margaret O'Brien, Nanette Fabray

Ana and the Wolves see *Ana y los Lobos*

22. *Ana y los Lobos (Ana and the Wolves)*

Ana (Geraldine Chaplin), an English governess, arrives at an old mansion in Spain where she becomes the sexual object of the three sons of a monstrous mother.

World Wide Pictures. Spain. 1972. 100m. C. *Writer-Director:* Carlos Saura *Cast:* Geraldine Chaplin, Fernando Fernan-Gomez, José Maria Prada, José Vivó

23. *Andaz (The Gesture)*

Sheetal (Hema Malini), left alone with a baby boy after the death of her husband and rejection from his family, becomes a teacher. She is drawn to widower Ravi (Shammi Kapoor), father of one of her students. They decide to marry despite the objections and the questions of honesty.

India. 1971. 166m. C. *Producer:* G. P. Sippy *Director:* Ramesh Sippy *Writers:* Javed Akhtar, Sacchin Bhowmick *Cast:* Shammi Kapoor, Rajesh Khanna, Hema Malini, Simi Garewal, Ajit, Aruna Irani, Achala Sachdev, David Abraham, Roopesh Kumar, Sonia Sahni, Alankar Joshi

24. *Angemaeul (Village in the Mist)*

A graduate teacher takes her first teaching post far from home and her fiancé. She finds the customs and comforts are very different, and learns that the villagers are comprised of one large clan.

Hwa-Chun Trading Company. South Korea. 1983. 90m. C. *Director:* Lim Kwon-Tack *Writer:* Song Kil-Han *Cast:* Ahn Song-Ki, Chong Yun-Hee, Lee Yea-Min, Kim Ji-Yung, Choi Dong-Jun, Jin Bong-Jin

The Angry Cosmos see *Seongnan cosmos*

25. *The Animals (Five Savage Men)*

A schoolteacher, raped by a sadistic killer and his gang, takes her revenge with the aid of a Native American, who saves her life.

MGM. US. 1970. 86m. C. *Writer-Producer:* Richard Bakalyan *Director:* Ron Joy *Cast:* Henry Silva, Keenan Wynn, Michele Carey, John Anderson, Joseph Turkel, Pepper Martin, Bobby Hall, Peter Hellmann

26. *Anjos do Arrabalde*

Three female teachers live and teach in a public school in the outskirts of Sao Paulo. The film begins on a violent note with a brutal rape. One woman attempts suicide and another faces a murder charge.

Embrafilme. Brazil. 1987. 90m. C. *Producer:* Antonio Polo Galante *Writer-Director:* Carlos Reichenbach *Cast:* Betty Faria, Clarisse Abujamra, Irene Stefânia, Vanessa Alves, Ênio Gonçalves, Emílio Di Biasi, Ricardo Blat, Carlos Koppa, Chica Burza, Kiko Guerra, Cilas Gregório, Elaine Marcondes, José de Abreu, Nicole Puzzi

27. *Anna and the King*

This is the story of Anna Leonowens (Jodie Foster), the English schoolteacher who came to Siam in the 1860s to teach the children of King Mongkut (Yun-Fat Chow). A subtle romance develops between them.

TCF. US. 1999. 148m. C. *Producers:* Lawrence Bender, Ed Elbert *Director:* Andy Tennant *Writers:* Steve Meerson, Peter Krikes *Cast:* Jodie Foster, Yun-Fat Chow, Ling Bai, Tom Felton, Syed Alwi, Randall Duk Kim, Kay Siu Lim, Melissa Campbell

28. *Anna and the King of Siam*

A proud English widow, Anna (Irene Dunne), arrives in Siam in 1862 to tutor the king's (Rex Harrison) 67 children. Anna is shocked and outraged at the feudal customs of Siam. The film is based on the biography written by Margaret Landon about the governess at the Siamese court.

TCF. US. 1946. 128m. B&W. *Producer:* Louis D. Lighton *Director:* John Cromwell *Writers:* Talbot Jennings, Sally Benson, Margaret Landon (novel) *Cast:* Irene Dunne, Rex Harrison, Linda Darnell, Gale Sondergaard, Lee J. Cobb, Mikhail Rasumny, Dennis Hoey, Tito Renaldo, Richard Lyon

29. *Anne of Green Gables*

Matthew and Marilla Cuthbert adopt a child named Anne Shirley (Mary Miles Minter). There are a few bumps in their relationship, but they all come to love each other. After her graduation, Anne becomes schoolmistress of the village. She is saving her money to pay for an operation for someone she cares about. One of her pupils falsely accuses her of beating him cruelly. Anne is vindicated and she marries her sweetheart Gilbert.

Realart Pictures Corp. 1919. B&W. *Director:* William Desmond Taylor *Writer:* Frances Marion *Cast:* Mary Miles Minter, Paul Kelly, Marcia Harris, Frederick Burton, F.T. Chailee, Leila Romer, Lincoln Stedman, Hazel Sexton, Russell Hewitt, Albert Hackett, Laurie Lovelle, Carolyn Lee, Jack B. Hollis, George Stewart

30. *Anne of Green Gables: The Sequel*

Anne Shirley, now a schoolteacher, decides to teach at Kingsport Ladies' College, an exclusive girls' school where she meets opposition from another teacher, Miss Brooke. Eventually she returns to Avonlea.

Buena Vista Television. Great Britain-Canada-US. 1987. 230m. C. *Producer-Director:* Kevin Sullivan *Writers:* Kevin Sullivan, Lucy Maud Montgomery (novels) *Cast:* Megan Follows, Colleen Dewhurst, Wendy Hiller, Frank Converse, Jonathan Crombie, Marilyn Lightstone, Schuyler Grant, Rosemary Dunsmore, Kate Lynch, Geneviève Appleton, Susannah Hoffman, Kathryn Trainor, Rosemary Radcliffe, Charmion King, Robert Collins

31. *Anne of Windy Poplars*

An ambitious young teacher (Anne Shirley) arrives in a small town to assume a job as vice-principal of the school. She is drawn into town politics, family feuds, and school hazings. Finally, she overcomes all the obstacles to win the townspeople's admiration.

RKO. US. 1940. 85m. B&W. *Producer:* Cliff Reid *Director:* Jack Hively *Writers:* Michael Kanin, Jerry Cady, L.M. Montgomery (novel) *Cast:* Anne Shirley, James Ellison, Henry Travers, Patric Knowles, Slim Summerville, Elizabeth Patterson, Louise Campbell, Joan Carroll, Katherine Alexander, Minnie Dupree, Alma Kruger, Marcia Mae Jones, Ethel Griffies, Gilbert Emery, Wright Kramer, Jackie Moran

32. *Annie*

Annie (Aileen Quinn), an orphan, and her dog Sandy are adopted by millionaire Daddy Oliver Warbucks (Albert Finney), but not before residing in a dreary orphanage supervised by the evil, drunken floozy Miss Hannigan (Carol Burnett). This big-budget film is based on the stage play *Annie,* created by Harold Gray, which was based on the comic strip "Little Orphan Annie."

Columbia. US. 1982. 126m. C. *Producer:* Ray Stark *Director:* John Huston *Writers:* Carol Sobieski, T. Bill Berloni *Cast:* Aileen Quinn, Carol Burnett, Albert Finney, Bernadette Peters, Ann Reinking, Tim Curry, Geoffrey Holder, Edward Herrmann, Bingo (dog).

33. *Annie's Coming Out (A Test of Love)*

The true story of Annie O'Farrell (Tina Arhondis), a teenager who suffers from cerebral palsy and was placed in a home for disabled children from the age of three. By doing everything possible to help Annie, therapist-teacher Jessica Hathaway (Angela Punch McGregor) conflicts with the doctors and staff.

Film Australia. Australia. 1984. 93m. C. *Producer:* Don Murray *Director:* Gil Brealey *Writers:* John Patterson, Chris Borthwick *Cast:* Angela Punch McGregor, Drew Forsythe, Tina Arhondis, Charles Tingwell, Monica Maughan, Mark Butler, Philippa Baker, Liddy Clark, Wallas Eaton, John Frawley, Alistair Duncan, Simon Chilvers

34. *Anthracite — Cet Âge Est Sans Pitié (This Age Without Pity* and *Cet Âge Sans Pitie)*

In a Jesuit school for young boys, a priest attempts to save face in the midst of a loss of funds and postwar changes. The priest finds one boy who seems to share his spirituality. However, having his own personal problems, the boy turns on the priest and joins the other boys in their assault upon him. The school director does nothing.

Rush Production. France. 1980. 90m. C. *Writer-Director*: Edouard Niermans *Cast*: Bruno Cremer, Jean Bouise, Roland Bertin, Jean-Pol Dubois, Jérôme Zucca, Jean-Pierre Bagot, Pierre Baldini

35. *Antonia (Antonia's Line)*

Antonia's (Willeke van Ammelrooy) daughter Danielle (Els Dottermans) is shy, but not too shy to stab the village rapist with a pitchfork. When Danielle herself decides to have a child, she and her mother negotiate with a handsome, quiet man. Therese is born and the women bring her up. Soon Danielle falls in love with Therese's beautiful teacher, imagining her as Botticelli's Venus. Therese develops into a woman and Antonia feels the pride of being a great woman.

First Look Pictures. Netherlands. 1996. 105m. C. *Producer:* Hans de Weers *Writer-Director:* Marleen Gorris *Cast:* Willeke van Ammelrooy, Els Dottermans, Jan Decleir, Mil Seghers, Catherine ten Bruggencate, Jan Steen

Antonia's Line see *Antonia*

Antônio das Mortes see *O Dragâo da Maldade Contra o Santo Guerreiro*

36. *Anu Bandham*

A widow Sunandha (Seema) lives in poverty with her child in rural Kerala. With the help of a secret admirer, she starts a kindergarten school. A tragic event causes everything to unravel.

India. 1985. C. *Director:* I.V. Sasi *Writer:* M.T. Vasudevan Nair *Cast:* Mammootty, Seema, Mohanlal, Sobhana, Master Prasobh, Thilakan, Sukumari, Kunchan, Sankaradi, Premji, Jagannatha Varma, Paravoor Bharathan, Bahadur, Kunjandi, Janardanan, Santha Devi, Thodupuzha Vasanthi

37. *Aranysárkány (The Golden Kite)*

The tragic story of an elderly schoolteacher in a Hungarian town of the 1920s.

Magyar Filmgyártó Vallalat. Hungary. 1966. 93m. C. *Directors:* László Ranódy, Imre Gyöngyössy *Writers:* Endre Illés, Dezsö Kosztolányi (novel) *Cast:* László Mensáros, Ilona Béres, Benedek Tóth, Imre Siakovits, Gyula Bodrogi, László Tahi Tóth, Margit Bara, Ferenc Bessenyei, Gyula Gózon, Zoltán Greguss, Teri Horváth, Zoltán Makláry, Sándor Pécsi, Sándor Szakács, Imre Sinkovits, Sándor Tompa, Zoltán Latinovits

38. *L'Argent de Poche (Small Change)*

In the summer of 1976, children learn about life from their teachers and parents. There are many examples of what the children are exposed to during the summer. For example, a teacher has his first child; a mom reaches out to Patrick, a motherless boy; a single mother hopes to meet Mr. Right, etc. One teacher proclaims, "Life is hard, but it's wonderful."

Films du Carosse/Artists Associé. France. 1976. 105m. C. *Producers:* Marcel Berbert, Roland Thenot *Director:* François Truffaut *Writers*: François Truffaut, Susan Schiffman *Cast:* Gerory Desmouceaux, Philippe Goldman, Claudio Deluca, Nicole Félix, Chantal Mercier, Jean- François Stèvenin, Virginie Thévenet

39. *As Young As We Are*

In Los Angeles, new schoolteachers Kim Hutchins (Pippa Scott) and Joyce Goodwin (Majel Barrett) meet at a job fair. With no experience they have difficulty finding positions. Principal Paul Evans (Harold Dyrenforth) reluctantly gives them a one-year contract and explains that his desert community has many seasonal farm and construction workers whose children are bitter. Evans believes that Rosario is a great training place but also stressful. Kim and Joyce are helped by a man when their car breaks down. Kim is attracted to him but shocked when she discovers that he is one of her students. He falls in love and kidnaps Kim to take her to Las Vegas to marry. An accident thwarts his plan. Everything is cleared up and Kim keeps teaching.

William Alland Production Corp. US. 1958. 76m. *Producer:* William Alland *Director:* Bernard Girard *Writer:* Meyer Dolinsky *Cast:* Robert Harland, Pippa Scott, Majel Barrett, Ty Hardin, Barry Atwater, Carla Hoffman, Ellen Corby, Harold Dyrenforth, Ross Elliott, Linda Watkins, Beverly Long, Mack W. Repp, Tyler McVey, Bill Boyett, James E. Kipling, James Anderson, Titus Moede, Tommie Moore

The Ascent see *Voskhozhdenie*

40. *Ashanti Sanket (Distant Thunder)*

In a small village in 1943, the schoolmaster-teacher-priest-doctor and his wife begin to see the causes and horrifying effects of a community-wide famine.

Balaka. India. 1973. 100m. C. *Producer:* Sarbani Bhattacharya *Writer-Director:* Satyajit Ray, Bibhutibhusan Banerjee (novel) *Cast:* Soumitra Chatterjee, Babita, Ramesh Mukherjee, Chitra Banerjee, Gobinda Chakravarti, Sandhya Roy

41. *At Bear Track Gulch*

The mining community of Bear Track Gulch has never had a woman visit until old Mr. Lorraine (John Sturgeon) and his schoolteacher daughter Alice (Edna Flugrath) come to stay. The Lorraines buy a cabin from Jack Turner (George Lessey), who falls in love with Alice. After her father dies, Alice is asked to stay and start a school.

General Film Co. US. 1913. B&W. *Director:* Harold M. Shaw *Writer:* R.P. Janette *Cast:* William West, Herbert Prior, George Lessey, Bigelow Cooper, Edna Flugrath, John Sturgeon.

42. *Au Revoir, les Infants (Goodbye, Children)*

This film was based on the director's life during the German occupation of France in World War II. 12-year-old Julien Quentin (Gaspard Manesse) is the smartest boy at a Catholic boarding school until new student Jean Bonnet (Raphael Fejtö) arrives. A brave priest headmaster, Father Jean (Philippe Morier-Genoud), has agreed to hide the boy at the school. A kitchen employee is discharged and gets revenge by tipping the Gestapo about the hiding of Jews. An agent arrives and asks the Jewish boy to reveal himself. Julien inadvertently glances at Jean and Jean is taken away.

Orion. France. 1988. 103m. C. *Writer-Producer-Director*: Louis Malle *Cast*: Gaspard Manesse, Raphael Fejtö, Francine Racette, Stanislas Carré de Malberg, Philippe Morier-Genoud, Francois Berléand, Francois Néget, Peter Fitz, Pascal Rivet, Benoît Henriet

43. *Auntie Mame*

Auntie Mame (Rosalind Russell) is the flamboyant and individualist aunt of young, impressionable Patrick Dennis (Jan Handzlik), who left in Mame's care when her brother (his father) drops dead. Patrick is quickly indoctrinated into his aunt's philosophy that "Life is a banquet — and some poor suckers are starving to death." His father knew how Mame lives, so he had executor Dwight Babcock (Fred Clark) do his best to help raise Patrick as a stuffy, conventional person. Mame tries to get past Babcock and allow Patrick to be a free spirit. One way is for Mame to enroll Patrick in an unconventional school run by Acacius Page (Henry Brandon). The older Patrick (Roger Smith) almost marries into the very conventional and upscale Upson family. A musical version starring Lucille Ball was made.

Warner. US. 1958. 144m. C. *Producer-Director:* Morton da Costa *Writers:* Betty Comden, Adolph Green, Jerome Lawrence (play), Patrick Dennis (novel) *Cast:* Rosalind Russell, Forrest Tucker, Coral Browne, Fred Clark, Roger Smith, Patric Knowles, Peggy Cass, Lee Patrick, Joanna Barnes, Jan Handzlik

Authorized Instructor see *L'Educatore Autorizzato*

Autobus see *Aux Yeux du Monde*

44. *Autumn Crocus*

Jenny Grey (Fay Compton), a British schoolmistress on holiday, falls for married Tyrolean innkeeper Andreas Steine (Ivor Novello).

ATP. Great Britain. 1934. 86m. B&W. *Producer-Director:* Basil Dean *Writer:* Dorothy Farnum *Cast:* Ivor Novello, Fay Compton, Frederick Ranalow, Jack Hawkins, Diana Beaumont, Muriel Aked, George Zucco, Esme Church, Gertrude Gould, Mignon O'Doherty

Autumn Marathon see *Osenny Marafon*

45. *Aux Yeux du Monde (Autobus)*

A frustrated youth hijacks a bus full of schoolchildren so he can visit a girlfriend.

Artificial Eyes/Les Productions Lazennec. France. 1991. 98m. C. *Producer:* Alain Rocca *Writer-Director:* Eric Rochant *Cast:* Yvan Attal, Kristin Scott-Thomas, Marc Berman, Charlotte Gainsbourg, Renan Mazeas

46. *Aw Aakare Aa*

Mini (Dipti Panda), a schoolteacher trying to change the present educational system, finds herself transferred from one school to another. Finally she starts her own school following her principles.

Om Films. India. 2003. 90m. C. *Writer-Producer-Director:* Subas Das *Cast:* Dipti Panda, Adyasha Mohapatra

47. *Back to Bataan (The Invisible Army)*

This is a story about guerrilla fighters in the Philippines. An army colonel's (John Wayne) task is to go into the hills and organize the resistance. Conjoined with the colonel's activities are the fates of a middle-aged schoolteacher Miss Barnes (Beulah Bondi), a native fighter, and his sweetheart, a spy.

RKO. US. 1945. 95m. C. *Producer:* Robert Fellows *Director:* Edward Dmytryk *Writers:* Ben Barzman, William Cordon *Cast:* John Wayne, Anthony Quinn, Beulah Bondi, Fely Franquelli, Richard Loo, Lawrence Tierney, Philip Ahn, "Ducky" Louie, Leonard Strong, Paul Fix, Abner Biberman, Vladimir Sokoloff, Alex Havier, John Miljan, Harold Fong

48. *Back to the Future Part III*

Doc and Marty's time travel adventures continue in the 1885 Old West town of Hill Valley. After Doc saves Clara Clayton, the new schoolmarm, from a runaway wagon, they fall in love. She was meant to die in a crash at the ravine. Even though Doc needs to go back to the future, he is very attracted to Clara.

Universal. US. 1990. 118m. C. *Producers:* Neil Canton, Bob Gale *Director:* Robert Zemeckis *Writers:* Robert Zemeckis, Bob Gale *Cast:* Michael J. Fox, Christopher Lloyd, Mary Steenburgen, Thomas F. Wilson, Lea Thompson, Elisabeth Shue, James Tolkan, Matt Clark, Dub Taylor, Harry Carey, Jr., Pat Buttram, Christopher Wynne, Sean Gregory Sullivan, Mike Watson, Marc McClure

49. *Bad Little Angel*

Patricia Victoria "Patsy" Sanderson (Virginia Weidler) is an orphan living with Mrs. Perkins (Elizabeth Patterson), an elderly woman. They love each other until the head of the orphanage comes looking for Patsy to bring her back. Mrs. Perkins dies of a heart attack. The orphanage supervisors (Arthur Aylesworth and Esther Dale) are of no support, and Patricia's spirits are actually lower in the dreadful orphanage. Patsy escapes with her dog to a small town in New Jersey. Trouble seems to follow her until she reads a verse from the Bible.

MGM. US. 1939. 72m. B&W. *Director:* William Thiele *Writers:* Dorothy Yost, Margaret Turnbull (novel) *Cast:* Virginia Weidler, Gene Reynolds, Guy Kibbee, Ian Hunter, Elizabeth Patterson, Reginald Owen, Henry Hull, Lois Wilson, Esther Dale, Arthur Aylesworth

50. *Baited Trap*

A young man heads west to avenge his father's death. He arrives in the town where the murderer lives and accomplishes his task. While there, he falls in love with schoolteacher Helen Alder (Neva Gerber).

Rayart Pictures. US. 1926. B&W. *Director:* Stuart Paton *Writer:* George Pyper *Cast:* Ben Wilson, Neva Gerber, Al Ferguson, Monty O'Grady, Ashton Dearholt, Lafe McKee, Fang (dog)

The Baker's Wife see *La Femme du Boulanger*

51. *Balanta (The Oak)*

Nela (Maia Morgenstern), a young schoolteacher, and her father, a former big shot in the secret police, live in squalor in a tiny flat in a Bucharest housing project. When her father dies she carries his ashes in a jar. Nela accepts a job outside of Bucharest, is gang-raped while traveling to her new assignment, learns that her father was not a hero, and meets Mitica (Razvan Vasilescu), a physician not in step with the government.

MK2/USA. Romania/France. 1992. 105m. C. *Producers:* Eliane Stutterheim, Sylvain Bursztejn, Lucian Pintilie *Writer-Director:* Lucian Pintilie, Ion Baiesu (novel) *Cast:* Maia Morgenstern, Razvan Vasilescu, Victor Rebengiuc, Dorel Visan, Mariana Mihut, Dan Condurache, Virgil Andriescu, Leopoldina Balanuta, Matei Alexandru, Gheorgh Visu, Magda Catone, Ionel Mahailescu, Ion Pavlescu

52. *La Balia (The Nanny)*

Wealthy psychiatrist Dr. Mori (Fabrizio Bentivoglio) must find a nanny-wet nurse for his infant when his wife (Valeria Bruni Tedeschi) can't take care of the baby. He selects a peasant, Annetta (Maya Sansa), who can't read or write, to come to Rome to care for his infant, forcing Annetta to leave behind her own child. The nanny bonds with the boy, which angers the mother. Annetta, whose lover is a jailed teacher, asks the doctor to teach her to read and write. Turmoil reigns in this scenario.

RaiTrade. Italy. 1999. 106m. C. *Producer:* Pier Giorgio Bellocchio *Director:* Marco Bellocchio *Writers:* Marco Bellocchio, Daniela Ceselli, Luigi Pirandello (novel) *Cast:* Fabrizio Bentivoglio, Maya Sansa, Valeria Bruni Tedeschi, Jacqueline Lustig, Pier Giorgio Bellocchio, Elda Alvigini, Gisella Burinato

The Bandit see *O Cangaceiro*

53. *Bannerline*

Mike Perrivale (Keefe Brasselle), a cub reporter, yearns for a big story and plans on marrying his schoolteacher girlfriend Richie Loomis (Sally Forrest). Richie suggests that Mike write a story about Hugo Trimble (Lionel Barrymore), a high school's longtime history teacher, who is near death in the hospital. Hugo's one regret is that he never motivated the town to take action against a gangster. Mike is so inspired by the words of the teacher that he makes it happen. Hugo dies knowing about the positive changes in town.

MGM. US. 1951. 87m. B&W. *Producer:* Henry Berman *Director:* Don Weis *Writer:* Charles Schnee *Cast:* Keefe Brasselle, Sally Forrest, Lionel Barrymore, Lewis Stone, J. Carrol Naish, Larry Keating, Spring Byington, Warner Anderson, Elisabeth Risdon, Michael Ansara, John Morgan, Mari Blanchard

54. *Barely Proper*

A pretty schoolteacher is a nudist and belongs to a nudist colony. She is brought up on charges of immorality before the local school board and the advisability of letting her continue teaching is debated.

Ambassador Film Distributors. US. 1975. C. *Producer-Director:* Brad F. Grinter *Writer:* Manny Dietz *Cast:* Brad F. Grinter, Carol Riccio, Ed Trostle, Cindy Walker

55. *The Basket*

During World War I, two teenage German war orphans from an internment camp appear in a Pacific Northwest farming community. They meet with hostile feelings as does the unconventional new schoolteacher, Martin Conlon (Peter Coyote), a Bostonian fleeing a secret past. Martin introduces the students to basketball and opera. The new arrivals generate conflict in the narrow-minded community.

Privileged Communications. US. 1999. 101m. C. *Producer-Director:* Rich Cowan *Writers:* Don Caron, Frank Swoboda, Tessa Swoboda *Cast:* Peter Coyote, Karen Allen, Robert Karl Burke, Amber Willenborg, Eric Dane, Brian Skala, Jock MacDonald

56. *Battle Hymn*

In this fact-based drama, clergyman Dean Hess (Rock Hudson) gives up his pulpit for pilot wings and goes to Korea with the Air Force to help train pilots. While there, he helps care for Korean children left orphaned and homeless by war. With the help of a pretty Korean teacher, he sets up an orphanage. He also airlifts many orphans to safety. The reason he is so driven is that during World War II, he accidentally bombed a German orphanage. The real Dean Hess served as an advisor on the film.

Universal. US. 1957. 108m. C. *Producer:* Ross Hunter *Director:* Douglas Sirk *Writers:* Charles Grayson, Vincent Evans *Cast:* Rock Hudson, Martha Hyer, Dan Duryea, Don DeFore, Anna Kashfi, Jock Mahoney, Alan Hale, Jr., Carl Benton Reid, Richard Loo, James Edwards, Philip Ahn

57. Baxter

A London speech therapist, Dr. Roberta Clemm (Patricia Neal), helps an American boy with a psychosomatic speech disorder.

National General. Great Britain. 1973. 105m. C. *Producer:* Arthur Lewis *Director:* Lionel Jeffries *Writer:* Reginald Rose *Cast:* Patricia Neal, Jean-Pierre Cassel, Britt Ekland, Lynn Carlin, Scott Jacoby, Sally Thomsett, Paul Eddington, Paul Maxwell, Ian Thompson

58. The Beautician and the Beast

An emissary of Slovetzia dictator Boris Pochenko (Timothy Dalton) believes Joy (Fran Drescher) to be a science teacher and hires her as governess to Pochenko's children. Joy, who is really a beauty school instructor, thinks he wants a beautician and accepts the position. Joy wins the children over, befriends the locals, organizes a union, and softens Boris.

Paramount. US. 1997. 107m. C. *Producers:* Howard W. Koch, Jr., Todd Graff *Director:* Ken Kwapis *Writer:* Todd Graff *Cast:* Fran Drescher, Timothy Dalton, Patrick Malahide, Ian McNeice, Lisa Jakub, Heather DeLoach, Adam LaVorgna

Beauties of the Night see **Les Belles de Nuit**

The Beekeeper see **O Mellissokomos**

Before the Revolution see **Prima della Rivvoluzione**

59. The Beguiled

During the Civil War, wounded Yankee soldier John McBurney (Clint Eastwood) is saved from certain death by a girl from a prim and proper Southern boarding school run by Martha Farnsworth (Geraldine Page). She gets him back to the school where he is cared for by the all-female staff and students. But they have a hidden agenda.

Universal. US. 1971. 109m. C. *Producer-Director:* Don Siegel *Writers:* John B. Sherry, Grimes Grice, Thomas Cullinan (novel) *Cast:* Clint Eastwood, Geraldine Page, Elizabeth Hartman, Jo Ann Harris, Darleen Carr, Mae Mercer

60. Bellamy Trial

A philandering teacher's testimony clears Stephen Bellamy and Sue Ives of murder charges stemming from Stephen's wife's death.

MGM. US. 1929. B&W. *Writer-Director:* Monta Bell *Cast:* Leatrice Joy, Betty Bronson, Edward Nugent, George Barraud, Margaret Livingston, Kenneth Thomson, Margaret Seddon, Charles Middleton, Charles Hill Mailes, William Tooker

61. Les Belles de Nuit (Beauties of the Night)

A young, idealistic, discounted composer, Claude (Gérard Philipe), is forced to teach music to unruly schoolchildren in order to survive financially.

Franco London/Rizzoli. France/Italy. 1952. 87m. B&W. *Writer-Director*: René Clair *Cast*: Gérard Philipe, Martine Carol, Gina Lollobrigida, Magali Vendeuil, Marilyn Buferd, Raymond Bussières, Raymond Cordy, Bernard La Jarrige, Albert Michel, Palau, Jean Parédès, Paolo Stoppa

62. *The Belles of St. Trinian's*

Princess Fatima, a sultan's daughter, arrives at the School for Young Ladies, creating chaos. Then her father's horse is due to run at the nearby track. Charles Fitton, bookie brother of headmistress Millicent, makes sure the sultan's daughter reports. The police plant a sergeant as a teacher in the school to keep an eye on things. Film is part of a series based on characters created by cartoonist Ronald Searle.

British Lion. Great Britain. 1954. 91m. B&W. *Producers:* Frank Launder, Sidney Gilliat *Director:* Frank Launder *Writers:* Frank Launder, Sidney Gilliat, Val Valentine *Cast:* Alastair Sim, Joyce Grenfell, George Cole, Hermione Baddeley, Betty Ann Davies, Beryl Reid, Mary Merrall, Renee Houston, Irene Handl, Joan Sims, Balbina, Guy Middleton, Sidney James, Arthur Howard, Richard Wattis, Eric Pohlmann, Lloyd Lamble, Belinda Lee, Jerry Verno, Jack Doyle

63. *The Bells of St. Mary's*

In the sequel to *Going My Way*, Father Charles "Chuck" O'Malley (Bing Crosby) heads a church-Catholic school that is in need of repair. The nuns drove the previous priest into a rest home. The nuns rest their hope on divine intervention while the singing priest convinces an ailing businessman to donate a new building. Sister Mary Benedict (Ingrid Bergman) says, "We have reason to know more things are wrought by prayer than this world dreams of." Sister Benedict is a tomboy but she also feels that academics are important as well, and she clashes with Father O'Malley over a number of issues. When Sister Benedict is diagnosed with tuberculosis she is told that she is to be transferred to Arizona because she cannot deal effectively with children. Of course she is tormented but accepts God's will. Father O'Malley comes to his senses and tells her of her illness. The film ends with Sister Benedict praying to understand God's will as she is sent away to recover from tuberculosis. It was reported that producer-director Leo McCarey based Bergman's character on his aunt, Sister Mary Benedict of the Immaculate Heart Convent in California. A made-for-TV version of the story starring Claudette Colbert, Robert Preston and Glenda Farrell was broadcast on CBS in 1959.

RKO. US. 1945. 126m. B&W. *Producer-Director*: Leo McCarey *Writers*: Leo McCarey, Dudley Nichols *Cast*: Bing Crosby, Ingrid Bergman, Henry Travers, William Gargan, Ruth Donnelly, Joan Carroll, Martha Sleeper, Rhys Williams, Richard Tyler, Una O'Connor

64. *Beneath Western Skies*

Longtime schoolteacher Carrie Stokes (Effie Laird) is angered by the terrorizing Bull Bricker gang, and her anger grows when one of her young students is accidentally shot. Carrie wants help from the sheriff and his deputy. When Carrie is voted town commissioner, she seeks help from a former pupil. A banker and the deputy are cohorts of the outlaws and are working to take complete control of the town. Stranger Johnny Revere (Bob Livingston), Carrie's former pupil, arrives in town, and Carrie appeals to him for help. At one point Johnny loses his memory and joins the outlaws. He regains his memory and stops the bad guys.

Republic. US. 1944. 56m. B&W. *Director:* Spencer Bennet *Writers:* Albert DeMond, Bob Williams *Cast:* Bob Livingston, Smiley Burnette, Effie Laird, Frank Jaquet, Tom London, Charles Miller, Joe Strauch, Jr., LeRoy Mason, Kenne Duncan, Charles Dorety, Jack Kirk, Bud Geary, Bob Kortman, Budd Buster, Jack Ingram, Maxine Doyle, Mickey Kuhn, Forrest Simmons

65. *Bengelchen Liebt Kreuz und Quer (Twenty-four Hour Lover)*

George Weissborn (Harald Leipnitz) is a middle-aged bachelor whose promiscuity is an embarrassment to his family, especially his brother Alfred (Herbert Bötticher), an elementary schoolteacher. Alfred's chance for a promotion depends on George's settling down. His family's hopes are high when he comes home from the hospital engaged, but then he soon begins to bring home a different fiancée every night.

AIP. West Germany. 1970. 90m. C. *Producer:* Rob Houwer *Director:* Marran Gosov *Cast:* Harald Leipnitz, Sybille Maar, Herbert Bötticher, Brigitte Skay, Monika Lundi, Renate Roland, Marianne Wischmann, Claudia Wedekind, Sylvie Beck, Isolde Brauner, Werner Schwier, Jana Novakova, Doris Kiesow, Herbert Weissbach, Inge Langen, Sammy Drechsel, Henry van Ly, Nono Korda

The Best Way to Walk see La Meilleure Façon de Marcher

66. *Bice Skoro Propast Sveta (It Rains in My Village)*

A simple young pig farmer defends a slow village girl, who has been with many men, by fighting with the innkeeper. When the farmer gets drunk, the innkeeper gets his revenge by having him marry the girl. Soon a female schoolteacher arrives to teach painting to the women of the village. She convinces the farmer to be her model and then lover. He is in love until he is replaced by a crop duster. When the townspeople joke about his marriage, he kills his wife and lets his father take the blame. The father dies in prison just after confessing that he did not kill the wife. The enraged townspeople kill the farmer.

UA. France/Yugoslavia. 1968. 84m. C. *Writer-Director:* Aleksandar Petrovic *Cast:* Annie Girardot, Ivan Palúch, Mija Aleksic, Eva Ras, Dragomire "Gidra" Bojanic

67. *Bidar Show, Arezoo! (Wake Up, Arezu!)*

A young teacher in a small village survives an earthquake which kills her colleagues. She sets out for help only to find more devastation. She can hear cries of help and the hospital is full of injured people. A cleric recommends she get help by washing the dead bodies of women. A prisoner who has escaped asks her to wash the bodies of his dead mother, wife and child.

Iran. 2005. 90m. C. *Writer-Producer-Director:* Kianoush Ayari *Cast:* Behnaz Jafari, Mahdi Jafari, Ehsan Rezvani, Sahar Salari, Zaynab Zamani

68. *The Big Green*

A new foreign exchange teacher, Anna Mongomery (Olivia d'Abo), and a former local sports hero turn a bunch of misfit kids into a soccer team.

Buena Vista. US. 1995. 100m. C. *Producer:* Roger Birnbaum *Writer-Director:* Holly Goldberg Sloan *Cast:* Steve Guttenberg, Olivia d'Abo, Jay O. Sanders, John Terry, Chauncey Leopardi, Patrick Renna, Billy L. Sullivan, Yareli Arizmendi, Bug Hall, Jessie Robertson, Anthony Esquivel, Jordan Brower, Hayley Kolb, Haley Miller, Ashley Welch

69. *The Big Tip Off*

Newspaper columnist Johnny Denton (Richard Conte) is taken in by his hoodlum friend Bob (Bruce Bennett), who makes his money by operating a professional fund-raising organization for charity drives such as one for St. Anne's Parochial School. Sister Joan (Cathy Downs) is the nun for whom Johnny convinces his friend to run a legitimate charity event. Sister Joan discovers that Bob is a crook and that he is supplying news tips to Johnny. She finally convinces Johnny to tell the police what he knows and to stop Bob.

AA. US. 1955. 79m. B&W. *Producer*: William F. Broidy *Director*: Frank McDonald *Writer*: Steve Fisher *Cast*: Richard Conte, Constance Smith, Bruce Bennett, Cathy Downs, James Millican, Dick Benedict, Sam Flint, Mary Carroll, Murray Alper, Lela Bliss, G. Pat Collins, Frank Hanley, Harry Guardino, Virginia Carroll, Robert Carraher, Cecil Elliott, Pete Kellett, Tony Rock, Allen Wells, Tony DeMario

70. *Big Top Pee-wee*

Pee-wee Herman (Paul Reubens) is a farmer and agricultural scientist who has invented a hot-dog tree. His best friend is a talking pig named Vance. Pee-wee is engaged to a pretty, sweet schoolteacher until the circus and a beautiful trapeze artist blows into town.

Paramount. US. 1988. 82m. C. *Producers:* Paul Reubens, Debra Hill *Director:* Randal Kleiser *Writers:* Paul Reubens, George McGrath *Cast:* Paul Reubens, Penelope Ann Miller, Kris Kristofferson, Valerie Golino, Wayne White Midge, Susan Tyrrell, Albert Henderson, Jack Murdock

71. *Bigger Than Life*

Grade school teacher Ed Avery (James Mason) undergoes a series of experiments with cortisone in the hopes of curing a usually fatal disease he has contracted.

At first it seems to be working, but when he begins to overdose himself, his personality changes for the worse. His family and friends are greatly upset by his illness.

TCF. US. 1956. 95m. C. *Producer:* James Mason *Director:* Nicholas Ray *Writers:* Cyril Hume, Richard Maibaum *Cast:* James Mason, Barbara Rush, Walter Matthau, Robert Simon, Christopher Olsen, Roland Winters, Kipp Hamilton, Rachel Stephens, Lewis Charles, Gus Schilling, Rusty Lane

72. *Billy Elliot*

Working class 11-year-old Billy Elliot (Jamie Bell) discovers a local ballet class and it captures his imagination. His family is outraged, but his headstrong ballet teacher (Julie Walters) convinces him to accept free private training and audition for a ballet school.

Universal Focus. Great Britain/France. 1999. 110m. C. *Producers:* Greg Brenman, Jon Finn *Director:* Stephen Daldry *Writer:* Lee Hall *Cast:* Julie Walters, Gary Lewis, Jamie Bell, Jamie Draven

73. *Billy Jack*

Onetime Green Beret Billy Jack is half Native American, half white. He hates violence but it seems that he cannot get away from it in the white man's world. When the locals terrorize the teachers and students of the free-arts school in the desert, Billy Jack is there to help. The teachers lecture on love and peace and many '60s themes come out (anti-establishment, make love not war, basic socialist ideals).

Warner/National Student Film Corporation. US. 1971. 113m. C. *Producer:* Mary Rose Solti *Director:* Tom Laughlin *Writer:* Tom Laughlin, Delores Taylor *Cast:* Tom Laughlin, Delores Taylor, Bert Freed, Clark Howat, Julie Webb, Ken Tobey, Victor Izay

74. *Billy Madison*

Loafer Billy Madison (Adam Sandler) is forced to repeat grades one through twelve by his millionaire father Brian Madison (Darren McGavin) if he ever wants to take control of his father's hotel chain. Billy devotes two weeks to each grade. First grade teacher Miss Lippy (Dina Platias) enthralls Billy with a story of a happy puppy. He does become attracted to one teacher (Bridgette Wilson).

Universal. US. 1995. 88m. C. *Producer:* Robert Simonds *Director:* Tamra Davis *Writers:* Tim Herlihy, Adam Sandler *Cast:* Adam Sandler, Bradley Whitford, Josh Mostel, Bridgette Wilson, Norm MacDonald, Darren McGavin, Dina Platias

75. *The Bionic Woman*

Television pilot spin-off from *The Six Million Dollar Man*. This time tennis pro Jamie Sommers (Lindsay Wagner) is put back together with bionic parts by the medical team that restored Steve Austin (Lee Majors). She becomes an agent and goes undercover as a schoolteacher.

ABC. US. 1976. 96m. C. *Director:* Henry Mankiewicz *Cast:* Lindsay Wagner, Monica Randall, Bob Sullivan, Alan Oppenheimer, Richard Anderson, Lee Majors

76. *The Birds*

Impulsive and wealthy Melanie Daniels (Tippi Hedren) is attracted to Mitch Brenner (Rod Taylor) when they meet in a San Francisco pet shop. Melanie buys two lovebirds and secretly delivers them herself to Bodega Bay for Mitch's little sister Cathy (Veronica Cartwright) for her birthday. Strange bird attacks start happening. Melanie meets Annie Hayworth (Susanne Pleshette), the schoolteacher, and pretends to know her to confuse Mitch. Melanie spends the night with Annie and learns that she was also interested in Mitch. Mitch's mother (Jessica Tandy) stopped any developing romance. The next day at the small one-room school, the birds attack. Annie heroically saves the children but is pecked to death. The Brenners and Melanie decide to leave after being boarded up in the house with birds attacking. The premise of the film is based on Daphne du Maurier's short story "The Birds."

Universal. US. 1963. 120m. C. *Producer-Director:* Alfred Hitchcock *Writer:* Evan Hunter *Cast:* Rod Taylor, Tippi Hedren, Jessica Tandy, Suzanne Pleshette, Veronica Cartwright, Ethel Griffies, Charles McGraw

Birth of a Butterfly see *Tavalod-E Parvaneh*

77. *Black*

An Indian "Miracle Worker" tale. The film spans many years in the life of Michelle McNally (portrayed as a child by Ayesha Kapoor and as a woman by Rani Mukherjee) who is born deaf, mute and blind. Unlike other children she lives in darkness, a "black world," and cannot express herself except through violent tantrums. Fortunately a teacher for the blind and deaf, Debraj Sahai (Amitabh Bachchan) enters her life. He is an alcoholic who has never been able to attain the success he desired in teaching blind and deaf children. Through his teaching efforts Debraj turns around Michelle's life, enabling her to leave the darkness and eventually attend college and gain her independence. Roles are reversed when years later Michelle discovers that her teacher is suffering from Alzheimer's disease.

Yash Raj Films. India. 2005. 122m. C. *Producer:* Anshumaan Shwami, Sanjay Leela Bhansali *Director:* Sanjay Leela Bhansali *Writers:* Sanjay Leela Bhansali, Bhavani Iyer, Prakash Kapadia *Cast:* Amitabh Bachchan, Rani Mukherjee, Shernaz Patel, Ayesha Kapoor, Dhritiman Chatterjee, Sillo Mahava, Chippy Gangjee, Mahabanoo Mody-Kotwal, Salomi Roy Kapur, Kenny Desai, Arif Shah, Bomie E. Dotiwala, Jeroo Shroff, Bomi Kapadia, Kamal Adib

78. *Black Sheep of Whitehall*

A professor (Will Hay) teaching at a correspondence school discovers that a Nazi agent is trying to prevent a trade treaty between England and South America. The agent is impersonating an economics expert.

Ealing. Great Britain. 1941. 80m. B&W. *Producer:* Michael Balcon *Directors:* Will Hay, Basil Dearden, *Writers:* Angus Macphail, John Dighton *Cast:* Will Hay, Basil Sydney, John Mills, Frank Cellier, Felix Aylmer, Henry Hewitt, Joss Ambler, Thora Hird, Leslie Mitchell, Frank Allenby, Babs Valerie, Brefni O'Rorke, George Ralph, Ronald Shiner, Aubrey Mallalieu, Geroge Merritt

Blackboards see Takhté slah

79. The Blacklist

Colorado Mine president Warren Harcourt (Charles Clary) arrives to see for himself why the miners are upset. The conditions are so bad that schoolmistress Vera Maroff (Blanche Sweet) has been given the task of killing Warren. She falls in love with Warren and ends up only wounding him. She then fails in her own suicide attempt. Warren gives the miners rights and plans to run the mine with Vera.

Paramount. US. 1916. B&W. *Director:* William C. de Mille *Writers:* Marion Fairfax, William C. de Mille *Cast:* Blanche Sweet, Charles Clary, Ernest Joy, Billy Elmer, Horace B. Carpenter, Lucien Littlefield, Jane Wolf

80. Blanche Fury

Ambitious but poor Blanche Fuller (Valerie Hobson) becomes governess to her wealthy cousins, who have adopted the name Fury since they inherited the ancestral home via marriage the Fury family. Blanche plots to become mistress of the home but her lust for vengeful Philip Thorn (Stewart Granger) may get in the way. Philip claims that the estate is his but he can't prove his birthright.

GFD/Cineguild. Great Britain. 1948. 95m. C. *Producer:* Anthony Havelock Allan *Director:* Marc Allégret *Writers:* Audrey Erskine Lindop, Hugh Mills, Cecil McGivern, Joseph Shearing (novel) *Cast:* Valerie Hobson, Stewart Granger, Walter Fitzgerald, Michael Gough, Maurice Denham, Sybilla Binder

81. Der Blaue Engel (The Blue Angel)

An aging and proper schoolteacher, Uhrath (Emil Jannings), becomes attracted to and marries Lola-Lola (Marlene Dietrich), a night club singer who deceives and humiliates him.

Paramount. Germany. 1930. 98m. B&W. *Director:* Josef von Sternberg *Writer:* Robert Liebmann, Karl Zückmayer, Karl Vollmüller *Cast:* Emil Jannings, Marlene Dietrich, Kurt Gerron, Hans Albers

82. The Blazing Trail

A young doctor suffering from a blood condition goes to the Blue Ridge Mountains to relax. While there, he takes a job as a lumberjack and falls in love with a schoolteacher who has been sent to enforce state school laws. Misunderstandings occur until his medical partner arrives with a lifesaving serum and everything turns out fine.

Universal. US. 1921. B&W. *Director:* Robert Thornby *Writer:* Lucien Hubbard *Cast:* Frank Mayo, Frank Holland, Verne Winter, Bert Sprotte, Madge Hunt, Mary Philbin, Lillian Rich, Ray Ripley, Joy Winthrop, Helen Gilmore

83. *Blondie's Big Moment*

By putting a big deal in jeopardy, Dagwood (Arthur Lake) is in trouble with his new boss George M. Radcliffe before they even meet. Dagwood's wife Blondie (Penny Singleton) invites Radcliffe and a feisty and attractive blonde schoolteacher Harriet Gary (Anita Louise) over for dinner to try and mend the problem. Miss Gary is there to get permission from Dagwood to take her class to see Dagwood's office.

Columbia. US. 1947. 69m. B&W. *Producer:* Burt Kelly *Director:* Abby Berlin *Writer:* Connie Lee *Cast:* Penny Singleton, Arthur Lake, Larry Simms, Marjorie Ann Mutchie, Anita Louise, Jerome Cowan, Danny Mummert, Jack Rice, Jack Davis, Johnny Granath, Hal K. Dawson, Eddie Acuff, Alyn Lockwood, Robert De Haven, Robert Kellard

84. *Blossoms in the Dust*

Edna Gladney (Greer Garson), who has lost her own child, opens an orphanage when she sees how the law treats unwanted children. The film is based on the true story of Edna Gladney.

MGM. US. 1941. 99m. C. *Producer:* Irving Asher *Director:* Mervyn Le Roy *Writer:* Anita Loos *Cast:* Greer Garson, Walter Pidgeon, Felix Bressart, Marsha Hunt, Fay Holden, Samuel S. Hinds

The Blue Angel see Der Blaue Engel

85. *Blue Murder at St. Trinian's*

To the horror of the Ministry of Education, the schoolgirls win an essay contest with a European "Goodwill" trip to Rome as the prize. They become involved with a jewel thief who travels with them, disguised as their headmistress.

British Lion/John Marvel. Great Britain. 1957. 86m. B&W. *Producers:* Frank Launder, Sidney Gilliat *Director:* Frank Launder *Writers:* Frank Launder, Val Valentine, Sidney Gilliat *Cast:* Terry-Thomas, George Cole, Joyce Grenfell, Alastair Sim, Judith Furse, Sabrina, Lionel Jeffries, Lloyd Lamble, Thorley Walters, Kenneth Griffith, Eric Barker, Richard Wattis, Michael Ripper, Lisa Gastoni, Dilys Laye, Kenneth Griffith, Guido Lorraine, Peter Jones, Terry Scott, Alma Taylor

86. *The Blue Peter (Navy Heroes)*

A confused war hero becomes a trainer at an Outward Bound school for boys.

British Lion/Beaconsfield. Great Britain. 1955. 93m. C. *Producer:* Herbert Mason *Director:* Wolf Rilla *Writers:* Don Sharp, John Pudney *Cast:* Kieron Moore, Greta Gynt, Sarah Lawson, Mervyn Johns, Ram Gopal, Edwin Richfield, Harry Fowler, John Charlesworth

87. *The Blue Veil*

After the death of her newborn son, war widow Louise "LouLou" Mason (Jane Wyman) accepts a temporary job as a nursemaid-nanny. One position leads to another as she forsakes love and other options to care for children. Now elderly and poor, LouLou is told that she is too old to be a nanny, so she takes a janitorial job in an elementary school to be near children. One of her now grown charges recognizes her and invites her to dinner. He has arranged for many of her former "children" to be there. He also asks her to be nanny to his two small children. This is a remake of the French film *Le Voile Bleu* with Gaby Morlay as the governess.

RKO. US. 1951. 114m. B&W. *Producers*: Jerry Wald, Norman Krasna, Raymond Hakim *Director*: Curtis Bernhardt *Writer*: Norman Corwin *Cast*: Jane Wyman, Charles Laughton, Richard Carlson, Joan Blondell, Agnes Moorehead, Don Taylor, Audrey Totter, Everett Sloane, Cyril Cusack, Natalie Wood, Warner Anderson, Alan Napier, Henry Morgan, Vivian Vance, Les Young, John Ridgely, Dan O'Herlihy, Carleton Young

The Blue Veil (French version) see *Le Voile Bleu*

The Boarding School see *La Residencia*

88. *A Boarding School Prank*

Three boarding school girls play a prank on their schoolmistress, which results in her being covered in soot.

American Mutoscope and Biograph Co. US. 1903. B&W.

89. *Bokuto kidan (The Twilight Story)*

A small-town girl (Fujiko Yamamoto) becomes a prostitute in Tokyo to support her sick mother. She hopes someday to marry a teacher (Hiroshi Akutagawa) who has told her that he is single. Actually, he is unhappily married to a woman whose child is not his. The teacher returns to his wife. The prostitute's unhappiness deepens when her uncle squanders funds entrusted to him, her mother dies, and she becomes sick.

Toho. Japan. 1962. 150m. B&W. *Producer*: Ichiro Sato *Director*: Shiro Toyoda *Writer*: Toshio Yasumi. *Cast*: Hiroshi Akutagawa, Fujiko Yamamoto, Masao Oda, Michiyo Aratama, Eijiro Tono, Nobuko Otowa, Keiko Awaji, Shikaku Nakamura

90. *Borrowed Trouble*

Hoppy and the boys head into town after finishing a trail drive. There is a conflict between prim middle-aged schoolteacher Miss Abott (Anne O'Neal) and the next door saloon owner Mawson (John Parrish). Miss Abott disappears, and Hoppy suspects that Mawson is the culprit. Hoppy takes over as teacher when the children start to run wild. Hoppy learns about Mawson's cabin where he finds Miss

Abott but it seems that she was kidnapped by Mawson's saloon rival, who wanted to make trouble for Mawson.

UA. US. 1948. 59m. B&W. *Producers:* William Boyd, Lewis J. Rachmil *Director:* George Archainbaud *Writer:* Charles Belden *Cast:* William Boyd, Andy Clyde, Rand Brooks, Anne O'Neal, John Parrish, Cliff Clark, Helen Chapman, Earle Hodgins, Herbert Rawlinson, Don Haggerty, James Harrison, Clarke Stevens, George Sowards, Nancy Stone, Jimmy Crane, Billy O'Leary

91. *Bottoms Up*

A seedy schoolmaster passes off his bookie's son as an eastern prince.

ABPC. Great Britain. 1960. 89m. B&W. *Producer-Director:* Mario Zampi *Writers:* Michael Pertwee, Frank Muir, Denis Norden *Cast:* Jimmy Edwards, Arthur Howard, Martita Hunt, Sidney Tafler, Raymond Huntley, Reginald Beckwith, Vanda Hudson, Melvyn Hayes, John Mitchell, Richard Briers, Gordon Phillot

92. *Le Boucher (The Butcher)*

Gentle butcher Popaul (Jean Vanne), who may be a serial killer, falls in love with lovely schoolmistress Mlle. Hélène (Stéphane Audran). Hélène is no ordinary teacher in the small village. She wears stylish clothing and smokes in the street. Popaul courts her with meat and Hélène teaches him to dance.

La Boétie/Euro International. France/Italy. 1969. 94m. C. *Producer:* André Génoves *Writer-Director:* Claude Chabrol *Cast:* Stéphane Audran, Jean Vanne, Antonio Passalia, Marlo Beccaria, Roger Rudel, William Guerault

93. *A Boy Named Charlie Brown*

The first full-length cartoon based on the *Peanuts* comic strip features Charlie Brown, Lucy, Linus, Shroeder, and Snoopy. The story centers on Charlie Brown entering a spelling bee. Adults (including teachers) are never shown and don't speak in words.

National General Pictures Corp. US. 1969. 86m. C. Animated. *Producers:* Lee Mendelson, Bill Melendez *Director:* Bill Melendez *Writer:* Charles M. Schulz *Voices:* Peter Robbins, Pamelyn Ferdin, Glenn Gilger, Andy Pforsich, Sally Dryer, Anne Altieri, Erin Sullivan, Bill Melendez, Linda Mendelson, Christopher De Faria

94. *Boy Student Jia Li*

An unassuming student runs for "Best Boy Student." Soon the teachers begin to recognize his hidden talents.

China. 1996. 90m.C. *Director:* Yuqiang Zhang *Cast*: Jiangnan Chen, Qian He, Li Guandfu.

95. *The Boys of St. Vincent*

Brother Peter Lavin (Henry Czerny) is the evil but pathetic superintendent of The Boys of Saint Vincent, an orphanage. Many of the boys suffer physical, emotional, and sexual abuse at the hands of the brothers. Lavin's reign of horror is ended by a janitor, a police detective, and a Brother. Followed by the sequel *The Boys of St. Vincent: 15 Years Later*.

Alliance. Canada. 1992. 186m. C. *Producers*: Sam Grana, Claudio Luca, Colin Neale *Director:* John N. Smith *Writers:* Sam Grana, John N. Smith, Des Walsh *Cast:* Henry Czerny, Johnny Morina, Brain Dooley, Philip Dinn, Brian Dodd, Ashley Billard, Greg Thomey, Maurice Podbrey, Sam Grana, Aidan Devine

96. *The Boys of St. Vincent: 15 Years Later*

Sequel to *The Boys of St. Vincent* in which boys involved in the events of the earlier film testify against the brothers. Peter Lavin (Henry Czerny) is now married with two children and proclaims his innocence. The men must revisit their horrible childhoods.

Alliance. Canada. 1993. 90m. C. *Producer*: Colin Neale *Director*: John N. Smith *Writers:* Des Walsh, Sam Grana *Cast*: Henry Czerny, Lise Roy, David Hewlett, Timothy Webber, Kristine Demers, Mary Walsh, Sheena Larkin, Pierre Gauthier, Brian Dooley, Michael Chiasson

Boys' School see Les Disparus de St-Agil

97. *Boys Town*

Spencer Tracy won an Academy Award for his performance as the tough but socially committed priest, Father Edward J. Flanagan, who began a home for troubled boys near Omaha. Initially, Father Flanagan creates an agency for down-and-out adults but soon realizes that working with at-risk boys would effect more change. With the help of a few supporters, Father Flanagan builds a "city" for wayward boys called Boys Town. The main sponsor is pawnbroker Dave Morris (Henry Hull), who really makes Boys Town possible. Fundraising and publicity work take up much of Flanagan's time. One day, Flanagan is summoned to the prison to meet with a convict who wants the father to help his brother Whitey (Mickey Rooney). After a few complications, Boys Town is well on its way to becoming a great facility and Father Flanagan turns his dream into a reality. *Boys Town* was one of the top money-making pictures of the year; the original story also received an Academy Award. Followed by *Men of Boys Town*.

Mickey Rooney played Father Flanagan in the 1995 television movie *Brothers' Destiny*, also known as *The Road Home*. The film is about two orphan brothers who travel across the country to reach Boys Town.

MGM. US. 1938. 93m. B&W. *Producer*: John W. Considine, Jr. *Director*: Norman Taurog *Writers*: John Meehan, Dore Schary *Cast*: Spencer Tracy, Mickey Rooney, Henry Hull, Leslie Fenton, Gene Reynolds, Edward Norris, Addison Richards, Minor Watson, Jonathan Hale, Bobs Watson, Martin Spellman, Mickey Rentschler, Frankie Thomas, Jimmy Butler, Sidney Miller, Robert Emmett Keane

98. *Boys Will Be Boys*

When Peep O'Day (Will Rogers) inherits a small fortune, a crooked lawyer tries to steal it. Peep's efforts to help schoolteacher Lucy (Irene Rich) are misunderstood. All is resolved and Lucy wins the man she loves.

Goldwyn Pictures. US. 1921. B&W. *Director:* Clarence G. Badger *Writer:* Edfrid A. Bingham *Cast:* Will Rogers, Irene Rich, C.E. Mason, Sydney Ainsworth, Edward Kimball, H. Milton Ross, C.E. Thurston, May Hopkins, Cordelia Callahan, Nick Cogley, Burton Halbert

99. *Boys Will Be Boys*

Dr. Smart Alec (Will Hay), a teacher in a prison, applies for the headship at a public school. This incompetent headmaster thwarts a jewel robber.

Gaumont/Gainsborough. Great Britain. 1935. 75m. B&W. *Producer:* Michael Balcon *Director:* William Beaudine *Writers:* Will Hay, Robert Edmunds *Cast:* Will Hay, Gordon Harker, Jimmy Hanley, Davy Burnaby, Norma Varden, Claude Dampier, Charles Farrell, Percy Walsh

100. *Brand of Fear*

Schoolteacher Anne Lamont arrives in the small town of Oreville, Arizona. She is hired by her guardian Marshal Black Jack Flint, who is secretly her father. Mine owner Frank Martin is concerned about Anne's safety while preparing for the opening of the school. A man learns of Black Jack's past and uses that information to blackmail him. After numerous gunfights and robberies, Black Jack is able to tell Anne that he is her father.

Monogram. US. 1949. 56m. B&W. *Producer:* Louis Gray *Director:* Oliver Drake *Writer:* Basil Dickey *Cast:* Jimmy Wakely, Cannonball Taylor, Tom London, William Ruhl, Holly Bane, Boyd Stockman, Myron Healey, Bob Curtis, Frank McCarroll, William Bailey, Bill Potter, Joe Galbreath, Dee Cooper

101. *The Bride Goes Wild*

Martha Terryton (June Allyson), a prim and proper grade school teacher living in Vermont with her two maiden aunts, becomes an illustrator of children's books at a New York publishing company. The company's top children's book author, Greg Rawling a.k.a. Uncle Bumps (Van Johnson), is threatening to leave before finishing his new book. He meets Martha and they go out for coffee (she doesn't realize he is Uncle Bumps). Greg spikes her coffee and they get drunk. Martha is livid when she learns that this playboy drunk is Uncle Bumps and threatens to expose him, but the publisher quickly makes up a story about Greg being a widower and a father with so much grief that he drinks. The publisher now must find a boy to play the part of the son. More complications ensue and then Martha's hometown sweetheart, Bruce Johnson, comes into the picture.

MGM. US. 1948. 97m. B&W. *Producer:* William H. Wright *Director:* Norman Taurog *Writer:* Albert Beich *Cast:* Van Johnson, June Allyson, Butch Jenkins,

Hume Cronyn, Una Merkel, Arlene Dahl, Richard Derr, Lloyd Corrigan, Elisabeth Risdon, Clara Blandick, Kathleen Howard

102. *Brides of Christ*

During the 1960s, six nuns and their students face personal crisis and great change within their Australian convent-girls' school as the Catholic Church enters modern times. Mother Ambrose (Sandy Gore) is the Mother Superior of Santo Spirito when the school hires a male teacher; Sister Agnes (Brenda Fricker) is a conservative nun; Sister Catherine (Josephine Byrnes) welcomes reform; Frances is a student whose parents are divorcing; and Rosemary (Kym Wilson) is a rebellious student.

Australian Broadcasting Corporation (a six-episode TV miniseries). Great Britain/ Australia/Ireland. 1991. C. *Producer:* Sue Masters *Director:* Ken Cameron *Writers:* John Alsop, Sue Smith *Cast:* Brenda Fricker, Sandy Gore, Josephine Byrnes, Lisa Hensley, Simon Burke, Melissa Jaffer, Philip Quast, Naomi Watts, Kym Wilson, Russell Crowe, Michael Craig

103. *The Brides of Dracula*

A young teacher on her way to a position in Transylvania unwittingly unleashes a vampire.

Universal/Hammer/Hotspur. Great Britain. 1960. 85m. C. *Producer:* Anthony Hinds *Director:* Terence Fisher *Writers:* Jimmy Sangster, Peter Bryan, Edward Percy *Cast:* David Peel, Peter Cushing, Freda Jackson, Martita Hunt, Yvonne Monlaur, Andrée Melly, Mona Washbourne, Henry Oscar, Miles Malleson

104. *Bridge to Terabithia*

Ten-year-old Jesse Aarons (Josh Hutcherson) is an introverted boy with four sisters, a financially strapped family, and a real talent for drawing. Jesse is regularly picked on by bullies and has a general tough time at school, especially when he wears his sister's old sneakers. Jesse's world changes with the arrival of new student Leslie Burke (AnnaSophia Robb), an artistic extrovert with neglectful parents. They become friends and together they create an imaginary world (Terabithia) in the woods complete with trolls, giants, and other magical beings. The woods turn dark though. The helpful music teacher Ms. Edmonds (Zooey Deschanel) discovers Jesse's artistic ability and helps him to nurture it. The encouragement of this teacher alters the course of Jesse's life.

Walt Disney Pictures. US. 2007. 95m. C. *Producers:* Lauren Levine, Hal Lieberman, David Paterson *Director:* Gabor Csupo *Writers:* Jeff Stockwell, David Paterson, Katherine Paterson (book) *Cast:* Josh Hutcherson, AnnaSophia Robb, Zooey Deschanel, Robert Patrick, Bailee Madison, Katrina Cerio, Devon Wood, Emma Fenton, Grace Branningan, Latham Grimes, Judy McIntosh, Patricia Aldersley, Lauren Clinton

105. Bright Road

In an all-black school, young, energetic teacher Miss Richards (Dorothy Dandridge) tries to help her fourth-grade problem student C.T. Young (Philip Hepburn). With his knowledge of bees, C.T. helps to chase away a swarm of bees in the classroom and finds his place. The principal, Mr. Williams (Harry Belafonte), likes the enthusiasm of the new teacher.

MGM. US. 1953. 69m. B&W. *Producer:* Sol Baer Fielding *Director:* Gerald Mayer *Writer:* Emmett Lavery *Cast:* Dorothy Dandridge, Harry Belafonte, Robert Horton, Philip Hepburn, Barbara Ann Saunders

106. Bring Your Smile Along

A lady schoolteacher goes to New York to write songs.

Columbia. US. 1955. 83m. C. *Writer-Director:* Blake Edwards *Cast:* Frankie Laine, Keefe Brasselle, Constance Towers, Lucy Marlow

107. The Brood

A father is trying to keep his daughter away from the mother, who is in psychotherapy at a posh retreat. Through therapy called psycho-plasmics in which patients change cell structure through internal anger, her doctor has the rage produce homicidal babies. His daughter's teacher, Ruth Meyer (Susan Hogan), befriends the girl and her father. Ruth is accused of trying to break up the family and she is soon murdered by the brood.

New World. Canada. 1979. 91m. C. *Producer:* Claude Heroux *Writer-Director:* David Cronenberg *Cast:* Oliver Reed, Samantha Eggar, Art Hindle, Cindy Hinds, Nuala Fitzgerald, Susan Hogan, Gary McKeehan, Henry Beckman

108. The Browning Version

Rigid and precise middle-aged English schoolmaster Andrew Crocker-Harris (Michael Redgraves) is unpopular with his students, and has a wife pursuing an affair with a younger master. Crocker-Harris is being forced out of his job when student Taplow (Brian Smith) gives him a copy of Robert Browning's translation of "Agamemnon," with an inscription from Taplow. Upon his departure, Crocker-Harris apologizes to the students for not caring and for being a failure as a teacher.

GFD/Javlin. Great Britain. 1951. 90m. B&W. *Producer:* Teddy Baird *Director:* Anthony Asquith *Writer:* Terrence Rattigan *Cast:* Michael Redgrave, Jean Kent, Nigel Patrick, Wilfred Hyde-White, Bill Travers, Ronald Howard, Brian Smith, Paul Medland. Ivan Samson, Josephine Middleton, Peter Jones, Sarah Lawson, Scott Harold, Judith Furse, Russell Waters

109. The Browning Version

It is the end of the term and unloved schoolmaster Andrew Crocker-Harris (Albert Finney) has been forced out of his job—and his wife is having an affair with his young colleague. Each year Andrew has become more dictatorial, humorless and rigid. A student, Taplow (Ben Silverstone), gives him a copy of Robert Browning's translation of "Agamemnon," inscribed by Taplow.

Paramount. Great Britain. 1994. 97m. C. *Producers:* Ridley Scott, Mimi Polk *Director:* Mike Figgis *Writer:* Ronald Harwood *Cast:* Albert Finney, Greta Sacchi, Matthew Modine, Ben Silverstone, Michael Gambon, Julian Sands

110. *Buckskin*

A villain steals the money of simple miners in his gambling houses and stops the water for homesteaders so he can get the land to sell to the railroad. One man wants to blow up the dam. Nora Johnson (Joan Caulfield) is a saloon tart who has just about given up hope of ever being a schoolmarm once more.

Paramount. US. 1968. 97m. C. *Producer:* A.C. Lyles *Director:* Michael Moore *Writer:* Michael Fisher *Cast:* Barry Sullivan, Joan Caulfield, Lon Chaney, Jr., John Russell, Richard Arlen, Barbara Hale, Bill Williams, Barton MacLane

111. *Buongiorno, Elefante! (Pardon My Trunk)*

After befriending an Indian prince, a poor schoolteacher is given a baby elephant. The family tries to keep it in their apartment but it ends up at the zoo. The teacher visits it daily.

Dear Film. Italy. 1952. B&W. *Producer:* Vittorio DeSica *Director:* Gianni Franciolini *Writers:* Suso Cecchi D'Amico, Cesare Zavattini *Cast:* Vittorio DeSica, Sabu, Maria Mercader

112. *Buried Alive*

A psychiatrist, made mad by his father's experiments, turns a former asylum into a school for disturbed girls.

TCF. US. 1991. 91m. C. *Producer:* Harry Alan Towers *Director:* Gérard Kikoine *Writers:* Jake Clesi, Stuart Lee *Cast:* Robert Vaughn, Donald Pleasence, Karen Witter, John Carradine, Nia Long, Ginger Lynn Allen, Bill Butler

113. *The Bushwhackers*

Confederate veteran Jeff Waring (John Ireland) arrives in Missouri after the Civil War vowing never again to use a gun. An evil land baron is pushing settlers away. Jeff sides with the good schoolmarm Cathy Sharpe (Dorothy Malone) and her dad, the newspaper editor, against the land baron.

Realart. US. 1952. 70m. B&W. *Director:* Rodney Amateau *Writers:* Rodney Amateau, Tom Gries *Cast:* John Ireland, Wayne Morris, Lawrence Tierney, Dorothy Malone, Lon Chaney, Jr., Bill Holmes, Jack Elam, Bob Woods, Charles Trowbridge, Myrna Dell

114. *Bustin' Loose*

Ex-con Joe Braxton (Richard Pryor) is given another chance after violating his probation. He has been hired by schoolteacher Vivian Perry (Cicely Tyson) to repair and drive an old school bus with a group of special kids to another home (their old home was shut down by the city of Philadelphia). The kids are a handful but Joe bonds with them and Vivian as they make their way to Vivian's farm. In pursuit is Vivian's boyfriend, a social worker who wants Joe back in jail.

Universal. US. 1981. 94m. C. *Producer:* William Greaves *Director:* Oz Scott *Writer:* Roger L. Simon *Cast:* Richard Pryor, Cicely Tyson, Angel Ramirez, Jimmy Hughes

115. *Butch Cassidy and the Sundance Kid*

Butch and the Sundance Kid are lovable crooks who switch to bank robbery when their old stealing ways no longer work. Their friend Etta Place (Katharine Ross) runs away from her life to help rob banks with Butch and Sundance. She explains, "I am 21 and single and a schoolteacher and that is the bottom of the pit."

TCF. US. 1969. 110m. C. *Producer:* John Forman *Director:* George Roy Hill *Writer:* William Goldman *Cast:* Paul Newman, Robert Redford, Katharine Ross, Strother Martin, Henry Jones, Jeff Corey, Cloris Leachman, Ted Cassidy, Kenneth Mars

The Butcher see Le Boucher

Butterfly see La Lengua de las Mariposas

116. *Ça Commence Aujourd'hui (It All Starts Today)*

Daniel Lefebvre (Philippe Torreton) is the director of a pre-school in a town devastated by the closing of the coal mines. Poverty, physical abuse and despair are realities that the children face daily. Under Daniel's guidance the school is a refuge for the children of this very economically depressed town. In the safety of the school, the children sing songs, play games, and hear stories. Daniel must also deal with the many frustrations caused by the system.

Independent Artists. France. 1999. 117m. C. *Producers:* Frédéric Bourboulon, Alain Sarde *Director:* Bertrand Tavernier *Writers:* Dominique Sampiero, Bertrand Tavernier, Tiffany Tavernier *Cast:* Philippe Torreton, Maria Pitarresi, Nadia Kaci, Véronique Ataly, Nathalie Bécue, Emmanuelle Bercot, Françoise Bette, Christine Citti, Christina Crevillén, Sylviane Goudal

117. *La Cage aux Rossignols (A Cage of Nightingales)*

An out-of-work writer, Clement, goes to teach at a reform school. The kids are out of control, but by treating them as adults and acknowledging them, Clement is able to bring them under control. He accidentally discovers that they have beautiful voices and organizes them into a choir. Clement writes about his experiences at the school and it is published.

Lopert Pictures Corp. France. 1945. 89m. B&W. *Director:* Jean Dréville *Writers:* Noël-Noël, Georges Chaperot *Cast:* Noël-Noël, Micheline Francey, Georges Biscot,

René Génin, René Blancard, Marguerite Ducouret, Marcelle Praince, Marthe Mellot, Georges Paulais, André Nicolle, Richard Francoeur, Jean Morel, Roger Vincent, Michel François, Roger Krebs

A Cage of Nightingales see *La Cage aux Rossignols*

Calabuch see *The Rocket from Calabuch*

118. Camila

The story takes place five years before Juan Manuel De Rosas was overthrown. Young Catholic socialite Camila (Susú Pecoraro) and Father Ladislao Gutierrez (Imanol Arais) meet and fall in love in Buenos Aires. Plagued by fear, bigotry and prejudice, they flee Buenos Aires and travel 500 miles up the Parana River where they settle and live happily for a time. They start a school for the children of nearby settlers. They are discovered by a priest, but are given a chance to escape by the local commander. However, after a night of praying they surrender the next morning. Because of pressure from the Church, society and political enemies, their execution is ordered and they are shot. The real-life story occurred in 1847. In 1909, director Mario Gallo filmed Camila's story as *Camila O'Gorman* with Blanca Podesta in the title role.

GEA. Argentina/Spain. 1984. 105m. C. *Producer:* Lita Stantic *Director:* Maria Luisa Bemberg *Writers:* Beda Docampo Feijóo, Juan Bautista Stagnaro, María Luisa Bemberg *Cast:* Susú Pecoraro, Imanol Arias, Héctor Alterio, Elena Tasisto, Mona Maris, Claudio Gallardou

119. The Campbells Are Coming

In 1857, Mary McLean (Grace Cunard) leaves her sweetheart and the Scottish Highlands to teach school in India, where her father is a missionary. Mary and her father are captured by rebels.

Universal Film Manufacturing Co. US. 1915. B&W. *Producer-Director:* Francis Ford *Writer:* Grace Cunard *Cast:* Francis Ford, Grace Cunard, Mr. Denecke, Duke Wome, Harry Schumm, Lew Short

120. O Cangaceiro (The Bandit)

A captured schoolteacher comes between the leader of a gang of cangaceiros (Brazilian bandits) and his young lieutenant.

Columbia. Brazil. 1953. 119m. B&W. *Director:* Lima Barreto *Writers:* Lima Barreto, Rachel De Queiroz *Cast:* Alberto Ruschel, Marisa Prado, Milton Ribeiro, Vanja Orico

121. Les Caprices de Marie (Give Her the Moon)

Life in a quaint French village life includes a retired, crusty military man, a businessman who prefers writing poetry, a dreamy cello-playing teacher, the cafe owner-mayor and his daughter. She loves the schoolteacher but yearns for the outside world. A rich American wants to marry her but she cannot leave her town. He buys the town and moves to an island near the Statue of Liberty. The townspeople can't fit in with the busy pace and are sent back to their old homes.

UA. Italy/France. 1970. 92m. C. *Producer:* Christian Ferry *Director:* Philippe de Broca *Writer:* Daniel Boulanger *Cast:* Philippe Noiret, Bert Convy, Valentina Cortese, Fernand Gravey, Jean-Pierre Marielle, François Périer, Marthe Keller, Didi Perego, Colin Drake, Henri Crémieux, Marc Dukicourt, Georges Guéret, Dorothy Marchini, Olga Valéry

122. *Captain Bill*

A bargee saves a schoolmistress from trouble with crooks.

Leslie Fuller. Great Britain. 1935. 81m. B&W. *Producer:* Joe Rock *Director:* Ralph Cedar *Writers:* Val Valentine, Syd Courtenay, George Harris *Cast:* Leslie Fuller, Georgie Harris, Judy Kelly, Hal Gordon, O.B. Clarence, D.J. Williams, Toni Edgar Bruce, Ralph Truman

Carla see *Karla*

123. *Carried Away*

Joseph Svenden (Dennis Hopper), a country schoolteacher, succumbs to a beautiful, sexually experienced teenager. This affair creates problems for Joseph, who has been involved in a stable long-term relationship with fellow teacher Rosealee Henson (Amy Irving), a middle-aged widow with two children.

Fine Line Features. US. 1996. 104m. C. *Producers:* Lisa M. Hansen, Paul Hertzberg *Director:* Bruno Barreto *Writers:* Ed Jones, Dale Herd, Jim Harrison (novel) *Cast:* Dennis Hopper, Amy Irving, Amy Locane, Julie Harris, Gary Busey, Hal Holbrook

124. *Carry On, Teacher*

Popular headmaster William Wakefield (Ted Ray) has applied for the headmaster's job at a new country school after 20 years at his present position. He is so beloved that his students will do anything to keep him there.

Anglo Amalgamated. Great Britain. 1962. 86m.B&W. *Producer:* Peter Rogers *Director:* Gerald Thomas *Writer:* Norman Hudis *Cast:* Ted Ray, Kenneth Williams, Charles Hawtrey, Leslie Phillips, Joan Sims, Kenneth Connor, Hattie Jacques, Rosalind Knight, Cyril Chamberlain, Richard O'Sullivan, Carol White

125. *Caterina in the Big City*

Giancarlo Iacovoni (Sergio Castellitto), a bitter teacher and aspiring novelist, lives with his timid wife Agatha (Margherita Buy) and their sweet 12-year-old daughter Caterina (Alice Teghil). He has secured a long-sought-after job in Rome. He considers his last position as "the most depressing waste of time in my life."

Upon arriving at her new school, Caterina finds herself in a tug of war between two cliques (leftist communist and right-winged fascist).

Empire Pictures. Italy. 2005. 106m. C. *Producers:* Riccardo Tozzi, Giovanni Stabilini, Marco Chimenz *Director:* Paolo Virzi *Writers:* Paolo Virzi, Francesco Bruni *Cast:* Alice Teghil, Sergio Castellitto, Margherita Buy, Zach Wallen, Federica Sbrenna, Carolina Iaquaniello, Galatea Ranzi, Claudio Amendola

Cats' Play see Macskajaték

Celine and Julie Go Boating see Céline et Julie Vont en Bateau

126. *Céline et Julie Vont en Bateau (Celine and Julie Go Boating)*

Céline (Juliet Berto), a magician in a cheap nightclub, and Julie (Dominique Labourier), a librarian, meet. Céline tells her how sometimes she works as governess to a little girl who lives in a strange house with her widowed father and two women. Céline and Julie enter the house and are drawn into the drama.

Les Films Du Losange. France. 1974. 192m. C. *Director:* Jacques Rivette *Writers:* Jacques Rivette, Eduardo Di Gregorio, Juliet Berto, Dominique Labourier *Cast:* Dominique Labourier, Juliet Berto, Bulle Ogier, Marie-France Pisier, Barbet Schroeder, Nathalie Asnar, Philippe Clevenot

Cet Âge Sans Pitié see Anthracite — Cet Âge Est Sans Pitié

127. *The Chalk Garden*

Governess Madrigal (Deborah Kerr) is a strong woman with a shadow of mystery who cares for an undisciplined girl named Laurel (Hayley Mills). Laurel's grandmother, Mrs. Maugham (Edith Evans), pampers and spoils the child. Governess Madrigal handles the child and the gardening in chalky soil.

Universal. Great Britain. 1963. 106m. C. *Producer:* Ross Hunter *Director:* Ronald Neame *Writers:* John Michael Hayes, Enid Bagnold (novel) *Cast:* Edith Evans, Deborah Kerr, Hayley Mills, John Mills, Felix Aylmer, Elizabeth Sellars, Lally Bowers, Toke Townley, Tonie MacMillan

128. *Chalk Marks*

Angelina Kilbourne (Marguerite Snow) becomes a teacher when Herbert Thompson (Ramsey Wallace) marries another. She does many good deeds as a teacher and later in life convinces Herbert to defend his son, Bert, against murder charges. Now aged, Angelina needs Bert's help to prevent a progress-minded school administrator from firing her.

Producers Distributing Corp. US. 1924. B&W. *Producer-Writer:* Frank E.

Woods *Director:* John G. Adolfi *Cast:* Marguerite Snow, Ramsey Wallace, June Elvidge, Lydia Knott, Rex Lease, Helen Ferguson, Priscilla Bonner, Harold Holland, Verna Mercereau, Fred Church, Lee Willard

129. *Charlie Chan in Panama*

Panama City is alive with spies, just as the United States fleet is preparing to travel through the Panama Canal. New arrivals who may be spies include novelist Clivedon Compton (Lionel Atwill), prim schoolteacher Miss Jennie Fitch (Mary Nash), scientist Dr. Rudolph Grosser (Lionel Royce), and café owner-singer-salesman-engineer-agent Godley (Addison Richards). Godley goes to Charlie Chan (Sidney Toler) to expose the true identity of a spy (code name: Reiner). He dies before he is able to tell Chan. Chan forces Miss Finch to expose herself as the saboteur and spy.

TCF. US. 1940. 67m. B&W. *Director:* Norman Foster *Writers:* John Larkin, Lester Ziffren *Cast:* Sidney Toler, Jean Rogers, Lionel Atwill, Mary Nash, Sen Yung, Kane Richmond, Chris-Pin Martin, Lionel Royce, Jack La Rue, Edwin Stanley, Don Douglas, Frank Puglia, Addison Richards, Edward Keane

130. *Cheers for Miss Bishop*

Midwestern schoolteacher Ella Bishop's (Martha Scott) fiancé runs off with her cousin. After the cousin dies in childbirth, Ella cares for the child. Her love life has been sad with many missed chances, but as she reaches retirement, she reflects back over her 50-year career as a schoolteacher which has been rich and rewarding. Students from over the years return to honor their beloved Miss Bishop.

UA. USA. 1941. 95m. B&W. *Producer:* Richard A. Rowland. *Director:* Tay Garnett *Writers:* Adelaide Heilbron, Bess Streeter Aldrich (novel) *Cast:* Martha Scott, William Gargan, Edmund Gwenn, Sterling Holloway, Sidney Blackmer, Mary Anderson, Dorothy Peterson, Donald Douglas, Marsha Hunt, John Archer, Lois Ranson, Rosemary DeCamp, Knox Manning, John Arledge, Dustin Farnum

131. *Chen Yi-Shin lao shi*

This film is based on a true incident from the '80s. A teacher (Mu Si-Cheng) takes his students on a field trip to the mountain and on the way they encounter a huge wasp attack. The teacher sacrifices his life by exposing his naked body to the wasps' stings to save the lives of his students.

Taiwan. 1986. 45m. C. *Writer-Producer-Director:* Josequ Kuo. *Cast:* Chen Qiu Yan, Mu Si-Cheng, Yin Yin, Yi Yuan, LanYu-Han, Li Zhong-Yi

132. *Chère Louise (Louise)*

After the death of her mother, divorcèe Louise starts a new life as a teacher in Annecy. There she befriends Luigi, a poor, much younger Italian. Soon he becomes her lover.

Les Films Ariane. France. 1972. 105m. C. *Director:* Philippe de Broca *Writer:*

Jean-Loup Dabadie *Cast:* Jeanne Moreau, Julian Negulesco, Didi Perego, Yves Robert, Pippo Starnazza

133. *Cheyenne Autumn*

The passionate and moving story of the mistreatment of Native Americans, who were deceitfully moved from rich lands to a bleak and barren area in the southwest. Deborah Wright (Carroll Baker), a sympathetic Quaker schoolteacher, accompanies the displaced natives on their desperate journey home. The original band of 1,000 has been reduced by disease and starvation to a mere 286. Pursuing them is Captain Thomas Archer (Richard Widmark), Deborah's betrothed, who hopes to resolve the situation peacefully. One young brave is ready to fight. The Cheyenne are captured and will be forced to return but Captain Archer intervenes and a treaty permitting the Cheyenne to return to their homeland is signed. Archer and Deborah remain with the Cheyenne.

Warner. US. 1964. 170m. C. *Producer:* Bernard Smith *Director:* John Ford *Writer:* James R. Webb *Cast:* Richard Widmark, Carroll Baker, Karl Malden, Dolores del Rio, Sal Mineo, Edward G. Robinson, Ricardo Montalban, Gilbert Roland, Arthur Kennedy, John Carradine, Victor Jory, Mike Mazurki, George O'Brien, Sean McClory, John Qualen, Elizabeth Allen, Patrick Wayne, James Stewart

134. *Chichi Ariki (There Was a Father)*

A widowed schoolteacher is very close to his son but they live separate lives with his son in boarding school and then university. Before he dies, he sees his son marry the daughter of his best friend.

Shochiku/Ofuna. Japan. 1942. 94m. B&W. *Director:* Yasujiro Ozu *Writers:* Tadao Ikeda, Takao Yanai, Yasujiro Ozu *Cast:* Chishu Ryu, Shuji Sano, Haruhiko Tsuda, Mitsuko Mito, Takeshi Sakamoto, Shin Saburi

135. *Chiedo Asilo (Seeking Asylum)*

The new, playful and highly spirited pre-school teacher (Roberto Benigni) takes the kids on field trips, entertains and educates in novel ways, and has a very unorthodox style of teaching. One of the first children he meets is mute. He is able to view life through a child's eyes and he really cares about the kids. He has a relationship with one child's mother and she becomes pregnant. He is very uncertain as to what to do now.

Gaumont Italia. Italy/France. 1979. 110m. C. *Producer:* Jacqueline Ferreri *Director:* Marco Ferreri *Writers:* Roberto Benigni, Gérard Brach, Marco Ferreri *Cast:* Roberto Benigni, Dominique Laffin, Luca Levi, Girolamo Marzano, Carlo Monni, Chiara Moretti, Roberto Amaro, Francesca De Sapio

136. *A Child Is Waiting*

Jean Hansen (Judy Garland) comes to teach at a school for disabled children. She becomes especially involved with young Reuben Widdicombe (Bruce Ritchey), an autistic boy whose parents have not visited in several years. Her involvement generates a crisis when she makes a personal appeal to the parents of the boy. The school principal, Dr. Matthew Clark (Burt Lancaster), is not pleased with her approach to teaching. He believes that mentally challenged children need to be taught to be self-reliant in an unemotional manner and not pampered. The film recounts how the teachers educate and train their students using unemotional responses.

UA. US. 1963. 104m. B&W. *Producer:* Stanley Kramer *Director:* John Cassavetes *Writer:* Abby Mann *Cast:* Burt Lancaster, Judy Garland, Bruce Ritchey, Steven Hill, Gena Rowlands, Paul Stewart, Lawrence Tierney

137. *A Child of God*

Francis Angel (Francelia Billington), schoolteacher in a western town, and Jim MacPherson (Sam de Grasse), a wealthy rancher, are attracted to each other. She initially refuses his proposal, but develops new respect for him after he saves her from unwanted advances. Her father asks her to come back east where he wants her to marry her former sweetheart Chet. She agrees to marry Chet when she learns that her penniless sister and baby are coming east. The train carrying Jane crashes near Jim's ranch and Jim consents to be the baby's godfather. Parson Perrin (Richard Cummings) baptizes the baby and agrees to bring the baby east. Jim, influenced by an evangelist, becomes a child of God. He travels east and meets Francis on her wedding day. Chet and Jim fight and Francis accepts Jim's proposal.

Mutual Film Corp. US. 1915. B&W. *Director:* John G. Adolfi *Writer:* Cyrus Townsend Brady *Cast:* Sam de Grasse, Francelia Billington, Richard Cummings

The Children see *Les Petits*

138. *Children of a Lesser God*

James Leeds (William Hurt) a renegade teacher of the deaf, ends up in a small New England school for the deaf. Dr. Franklin (Philip Bosco), the school administrator, warns him not to be too creative with his teaching style. Leeds' methods include playing loud rock music so the students will feel the vibrations. He also tries to teach them to speak phonetically. When he meets the attractive custodian Sarah (Marlee Matlin), who never left because of the cruel hearing world, his attention turns to helping her. Through the process they fall in love.

Paramount. US. 1986. 119m. C. *Producers:* Burt Sugarman, Patrick Palmer *Director:* Randa Haines *Writer:* Mark Medoff *Cast:* William Hurt, Marlee Matlin, Piper Laurie, Philip Bosco, Allison Gompf, John F. Cleary, Georgia Ann Cline, William D. Byrd, Frank Carter, Jr., Archie Hahn III, Bob Hilterman, E. Katherine Kerr, Gigi Vorgan, Jack Blessing, James Carrington, John Basinger, John Limnidis, Leigh French, Linda Bove, Lynne Stewart, Nicholas Guest, Philip Holmes

Children of Hiroshima see *Genbaku No Ko*

Children on the Island see *Nijushi no hitomi (1987)*

139. The Children's Hour

Spoiled schoolgirl Mary Tilford (Karen Balkin) spreads the rumor that her schoolmistresses Martha Dobie (Shirley MacLaine) and Karen Wright (Audrey Hepburn) are lesbians. The accusation hurts the relationship between Karen and her boyfriend Dr. Joe Cardin (James Garner). The lie grows and children are withdrawn from their school. The women sue for libel but Martha's aunt Mrs. Lily Mortar (Miriam Hopkins) refuses to testify. By the time Mary's lie is exposed, it is too late. Miriam Hopkins played the Martha Dobie role in an earlier (1936) film version of the Lillian Hellman story, *These Three*.

UA. US. 1961. 108m. B&W. *Producer-Director:* William Wyler *Writer:* Lillian Hellman *Cast:* Audrey Hepburn, Shirley MacLaine, James Garner, Miriam Hopkins, Fay Bainter, Karen Balkin

140. Child's Play

At an exclusive boy's school, the gym teacher is caught in a feud between two older instructors. He soon discovers that things are not as tranquil and harmless at the school as they seem.

Paramount. US. 1972. 100m. C. *Producer:* David Merrick *Director:* Sidney Lumet *Writer:* Leon Prochnik *Cast:* James Mason, Robert Preston, Beau Bridges, Ronald Weyand, Charles White, David Rounds, Kate Harrington, Jamie Alexander, Brian Chapin, Bryant Fraser, Mark Hall Haefeli, Tom Leopold, Julius Lo Iacono, Christopher Man, Paul O'Keefe

141. China Girl

In World War II China, American newsreel cameraman Johnny (George Montgomery) falls in love with a Eurasian schoolteacher, Miss Young (Gene Tierney).

TCF. US. 1943. 95m. B&W. *Producer-Writer:* Ben Hecht *Director:* Henry Hathaway *Cast:* Gene Tierney, George Montgomery, Lynn Bari, Victor McLaglen, Alan Baxter, Sig Rumann, Myron McCormick, Philip Ahn

142. Les Choristes (The Chorus)

Clément Mathieu (Gérard Jugnot), the new teacher at a very harshly run boarding school, is able to positively affect the students' lives through music and turn the misfits into an angelic choir. Two memorable students are Pierre Morhange (Jean-Baptiste Maunier), a soprano with a haunting voice, and Pepinot (Maxence Perrin), a young boy who waits every Saturday at the gate for parents who never come. At the end, Clément takes the young Pepinot with him when he leaves the school.

Miramax. France/Switzerland/Germany. 2004. 96m. C. *Director:* Christophe Barratier *Writers:* Georges Chaperot, René Wheeler *Cast:* Gérard Jugnot, François Berléand, Kad Merad, Jean-Paul Bonnaire, Marie Bunel, Jean-Baptiste Maunier, Maxence Perrin, Grégory Gatignol, Thomas Blumenthal, Cyril Bernicot, Simon Fargeot, Théodule Carré-Chassaigne, Philippe Du Janerand, Carole Weiss, Erick Desmarestz

The Chorus see *Les Choristes*

143. *Christmas Lilies of the Field*

Homer Smith (Billy Dee Williams) returns to the chapel which he built years before. The selfless behavior of the nuns, including Mother Maria (Maria Schell), motivates him to build an orphanage and school for the children. Sequel to *Lilies of the Field*.

NBC. US. 1979. 100m. C. *Producer-Director*: Ralph Nelson *Writers*: John McGreevey, Ralph Nelson *Cast*: Billy Dee Williams, Maria Schell, Fay Hauser, Lisa Mann, Hanna Hertelendy, Judith Piquet, Donna Johnston, Bob Hastings, Jean Jenkins, Fred Hart, Sam Di Bello

144. *A Christmas Story*

A small boy in 1940s Indiana is obsessed with getting a Red Ryder 200-shot Carbine Action Air Rifle for Christmas. A good deal of the movie takes place in his classroom. During recess, Ralph is part of a group that dares Flick to lick the flagpole; his tongue sticks to it and the others run back to class, leaving Flick alone. Miss Shields (Tedde Moore) asks where Flick is but no one will tell her. Finally a girl in the class points to the flagpole. Ralph turns in an essay to Miss Shields on what he wants for Christmas. He dreams of getting a good grade on his composition. He even tries to bribe Miss Shields with a large fruit basket. When his paper receives a C+, Ralph sees Miss Shields as a witch.

MGM/UA. US. 1983. 93m. C. *Producers:* René Dupont, Bob Clark *Director:* Bob Clark *Writers:* Jean Shepherd, Leigh Brown, Bob Clark *Cast:* Peter Billingsley, Melinda Dillon, Daren McGavin, Ian Petrella, Tedde Moore

Ciao, Professore! see *Io Speriamo Che Me la Cava*

145. *The Cider House Rules*

Maine orphanage director Dr. Wilbur Larch (Michael Caine) imparts his medical knowledge to Homer (Tobey Maguire). Unfortunately, Homer decides to leave the orphanage to see the world.

Mirimax Films. US. 1999. 126m. C. *Director:* Lasse Hallström *Writer:* John Irving *Cast:* Tobey Maguire, Charlize Theron, Delroy Lindo, Paul Rudd, Michael Caine, Jane Alexander, Kathy Baker, Erykah Badu, Kieran Culking, Kate Nelligan, Heavy D, K. Todd Freeman, Paz de la Huerta, J.K. Simmons, Evan Parke

146. *De Cierta Manera (One Way or Another)*

A middle-class schoolteacher and a mulatto factory worker are young lovers who learn about each other and class prejudices they knew before the revolution.

Instituto Cubano Del Arte E Industria Cinematográficos. Cuba. 1974. 79m. B&W. *Director:* Sara Gómez *Writers:* Sara Gómez, Tomás González Pérez *Cast:* Mario Balmaseda, Yolanda Cuéllar, Mario Limonta, Guillermo Diaz

147. *Ciscke — Ein Kind Braucht Liebe*

Thirteen-year-old Ciscke (Dick van der Velde) is a victim of parental neglect (his father is indifferent and his mother abuses him). He becomes so neurotic that he terrorizes his school and kills his mother. He is institutionalized and reforms but people continue to torment him. Thanks to a sympathetic teacher and his aunt, he has a chance.

Bakros Corp. West Germany. 1955. 88m. B&W. *Producer:* Alfred Bittins *Writer-Director:* Wolfgang Staudte *Cast:* Dick van der Velde, Kees Brusse, Riek Schagen, Heidi Everts, Piet van Leeuwen, Johan Valk, Paul Steenbergen, John Kaart, Lies Franken, Berhard Droog, Heli Finkenzeller, Berta Drews, Alexander Kerst, Günther Lüders, Walter Janssen

148. *The Class of Miss MacMichael*

Conor MacMichael (Glenda Jackson), a teacher in a trade school, is dedicated to her class of hoodlums. Principal Terence Sutton (Oliver Reed) has his own ideas and fellow teacher Una Ferrar (Rosalind Cash) has her own calming influence at the school.

Brut/Kettledrum. Great Britain. 1978. 90m. C. *Producer:* Judd Bernard *Director:* Silvio Narizzano *Writers:* Judd Bernard, Sandy Hutson (novel) *Cast:* Glenda Jackson, Oliver Reed, John Standing, Michael Murphy, Rosalind Cash, John Standing, Riba Akabusl, Phil Daniels, Patrick Murray, Sharon Fussey, Herbert Norville

The Clay Bird see *Matir moina*

149. *Clockwise*

Headmaster Brian Stimpson (John Cleese) of the Thomas Tompkin School has become a member of the prestigious Headmaster's Conference and is to give a speech at the annual meeting as chairman. He misses the train and gradually falls apart as he tries to get to the conference.

EMI/Moment. Great Britain. 1986. 97m. C. *Producer:* Michael Condron *Director:* Christopher Morahan *Writer:* Michael Frayn *Cast:* John Cleese, Alison Steadman, Penelope Wilton, Stephen Moore, Joan Hickson, Charon Maiden

Close to the Wind see *Oss Emellan*

Closed Pages see *Pagine Chiuse*

150. *Come Back, Miss Pipps*

"Our Gang" members Spanky, Froggy, Darla and Mickey will do anything to keep their great teacher Miss Pipps (Sara Haden). But school board chairman Alonzo K. Pratt (Clarence Wilson) wants her out.

MGM. US. 1941. B&W. *Director:* Edward L. Cahn *Writers:* Hal Law, Robert A. McGowan *Cast:* Barbara Bedford, Robert Blake, Billy Bletcher, Byron Foulger, Teresa Mae Glass, James Gubitosi, Sara Haden, Darla Hood, Billy "Foggy" Laughlin, George "Spanky" McFarland, Tommy McFarland, Christian Rub, Billie "Buckwheat" Tomas, Leon Tyler, Clarence Wilson

151. *Connecting Rooms*

This melodrama explores the relationship between tenants in a boarding house. Included are musician-cellist Wanda Fleming (Bette Davis), ex-schoolteacher James Wallraven (Michael Redgrave), and the angry young man Mickey Hollister (Alexis Kanner) who brings chaos to their quiet lives. James is a schoolmaster who has been dismissed for sexual misconduct with a student but he was unfairly accused.

Telstar. Great Britain. 1969. 102m. C. *Producers:* Harry Field, Jack Smith, Arthur S. Cooper *Writer-Director:* Franklin Gollings *Cast:* Bette Davis, Michael Redgrave, Alexis Kanner, Kay Walsh, Gabrielle Drake, Leo Genn, Olga Georges-Picot, Richard Wyler, Brian Wilde, John Woodnutt, Tony Hughes

152. *Conrack*

Liberal young Pat Conroy (Jon Voight) teaches fifth through eighth grades in a black school on an island off the coast of South Carolina. Conroy is paid $510 per month to teach there. He is shocked by the children's lack of knowledge and clashes with the grim black principal, Mrs. Scott (Madge Sinclair). Inevitably he is fired by the school superintendent Mr. Skeffington (Hume Cronyn), who considers him an outside agitator. After an attempt in court to save his job fails, he speaks his mind through a loudspeaker from his beat-up van on the mainland.

TCF. US. 1974. 106m. C. *Producers:* Martin Ritt, Irving Ravetch, Harriet Frank, Jr. *Director:* Martin Ritt *Writers:* Irving Ravetch, Harriet Frank, Jr., Pat Conroy (book) *Cast:* Jon Voight, Paul Winfield, Hume Cronyn, Madge Sinclair, Tina Andrews, Antonio Fargas, Ruth Attaway, James O'Reare

153. *Convict 99*

Benjamin Twist (Will Hay), a disgraced schoolmaster, goes to an employment agency to apply for a job at a reform school for difficult boys. The agency mistakenly believes he is a Mr. Benjamin, a prison warden, and he is assigned to one of the country's worst prisons for hardened criminals. Arriving there drunk, Benjamin is mistakenly assumed to be a prisoner, named "Convict 99" and jailed. Benjamin's innocence is soon discovered, and he takes over as warden, instituting some humane reforms. When corruption enters the picture, he must track down the crook and find a way of returning the money to the bank.

Gainsborough. Great Britain. 1938. 91m. B&W. *Producer:* Edward Black *Director:* Marcel Varnel *Writers:* Marriott Edgar, Val Guest, Ralph Smart, Jack Davies *Cast:* Will Hay, Graham Moffatt, Moore Marriott, Googie Withers, Garry Marsh, Peter Gawthorne, Basil Radford, Kathleen Harrison, Denis Wyndham, Wilfred Walter, Alf Goddard, Teddy Brown, Roy Emerton

154. Copper Sky

Proper schoolteacher Nora Hayes (Coleen Gray) arrives in the small town of Occident in a wagon driven by Charlie Martin (Paul Brinegar). The two find the streets littered with dead bodies. Charlie is shot and killed by a wounded Native American. Nora thinks she is alone until drunken Hack Williams (Jeff Morrow) appears. Hack is an ex-cavalryman wrongly accused and sentenced to die for the murder of a Native American. While he was waiting to be executed, the town was wiped out. At one point Hack asks Nora to teach him how to pray. Hack becomes a hero when he saves troops from an ambush.

TCF. US. 1957. 77m. B&W. *Producer:* Robert Stabler *Director:* Charles Marquis Warren *Writers:* Eric Norden, Robert Stabler *Cast:* Jeff Morrow, Coleen Gray, Strother Martin, Paul Brinegar, John Pickard, Jack Lomas, Bill Hamel, Dorothy Schuyler, Jerry Oddo, Rush Williams, Rodd Redwing

155. The Corn Is Green

Middle-aged, self-reliant spinster teacher Lilly Moffat (Bette Davis) is determined to bring enlightenment to a poor coal-mining Welsh village. She devotes her life to shaping the mind of a genius mining boy, Morgan Evans (John Dall). Her only reward is to see him move on. After Morgan receives a scholarship to Oxford, Miss Moffat hides the fact that a local girl is pregnant with his baby. To keep Morgan in school, she pays off the girl and then adopts the baby to rear as her own. Miss Moffat uses her Oxford education and inherited wealth to keep young boys in school.

Warner. US. 1945. 118m. B&W. *Producer:* Jack Chertok *Director:* Irving Rapper *Writers:* Casey Robinson, Frank Cavett *Cast:* Bette Davis, John Dall, Nigel Bruce, Joan Lorring, Rhys Williams, Rosalind Ivan, Mildred Dunnock, Arthur Shields, Gwenyth Hughes, Thomas Louden, Billy Roy

156. The Corn Is Green

A dedicated, strong-willed teacher is determined to educate the poor and illiterate youth of a small Welsh village. Lilly Moffat (Katharine Hepburn) soon discovers that one of her students is very intelligent.

CBS. US. 1979. 93m. C. *Director:* George Cukor *Writer:* Ivan Davis *Cast:* Katharine Hepburn, Ian Saynor, Bill Fraser, Patricia Hayes, Anna Massey, Artro Morris, Dorothea Phillips, Toyah Willcox, Huw Richards, Bryn Fôn, Dyfan Roberts, Robin John

157. Corralling a Schoolmarm

Local rancher-school board president Tom Simpson (Lee White) becomes attracted to new schoolmarm Alice Lorraine (Virginia Vale). Neighboring widow Martha Bakely (Jane Keckley) is jealous and asks Simpson's foreman Ray (Ray Whitley) for help. All is resolved with Ray winning over the schoolmarm.

RKO. US. 1940. 20m. B&W. *Director:* Charles E. Roberts *Writers:* George

Jeske, Charles E. Roberts *Cast:* Ray Whitley, Virginia Vale, Lee "Lasses" White, Jane Keckley, Willie Phelps, Frankie Marvin, Ken Card, Cactus Mack

158. *The Country Cupid*

Schoolteacher Edith (Blanche Sweet) breaks off her engagement after a fight with her fiancé. She writes a note about getting back together but throws it away. One of her students takes it out of the trash and sends it. Later, while she is grading papers, a man bursts into the classroom.

General Film. US. 1911. B&W. *Director:* D.W.Griffith *Cast:* Blanche Sweet, Edwin August, Edna Foster, Joseph Graybill, Kate Bruce, Claire McDowell, Frank Evans, Alfred Paget

159. *A Country Hero*

In the town of Jazzville, the blacksmith (Roscoe "Fatty" Arbuckle) and Cy Klone (Joe Keaton), owner of a garage, are rivals for the schoolteacher (Alice Lake). They do join forces when a new arrival, a city gent (Al St. John), also shows interest in the her. Buster Keaton performs at a village ball.

Paramount. US. 1917. B&W. *Writer-Director:* Roscoe "Fatty" Arbuckle *Cast:* Roscoe "Fatty" Arbuckle, Buster Keaton, Al St. John, Alice Lake, Joe Keaton, Stanley Pembroke

The Country Schoolmaster see Heideschulmeister Uwe Karsten

160. *Country Teacher*

Dedicated young teachers watch their simple way of life vanish in Hong Kong's rural New Territories. With their selfless efforts, these inspirational teachers learn about love and kindness. They vow to keep their small fishing community viable and its children cared for.

Hong Kong. 1994. 87m. C. *Cast*: Richard Ng, Chan Siu Ha

161. *Country Teacher and His Pupils*

In a typical country school, the schoolmaster asks each boy in his class a particular question. Each in turn misses the answer. When the teacher leaves the classroom for a short time, the boys start playing a game. When he returns to class, he catches them in the act. One child pours a bucket of water on the teacher.

S. Lubin. US. 1903. B&W.

Country Teachers see Feng huang qin

162. *Courting Courtney*

Budding filmmaker Nick has decided to make a documentary about his longtime pal Courtney, a schoolteacher. She has had a two-year on and off relationship with a man and can't commit. Nick's camera follows her around and seeks out others who know her.

Broken Twig. US. 1997. 83m. C. *Producers:* Serge Rodnunsky, Hadeel Reda, Paul Tarantino *Writer-Director:* Paul Tarantino *Cast:* Dana Gould, Eliza Coyle, Taylor Negron, Sean Masterson, Ann Mattingly, Al Schuermann

The Coward see *Zbabelec*

163. *The Cowboy and the School Marm*

No description available.
Edison Mfg. Co. US. 1908. B&W.

164. *The Cowboy and the School Marm*

No description available.
New York Motion Picture Co. US. 1910. B&W. *Director:* Fred J. Balshofer *Cast:* Young Deer, Red Wing

165. *Crash Dive*

During World War II, Ward Stewart (Tyrone Power), a lieutenant on leave, falls in love with schoolteacher Jean Hewlett (Anne Baxter) at a sub base. He later learns that she is the fiancée of his new submarine commander Dewey Connors (Dana Andrews).

TCF. US. 1943. 105m. C. *Producer:* Milton Sperling *Director:* Archie Mayo *Writers:* W.R. Burnett, Jo Swerling *Cast:* Tyrone Power, Anne Baxter, Dana Andrews, James Gleason, Dame May Whitty, Harry Morgan, Frank Conroy, Minor Watson

The Crash of Silence see *Mandy*

166. *Un Crime au Paradis (A Crime in Paradise)*

Farmer Jo Jo Braconnier (Jacques Villeret) and his nasty wife Lu Lu (Josiane Balasko) hate each other. Even though their farm is named Le Paradis, they spend their days tormenting each other as much as possible. Jo Jo's only peace comes when Lu Lu passes out from drinking too much wine. Then husband and wife decide to kill each other. La Maîtresse (Suzanne Flon) is the empathetic schoolteacher who has known Jo Jo since he was a child. Maître Jacquard (André Dussollier), Jo Jo's lawyer, helps him, not knowing no murder has occurred yet.

UGC-Fox Distribution. France. 2001. 89m. C. *Producer:* Christian Fechner *Director:* Jean Becker *Writers:* Sacha Guitry, Jean Becker *Cast:* Jacques Villeret, Josiane Balasko, André Dussollier, Suzanne Flon, Gérard Hernandez, Roland Magdane, Valérie Mairesse, Maryse Deol, Jenny Clève, Jacques Dacqmine, Jean Dell, Christine Delaroche, Eric Bougnon, Armand Chagot, Dominique Lavanant, Michel Bonnet, Jean-Michel Martial

A Crime in Paradise see *Un Crime au Paradis*

167. A Cry from the Streets

Orphaned, underprivileged and homeless youngsters are in a city children's shelter headed by Mrs. Daniels (Mona Washbourne). The tots are confused by a world they did not make. A pretty and very dedicated social worker, Ann Fairlee (Barbara Murray), and her understanding radio repairman beau try to make a difference in the children's lives

Film Traders. Great Britain. 1958. 100m. B&W. *Producer:* Ian Dalrymple *Director:* Lewis Gilbert *Writers:* Vernon Harris, Elizabeth Coxhead (novel) *Cast:* Max Bygraves, Barbara Murray, Colin Petersen, Dana Wilson, Kathleen Harrison, Eleanor Summerfield, Mona Washbourne

168. The Cub

Cub reporter Steve Oldham (John Hines) is sent to cover a feud between the Renlows and the Whites over a pig eating turnips. Steve falls in love with schoolteacher Alice Renlow (Martha Hedman). At a dance to raise money for Alice's salary, Steve drinks too much and kisses Peggy White, who tells her relatives that they are engaged. Steve is later seen kissing Alice's hand and is taken captive to be shot. A big ruckus occurs but all ends well.

World Film Corp. US. 1915. B&W. *Director:* Maurice Tourneur *Cast:* John Hines, Martha Hedman, Robert Cummings, Dorothy Farnum, Jessie Lewis, Bert Starkey

169. Cupid Forecloses

Geraldine Farleigh (Bessie Love) supports her poor but aristocratic family by teaching at the village school. A $3,000 debt and impersonations cause great grief but all is resolved with Geraldine finding love.

Vitagraph Co. of America. US. 1919. B&W. *Director:* David Smith *Writers:* Stanley Olmstead, Edward J. Montagne *Cast:* Bessie Love, Dorothea Wolbert, Wallace McDonald, Frank Hayes, Jim Donnelly, Aggie Herring, Jake Abrams, Anne Schaefer, Gordon Griffith, Otto Lederer, Ruth Fuller Golden

170. Curley

When the beloved elementary schoolteacher of Lakeview gets married, Curly and his classmates plot to get rid of their new teacher, whom they think will be grumpy middle-age Miss Johnson. The county supervisor discovers that the new teacher is Miss Johnson's pretty young niece Mildred. On the first day of school, Mildred gives Curly a ride and he tells her all the pranks they will be playing on their new teacher. Mildred teaches the children a lesson by making one a victim of his own prank. Curly is so humiliated he runs away. Curly is blamed for the other children's mischievous behavior. Miss Payne arrives to see apparent chaos and scolds Mildred on her inability to discipline. At a picnic, Miss Payne appears again and the children thank her for hiring Mildred. Curly is found and everything is cleared with cake and ice cream. Mildred picks up Curly's frog Croakey.

UA. US. 1947. 53m. C. *Producer:* Robert F. McGowan *Director:* Bernard Carr *Writer:* Dorothy Reid *Cast:* Larry Olsen, Frances Rafferty, Eilene Janssen, Dale Belding, Gerald Perreau, Arda Lynwood, Kathleen Howard, Edna Holland, Rene Beard, Donald King, Eugene Holland, Billy Gray, George Bentley, Ferris Taylor, Barbara Woodell, Eddie Dunn, Jim Farley, Guy Beach, Syd Saylor, Fred Trowbridge

171. *Daddy Day Care*

When two fathers (Eddie Murphy and Jeff Garlin) lose their product development jobs, they must remove their sons from the exclusive Chapman Academy. With no prospects they open their own day care center, "Daddy Day Care." As it gains in popularity, Chapman Academy's tough director (Anjelica Huston) begins to investigate. Then rivalry comes into the situation.

Sony. US. 2003. 92m. C. *Producers:* Matt Bereson, John Davies, Wyck Godfrey *Director:* Steve Carr *Writer:* Geoff Rodkey *Cast:* Eddie Murphy, Jeff Garlin, Steve Zahn, Regina King, Kevin Nealon, Jonathan Katz, Siobhan Fallan, Lacey Chabert, Lisa Edelstein, Laura Kightlinger, Leila Arcieri, Anjelica Huston, Khamani Griffin, Max Burkholder, Arthur Young, Elle Fanning, Cesar Flores, Hailey Noelle Johnson, Felix Achille, Shane Baumel, Jimmy Bennett, Connor Carmody, Kennedy McCullough, Alyssa Shafer, Bridgette Ho

172. *Dancing at Lughnasa*

On the family farm in 1936, five unmarried sisters struggle to maintain their independence. Kate Munday (Meryl Streep) teaches in the parish school. Christina (Catherine McCormack), the most beautiful sister, has a love child. One day their brother Jack (Michael Gambon) returns from Uganda after nearly 20 years as a missionary priest in a leper colony. He arrives home a shattered man who confuses his own faith with African religion.

Sony. Ireland/Great Britain/US. 1999. 96m. C. *Producer:* Noel Pearson *Director:* Pat O'Connor *Writers:* Frank McGuinness, Brian Friel (play) *Cast:* Meryl Streep, Michael Gambon, Catherine McCormack, Rhys Ifans, Sophie Thompson, Kathy Burke, Brid Brennan

173. *The Dangerous Lives of Altar Boys*

This coming-of-age story, set in the 1970s, follows a group of Catholic schoolboys who battle the strict rules of wicked peg-legged Sister Assumpta (Jodie Foster). The glue of the friendship between Francis Doyle and Tim Sullivan is their collaboration on an action-adventure comic book in which their hero battles school officials like Sister Assumpta. Chain-smoking, soccer-loving Father Casey (Vincent D'Onofrio) knows what the boys are up to but is also wary of Sister Assumpta. He is more amused than appalled by the confiscated comic book.

ThinkFilm. US. 2002. 104m. C. *Producers:* Jodie Foster, Meg LeFauve, Jay

Shapiro *Director:* Peter Care *Writers:* Michael Petroni, Chris Fuhrman (novel), Jeff Stockwell *Cast:* Jodie Foster, Kieran Culkin, Jena Malone, Emile Hirsch, Vincent D'Onofrio, Jake Richardson, Tyler Long, Arthur Bridgers

174. Dangerous Love

A young schoolteacher (Carol Halloway) convinces likable Ben (Pete Morrison) to give up his vices. Their romance is threatened when another of the teacher's suitors lies about Ben. She leaves for the East to study music but returns just in time to foil the plot against Ben.

State Rights; C.B.C. Film Sales Corp. US. 1920. B&W. *Director:* Charles E. Batlett *Writer:* Hal Hoadley *Cast:* Pete Morrison, Carol Halloway, Ruth King, Spottiswoode Aitken, Harry Van Meter, William Lyons West, Jack Richardson, Verne Layton, William Walsh, Claire Hatton, Zelma Edwards

175. Daring Chances

Agnes Rushton (Alta Allen) has two rivals for her attention. The teacher is won over by Jack (Jack Hoxie), a good man.

Universal. US. 1924. B&W. *Director:* Clifford S. Smith *Writers:* Isadore Bernstein, Wyndham Gittens *Cast:* Jack Hoxie, Alta Allen, Claude Payton, Jack Pratt, Catherine Wallace, Doreen Turner, Genevieve Danninger, Newton Campbell, William McCall, Scout (horse)

176. Dark Command

In Lawrence, Kansas, in the late 1800s, mild-mannered Will Cantrell (Walter Pidgeon) is a music teacher. Bob Seaton (John Wayne) is passing through town with a traveling doctor-dentist. Will and Bob become rivals when both run for the job of town marshal and also vie for the attention of Mary McCloud. Even though Will hates being a teacher, he offers to help Bob learn to read and write. Losing the town marshal election to Bob, Will turns bitter and becomes a gun runner. After the town is burned down, Bob and Mary head for Texas together.

Republic. US. 1940. 92m. B&W. *Producer:* Sol C. Siegel *Director:* Raoul Walsh *Writers:* Grover Jones, Lionel Houser, F. Hugh Herbert, W.R. Burnett (novel) *Cast:* John Wayne, Claire Trevor, Walter Pidgeon, Roy Rogers, George "Gabby" Hayes, Porter Hall, Marjorie Main

177. Dark Water

A newly separated mother Dahlia (Jennifer Connelly) and her daughter move to a strange apartment building haunted by ghosts and water. A very concerned schoolteacher (Camryn Manheim) tries to help them. A remake of the Japanese horror flick *Honogurai mizu no soko kara*.

Touchstone Pictures. US. 2005. 103m. C. *Producers:* Bill Mechanic, Roy Lee, Doug Davison *Director:* Walter Salles *Writers:* Rafael Yglesias, Koji Suzuki (novel) *Cast:* Jennifer Connelly, John C. Reilly, Tim Roth, Dougray Scott, Pete Postlethwaite, Camryn Manheim, Ariel Gade

178. David Harum

Country banker and horse trader David Harum (William H. Crane), who lives with his sister, is secretly a soft-hearted man. His friend General Wolsey sends honest man John Lenox (Harold Lockwood) to replace David's crooked bookkeeper Chet Timson (Hal Clarendon). The general also sends Mary Blake (May Allison), who wants to be independent of her inherited fortune, to David's town to be the new schoolmarm. John loves Mary and with David's encouragement they become engaged. Timson falsely accuses John of counterfeiting but David steps in and clears his name.

Paramount. US. 1915. B&W. *Cast:* William H. Crane, Kate Meeks, May Allison, Harold Lockwood, Hal Clarendon, Guy Nichols

179. A Day in the Death of Joe Egg

A schoolteacher (Alan Bates) tries to kill his very ill daughter.

Columbia. Great Britain. 1971. 106m. C. *Producer:* David Deutsch *Director:* Peter Medak *Writer:* Peter Nichols *Cast:* Alan Bates, Janet Suzman, Peter Bowles, Sheila Gish, Joan Hickson, Elizabeth Robillard, Murray Melvin, Fanny Carby, Constance Chapman, Elizabeth Tyrell

Day of the Wacko see Dzien swira

180. Dead Men Tell No Tales

The matron of a school for boys is murdered after winning a lottery.

British National. Great Britain. 1938. 80m. B&W. *Producer:* John Corfield *Director:* David McDonald *Writers:* Walter Summers, Stafford Dickens, Emlyn Williams, Doreen Montgomery, Francis Beeding (novel) *Cast:* Emlyn Williams, Hugh Williams, Marius Goring, Lesley Brook, Sara Seegar, Christine Silver, Clive Morton, Anne Wilton, Hal Gordon

181. The Dead Zone

Schoolteacher Johnny Smith (Christopher Walken), injured in an auto accident, is in a coma for five years. When he awakens, he has lost his fiancée Sarah Bracknell (Brooke Adams) but has gained psychic abilities.

Paramount. US. 1983. 103m. C. *Producer:* Debra Hill *Director:* David Cronenberg *Writers:* Jeffrey Boam, Stephen King (novel) *Cast:* Christopher Walken, Brooke Adams, Tom Skerritt, Herbert Lom, Anthony Zerbe, Colleen Dewhurst, Martin Sheen, Nicholas Campbell, Sean Sullivan, Jackie Burroughs, Geza Kovacs

182. The Dear Little Teacher

A schoolmistress falls for a new teacher after he has an accident.

Hepworth. Great Britain. 1912. B&W. *Director:* Warwick Buckland *Cast:* Alec Warcester, Alma Taylor

183. *Death Goes to School*

A girl's school music teacher proves a colleague is a strangler.
Independent Artists. Great Britain. 1953. 65m. *Producer:* Victor Hanbury *Director:* Stephen Clarkson *Writers:* Maisie Sharman, Stephen Clarkson *Cast:* Barbara Murray, Gordon Jackson, Pamela Allan, Jane Aird, Beatrice Varley, Stanley Rose, Robert Long, Sam Kydd

Death in a French Garden see Péril en la Demeure

The Deserted Station see Istgah-Matrouk

The Deserted Valley see Thung lung hoang vang

Desire see Fatale Sehnsucht

184. *The Desired Woman*

Vacationing in the country, dishonest New York stockbroker Richard Mostyn meets charming teacher Dolly Drake (Jean Paige). The two fall in love and he returns to New York to tie up loose ends. He finds a new love and never returns. After a failed marriage and the death of his son, he finally returns to Dolly, but she has found another.
Greater Vitagraph, Inc. US. 1918. B&W. *Producer:* Albert E. Smith *Director:* Paul Scardon *Writer:* Edward J. Montagne *Cast:* Harry Morey, Florence Deshon, Jean Paige, Charles Hutchinson, William Cameron, Eulalie Jensen, Harold Foshay, Aida Horton, Julia Swayne Gordon, Herbert Potter

185. *Destination Big House*

During a car chase, mobsters shoot their double-crossing partner, Joe Bruno. He escapes and makes his way to a cabin where schoolteacher Janet Brooks (Dorothy Patrick) takes him in. Janet nurses him, thinking he was hurt in a hunting accident. He hides a roll of money in one of her rooms. Janet goes on an errand and Joe leaves. When Janet returns to her small-town home, reporters are eager to question her about the money left to her by a dying Joe. When the school hears of the story, she is suspended indefinitely. Finally she decides that if the money is found, it will be turned over to Walter, her fiancé. Now everyone is looking for the $80,000. Janet finally receives the money and gives it to a new hospital.
Republic. US. 1950. 60m. B&W. *Director:* George Blair *Writers:* Eric Taylor, Mortimer Braus *Cast:* Dorothy Patrick, Robert Rockwell, James Lydon, Robert Armstrong, Larry J. Blake, John Harmon, Claire DuBrey, Richard Benedict, Olan Soule, Peter Prouse, Norman Field, Mira McKinney, Virginia Farmer, Hal Fieberling, Robert Griffin, Jess Kirkpatrick, William E. Green, Sammy McKim, Mickey Knox, Danny Morton, Mack Williams

The Devil's Backbone see El Espinazo del diablo

186. *The Devil's Own*

While teaching at a missionary school in Africa, Gwen Mayfield (Joan Fontaine) has a traumatic encounter with a witch doctor and suffers a nervous breakdown. Now in good health, she returns to England and accepts a job as headmistress of a small private school run by Alan Bax (Alec McCowen) and his sister Stephanie (Kay Walsh). Everything seems very pleasant, until talk of witchcraft, curses, death and sacrifice abounds. Gwen has another breakdown when she spies a voodoo image in her room. Aided by Alan, she learns that Stephanie has the entire village in her control through witchcraft. Gwen is able to kill Stephanie and break the spell. She decides to stay as headmistress at the school.

Hammer Film Productions. Great Britain. 1967. 90m. C. *Producer:* Anthony Nelson-Keys *Director:* Cyril Frankel *Writers:* Nigel Kneale, Peter Curtis (novel) *Cast:* Joan Fontaine, Kay Walsh, Alec McCowen, Gwen Frangcon-Davies, Duncan Lamont, Leo Rossiter, Martin Stephens, Carmel McSharry, Viola Keats, Shelagh Fraser, Bryan Marshall

187. *The Devil's Playground*

The film concentrates on the emotional sexual seething amidst young boys at a Roman Catholic boarding school. Of course the Brothers run a chaste and sterile environment.

EMC. Australia. 1976. 107m. C. *Writer-Producer-Director:* Fred Schepisi *Cast:* Arthur Dignam, Nick Tate, Simon Burke, Charles McCallum, John Frawley, Jonathan Hardy, Gerry Duggan, Peter Cox, John Diedrich, Thomas Keneally, Sheila Florance, Alan Cinis

188. *The Devonsville Terror*

A schoolteacher is a supernatural agent sent to wreak vengeance on a man who has just killed his wife. There is a subplot of the local doctor suffering from a curse in which his body is infested with worms.

Motion Picture Marketing. US. 1983. 83m. C. *Producer-Director:* Ulli Lommel *Writers:* Ulli Lommel, George T. Lindsey, Suzanna Love *Cast:* Suzanna Love, Robert Walker, Donald Pleasence, Paul Wilson

189. *Devotion*

A woman falls in love with a barrister and takes a job as governess to his son.
RKO/Pathé. US. 1931. 84m. B&W. *Director:* Robert Milton *Writers:* Graham John, Horace Jackson, Pamela Wynne (novel) *Cast:* Ann Harding, Leslie Howard, Robert Williams, O.P. Heggie, Louise Closser Hale, Dudley Digges

190. *Di zi ye feng kuang (Enter the 36th Chamber of Shaolin)*

Disguised as schoolteachers, anti-Ching patriots set up in a school. After a brutal Manchu attack, one man must master martial arts before he can begin his mission of vengeance.

Hong Kong. 1985. C. *Director:* Kar-Hung Yau *Cast:* Shen Chan, Siu-hou Chin, Philip Kwok, Hoi San Lee, Chia Hui Liu, Lieh Lo, Meng Lo, Yue Wong, Qiu Yuen

191. *Les Diaboliques (Diabolique)*

Michel Delasalle (Paul Meurisse), tyrannical headmaster of a boys' school, bullies his students, faculty and wife Christina (Vera Clouzot). Christina and Michel's mistress Nicole Horner (Simone Signoret), a teacher at the school, plot revenge. Appearances are deceiving in this thriller.

Filmsonor. France. 1954. 114m. B&W. *Producer-Director:* Henri-Georges Clouzot *Writers:* Henri-Georges Clouzot, G. Geronimi, Pierre Boileau, Thomas Narcejac (novel) *Cast:* Simone Signoret, Vera Clouzot, Charles Vanel, Paul Meurisse, Noel P. Roquevert, Therese Dorny, Pierre Larquey, Pierre Larquey, Michel Serrault, Jean Brochard, Georges Chamarat, Jacques Verennes

192. *Diabolo Menthe (Peppermint Soda)*

Thirteen-year-old Anne Weber (Eleonore Klarwein), withdrawn and solemn, and her sister Frédérrique (Odile Michel) are the daughters of a divorced Jewish couple. They live with their mother and attend a strict school. Anne's math teacher is afraid of her students; the gym teacher wears a fur coat while the girls suffer wearing shorts outside; and the art teacher is an evil old woman who harps on their drawings of Bambi. Peppermint Soda refers to an adult beverage which Anne orders but doesn't get to drink.

Gaumont/New York Films. France. 1997. 101m. C. *Writer-Director:* Diane Kurys *Cast:* Eleonore Klarwein, Odile Michel, Coralie Clement, Marie Veronique Maurin, Valerie Stano, Anne Guillard, Corinne Dacla, Veronique Vernon, Francoise Bertin, Arlette Bonnard, Jacqueline Boyen, Dora Doll, Tsila Chelton, Jacques Rispal, Anouk Feriac, Pterflam, Yves Regnier, Robert Rimbaud

Die to Live see *Jukeumyeon salrira*

193. *Dilemma*

A respectable schoolmaster returns home from work on the eve of his wedding anniversary to find the dead body of a man in their bathroom. His wife is missing. He wraps up the body and plans on hiding it under the floorboards, but keeps getting interrupted. Finally he finishes and his wife appears.

ACT Films. Great Britain. 1962. 70m. B&W. *Producer:* Edward Lloyd *Writer-Director:* Peter Maxwell *Cast:* Peter Halliday, Ingrid Haffner, Patricia Burke, Patrick Jordan, Alan Rolfe, Robert Dean

194. *Los Dioses Ajenos (Strange Gods)*

A love story between an archaeologist and a schoolteacher unfolds in a mountainous region in the northern part of Argentina.

Argentina. 1958. 84m. C. *Director:* Román Viñoly Barreto *Writer:* Hugo Moser *Cast:* Enrique Fava, Olga Zubarry

195. *Les Disparus de St Agil (Boys' School)*

The boys' school of St. Agil is like any other in France with one big exception: The director counterfeits 100-franc notes. His press is located behind the blackboard in the science classroom. One student is abducted because he sits near the press and interferes with the printing. The director murders the drunken art teacher, who made the drawings of the fake money, because he fears he may talk when drunk.

Vog Films. France. 1938. 95m. B&W. *Director:* Christian-Jaque *Writers:* J.H. Blanchon, Pierre Véry (novel) *Cast:* Michel Simon, Erich von Stroheim, Almé Clariond, Armand Bernard

Distant Thunder see *Ashanti Sanket*

196. *Do Aur do Paanch*

Bittu, an only child of a rich businessman, is the target in many kidnapping attempts. A schoolteacher Shaalu tries to help him. Vijay, a kind-hearted burglar, fakes his identification papers and joins the boarding school as a P.T. instructor. Underworld boss "Uncle" has Sunil join the school as music teacher Lakshman and both try to outdo each other in their attempts to kidnap the boy. Shaalu falls in love with one of the crooks.

Digital Entertainment. India. 1980. C. *Producer:* C. Dhandayuthapani *Director:* Rakesh Kumar *Writers:* Sachin Bhowmick, Gyandev Agnihotri *Cast:* Shashi Kapoor, Amitabh Bachchan, Hema Malini, Parveen Babi, Lalita Pawar, Aarti, Shreeram Lagoo, Sajjan, Master Bittoo, Om Prakash, Kader Khan, Om Prakash, Jagdeep, Ram Sethi, Goga Kapoor, Jagdish Raj, Mohan Sherry, Vikas Anand, Kiti Kumar, Jagdeep, Ram Sethi

197. *Dom s Mezoninom (House with an Attic)*

A landscape painter from St. Petersburg spends his summer at an estate. He meets Misyus, her older sister Lidiya, who teaches school, and their mother. The artist is attracted to youthful Misyus but the family is dominated by Lidiya, who also devotes herself to projects for the peasants. The artist and Lidiya argue about the new Russia. Lidiya hates the artist so much she sends her sister and mother away.

Artkino Pictures. Soviet Union. 1964. 86m. C. *Director:* Yakov Bazelyan *Writer:* P. Yerofeyev *Cast:* Sergey Yakovlev, Ninel Myshkova, Lyudmila Gordeychyk, Olga Zhizneva, Yu. Leonidov, Vera Altayakaya, V. Ananina, Sergey Kalinin, G. Smirnova, N. Oleshchenko, D. Tarasov, A. Pokorskiy

198. *Domani È Troppo Tardi (Tomorrow Is Too Late)*

Progressive schoolteachers Landi (Vittorio de Sica) and Anna (Lois Maxwell)

decide to provide a proper sex education for youngsters. Two children practice what they have learned with devastating results.

Rizzoli. Italy. 1950. 101m. B&W. *Producer:* Guiseppe Amato *Director:* Leonide Moguy *Writers:* Alfred Machard, Lionide Moguy *Cast:* Vittorio de Sica, Lois Maxwell, Gabrielle Dorziat, Anna Maria Pierangeli, Gino Leurini

199. *La Donna È Mobile (The Lady Is Fickle)*

Ferruccio Landini (Ferruccio Tagliavini), a small-town schoolteacher, aspires to become an opera singer. He is aided by his friend Cristoforo (Carlo Campanini), the chauffeur for an opera star. Ferruccio must endure a series of clichés before reaching the final opera audition.

Superfilm Distributing. Italy. 1948. 76m. B&W. *Director:* Mario Mattole *Writers:* Leo Cattozzo, Marcello Marchesi, Mario Monicelli *Cast:* Ferruccio Tagliavini, Fioretto Dolfi, Carlo Campanini, Carlo Micheluzzi, Dora Bini, Arturo Bragaglia, Rosina Anselmi

200. *Don't Go Near the Water*

During World War II, on a small South Pacific island, the P.R. department of the Navy is run by inept Lt. Comdr. Clinton Nash (Fred Clark). His second-in-command, Max Siegal (Glenn Ford), is happy not to be at sea. Max must deal with keeping everyone happy — correspondents, writers, etc. Through all this turmoil he is wooing European-educated schoolteacher Melora (Gia Scala).

MGM/Avon. US. 1957. 107m. C. *Producer:* Lawrence Weingarten *Director:* Charles Walters *Writers:* Dorothy Kingsley, George Wells, William Brinkley (novel) *Cast:* Glenn Ford, Fred Clark, Gia Scala, Romney Brent, Mickey Shaughnessy, Earl Holliman, Anne Francis, Keenan Wynn, Eva Gabor, Russ Tamblyn, Jeff Richards, Mary Wickes

201. *Dopamine*

Rand, a computer programmer, has created Koy Koy, a big-eyed, birdlike creature. Rand and his business associates install Koy Koy in a kindergarten classroom for testing. Koy Koy lives all alone in an artificial environment inside the computer, but he does respond to those who approach his interface. Rand meets Sarah (Sabrina Lloyd), an idealistic but neurotic young teacher. Rand, immediately attracted to her, attributes it to a rush of the chemical dopamine.

Sundance Film Series. US. 2003. 79m. C. *Director:* Mark Decena *Writer:* Timothy Breitbach Decena *Cast:* John Livingston, Sabrina Lloyd, Bruno Campos, Reuben Grundy, Kathleen Antonio, Nicole Wilder

202. *Dotheboys Hall; or, Nicholas Nickleby*

A stupid teacher beats a pupil, and then a new teacher canes the teacher.

Gaumont. Great Britain. 1903. B&W. *Director:* Alf Collins *Writer:* Charles Dickens (novel) *Cast:* William Carrington

The Double Life of Véronique see *La Double Vie de Véronique*

203. La Double Vie de Véronique (The Double Life of Véronique)

The film explores the mystical bond between two identical young women, Véronique and Veronika (Irene Jacob). Véronique is Polish and Veronika is French and neither knows of the other. Véronique devotes her energies to teaching music to grammar school students.

Gala/Sidéral/Canal Plus/TOR/Norske Film. France/Poland. 1991. 98m. C. *Producer:* Leonardo de la Fuente *Director:* Krzysztof Kiéslowski *Writers:* Krzysztof Kiéslowski, Krzysztof Piesiewicz *Cast:* Irène Jacob, Philippe Volter, Halina Gryglaszewska, Kalina Jedrusik, Aleksander Bardini, Wladyslaw Kowalski, Jerzy Gudejko, Sandrine Dumas, Louis Ducreus, Claude Duneton

204. Down Dakota Way

En route to a Wild West show, cowboy Roy Rogers and his men become involved in the hunt for Steve, a hired killer and blackmailer. Roy detours to visit his old schoolteacher Dolly Paxton (Elisabeth Risdon), who happens to be Steve's stepmother, and finds Ruth Shaw (Dale Evans) instead. She explains that Dolly was dismissed after learning about her stepson. Roy goes to Dolly's house, where she is hiding Steve. Steve escapes and Dolly surrenders to the authorities. Roy discovers that someone is hiding evidence of hoof-and-mouth disease. Steve is killed, the plot is revealed and Dolly is reinstated at the school.

Republic. US. 1949. 67m. B&W. *Director:* William Witney *Writers:* John Butler, Sloan Nibley *Cast:* Roy Rogers, Trigger, Dale Evans, Pat Brady, Montie Montana, Elisabeth Risdon, Byron Barr, James Cardwell, Roy Barcroft, Emmett Vogan, Foy Willing, The Riders of the Purple Sage

Downpour see *Ragbar*

205. Dozhivyom do Ponedelnika (We'll Live Till Monday and Until Monday)

Grades one through twelve co-exist in a large urban Russian school. The film focuses on one upper-class home room and their teachers on a Thursday and Friday. The history teacher (Vyacheslav Tikhonov) and the pretty English teacher (Irina Pechernikova) are probably in love with each other, but it goes unspoken. They are both having difficulties, such as the history teacher's crisis of conscience and the English teacher's difficulty in keeping discipline while maintaining a rapport with her students. The history teacher is well-liked and respected by students and colleagues but is so upset by a rumor about him and the English teacher that he wants to resign. He still lives with his elderly mother, who waits at home and cooks his meals.

Soviet Union. 1969. 106m. B&W. *Director:* Stanislav Rostotsky *Writer:* Georgi Polonsky *Cast:* Vyacheslav Tikhonov, Irina Pechernikova, Nina Menshikova, Mikhail Zimin, Olga Zhiznyeva, Lyudmila Arkharova, Valleri Zbarev, Olga Ostroumova, Igor Starygin, Yuri Chernov, Roza Grigoryeva, Lyubov Sokolova, German Kachin, Dalvin Shckerbakov, Nina Grebeshkova

206. *O Dragão da Maldade Contra o Santo Guerreiro (Antônio das Mortes)*

In Brazil, bandits named Congaciero try to help the poor and fight the authorities and the rich. Tyrannical landowner Col. Horatio (Jofre Soares) and the corrupt police chief hire Antônio das Mortes (Maurício do Valle) to wipe out the Congaciero and the poor on his land. Antônio realizes that the Congaciero are not his enemy. The local schoolteacher (Othon Bastos) rises from his despair to help wipe out the evildoers in a heroic gun battle.

Grove Press. France/Brazil/West Germany. 1969. 100m. C. *Producers:* Claude-Antoine Mapa, Glauber Rocha *Writer-Director:* Glauber Rocha *Cast:* Maurício do Valle, Odete Lara, Hugo Carvana, Othon Bastos, Jofre Soares, Lorival Pariz, Rosa Marie Penna, Mário Gasmão, Vinicius Salvatori, Emanuel Cavalcanti, Sante Scaldaferri, The People of Milagres

207. *Drawing Teacher*

No description available.
Kliene Optical Co., France or Great Britain. 1907. B&W.

208. *Dreamchild*

In 1932, Alice Hargreaves (Coral Browne) is in America to celebrate Lewis Carroll's 100th birthday and to receive a honorary degree from Columbia University. She remembers Rev. Charles Dodgson (Ian Holm), also known as Lewis Carroll, as a shy, stuttering teacher at her father's prep school. It seems that then-young Alice was the model for Alice in Wonderland.

Universal. Great Britain. 1985. 94m. C. *Producers:* Rick McCallum, Kenith Trodd *Director:* Gavin Millar *Writer:* Dennis Potter *Cast:* Coral Browne, Ian Holm, Peter Gallagher, Nicola Cowper, Jane Asher, Amelia Shankley, Imogen Boorman, Emma King, Rupert Wainwright, Roger Ashton-Griffiths, Shane Rimmer, Caris Corfman, James Wilby

209. *Driftwood*

In the west, orphan Jenny (Natalie Wood) is informally adopted by young doctor Steve Webster (Dean Jagger) and a druggist (Walter Brennan). Susan (Ruth Warrick), the town schoolteacher, loves the doctor, who is combating an epidemic of spotted fever.

Republic. US. 1947. 88m. *Director:* Allan Dwan *Writers:* Mary Loos, Richard Sale *Cast:* Ruth Warrick, Walter Brennan, Dean Jagger, Charlotte Greenwood,

Natalie Wood, Jerome Cowan, H.B. Warner, Margaret Hamilton, Hobart Cavanaugh, Francis Ford, Howland Chamberlin, Alan Napier, James Bell, Teddy Infuhr, James Kirkwood, Ray Teal

210. *A Dry White Season*

Afrikaner Ben du Toit (Donald Sutherland) teaches history and considers himself a caring and just man. When the son of Gordon (Winston Ntshona), Ben's gardener, is beaten at a demonstration and then jailed, Gordon asks for Ben's help. Gordon dies in police custody. As Ben starts to investigate, he realizes his society is built on injustice, exploitation and corruption.

Universal/MGM. US. 1989. 107m. C. *Director:* Euzhan Palcy *Writers:* Colin Welland, Euzhan Palcy, André Brink (novel) *Cast:* Donald Sutherland, Janet Suzman, Zakes Mokae, Jürgen Prochnow, Susan Sarandon, Marlon Brando, Winston Ntshona, Thoko Nishinga, Leonard Maguire

211. *Du Sjak Aere Din Hustru (Master of the House)*

Since a business failure, Victor (Johannes Meyer) has grown morose, selfish and ill-tempered. He treats his wife so badly that she has a nervous breakdown and is sent away to get better. His old nanny (Mathilde Nielson) moves in and teaches him to mend his ways.

Palladium. Denmark. 1925. 95m. B&W. *Director:* Carl Theodor Dreyer *Writers:* Carl Theodor Dreyer, Svend Rindom *Cast:* Johannes Meyer, Astrid Hölm, Mathilde Neilson, Clara Schönfeld

The Dull-Ice Flower see *Lubinghua*

212. *Dzien Swira (Day of the Wacko)*

A day in the life of a bitter 49-year-old schoolteacher who hates his life and feels that everyone *else* is to blame for his misery. He can recite poetry during class and later swear at his neighbors.

Vision Film Production. Poland. 2002. 93m. C. *Producers:* Juliusz Machulski, Wlodzimierz Otulak *Writer-Director:* Marek Koterski *Cast:* Marek Kondrat, Janina Traczykówna, Michal Koterski, Joanna Sienkiewicz, Monika Donner-Trelinska, Aleksander Bednarz, Piotr Machalica, Ewa Zietek, Cezary Pazura, Andrzej Grabowski

Early Autumn see *Kohayagawa-ke no aki*

213. *L'École Buissonière (I Have a New Master)*

In a small village, the new and very dedicated schoolteacher Pascal Laurent tries to introduce fresh ideas and modern approaches to the classroom. He meets with opposition from parents and other teachers, but the children are eager to learn.

UGC/CGCF. France. 1948. 89m. B&W. *Director:* Jean-Paul Le Chanois *Writers:* Jean-Paul Le Chanois, Elise Freinet *Cast:* Bernard Blier, Juliette Fabre, Edouard Delmont, Pierre Coste, Jean-Louis Allibert, Danny Caron

214. L'École Infernale (The Trials of a Schoolmaster)

No description available.
France. 1901. B&W. *Director:* Georges Méliès

215. Édes Emma, Dróga Böbe — Vázlatok, Aktok (Sweet Emma, Dear Böbe)

Two female schoolteachers share a hotel room and become good friends.
Objektiv/Manfred Dumick Frilproduction. Hungary. 1992. 78m. C. *Producers:* Lajos Ovari, Gabriella Groz *Director:* Istaván Szabó *Writers:* Istaván Szabó, Andrea Veszits *Cast:* Johanna Ter Steege, Eniko Börcsök, Peter Andorai

216. Edge of Darkness

The story of tension and bitterness between the residents of a tiny Norwegian fishing village and the Nazi invaders. We meet the storekeeper, owner of the canning factory, the old schoolteacher who wrongly thinks this is an individual's fight, and the leader of the underground. The villagers are filled with horror when the old schoolteacher is tortured. When armed with guns from England, the whole village is able to fight.
Warner. US. 1943. 119m. B&W. *Producer:* Henry Blanke *Director:* Lewis Milestone *Writers:* Robert Rossen, William Woods (novel) *Cast:* Errol Flynn, Ann Sheridan, Walter Huston, Nancy Coleman, Tom Fadden, Judith Anderson, Helmut Dantine, Ruth Gordon, Charles Dingle, John Beal, Roman Bohnen, Helene Thimig, Monte Blue, Dorothy Tree, Richard Fraser, Morris Carnovsky, Art Smith, Henry Brandon, Tonio Selwart, Torben Meyer

217. Education of Little Tree

After losing his parents, eight-year-old orphan Cherokee Little Tree (Joseph Ashton) goes to live with his grandparents (Tantoo Cardinal, James Cromwell). His grandfather is white and his grandmother is Cherokee. His grandmother homeschools him using dictionaries and other books. He also learns about life by spending time outdoors with his grandparents and spiritual Cherokee Willow John (Graham Greene). The State Department of Welfare has a complaint that Little Tree is not going to school and that there are illegal activities in the household. They force him to attend the Notched Gap Indian School, a boarding school. Little Tree encounters difficulties at the school as it is harsh and regimented and he cannot speak in his native tongue. The headmaster renames him Joshua. When he answers a teacher with an innocent statement, he is beaten with a cane and put in solitary confinement to reflect on his answer. His grandfather breaks him out of the school

and they go into the high country to avoid the authorities that come for Little Tree. When his grandparents die, he goes to live with Willow John.
 Paramount. US. 1996. 112m. C. *Producer:* Jake Eberts *Director:* Richard Friedenberg *Writers:* Richard Friedenberg, Forrest Carter (novel) *Cast:* James Cromwell, Tantoo Cardinal, Joseph Ashton, Graham Greene

218. *L'Educatore Autorizzato (Authorized Instructor)*

Gianni Frontini (Gianfranco De Grassi), once an inmate at a reform school, becomes a teacher at another reform school. He tries to introduce humanity to that very repressive institution.
 Italy. 1979. 120m. C. *Writer-Director:* Luciano Odorisio *Writers* Luciano Odorisio, Armando Rossini (novel) *Cast:* Gianfranco De Grassi, Guido Celano, Antonio Orlando, Giuseppe Piciccio

Eeny Meeny Miny Moe see *Ole Dole Doff*

219. *Les Égarés (Strayed)*

In 1940, widowed schoolteacher Odile (Emmanuelle Béart) and her two children, teenage Philippe (Grégoire Leprince-Ringuet) and seven-year-old Cathy (Clémence Meyer), flee Nazi-occupied Paris. A German plane attacks the refugees. A youthful drifter with a shaven head, Yvan (Gaspard Ulliel), suddenly appears and saves them by leading them into the forest. Yvan is 17 years old and lives in isolation from the rest of the world.
 Wild Bunch/Wellspring. France/Great Britain. 2003. 95m. C. *Producer:* Jean-Pierre Ramsay-Levi *Director:* André Téchiné *Writers:* Gilles Taurand, André Téchiné, Gilles Perrault (novel) *Cast:* Emmanuelle Béart, Gaspard Ulliel, Grégoire Leprince-Ringuet, Clémence Meyer, Samuel Labarthe, Jean Fornerod, Eric Kreikenmayer, Nicholas Mead, Robert Elliot, Nigel Hollidge

220. *Ekti Jiban (Portrait of a Life)*

In the 1930s, a humble schoolteacher at a poor country school becomes interested in the origin of Bengali words. He decides to write the first Bengali dictionary and devotes the rest of his life to the task, only gaining recognition on his deathbed.
 Chalchitra Productions. India. 1988. 130m. C. *Writer-Director:* Raja Mitra *Cast:* Soumitra Chatterjee, Madhavi Chakrabarty, Avory Dutta, Munna Chakrabarty

Elementary School see *Obecna Skola*

End of a Priest see *Faráruv Konec*

The End of Summer see *Kohayagawa-ke no aki*

221. L'Enfant Sauvage (The Wild Child)

Dr. Jean Itard (François Truffaut) of Paris' Institute for the Deaf and Dumb is determined to teach a wild boy to read and write, wear clothes, and live in society. The film is based on a true story of the 19th century education of an illiterate, non-socialized boy found in the wilds of France.

UA/Film du Carosse. France. 1970. 84m. B&W. *Producer:* Marcel Berbert *Director:* François Truffaut *Writers:* François Truffaut, Jean Gruault *Cast:* Jean-Pierre Cargol, François Truffaut, Jean Dasté, Françoise Seigner

222. Eno nakano bokuno mura (Village of Dreams)

Nine-year-old twins (Keigo Matsuyama and Shogo Matsuyama) grow up in a rural village just after World War II. Their mother (Mieko Harada), who recently moved with her sons and daughter, teaches school at the local grade school while her husband works for the government. The children have a grand time exploring, playing pranks, and befriending lonely children, all while being watched over by a trio of witches.

Milestone Film and Video. Japan. 1996. 112m. C. *Producers:* Koshiro Sho, Tetsujiro Yamagami, Kaneko Iwasaki, Kôichi Ueda *Director:* Yoichi Higashi *Writers:* Yoichi Higashi, Takehiro Nakajima *Cast:* Mieko Harada, Keigo Matsuyama, Shogo Matsuyama, Kyozo Nagatsuka

Enter the 36th Chamber of Shadin *see* Di zi ye feng kuang

223. Escapade

Pacifist John Hampden (John Mills) is so involved in his causes that he neglects his wife and sons. One day the schoolmaster Dr. Skillingworth (Alastair Sim) tells John that his sons are going to be expelled for fighting. The boys disappear with a peace petition in a stolen plane.

Pinnacle. Great Britain. 1955. 87m. B&W. *Producer:* Daniel Angel *Director:* Philip Leacock *Writer:* Gilbert Holland *Cast:* John Mills, Alastair Sim, Yvonne Mitchell, Colin Gordon, Marie Lohr

224. Escape to Danger

The movie follows the adventures of an English schoolteacher in Denmark when the Germans invade.

RKO. Great Britain. 1943. 92m. B&W. *Producer:* William Sistrom *Directors:* Lance Comfort, Mutz Greenbaum *Writers:* Wolfgang Wilhelm, Jack Whittingham *Cast:* Eric Portman, Ann Dvorak, Karel Stepanek, Ronald Ward, Ronald Adam, Lily Kann, David Peel, Felix Aylmer, A.E. Matthews, Brefni O'Rourke, Charles Victor, Marjorie Rhodes, Frederick Cooper, Ivor Bernard

225. El Espinazo del Diablo (The Devil's Backbone)

Late in the Spanish Civil War, a lonely boarding school has become an orphanage for the sons of dead Republicans. Stoical old leftists Dr. Cásares and Carmen run the orphanage, where an unexploded Fascist bomb sits in the courtyard. Sexual frustration, class hatred, and greed all collide and the children must band together against their oppressors. A ghost of a boy, killed the night the bomb fell, tries to communicate with the new boy Carlos.

Sony Picture Classics. Spain/Mexico. 2001. 106m. C. *Producers:* Agustín Almodóvar, Bertha Navarro *Director:* Guillermo del Toro *Writers:* Guillermo del Toro, Antonio Trashorras, David Muñz *Cast:* Eduardo Noriega, Marisa Paredes, Federico Luppi, Iñigo Garcés, Fernando Tielve, Irene Visedo, Berta Ojea

226. *L'Estate di Bobby Charlton (The Summer of Bobby Charlton)*

During the summer that soccer great Bobby Charlton leads England's victorious team, a divorced man kidnaps his children from his ex-wife's parents' home in Austria. The father is a schoolteacher from the south of Italy south and the mother is from Italy's north. Father and son set out on a road trip in a VW Bug. Through flashbacks we learn about happier times.

Italy. 1995. 99m. B&W/C. *Director:* Massimo Guglielmi *Cast:* Agnese Nano, Carlotta Natoli, Francesca Prandi, Francesco Carnelutti, Sian Marco Tognazzi, Giulio Scarpati, Irene Grazioli, Katarina Vasilliessa, Roberto De Francesco

Eternal Love see *Heideschulmeister Uwe Karsten*

227. *Eve and the Merman*

Prudish young schoolteacher Eve (Lori Dawson), dance teacher Suzette (Marcia LeRoux) and legal secretary Brenda (Laura Kane) rent a house on a secluded island with a nudist camp director. Brenda and Suzette remove their clothes and enjoy the sun. Eve goes off to explore the other side of the island where she takes off her bikini. Becoming aware of a man staring at her, she is not scared but rather finds herself drawn towards him. He tells the strange story of his merman life and disappears. She keeps the secret and waits for the next visit.

Thunderbird International Pictures. US. 1965. 73m. *Producer:* Rod Vincent *Director:* Chev Royton *Cast:* Johnny Salvo, Lori Dawson, Marcia LeRoux, Laura Kane, Guy Lawrence, Jackie Prince, Paula Guest, Dolores Mandel, Brenda Morris, June Perez, Christine Lee, Christine Paulson, Ruth Michaels, Harry Mann, John Mabbitt, Betty Meister, Miriam Roberts, Amelia Marshall, Janice London, Jane Mitchell

228. *Everything but the Truth*

Small-town fourth grade schoolboy Willie (Tim Hovey) takes to heart his admired teacher's lessons about truthfulness. He tells the truth in public about paying a kickback to the mayor. As a result, he is suspended from school by the principal, Miss Dabney. His teacher Joan Madison (Maureen O'Hara) enlists the help of columnist Ernie Miller to take his case to the public.

Universal. US. 1956. 83m. C. *Producer:* Howard Christie *Director:* Jerry Hopper *Writer:* Herb Meadow *Cast:* Maureen O'Hara, John Forsythe, Tim Hovey, Frank Faylen, Barry Atwater

229. *Das Ewige Lied*

Country priest Joseph Mohr (Tobias Moretti) arrives at his new parish in a divided village. There is a bitter ongoing struggle between the wealthy merchants and the poor workers. Joseph and his friend Franz Xaver Gruber (Heio von Stetten), the village schoolteacher, compose the song "Silent Night, Holy Night" to comfort the poor.

MC-One (Media Cooperation One) GmbH. Germany/Austria. 1997. 120m. C. *Producer:* Arno Ortmair *Writer-Director:* Franz Xaver Bogner *Cast:* Tobias Moretti, Heio von Stetten, Erwin Steinhauer, Michael Mendl, Johannes Thanheiser, Jörg Hube, Karl Merkatz, Norman Schenk, Bernadette Heerwagen, Aaron Karl, Krista Posch, Andrea Eckert, Paul Faßnacht, Christine Mayr, Rainer Frieb

Eyes, the Sea and a Ball see Natsukashiki fue ya taiko

230. *The Face of Fear*

Young schoolteacher Sally Dillman (Elizabeth Ashley), thinking she is terminally ill, travels to San Francisco and hires a killer to take her life. She decides to get a second opinion and learns that she is not dying. Sally goes to the police to stop her own killing.

CBS. US. 1971. 75m. C. *Director:* George McCowan *Writers:* Edward Hume, Howard Fast (novel) *Cast:* Ricardo Montalban, Jack Warden, Elizabeth Ashley, Dane Clark, Roy Poole, Charles Dierkop, Burr DeBenning, Regis Cordic, Fred Sadoff, Brooke Mills, Dallas Mitchell

231. *Fahrenheit 451*

Montag (Oskar Werner) is a futuristic fireman who burns books instead of putting out fires. All reading matter is forbidden. His sexy wife (Julie Christie) only watches television. Montag falls in love with a schoolteacher (also Christie) who owns a secret copy of the Memoirs of Saint-Simon.

Universal. Great Britain. 1966. 112m. C. *Producer:* Lewis M. Allen *Director:* François Truffaut *Writers:* François Truffaut, Jean-Louis Richard, Ray Bradbury (novel) *Cast:* Oskar Werner, Julie Christie, Cyril Cusack, Anton Diffring, Jeremy Spenser, Alex Scott, Bee Duffell, Gillian Lewis

232. *The Falcon and the Co-Eds*

When a student at the Blue Cliff Seminary for Girls asks for help, "The Falcon" Tom Lawrence (Tom Conway) is drawn into the investigation of the death of a teacher. He pretends to be an insurance investigator looking into the death.

RKO. US. 1943. 68m. B&W. *Producer:* Maurice Geraghty *Director:* William

Clemens *Writers:* Ardel Wray, Gerald Geraghty *Cast:* Tom Conway, Jean Brooks, Rita Corday, Amelita Ward, Isabel Jewell, George Givot, Cliff Clark, Ed Gargan, Barbara Brown, Juanita Alvarez, Ruth Alvarez, Nancy McCollum, Patti Brill, Olin Howlin, Ian Wolfe, Margie Stewart, Carole Gallagher, Barbara Lynn, Margaret Landry, Elaine Riley, Anne O'Neal, Dorothy Christy

233. *Fallen Angels*

At Holy Angel School for Girls, a New England boarding school, Nell Fisher is abducted by a mysteriously disguised man. She escapes and exposes history teacher Leighton as her attacker. During an ensuing struggle, the school dorm burns down with loss of life. Five years later, some girls return for the making of a documentary — as well as the mysterious killer.

Seventh Twelfth Collective Ltd. Great Britain. 2002. 100m.C. *Producer:* Michael Derbas *Director:* Ian David Diaz *Writers:* Julian Boote, Ian David Diaz *Cast:* Esme Eliot, Michael Ironside, Kai Wiesinger, Jeff Fahey

234. *False Kisses*

Jennie Blake (Miss Du Pont), a schoolteacher from the city, comes between fishing partners. She chooses one of the men after they fight over her. Later, when the husband is out of work, the rival returns with a job offer. The husband loses his sight and thinks that Jennie is having an affair. When he regains his sight, he finds out that Jennie has been faithful.

Universal. US. 1921. B&W. *Producer:* Carl Laemmle *Director:* Paul Scardon *Writers:* Wallace Clifton, Winifred Reeve *Cast:* Miss Du Pont, Pat O'Malley, Lloyd Whitlock, Camilla Clark, Percy Challenger, Madge Hunt, Fay Winthrop, Joseph Hazelton, Mary Philbin

235. *Faráruv Konec (End of a Priest)*

A verger, who dresses as a priest, is invited by a villager to assume the position of pastor at a vacant church. An atheist teacher (Jan Libicek) tries to embarrass him in various ways because the people confess to him and prefer him to the teacher. The teacher speaks for the government at every opportunity. The false priest is crucified by the people who demand too much of him, the police, and the cardinal.

Grove Press. Czechoslovakia. 1969. 98m. B&W. *Director:* Evald Schorm *Writers:* Evald Schorm, Josef Skvorecky *Cast:* Pavel Bosek, Jana Brejchová, Vlastimil Brodsk, Gueye Cheick, Vladimir Jedenáctik, Václav Kotva, Maria Landova, Pavel Landovsk, Jan Libícek, Jirí Lír, Josefa Pechlatová, Eva Repiková, Martin Ruzek, Helena Ruzicková, Jaroslav Satoransk, Zdena Skvorecka, Vladimir Valenta

236. *Fatal Lessons: The Good Teacher*

Schoolteacher Victoria Paige (Erika Eleniak) tutors a student. The teacher and mother Samantha Stephens (Patricia Kalember) become friends, without Samantha realizing the teacher's intent on taking over the family. Using poisonous herbal teas and psychological devices, Victoria manipulates the husband into thinking his wife is going crazy.

PorchLight. Canada/US. 2004. 100m. C. *Director:* Michael Scott *Writer:* Casey T. Mitchell *Cast:* Erika Eleniak, Patricia Kalember, Ken Tremblett, Lori Ann Triolo, William MacDonald, Rowen Kahn, Keely Purvis, Jerry Rector, Dean Redman, Pamela Perry, Ryan Booth

237. *Fatalel Schnsucht (Desire)*

A Canadian schoolteacher who falls for a young music student may not be what he seems.

Advanced. Canada/Germany. 2000. 97m. C. *Producers:* Eberhard Junkersdorf, Elizabeth Yake *Writer-Director:* Colleen Murphy *Cast:* Katja Riemann, Zachary Bennett, Elizabeth Shepherd, Joost Siedhoff, Alberta Watson, Graham Greene, Martin Donovan

238. *Father Goose*

During World War II, while running from the Japanese, schoolteacher Catherine Frenay (Leslie Caron) disrupts the life of South Sea beachcomber Walter Eckland (Cary Grant) when she arrives with her students Catherine wastes no time taking over his life by hiding liquor, evicting him, and taking his supplies.

Universal. US. 1964. 116m. C. *Producer:* Robert Arthur *Director:* Ralph Nelson *Writers:* Peter Stone, Frank Tarloff *Cast:* Cary Grant, Leslie Caron, Trevor Howard

239. *Fear in the Night*

Michael Carmichael (Peter Cushing) is the headmaster of a private school where instructor Robert Heller (Ralph Bates) is having an affair with Michael's wife Molly (Joan Collins). Robert and Molly decide to drive his wife insane and cause her to kill Michael.

MGM. Great Britain. 1972. 85m. C. *Producer-Director:* Jimmy Sangster *Writers:* Jimmy Sangster, Michael Syson *Cast:* Judy Geeson, Joan Collins, Ralph Bates, Peter Cushing, Gillian Lind, James Cossins, John Brown, Brian Grellis

Fear o' God see *The Mountain Eagle*

240. *La Femme du Boulanger (The Baker's Wife)*

The new baker's wife runs off with the marquis' shepherd on the marquis' best horse. The baker becomes too depressed to bake bread. The marquis, a righteous priest, and a heretical schoolteacher (Robert Bassac) unite to bring back the wife. After all, they must have their bread.

Les Films. France. 1938. 130m. B&W. *Producers:* Robert Hakim, Raymond Hakim *Director:* Marcel Pagnol *Writers:* Marcel Pagnol, Jean Giono (novel) *Cast:*

Raimu, Ginette Leclerc, Charles Moulin, Robert Vattier, Robert Bassac, Fernand Charpin

241. *Feng Huang Qin (Country Teachers)*

A committed teacher takes a position with very little pay in a small Chinese village hoping to improve the lives of her students. She gives of herself and learns about herself.

China. 1994. 90m. C. *Director:* Qun He *Writers:* Yangui Bu, Sheng Ju *Cast:* Baotian Li, Xue Ju, Xueqi Wang, Zongdi Xiu, Qian Sun, Jiali Ding, DaWei Xu, Fan Zhang, Shunzi Jin, Jianxin Zhang, Meng Pang, Xinying Yu, Mei Li, Nenran Ma, Jianyi Li, Xuexin Wang

242. *Ferry to Hong Kong*

A pompous and tyrannical Cecil Hart (Orson Welles) is the skipper of a broken-down ferry running between Hong Kong and Macao. When he is forced to take Mark Conrad (Curt Jurgens), he finds that must stay aboard permanently because no country will allow Mark to step foot there. Mark does have friends in the crew and schoolteacher Liz Ferrers (Sylvia Syms). Conrad redeems himself by being a hero several times, including defeating pirates.

TCF. Great Britain. 1961. 103m. C. *Producer:* George Maynard *Director:* Lewis Gilbert *Writer:* Vernon Harris *Cast:* Curt Jurgens, Orson Welles, Sylvia Syms, Jeremy Spenser, Noel Purcell, Margaret Withers, John Wallace, Roy Chiao Hung, Shelley Shen, Louis Seto, Milton Reid, Ronald Decent, Don Carlos, Nick Kendall

243. *Fever Pitch*

Lindsey Meeks (Drew Barrymore), a Boston consultant, finds herself at a career show-and-tell for some elementary school math students and their nerdy teacher, Ben Wrightman (Jimmy Fallon). She and Ben start to date and she learns of his obsession with the Red Sox.

Fox Pictures. US. 2005. 98m. C. *Producers:* Alan Greenspan, Amanda Posey, Gil Netter, Drew Barrymore, Nancy Juvonen, Bradley Thomas *Directors:* Peter Farrelly, Bobby Farrelly *Writers:* Lowell Ganz, Babaloo Madel, Nich Hornby (novel) *Cast:* Drew Barrymore, Jimmy Fallon, Jason Spevack, Jack Kehler, Scott H. Severance, Jessamy R. Finet

244. *The Fifth Form at St Dominic's*

A school prefect's brother is blamed for the theft of examination papers.

I.B. Davidson. Great Britain. 1921. B&W. *Director:* A.E. Coleby *Writers:* A.E. Coleby, Dave Aylott, Talbot Baines Reed (novel) *Cast:* Ralph Forbes, Maurice Thompson, Humberston Wright, Phyllis Shannaw, William Freshman, Percy Field, Clifford Cobbe, Sam Austin, Douglas Phair, Cecil Susands, Royce Milton

The Fifth Reaction see Vakonesh panjom

245. *The Fighting Schoolmarm*
No description available.
Universal. US. 1925. B&W *Director:* Ernst Laemmle *Writer:* Isadore Bernstein *Cast:* Josie Sedgwick

Final Chord see *Schlussakkord*

The First Teacher see *Pervy Uchitel*

Five from Barska Street see *Piatka z Ulicy Barskiej*

Five Savage Men see *The Animals*

246. *The Five Thousand Fingers of Doctor T*
Ten-year-old Bart (Tommy Rettig) hates piano lessons and, in his dreams, sees his music teacher Dr. Terwilliker (Hans Conried) as an evil man holding 500 children as prisoners.
Columbia. US. 1953. 88m. C. *Producer:* Stanley Kramer *Director:* Roy Rowland *Writers:* Theodore Geisel (Dr. Seuss), Alan Scott *Cast:* Hans Conried, Tommy Rettig, Peter Lind Hayes, Mary Healy, John Heasley, Robert Heasley, Noel Cravat, Henry Kulky

247. *Flame in the Streets*
Jacko Palmer (John Mills) considers himself as fair-minded toward black employees and at union meetings he defends their rights. One night he learns that his schoolmistress daughter, Kathie (Sylvia Syms), plans to marry young Jamaican schoolteacher Peter Lincoln (Johnny Sekka). Jacko's wife Nell (Brenda De Banzie) is very opposed to the match, but the young couple are in love and aware of a tough future. Some white hoodlums menacing Jamaicans burn one of Jacko's co-workers.
Atlantic Releasing. Great Britain. 1961. 93m. C. *Producer-Director:* Roy Ward Baker *Writer:* Ted Willis *Cast:* John Mills, Sylvia Syms, Brenda De Banzie, Johnny Sekka, Ann Lynn, Earl Cameron, G. Brambell, Meredith Edwards, Newton Blick, Michael Wynne, Dan Jackson, Gretchen Franklin, Harry Baird

The Flirtation of Girls see *Ghazal al-banat*

248. *Flora the Schoolteacher*
No description available.
US. 1917. B&W. *Cast:* Flora Finch

249. *Follow Me, Boys*
Traveling musician Lem Siddons (Fred MacMurray) decides to settle down in

a small town, finding work as a stock boy and falling in love with bank teller Vida Downey (Vera Miles). Volunteering to be a scoutmaster, Lem begins a scout troop. After a few complications, he is able to make a difference.

Walt Disney. US. 1966. 132m. C. *Producer:* Winston Hibler *Director:* Norman Tokar *Writers:* Louis Pelletier, MacKinlay Kantor (novel) *Cast:* Fred MacMurray, Vera Miles, Lillian Gish, Charlie Ruggles, Elliott Reid, Kurt Russell, Luana Patten, Ken Murray

250. *Follow Your Leader and the Master Follows Last*

Teacher chases pupil and is followed.

Clarendon. Great Britain. 1908. B&W. *Director:* Percy Stow *Writer:* Langford Reed

251. *The Foolish Virgin*

Young schoolteacher Mary Adams (Clara Kimball Young) marries Jim Anthony (Conway Tearle), a failed inventor turned burglar. Mary doesn't know of his dishonesty and accompanies him to North Carolina to see his mother who had deserted him. His mother tries to kill him for his hidden jewels. Jim repents and reconciles with Mary.

Selznick Pictures. US. 1916. B&W. *Writer-Director:* Albert Capellani *Cast:* Clara Kimball Young, Conway Tearle, Paul Capellani, Catherine Proctor, Sheridan Tansey, William Welsh, Marie Lines, Agnes Mapes, Edward Elkas, Jacqueline Morhange

For the Children see Meili de dajiao

Forever Mary see Mery per sempre

252. *Forever Young*

In Great Britain, Jimmy and Mike dreamed of being rock stars but went their separate ways. Mike (Nicholas Gecks) became an idealistic priest and Jimmy (James Aubrey) a cynical teacher. The two unexpectedly meet again 20 years later and their initial joy at seeing each other changes to discovery that what they share are frustrated musical dreams, sadness and resentment. There is also a subplot about a young boy who idolizes the priest and learns about betrayal from him.

TCF. Great Britain. 1983. 84m. B&W/C. *Producer:* Chris Griffin *Director:* David Drury *Writer:* Ray Connolly *Cast:* James Aubrey, Nicholas Gecks, Alec McCowen, Karen Archer, Joseph Wright, Liam Holt, Jane Forster, Jason Carter, Oona Kirsch

Forty Little Mothers see Le Mioche

253. *Forty Naughty Girls*

When Windy Bennett turns up dead in the dressing room of the popular Broadway musical "Forty Naughty Girls," audience members Inspector Oscar Pipper

(James Gleason) and schoolteacher Hildegarde Withers (ZaSu Pitts) are on the case. Oscar thinks he has his man, Tommy Washburn (Alden Chase), the author who actually stole the manuscript, but he too is murdered. Clumsy but clever Hildegarde discovers the real murderer.

RKO. US. 1937. 68m. B&W. *Producer:* William Sistrom *Director:* Edward Cline *Writers:* John Grey, Harold Kusell, Stuart Palmer (short story) *Cast:* James Gleason, ZaSu Pitts, Marjorie Lord, George Shelley, Joan Woodbury, Frank M. Thomas, Tom Kennedy, Alan Edwards, Alden Chase, Edward Marr, Ada Leonard, Barbara Pepper, Donald Kerr

254. *Four Frightened People*

Newspaper correspondent Stewart Corder, chemist Arnold Ainger, lecturer Fifi Marsdick and meek schoolteacher Judith Jones find themselves on a Malaysian jungle island infected with cholera and infested with jungle beasts, and angry natives. (They had fled a bubonic plague-infected steamer.) They hire Montage, a half-caste native, to guide them to a more healthy part of the island. The trip costs lives, but Judith becomes very brave and sheds her schoolteacher limitations.

Paramount. 1934. US. 95m. B&W. *Director:* Cecil B. DeMille *Writer:* E. Arnot Robertson (novel) *Cast:* Claudette Colbert, Herbert Marshall, Mary Boland, William Gargan, Leo Carrillo, Nella Walker, Tetsu Komai, Chris Pin Martin, Joe De La Cruz, Minoru Nisheda, Teru Shimada, E.R. Jinadas, Delmar Costello

The Four Hundred Blows see *Les Quatre Cents Coups*

255. *Freckles*

Mischievous young Laurie-Lou Duncan (Virginia Weidler) and her bear Cubby meet orphan Freckles (Tom Brown) wandering in the forest. Laurie-Lou introduces Freckles to her pretty schoolteacher Mary Arden (Carol Stone), who helps Freckles get a job as guard of the Limberlost forest. Laurie-Lou helps him adjust and Mary gives him botany books and invites him to visit her home. Freckles saves Laurie-Lou and Cubby from a falling tree. A convicted timber thief is there planning a heist and Laurie-Lou ends up captured. Freckles saves the day and gets the teacher.

RKO. US. 1935. 69m. B&W. *Producer:* Pandro S. Berman *Director:* Edward Killy *Writers:* Dorothy Yost, Gene Stratton-Porter (novel) *Cast:* Tom Brown, Virginia Weidler, Carol Stone, Lumsden Hare, James Bush, Dorothy Peterson, Addison Richards, Richard Alexander, George Lloyd, Louis Natheaux, Wade Boteler

Freedom Is Paradise see *SER*

256. *The Freeze Out*

Zoe Whipple (Helen Ferguson) is the local schoolteacher and owner of a variety store. Her brother operates a gambler-infested saloon. When a stranger threatens to open a rival business, Zoe convinces him to open a new school and library. In the end, he wins Zoe's heart.

Universal Film Manufacturing Co. US. 1921. B&W. *Director:* Jack Ford *Writers:* George Hull, Jack Ford *Cast:* Harry Carey, Helen Ferguson, Joe Harris, Charles Le Moyne, J. Farrell MacDonald, Lydia Yeamans Titus

257. *A French Mistress*

The boys of Melbury Primary School are pleasantly surprised when the new French master turns out to be a mistress. Soon all the boys want extra French lessons. When the head discovers that mademoiselle's mother was an old flame, the new teacher must go. The boys take action to prevent her dismissal.

British Lion/Charter. Great Britain. 1960. 98m. B&W. *Producer:* John Boulting *Director:* Roy Boulting *Writers:* Roy Boulting, Jeffrey Dell *Cast:* James Robertson Justice, Cecil Parker, Raymond Huntley, Ian Bannen, Agnes Laurent, Thorley Walters, Edith Sharpe, Athene Seyler, Kenneth Griffith, Paul Sheridan, Irene Handl, Schot Finch, Michael Crawford

Frenzy see *Hets*

258. *Friends*

At the end of the 1980s, three female friends share a house in Johannesburg, South Africa: non-violent black schoolteacher Thoko (Dambisa Kente); white militant Sophie (Kerry Fox); and Annika (Michele Burgers), who hides in her archaeological studies. Their worlds will be changed by a bomb.

South Africa/UK/France. 1993. 105m. C. *Producer:* Judith Hunt *Writer-Director:* Elaine Proctor *Cast:* Kerry Fox, Dambisa Kente, Michele Burgers, Marius Weyers, Tertius Meintjes, Dolly Rathebe, Wilma Stockenström, Carel Trichardt, Anne Curteis, Ralph Draper, Mary Twala, Maphiki Mabohi, Job Kubatsi, Vanessa Cooke, Jerry Mofokeng, Trevi Jean Le Pere, Motshabi Tyelele, Archie Mgwenya

259. *The Frontiersman*

In the wilds of New Mexico, spoiled boy Artie (Dickie Jones) lives on a ranch with his aunt and uncle. Artie refuses to go to school because old schoolmarm Snooksie disciplines with a switch. When the students tie her up, Mayor Jud Thorpe (Charles A. Hughes) asks Hoppy (William Boyd) to restore peace. Unbeknownst to Hoppy, Thorpe is really a rustler who uses diversions to steal cattle. Thorpe sends for a strict schoolmarm but Hoppy asks for a gentle schoolmarm. Pretty June Lake (Evelyn Venable) arrives from Boston and quickly wins the affections of everyone. The ranch hands are distracted from their work by the schoolmarm, who is staying at the ranch. Thorpe courts June but Hoppy warns her to be careful. During graduation ceremony, Thorpe's men are planning to rustle the ranch's cattle. A shootout occurs and the villains are defeated. June promises to return to the ranch in September.

Paramount. US. 1938. 72m. B&W. *Director:* Lesley Selander *Writer:* Norman Houston *Cast:* William Boyd, George Hayes, Russell Hayden, Evelyn Venable, Charles A. Hughes, Jud Thorpe, William Duncan, Clara Kimball Young, Emily Fitzroy, Dickie Jones, John Beach, Roy Barcroft, Robert Mitchell, St. Brendan's Boys Choir

260. *Genbaku No Ko (Children of Hiroshima)*

A young teacher returns to Hiroshima seven years after the bomb to visit her parents' grave and to see how her friends and ex-pupils have lived since the bombing.

Kendai Eiga Lyokai. Japan. 1952. 97m. B&W. *Producer:* Gekidan Mingei *Writer-Director:* Kaneto Shindo, Arata Osada (novel) *Cast:* Nobuko Otowa, Chikako Hoshawa, Niwa Saito

261. *Gente Così (Mistress of the Mountains)*

Parish priest Don Candido (Camillo Pilotto) and mayor-barber Mayor Giusà (Saro Urzì) watch over their small mountain village. Giàn (Adriano Rimoldi), a young smuggler, falls in love with schoolteacher Theresa (Vivi Gioi), a Communist. Due to a misunderstanding, they are separated when she becomes pregnant and leaves. She wants him to have his freedom. They come together but unfortunately Giàn is shot. While he lies dying, Don Candido marries the couple. This film was not released until 1954 in the United States.

Artista Associati. Italy. 1949. 90m. B&W. *Producer:* Giorgio Venturini *Director:* Fernando Cerchio *Writer:* Giovanni Guareschi *Cast:* Vivi Gioi, Adriano Rimoldi, Camillo Pilotto, Renato De Carmine, Marisa Mari, Saro Urzì

262. *Gente di Rispetto (The Masters)*

A naïve schoolteacher arrives in a Sicilian town and becomes involved with the corrupt government and the Mafia. A local man is murdered after insulting the teacher.

Campagnia Cinematografica Champion. Italy. 1975. 100m. C. *Producer:* Carlo Ponti *Director:* Luigi Zampa *Writers:* Leo Benevenuti, Peiro de Bernardi, Luigi Zampa *Cast:* James Mason, Jennifer O'Neill, Franco Nero, Orazio Orlando, Claudio Gora, Franco Fabrizi, Aldo Giuffré

Gentlemen of Fortune see *Gentlemeny Udachy*

263. *Gentlemeny Udachy (Gentlemen of Fortune)*

Kindergarten director Troshkin (Yevgeni Leonov) is a dead ringer for a criminal named Docent, who has stolen a priceless archaeological piece. Troshkin is soon thrust into the criminal world.

Mosfilm. Soviet Union. 1972. 88m. *Director:* Aleksandr Seryj *Writers:* Georgi Daneliya, Viktoriya Tokareva *Cast:* Yevgeni Leonov, Georgi Vitsin, Radner Muratov, Saveli Kramarov, Natalya Fateyeva, Erast Garin

The Gesture see *Andaz*

264. Get a Clue

Twelve-year-old Lexy writes in her school paper about the relationship of two teachers. When the story is published in the city's daily paper, one of the teachers (Ian Gomez) goes missing. With the help of her friends, Lexy tries to solve the mystery.

The Disney Channel. US. 2002. 83m. C. *Producer:* Josette Perrotta *Director:* Maggie Greenwald *Writer:* Alana Sanko *Cast:* Lindsay Lohan, Bug Hall, Ian Gomez, Brenda Song, Ali Mukaddam, Dan Lett, Amanda Plummer, Charles Shaughnessy, Kim Roberts, Eric Fink, Jennifer Pisana, Judy Sinclair, Marilyn Boyle, Keenan Macwilliam, Sugith Varughese

265. Gharbar (The Householder)

Young schoolteacher Prem Sagar (Shashi Kapoor) helps a friend deal with his recent marriage by telling of his experience. When Prem started his first teaching job, he was a newlywed and learned that wife was pregnant. Unable to cope, he sent for his mother. After a few more missteps, he discovered that marriage is important.

Royal Films International. India. 1963. 100m. B&W. *Producer:* Ismail Merchant *Director:* James Ivory *Writer:* Ruth Prawer Jhabvala *Cast:* Shashi Kapoor, Leela Naidu, Durga Khote, Hariendernath Chattopadaya, Pro Sen, Romesh Thappar, Indu Iele, Achla Sachdev, Pincho Kapoor, Pra Raaj, Shama Beg, Usha Amin, Praveen Paul, Pahar Snayal, Jabeen Jalil, Patsy Dance, Walter King, Ernest Castaldo

266. Ghazal al-banat (The Flirtation of Girls)

Teacher Hamam (Naguib Al Rihani) is fired from a girls' elementary school because he can't control his students. A friend finds him a job as a private teacher for Laila (Laila Mourad). Through his friendship with her, Hamam comes to appreciate life.

Egypt. 1949. 120m. B&W. *Director:* Anwar Wagdi *Writers:* Naguib Al Rihani, Anwar Wagdi *Cast:* Naguib Al Rihani, Laila Mourad, Anwar Wagdi, Mahmoud El-Meliguy, Suleiman Naguib, Abdel Waress Assar, Youssef Wahby, Stephan Rosti, Zeinat Sedki, Mohamend Abdel Wahab, Farid Shawqi, Said Abu Bakr, Ferdoos Mohammed

267. The Ghost of St. Michaels

William Lamb (Will Hay), an incompetent teacher, is hired by a school in remote Scotland. Soon the school is haunted by a murderous, bagpipe-playing ghost. Hilary Teasdale (Claude Hulbert) and Percy Thorne (Charles Hawtrey) assist in unraveling the mystery.

Ealing. Great Britain. 1941. 82m. B&W. *Producer:* Basil Dearden *Director:* Marcel Varnel *Writers:* Angus Macphail, John Dighton *Cast:* Will Hay, Claude Hulbert, Felix Aylmer, Raymond Huntley, Elliot Mason, Charles Hawtrey, John Laurie, Hay Petrie, Roddy Hughes, Manning Whiley, Derek Blomfield, Brefni O'Rourke

268. *A Giant of His Race*

The son of an African slave graduates from medical school. He devotes himself to trying to find a cure for the yellow plague decimating the black community. A young woman teacher offers to test the serum. He finds the cure and wins the teacher.

Norman Film Manufacturing. C. US. 1921. B&W. *Director:* Ben Strasser *Cast:* Mr. Billopps, Miss Young, Mabel Holmes, Walter Holeby, Walter Long, Ruth Freeman

269. *The Girl from Jones Beach*

The producers of a television program are searching for the perfect girl to be "The Randolph Girl." It takes time but they find Ruth Wilson (Virginia Mayo), a beautiful teacher living with her mother and brother. Ruth loses her teaching job amid all the chaos.

Warner. US. 1949. 78m. B&W. *Producer:* Alex Gottlieb *Director:* Peter Godfrey *Writer:* I.A.L. Diamond *Cast:* Ronald Reagan, Virginia Mayo, Eddie Bracken, Dona Drake, Henry Travers, Florence Bates, Lois Wilson, Jerome Cowan, Helen Westcott, Paul Harvey, Lloyd Corrigan, Gary Gray, Myrna Dell, William Forrest, Mary Stuart

270. *The Girl Who Ran Wild*

A new schoolmaster (Vernon Steele) persuades M'liss (Gladys Walton) to clean up and get some education. The school master fights his rival to convince her to stay.

Universal Film Manufacturing Co. US. 1922. B&W. *Director:* Rupert Julian *Writers:* Rupert Julian, George C. Hull *Cast:* Gladys Walton, Marc Robbins, Vernon Steele, Joseph Dowling, William Burress, Al Hart, Nelson McDowell, Lloyd Whitlock, Lucille Ricksen

Girls' Boarding School see *Internado para Señoritas*

Girls in Uniform see *Mädchen in Uniform (1931, 1958)*

271. *Girls Please*

Trampleasure (Sydney Howard), a girls' school's physical education teacher, is left in charge of the school in the headmistress' absence. Complications arise when one of the girls decides to elope.

B&D. Great Britain. 1934. 73m. B&W. *Producer:* Herbert Wilcox *Director:* Jack Raymond *Writers:* R.P. Weston, Bert Lee, Jack Marks *Cast:* Sydney Howard,

Jane Baxter, Meriel Forbes, Edward Underdown, Peter Gawthorne, Lena Halliday, Cecily Oates, Sybil Arundate, Moore Marriott

Give Her the Moon see *Les Caprices de Marie*

272. Glamour

The trials and tribulations of a Hungarian Jewish family from World War I through the Nazi and Communist regimes. During the 1930s, the patriarch's son falls in love with a pretty German nursery schoolteacher, but they are prohibited from marriage because of the strict laws. She must first be a divorced woman. Therefore, for three months she becomes the wife in name only to a family worker. The love between the son and his German wife remains strong through all the adversities.

Bunyik Entertainment. Hungary. 2000. 114m. C. *Producer:* Kornel Sipos, Ilona Grundman, Gerald W. Kruse *Writer-Director:* Frigyes Godros *Cast:* Karoly Eperjes, Eszter Onodi, Gyorgy Barko, Jonas Togay, Miklos Lang

The Golden Kite see *Aranysárkány*

273. The Good Companions

An unlikely musical trio consists of Inigo Jolifant (John Gielgud), master of a small school run by a tight-lipped, puritanical battle-axe; Jess Oakroyd (Edmund Gwenn); and chorus girl Susie Dean (Jessie Matthews). Miss Trant (Mary Glynne), a woman looking for adventure, is persuaded by the men to financially back "The Dinky Do's."

Gaumont-Welsh-Pearson. Great Britain. 1933. B&W. *Producers:* T.A. Welsh, George Pearson *Director:* Victor Saville *Writers:* W.P. Lipscomb, Angus Macphail, Ian Dalrymple *Cast:* Jessie Matthews, Edmund Gwenn, John Gielgud, Mary Glynne, Percy Parsons, A.W. Baskcomb, Dennis Hoey, Viola Compton, Richard Dolman, Marger Binner, D.A. Clarke-Smith, Florence Gregson, Frank Pettingell, Alex Fraser, Finlay Currie, Max Miller, Ivor Barnard, Olive Sloane, Muriel Aded, J. Fisher White, Jack Hawkins, Cyril Smith, Lawrence Hanray, Annie Esmond, Ben Field, George Zucco, Arnold Riches, Wally Patch, Barbara Gott, Margaret Yarde, Hugh E. Wright, Pollie Emery

274. Good Luck, Miss Wyckoff

In 1956 Kansas, Dr. Steiner (Donald Pleasence) and Dr. Neal (Robert Vaughn) attempt to help a 35-year-old white schoolteacher Evelyn Wyckoff (Anne Heywood), who was a virgin, deal with a brutal rape. The incident is complicated because her attacker is a young janitor at the school where she worked (and had been trying to help the man). There are also racial implications.

IFI/Scope III Inc. US. 1979. 90m. C. *Producer:* Raymond Stross *Director:* Marvin J. Chomsky *Writers:* Polly Platt, William Inge (novel) *Cast:* Anne Heywood,

Donald Pleasence, Robert Vaughn, Earl Holliman, Carolyn Jones, Ronee Blakley, Dorothy Malone, Doris Roberts, John Lafayette, Jocelyn Brando, R.G. Armstrong, Dana Elcar, J. Patrick McNamara, Gary Prendergast, Rip Clark

275. *Good Luck, Mr. Yates*

Teacher Oliver Yates (Jess Barker) feels that he is losing the admiration of his pupils at Carlyle Military Academy because he has not enlisted. The head of the school convinces Oliver that teaching is just as important as fighting. But circumstances change and Oliver decides to enlist, but fails the physical due to a perforated eardrum. He meets an old friend, Joe (Frank Sully), who introduces him to a doctor who can operate on his ear. Yates doesn't want the boys to know so he takes a job at the shipyard and stays at a boardinghouse. Misunderstandings and jealousy reign in this plot. Yates finds love and his ear injury worsens because of his heroic actions. The boys are still proud but Yates continues his important work at the shipyard.

Columbia. US. 1943. 69m. B&W. *Producer:* David J. Chatkin *Director:* Ray Enright *Writers:* Lou Breslow, Adele Comandini *Cast:* Claire Trevor, Jess Barker, Edgar Buchanan, Tom Neal, Albert Basserman, Henry Armetta, Scotty Beckett, Tommy Cook, Frank Sully, Douglas Leavitt, Rosina Galli, Billy Roy, Conrad Binyon, Rudy Wissler, Barbara Brown, Shimen Ruskin, Adia Kuznetzoff, Edward Fielding, David McKim

276. *Good Morning, Boys*

Dr. Benjamin Twist (Will Hay) is headmaster of a seedy boarding school where an escaped convict is living, posing as an older student. The school is part of a plot to steal the Mona Lisa.

GFD/Gainsborough. Great Britain. 1937. 79m. B&W. *Producer:* Edward Black *Director:* Marcel Varnel *Writers:* Marriott Edgar, Val Guest, Anthony Kimmins *Cast:* Will Hay, Graham Moffatt, Lilli Palmer, Mark Daly, Peter Gawthorne, Martita Hunt, Charles Hawtrey, Will Hay, Jr., Fewlass Llewellyn, Basil McGrail, Jacques Brown

277. *Good Morning, Miss Dove*

In the small town of Liberty Hill, prim schoolteacher "Terrible Miss Dove" (Jennifer Jones), a strict disciplinarian, lies ill waiting for a doctor. As she waits, she remembers how she gave up her love and future to teach in order to repay her deceased father's debt. While hospitalized, former pupils come to pay their respects for all the good she has done for them and others. Miss Dove's impact on her students has really made a difference in their lives. The operation is a success and she asks the principal to resume classes.

TCF. US. 1955. 107m. C. *Producer:* Samuel G. Engel *Director:* Henry Koster *Writers:* Eleanore Griffin, Frances Gray Patton (novel) *Cast:* Jennifer Jones, Robert Stack, Robert Douglas, Kipp Hamilton, Peggy Knudsen, Marshall Thompson, Chuck Connors, Mary Wickes, Biff Elliot, Jerry Paris, Leslie Bradley, Edward Firestone, Richard Deacon, Ted Marc, Dick Stewart, Than Wyenn, Martha Wentworth, Aifred Calazza, John Hensley, Gary Pagett

Goodbye, Children see Au Revoir, les Infants

278. Goodbye, Mr. Chips

A sentimental tribute to the English public school system and to its institutional Mr. Charles Chipping (Robert Donat) of Brookfield. As the years go by, he transitions from a young schoolmaster to a very old man. Katherine Ellis (Greer Garson) is the woman who brings him out of his shell. She shows him that it is better to teach with benevolence and changes Mr. Chipping into the lovable Mr. Chips.

MGM. Great Britain. 1939. 114m. B&W. *Producer:* Victor Saville *Director:* Sam Wood *Writers:* R.C. Sherriff, Claudine West, Eric Maschwitz, Sidney Franklin, James Hilton (novel) *Cast:* Robert Donat, Greer Garson, Paul Henreid, Lyn Harding, Austin Trevor, Terry Kilburn, John Mills, Milton Rosmer, Judith Furse, Louise Hampton, Austin Trevor, David Tree, Edmond Brean, Jill Furse, Guy Middleton, Nigel Stock, John Longden, Peter Gawthorne, Martita Hunt, J.H. Roberts, Cyril Raymond, Michael Shepley

279. Goodbye, Mr. Chips

Another film version of the classic tale of Mr. Charles Chipping's years as a schoolteacher.

MGM/APJAC. Great Britain. 1969. 147m. C. *Producer:* Arthur P. Jacobs *Director:* Herbert Ross *Writers:* Terrence Rattigan, James Hilton (novel) *Cast:* Peter O'Toole, Petula Clark, Michael Bryant, Michael Redgrave, George Baker, Jack Hedley, Stan Phillips, Alison Leggatt, Michael Culver, Barbarra Couper, Elspeth March, Clive Morton

280. Goodbye, Mr. Chips (TV)

This made-for-TV film chronicles a man's journey to becoming an inspirational schoolteacher.

Independent TeleVision. Great Britain, 2002. 101m. C. *Producer:* Margaret Mitchell *Director:* Stuart Orme *Writers:* Frank Delaney, James Hilton (novel) *Cast:* Martin Clunes, Victoria Hamilton, Conleth Hill, John Wood, Patrick Malahide, David Horovitch, Christopher Fulford, John Harding

281. The Goose Steps Out

Bumbling teacher William Potts (Will Hay) turns out to be the double of a German general. He is flown to Germany to impersonate the general and cause trouble at the Hitler youth school. Exposing German spies in Britain, Potts saves the day.

Ealing. Great Britain. 1942. 79m. B&W. *Producer:* Michael Balcon *Directors:* Will Hay, Basil Dearden *Writers:* Angus Macphail, John Dighton *Cast:* Will Hay, Frank Pettingell, Julien Mitchell, Charles Hawtrey, Peter Croft, Anne Firth, Leslie Harcourt, Jeremy Hawk, Raymond Lovell, Aubrey Mallalieu, Barry Morse, Lawrence O'Madden, Peter Ustinov

282. *The Gospel According to Vic (Heavenly Pursuits)*

In Scotland, a Catholic school named after Blessed Edith Semple is devoted to finding two more miracles that would promote Semple to sainthood. Non-believer Scottish teacher Mathews (Tom Conti) is involved in a possible miracle.

Island Films/Skreba. Great Britain. 1985. 92m. C. *Producer:* Michael Relph *Writer-Director:* Charles Gormley *Cast:* Tom Conti, Helen Mirren, David Hayman, Brain Pettifer, Jennifer Black, Ewen Bremner, Tom Busby

283. *The Governess*

Jewish, rebellious Rosina's (Minnie Driver) life is shattered when her father is murdered and the family is in debt. Rosina disguises her Jewishness to fit into 1840s English society. She poses as Mary Blackchurch, a Protestant of Italian descent, and takes a position as a governess to the Cavendish family on a remote Scottish island. Charles Cavendish (Tom Wilkinson) is a scientist and with Rosina's idea makes a new discovery. The two conduct a secret, wildly passionate affair.

Sony Pictures Classics. Great Britain. 1998. 114m. C. *Producer:* Sarah Curtis *Writer-Director:* Sandra Goldbacher *Cast:* Minnie Driver, Tom Wilkinson, Harriet Walter, Florence Hoath, Bruce Myers, Jonathan Rhys Meyers

284. *Le Grand Meaulnes*

In turn-of-the-century France, a friendship develops between an older student and the timid son of a private school director. The dashing older student is searching for a certain girl and, when he doesn't find her, he travels to Paris. The younger boy is living through him.

CFDC. France. 1967. 116m. C. *Director:* Jean-Gabriel Albicocco *Writers:* Isabelle Riviere, Alain-Fournier (novel) *Cast:* Jean Blaise, Brigitte Fossey, Alan Libolt, Alaine Jean, Marcel Cuvelier, Juliette Vitar

The Great Love see *Al-Hob al kabir*

285. *Great Stagecoach Robbery*

A film based on the comic strip "Red Ryder" created by Fred Harman. One afternoon in a small town, schoolteacher Jed Quinlan (Don Costello) breaks up a fight between tomboy Boots Hollister (Sylvia Arslan) and Little Beaver (Bobby Blake) and switches them both. Quinlan is just posing as a teacher to cover his many criminal activities. This time he is involved with plotting a $150,000 robbery.

Wounded during a shootout, he is discovered by Boots. Jed shoots and kills her and tries to blame good guy Red Ryder. After all is cleared up, Quinlan is sentenced to hang.

Republic. US. 1945. 56m. B&W. *Director:* Lesley Selander *Writer:* Randall Faye *Cast:* Wild Bill Elliott, Bobby Blake, Alice Fleming, Don Costello, Francis McDonald, John James, Sylvia Arslan, Bud Geary, Leon Tyler, Freddie Chapman, Dickie Dillon, Bobby Dillon, Patsy May, Chris Wren, Ginny Wren, Frederick Howard, Grace Cunard, Hank Bell, Horace Carpenter

286. *The Great St. Trinian's Train Robbery*

Amber Spottiswood (Dora Bryan), headmistress of St. Trinian's School, receives a grant from her lover, the new minister of schools, to reopen the institution. She gathers her staff from prison, stripping and modeling positions. Classes are underway but it seems train robbers have hidden their loot under the school's ballroom stage. The gang leader enrolls his two daughters in the school to help their cause. Soon there is an all-out chase for the money.

British Lion. Great Britain. 1967. 94m. C. *Producer:* Leslie Gilliat *Directors:* Frank Launder, Sidney Gilliat *Writers:* Frank Launder, Ivor Herbert, Sidney Gilliat, Leslie Gilliat *Cast:* Frankie Howerd, Dora Bryan, Reg Varney, Desmond Walter-Ellis, Raymond Huntley, Richard Wattis, George Benson, Eric Barker, Godfrey Winn, George Cole, Colin Gordon, Barbara Couper, Elspeth Duxbury, Portland Mason, Terry Scott, Carole Ann Ford, Arthur Mullard, Stratford Johns, Meredith Edwards, Michael Ripper

Grimaces see Gyerekbetegségek

287. *Gryphon*

When substitute teacher Miss Ferenczi (Amanda Plummer) appears before a class at a predominately Hispanic inner city middle school, things change for the better. Her teaching philosophy encourages students to expand their minds. Art student Ricky (Alexis Cruz) gets the message and organizes the class to spray paint the back of the school with a Gryphon.

Wonder Works. US. 1990. 55m. C. *Director:* Mark Cullingham *Writers:* Manuel Arce, Carl Haber *Cast:* Alexis Cruz, Nico Hughes, Edward O'Connor, Virgilio Martí, Paul Stolarsky, Hamadi Izzard, Hassan Izzard, Lourdes Benedicto, Edna Harris, Carol Jean Lewis, Ophelia Gonzalez, Sully Diaz, Aurelio Padrón, Kira Delgado, Amanda Plummer

288. *The Guardian*

Nancy Camilla has special plans for the babies for whom she cares — and she may not be human.

Universal. US. 1990. 93m. C. *Producer:* Joe Wizan *Director:* William Friedkin *Writers:* Stephen Volk, Dan Greenburg *Cast:* Jenny Seagrove, Dwier Brown, Carey Lowell, Brad Hull, Miguel Ferrer, Natalia Nogulich, Pamela Brull, Gary Swanson

289. *The Guinea Pig (The Outsider)*

To democratize the English public school system, the Ministry of Education sends a less privileged boy, Jack Read (Richard Attenborough), to such a school. Snobbery runs amok and many of the masters think the system is perfect as is. Mr. Hartley (Cecil Trouncer) is a stern aging headmaster and Nigel Lorraine (Robert Flemyng) is a new master at the school. Mr. Hartley's daughter Lynne (Sheila Sim) falls in love with Jack.

Pilgrim. Great Britain. 1948. 97m. B&W. *Producer:* John Boulting *Director:* Roy Boulting *Writers:* Bernard Miles, Warren Chetham Strode, Roy Boulting *Cast:* Richard Attenborough, Robert Flemyng, Cecil Trouncer, Sheila Sim, Bernard Miles, Joan Hickson, Edith Sharp, Peter Reynolds, Timothy Bateson, Clive Baxter, Basil Cunard, John Forrest, Maureen Glynne, Brenda Hogan, Herbert Lomas, Anthony Newley, Anthony Nicholls, Wally Patch, Hay Petrie, Kynaston Reeves, Olive Sloane, Anthony Wager

290. *Gyerekbetegségek (Grimaces)*

Story centers on a six-year-old boy starting school and his fantasies about entering the real world.

Hungarofilm. Hungary. 1965. 77m. C. *Writer-Directors:* Ferenc Kardos, János Rózsa *Cast:* István Géczy, Tündi Kassai, Rita Bartanyai, Gabor Lontay, Emil Keres, Judit Halász, Dóri Bánfalvi, Béla Horváth, Mária Mamusich, Irma Patkós

291. *Hai Zi Wang (King of the Children)*

During the Cultural Revolution, a laborer sent from the city into a mountainous area helps cultivate the fields alongside the peasants. Suddenly he is asked to become a teacher even though is not qualified. Besides teaching his pupils the basics, he also teaches them to understand the world around them. When the authorities find out, he incurs their anger.

Xi'an Film Studio. China. 1988. 107m. C. *Director:* Chen Kaige *Writers:* Chen Kaige, Wan Zhi *Cast:* Xie Yuan, Yang Xuewen, Chen Shaohua, Zhang Caimei, Xu Guoqing

292. *Hakai (The Sin)*

Segawa (Raizo Ichikawa), born at the bottom of Japan's social scale, receives his education and promises his dying father to hide his roots forever. Now a popular schoolteacher, Segawa can no longer live a lie and must campaign for human rights.

Daiei. Japan. 1961. 119m. B&W. *Director:* Kon Ichikawa *Writer:* Natto Wada *Cast:* Raizo Ichikawa, Rentaro Mikune, Hiroyuki Nagato, Eiji Fugimura, Ganjiro Nakamura

293. *Half a Sinner*

Against her grandmother's advice, straight-laced schoolteacher Anne Gladden (Heather Angel) gets rid of her glasses, buys a new outfit and does what she wants for the day. Anne jumps into a parked limousine and drives away to avoid unwelcome advances. Anne doesn't realize that the car is stolen and has a dead body in the back seat. Larry Cameron (John King), the owner of the car, stops her and pretends to be a crook. They keep getting into trouble but with the help of Mrs. Breckenridge (Constance Collier) they escape and decide to marry.

Universal. US. 1940. 59m. B&W. *Producer:* Jack Skirball *Director:* Al Christie *Writer:* Frederick Jackson *Cast:* Heather Angel, John King, Constance Collier, Walter Catlett, Tom Dugan, Robert Elliot, Clem Bevans, Emma Dunn, Henry Brandon, William B. Davidson, Fern Emmett, Sonny Bupp, Wilbur Mack, Joe Devlin, Antonio Oland

294. *Half Nelson*

This small independent film tells the story of the relationship between a white man and a black girl. Dan (Ryan Gosling) teaches junior high school history in a Brooklyn neighborhood where he also purchases his drugs. He lives with a cat in an apartment filled with books and unfinished dreams. Dan befriends one of his students, lonely Drey (Shareeka Epps), after she finds him almost passed out in the bathroom with crack pipe in hand.

ThinkFilm. US. 2006. 107m. C. *Producers*: Jamie Patricof, Alex Orlovsky, Lynette Howell, Anna Boden, Rosanne Korenberg *Director*: Ryan Fleck, *Writers*: Ryan Fleck, Anna Boden. *Cast*: Ryan Gosling, Shareeka Epps, Anthony Mackie, Monique Gabriela Curnen, Karen Chilton, Tina Holmes

295. *The Hand That Rocks the Cradle*

Peyton Flanders (Rebecca De Mornay) seems to be the perfect nanny for the Bartel family. Appearances can be deceiving: She is out to wreck the family because she blames Claire Bartel (Annabella Sciorra) for a miscarriage. Claire suspects nothing because she has never met Peyton before.

Buena Vista. US. 1991. 110m. C. *Producer:* David Madden *Director:* Curtis Hanson *Writer:* Amanda Silver *Cast:* Annabella Sciorra, Rebecca De Mornay, Matt McCoy, Ernie Hudson, Julianne Moore, Madeline Zima, John de Lancie, Kevin Skousen

296. *Handgun*

A young Boston teacher moves to Dallas and meets a lawyer. After he rapes her at gunpoint, she joins a gun club, buys a gun and plots her revenge.

EMI/Kestrel. US. 1982. 101m. C. *Writer-Producer-Director:* Tony Garnett *Cast:* Karen Young, Clayton Day, Suzie Humphreys, Helena Humann, Ben Jones

297. *Happiest Days of Your Life*

As a result of a mistake at the Ministry of Education, students from a girls' school are evacuated to a boys' school. Harassed headmaster Wetherby Pond (Alastair Sim) butts heads with overpowering headmistress Miss Whitchurch (Margaret Rutherford). Miss Gossage (Joyce Grenfell) is an eager physical education teacher.

British Lion. Great Britain. 1950. 91m. B&W. *Producers:* Frank Launder, Sidney Gilliat *Director:* Frank Launder *Writers:* Frank Launder, John Dighton *Cast:* Alastair Sim, Margaret Rutherford, John Turnbull, Richard Wattis, Guy Middleton, Arthur Howard, John Bentley, Edward Rigby, Muriel Aked, Joyce Grenfell, Millicent Wolfe, Myrette Morven, Bernadette O'Farrell, Russell Waters, Gladys Henson, John Turnbull, Percy Walsh, Laurence Naismith, Patricia Owens, Stringer Davis, George Benson, George Cole

298. *The Happy Years*

In the early twentieth century, a habitual troublemaker (Dean Stockwell) is sent to a boys' prep school. The teachers work to straighten him out and make a man of him. At first the older students bully him but he earns their respect by being strong.

MGM. US. 1950. 86m. B&W. *Producer:* Carey Wilson *Director:* William Wellman *Writers:* Harry Ruskin, Owen Johnson (novel) *Cast:* Dean Stockwell, Leo G. Carroll, Darryl Hickman, Scotty Beckett, Leon Ames, Margalo Gillmore

299. *Harry Potter and the Chamber of Secrets*

Harry Potter (Daniel Radcliffe) has an encounter with a house elf named Dobby who warns him not to return to Hogwarts. Harry escapes to the Weasley house with Ron Weasley (Rupert Grint) in a flying car. When they get to the school, unusual events ensue. Harry learns that he has the ability to talk to snakes. "Mudbloods" (people of Muggle families) are "petrified" by an evil monster lurking on the grounds. The new "Defense Against the Dark Arts" teacher, Professor Gilderoy Lockhart (Kenneth Branagh), seems to be more into himself than his teachings.

Warner. Great Britain/US. 2002. 161m. C. *Producer:* David Heyman *Director:* Chris Columbus *Writers:* Steve Kloves, J.K. Rowling (novel) *Cast:* Daniel Radcliffe, Rupert Grint, Emma Watson, Tom Felton, Kenneth Branagh, John Cleese, Robbie Coltrane, Warwick Davis, Richard Griffiths, Richard Harris, Jason Isaacs, Alan Rickman, Fiona Shaw, Maggie Smith, Julie Walters, Shirley Henderson

300. *Harry Potter and the Goblet of Fire*

Harry's fourth year at Hogwarts brings new challenges. He is one of the young wizards and witches who are selected to compete in the Triwizard Tournament. Will Harry rise to the challenge? Will He Who Must Not Be Named Voldemort's rebirth be too much for the young hero? Will Harry survive?

Warner. Great Britain/US. 2005. 157m. C. *Producer:* David Heyman *Director:* Mike Newall *Writers:* Steven Kloves, J.K. Rowling (novel) *Cast:* Daniel Radcliffe, Eric Sykes, Timothy Spall, David Tennenat, Emma Watson, Rupert Grint, Mark Williams, James Phelps, Oliver Phelps, Bonnie Wright, Jeff Rawle, Robert Pattinson, Jason Isaacs, Tom Felton, Stanislav Ianevski

301. *Harry Potter and the Prisoner of Azkaban*

During Harry's third year at Hogwarts, he has a new "Defense Against the Dark Arts" teacher. Convicted murderer Sirius Black (Gary Oldman) has escaped the Wizards' Prison and is coming after Harry. The school calls in supernatural help against Black in the form of Dementors, but unusual things continue to put Harry in peril. Professor Dumbledore (Michael Gambon) is worried about Harry's safety.

Warner. Great Britain/US. 2004. 136m. C. *Producer:* David Heyman *Director:* Alfonso Cuarón *Writers:* Steve Kloves, J.K. Rowling (novel) *Cast:* Daniel Radcliffe, Rupert Grint, Emma Watson, Robbie Coltrane, Michael Gambon, Richard Griffiths, Gary Oldman, Alan Rickman, Fiona Shaw, Maggie Smith, Timothy Spall, David Thewlis, Emma Thompson, Tom Felton

302. *Harry Potter and the Sorcerer's Stone*

Harry Potter (Daniel Radcliffe) is mistreated by his aunt and uncle and lives under the stairs. On his eleventh birthday, a gigantic man named Rubeus Hagrid (Robbie Coltrane) brings him a mysterious letter from the Hogwarts School of Witchcraft and Wizardry, telling him that he has been chosen as one of the new students. He also learns about the death of his powerful wizard parents and how he got the mark on his forehead. At Hogwarts, Harry meets his teachers and the wonderful wizard Albus Dumbledore (Richard Harris), and becomes friends with gawky Ron Weasley (Rupert Grint) and bossy Hermione Granger (Emma Watson). Harry learns the game of Quidditch and Wizard Chess, all the while facing a Dark Wizard who is bent on destroying his teachers. Professor Severus Snape (Alan Rickman) doesn't care for Harry. Harry's other teachers include Professor Quirrell (Ian Hart) and Professor McGonagal (Maggie Smith).

Warner. Great Britain/US. 2001. 146m. C. *Producer:* David Heyman *Director:* Chris Columbus *Writers:* Steve Kloves, J.K. Rowling (novel) *Cast:* Daniel Radcliffe, Rupert Grint, Emma Watson, John Cleese, Robbie Coltrane, Warwick Davis, Richard Griffiths, Richard Harris, Ian Hart, John Hurt, Alan Rickman, Fiona Shaw, Maggie Smith, Julie Walters, Zoë Wanamaker, Tom Felton, Harry Melling, David Bradley, Richard Bremmer

303. *He ni Zai Yi Qi (Together)*

Thirteen-year-old Liu Xiaochun (Tang Yun) is a talented violinist who lives with his father Liu Chang (Lui Peiqi) in a small rural area. The father is willing to do anything for his son, even moving to Beijing so that Liu can get the best education. Liu fails to make the cut for a musical scholarship but his father convinces one of the judges to become the boy's private tutor.

UA. China/South Korea. 2002. 117m. C. *Producers:* Hong Chen, Kaaige Chen, Joo-ik Lee, Bolun Li, Ernst Etchie Stroh, Buting Yang, Xiaoming Yan *Director:* Kaige Chen *Writers:* Kaige Chen, Xiao Lu Xue *Cast:* Yun Tang, Peiqi Liu, Hong Chen, Zhiwen Wang, Kaige Chen, Qiang Chen, Qing Zhang, Hye-ri Kim, Bing Liu

304. *The Headless Horseman*

The village of Sleepy Hollow is getting a new schoolteacher, Ichabod Crane (Will Rogers). He is not immediately accepted, but gets attention when Katrina Van Tassel (Lois Meredith) shows interest in him. His rival "Brom" Bones (Ben Hendricks, Jr.) disguises himself as the legendary headless horseman and scares Ichabod away.

W.W. Hodkinson Corp. US. 1922. B&W. *Director:* Edward Venturini *Writer:* Carl Stearns Clancy *Cast:* Will Rogers, Lois Meredith, Ben Hendricks, Jr., Mary Foy, Charles Graham

305. *The Headmaster*

A headmaster seeks a new position by forcing his daughter to marry a rich woman's son.

Astra Films. Great Britain. 1921. B&W. *Producer:* H.W. Thompson *Writer-Director:* Kenelm Foss *Cast:* Cyril Maude, Margot Drake, Miles Malleson, Marie Illington, Lionelle Howard, Sir Simeon Stuart, Ann Trevor, Louie Freear, Will Corrie, Alan Selby, Gordon Craig

Heart and Guts see *Das Tripas Coração*

306. *The Heartbreak Kid*

Greek-Australian student Nick (Alex Dimitriades) falls in love with his Greek-Australian schoolteacher Christina (Claudia Karvan). Christina is engaged to be married to a man who represents the Greek Orthodox lifestyle that she has been brought up in, but wishes to leave.

Roadshow Entertainment. Australia. 1993. 97m. C. *Producer:* Ben Gannon *Director:* Michael Jenkins *Writer:* Richard Barrett *Cast:* Claudia Karvan, Alex Dimitriades, Nico Lathouris, Steve Bastoni, Doris Younane

Heavenly Pursuits see *The Gospel According to Vic*

307. *Heideschulmeister Uwe Karsten (The Country Schoolmaster)*

In a country village, a teacher (Hans Schlenck) meets the love of his life: a rich woman (Marianne Hoppe) from Hamburg, fleeing a loveless marriage.

UFA. Germany. 1934. 94m. B&W. *Producer:* Alfred Zeisler *Director:* Carl Heinz Wolff *Writers:* Kurt Heynicke, Felicitas Rose (novel) *Cast:* Hans Schlenck, Marianne Hoppe, Heinrich Keilinger, Brigitte Horney, Olga Tschechowa, Walter Steinbeck, Carl Auen, Günther Ballier, Jeanette Bethge, Eberhard Leithoff, Ernst Bahmer, Paul Henckels, Maria Karsten, Paul Moleska

308. *Heideschulmeister Uwe Karsten (Eternal Love)*

A woman discovers that her fiancé has fathered the child of her closest friend. She breaks the engagement and moves to the country, where she falls in love with a handsome schoolmaster. Unable to cope with the local gossip, she leaves. She returns when she learns that the schoolmaster has been badly burned while saving someone from a fire. Unfortunately she catches diphtheria and dies.

Casino Film. West Germany. 1954. 95m. C. *Producer-Director:* Hans Deppe *Cast:* Heidi Bruhl, Käthe Haacke, Carola Hoehn, Claus Holm, Herbert Hübner, Wolfgang Lukschy, Hans Quest, Barbara Rutting, Franz Schafheitlin, Josef Sieber

309. *Heidi*

Orphan Heidi (Shirley Temple) is in the care of her bitter, grumpy grandfather Adolph Kramer (Jean Hersholt), whose icy heart quickly melts. Heidi's cruel aunt forces her into servitude in the home of a wealthy family. Heidi is a positive influence on their invalid daughter, encouraging her to walk after many years. Heidi is promised that she will be reunited with her grandfather but the evil wicked governess has other plans. Pauline Moore plays Heidi's schoolteacher. There originally was a love interest between the schoolteacher and the minister that never showed up in the final release. *Heidi* has been filmed many times.

TCF. US. 1937. 88m. B&W. *Producer:* Raymond Griffith *Director:* Allan Dwan *Writers:* Walter Ferris, Julian Josephson, Johanna Spyri (novel) *Cast:* Shirley Temple, Jean Hersholt, Arthur Treacher, Helen Westley, Pauline Moore, Mary Nash, Thomas Beck, Sidney Blackmer, Mady Christians, Sig Rumann, Marcia Mae Jones, Christian Rub, Delmar Watson

310. *Heimatland (Homeland)*

Young poacher Hans (Adrian Hoven) is battling for the affections of schoolteacher Helga Sonnleithner (Marianne Hold). Hans' rival, forest warden Thomas (Rudolph Prack), is always there to impede his progress. Hans' dog Krambambuli indirectly causes his death.

Casin Film. Austria. 1955. 95m. C. *Producer:* Herbert Gruber *Director:* Franz Antel *Writers:* Kurt Nachmann, Hans Holt *Cast:* Rudolf Prack, Adrian Hoven, Marianne Hold, Hannelore Bollman, Oska Sima, Ernst Waldbrunn.

Hello Elephant see *Buongiorno, Elefante!*

311. *Her Adventurous Night*

Junior (Scotty Beckett) gets into trouble when he tries to bring a gun to school. He makes up a story involving his parents Bill (Dennis O'Keefe) and Constance (Helen Walker) and his headmaster (Tom Powers). As a result of the boy's lies, his parents and headmaster end up in jail. They are freed when Junior solves a fifteen-year-old mystery.

Universal. US. 1946. 75m. B&W. *Producer:* Marshall Grant *Director:* John Rawlins *Writer:* Jerry Warner *Cast:* Dennis O'Keefe, Helen Walker, Tom Powers, Fuzzy Knight, Scotty Beckett

312. *Her Twelve Men*

Jan Stewart (Greer Garson), the new teacher at the Oaks, a boys' boarding school, becomes educator and "mother" to a class of twelve. Joe Hargrave, head of the lower school, disapproves of her lack of experience.

MGM. US. 1954. 91m. C. *Producer:* John Houseman *Director:* Robert Z. Leonard *Writers:* William Roberts, Laura Z. Hobson *Cast:* Greer Garson, Robert Ryan, Richard Haydn, Barry Sullivan

313. Hets *(Frenzy and Tormet)*

A sensitive schoolboy, tortured by a sadistic Latin teacher and misunderstood at home, turns to a young alcoholic prostitute for love.

Svensk Filmindustri. Sweden. 1944. 101m. B&W. *Director:* Alf Sjöberg *Writer:* Ingmar Bergman *Cast:* Stig Järrel, Alf Kjellin, Mai Zetterling, Olof Winnerstrand, Märta Arbin, Gunnar Björnstrand

314. Hey! Hey! USA

On an ocean liner bound for America Porter, Benjamin Twist (Will Hay) finds himself impersonating a teacher. He teams with a gangster stowaway and becomes ensnarled with a kidnapping plot.

Gainsborough. Great Britain. 1938. 92m. B&W. *Producer:* Edward Black *Director:* Marcel Varnel *Writers:* J.O.C. Orton, Val Guest, Marriott Edgar *Cast:* Will Hay, Edgar Kennedy, David Burns, Fred Duprez, Tommy Bupp, Edmon Ryan, Fred Duprez, Paddy Reynolds, Peter Gawthorne, Gibb McLaughlin, Arthur Goullet, Eddie Pola, Roddy McDowall

Hidden River *see* Río Escondido

315. Hide-Out

Lucky Wilson (Robert Montgomery), playboy and strong arm of the gangsters, is shot while fleeing from the police. The wounded man finds soon himself in Connecticut with the Millers, a farm family. Lucky is eager to leave until he meets their daughter Pauline (Maureen O'Sullivan), a twenty-year-old schoolteacher. Lucky falls in love and is willing to become an honest man.

MGM. US. 1934. 82m. B&W. *Producer:* Hunt Stromberg *Director:* W.S. Van Dyke *Writers:* Frances Goodrich, Albert Hackett *Cast:* Robert Montgomery, Maureen O'Sullivan, Edward Arnold, Elizabeth Patterson, Whitford Kane, Mickey Rooney, C. Henry Gordon, Muriel Evans, Edward Brophy, Henry Armetta, Herman Bing, Louise Henry, Harold Huber

316. Hills of Kentucky

In a poverty-stricken area of Kentucky, the mountain people turn out their dogs. The Grey Ghost (Rin Tin Tin) leads the dog pack. Ben, a bully, and Steve, his shy half brother, vie for the attentions of schoolteacher Janet (Dorothy Dwan). Little Davey secretly saves Grey Ghost and they become friends. In a jealous state,

Ben causes the farmers to turn against Janet. The Grey Ghost saves Steve from Ben and Janet from the rapids.

Warner. US. 1927. B&W. *Director:* Howard Bretherton *Writer:* Edward Clark *Cast:* Rin Tin Tin, Jason Robards, Dorothy Dwan, Tom Santschi, Billy Kent Schaeffer, Rin Tin Tin, Jr.

317. *His Own People*

Town blacksmith and leader of the people Hugh O'Donnell (Harry T. Morey) is in love with Molly Conway (Gladys Leslie). The lord of the area is hated by the people because of his war on poachers. There is turmoil and jealousy, but all is forgiven. According to the January 4, 1918, *Variety,* "Arthur Donaldson as the local schoolmaster is probably the most consistently good type in the cast."

Greater Vitagraph. US. 1917. B&W. *Director:* William P.S. Earle *Writer:* William Addison Lathrop *Cast:* Harry T. Morey, Gladys Leslie, Arthur Donaldson, William Dunn, Betty Blythe, Stanley Dunn

318. *La Historia Oficial (The Official Story* and *The Official Version)*

Schoolteacher Alicia (Norma Aleandro) and her businessman husband live a comfortable life with their adopted little daughter. The upper-middle-class teacher is forced to acknowledge her husband's role in horrific government programs. When she learns about parents being tortured and children taken away, she begins to suspect her child might be one of them.

Virgin. Argentina. 1985. 115m. C. *Producer:* Marcelo Pineyro *Director:* Luis Puenzo *Writers:* Aida Bortnik, Luis Puenzo *Cast:* Hector Alterio, Norma Aleandro, Chela Ruiz, Chunchuna Villafane, Hugo Arana, Patricio Contreras

319. *Historias de la Radio (Radio Stories)*

In a small Spanish country village, a schoolteacher reluctantly agrees to participate in a quiz radio show to raise money needed for a child's operation in Sweden. On the day of the program, the entire village gathers around the only radio to cheer him on. The schoolteacher does so well that the host switches to sports trivia. The film consists of three vignettes linked by a radio show: the story of the schoolteacher, one about an aging inventor dressing like an Eskimo, and one about a landlord, tenant and priest.

Cesáreo González Producciones Cinematográficas. Spain. 1955. 95m. B&W. *Writer-Director:* José Luis Sáenz de Heredia *Cast:* Carlos Acevedo, Alicia Altabella, Margarita Andrey, Rafael Bardem, Francisco Bernal, Xan das Bolas, Félix Briones, Juan Calvo, Ángel de Andrés, Bobby Deglané, Antonio Fernández, José María Lado, Juanjo Menéndez, Pedro Porcel, Francisco Rabal, Gustavo Re, Alberto Romea

History see La Storia

320. *Al-Hob al kabir (The Great Love)*

A young schoolteacher falls in love with a famous singer.
Lebanon. 1969. B&W. *Producer-Director:* Henry Barakat *Writers:* Henry Barakat, Kaman El-Telmessani *Cast:* Farid Al Atrache, Abdel Salam Al Nabulsy, Faten Hamama, Youssef Wahby

321. *Hold Back the Dawn*

Georges Iscovescu (Charles Boyer), a European ladies' man, marries American schoolteacher Emmy Brown (Olivia de Havilland) in a Mexican border town merely to gain entrance into the United States.
Paramount. US. 1941. 115m. B&W. *Producer:* Arthur Hornblow, Jr. *Director:* Mitchell Leisen *Writers:* Charles Brackett, Billy Wilder *Cast:* Charles Boyer, Olivia de Havilland, Paulette Goddard, Victor Francen, Walter Abel, Curt Bois, Rosemary de Camp, Nestor Paiva, Mitchell Leisen, Billy Lee, Eric Feldary

322. *Holiday's End*

The boy king of a small European country is being sent to an English prep school. Rivalry amongst the masters leads to the death of the science master just before the boy arrives.
B&D/Paramount British. Great Britain. 1937. 70m. B&W. *Producer:* Anthony Havelock-Allan *Director:* John Paddy Carstairs *Writer:* Gerald Elliott *Cast:* Sally Stewart, Wally Patch, Rosalyn Boulter, Aubray Mallalieu, Kenneth Buckley, Henry Victor, Leslie Bradley, Robert Field

323. *Home-Keeping Hearts*

Convicted on circumstantial evidence for causing his employer's death, diver Robert Colton is imprisoned for ten years. His motherless daughter Mary is brought up by the stern Teads. Robert goes to work for them at their creamery where he discovers corruption. Everything is resolved and Robert can now woo and marry schoolmistress Laurel Stewart (Louella Carr).
Playgoers Pictures. US. 1921. B&W. *Director:* Carlyle Ellis *Writers:* Carlyle Ellis, Charles W. Barrell *Cast:* Thomas H. Swinton, Mary Ryan, Louella Carr, Edward Grace, Henry West

324. *A Home of Our Own*

The film is based on the work of Father William Wasson (Jason Miller), founder and director of a home for orphaned children in Mexico. He takes a particular interest in a boy named Julio, who has lost his parents. Julio succeeds and becomes a doctor. One day his wife and daughter are killed and he visits Father Wasson.
CBS. US. 1975. 120m. C. *Producer:* Fred Baum *Director:* Robert Day *Writer:* Blanche Hanalis *Cast:* Jason Miller, Pancho Córdova, Enrique Novi, Pedro Armen-

dariz, Jr., Richard Angarola, Carmen Zapata, Farnesio de Bernal, Rosario Álvarez, Nancy Rodman

Homeland see *Heimatland*

325. *L'Homme du Train (Man on a Train)*

Retired schoolteacher Manesquier (Jean Rochefort) befriends a thief named Milan (Johnny Hallyday). They share a need to prove they are still alive. In one scene, Manesquier challenges a group of louts at a bar and Milan prepares for action. But it seems that one of the young men was a student of Manesquier and admired his teaching. Instead of fighting, he honors the teacher with a poem.

Paramount Classics. France. 90m. C. *Producer:* Philippe Carcassonne *Director:* Patrice Leconte *Writer:* Claude Klotz *Cast:* Johnny Hallyday, Jean Rochefort, Pascal Parmentier

326. *Hoosier Schoolboy*

Schoolteacher Mary Evans (Anne Nagel) arrives in Ainsley, Indiana, in the middle of a milk strike. Student Shockey Carter (Mickey Rooney), the son of an alcoholic, shell-shocked war hero, gets into trouble at school when his father is insulted. Mary prevents him from going to an institution by assuming full responsibility for him. Shockey's father dies during the strike, thereby ending it.

Monogram Pictures Corp. US. 1937. 62m. *Director:* William Nigh *Writers:* Robert Lee Johnson, Edward Eggleston (novel) *Cast:* Mickey Rooney, Anne Nagel, Frank Shields, Edward Pawley, William Gould, Dorothy Vaughan, Anita Deniston, Harry Hayden, Bradley Metcalf, Doris Rankin, Walter Long, Helena Grant, Cecil Weston, Mary Field

327. *The Hoosier Schoolmaster*

In 1831, Ralph Hartsock (Max Figman) goes to rural Flat Creek, Indiana, to open a school. All other aspiring schoolmasters have been driven away by hostile townspeople. His opponents are a politician and a local bully. Complicating matters, Ralph falls in love with Hannah Thompson and is falsely accused of a crime.

Alliance Films Corp. 1914. B&W. *Producer:* M. De la Parelle *Director:* Max Figman *Cast:* Max Figman, Lolita Roberts

328. *The Hoosier Schoolmaster*

Ralph Hartsook (Henry Hull), schoolmaster of the Indiana Flat Creek district, falls in love with Hannah Thompson (Jane Thomas), a 20-year-old orphan. Hannah's brother and Ralph save an innocent man from being lynched. Ralph is falsely accused of robbery but successfully defends himself and gets the girl.

W.W. Hodkinson Corp. US. 1924. B&W. *Producer:* Whitman Bennett *Director:* Oliver L. Sellers *Writer:* Eve Stuyvesant *Cast:* Henry Hull, Jane Thomas, Frank

Dane, Mary Foy, Walter Palm, Nat Pendleton, Dorothy Allen, G.W. Hall, George Pelzer, Arthur Ludwig, Frank Andrews, Harold McArthur, Tom Brown, Adolf Link, Jerry Sinclair, Dorothy Walters, Dick Lee

329. *The Hoosier Schoolmaster*

Yankee Civil War veteran Ralph Hartsook (Norman Foster) comes for land promised in Indiana for veterans but becomes a schoolteacher in Flat Creek. Ralph wins his class' respect and falls in love. Nightriders and crooked politicians cause Ralph to write to the federal government. This raises the anger of the corrupt men, who discredit Ralph and fire him. Ralph learns about more problems and is almost lynched but veterans come to his rescue. Ralph regains his teaching position.

Monogram Pictures Corp. US. 1935. 75m. *Director:* Lewis D. Collins *Cast:* Norman Foster, Charlotte Henry, Dorothy Libaire, Tommy Bupp, Otis Harlan, Fred Kohler, Jr., William V. Mong, Russell Simpson, J.E. Bernard, Wallace Reid, Jr., George Hayes, Sarah Padden

330. *Horvator Izbor (Vucjak)*

In 1918, the eve of the Great Warn chaos reigns in Croatia. A city journalist becomes a country schoolteacher to find some peace in the restless times. He soon discovers that no place is safe, not even a small village.

Yugoslavia. 1985. 114m. C. *Director:* Eduard Galic *Writer:* Ivo Stivicic *Cast:* Rade Serbedzija, Milena Dravic, Mira Furlan, Fabijan Sovagovic, Zvonko Lepetic, Mustafa Nadarevic, Edo Perocivic, Zvonimir Ferencic, Bozidar Smiljanic, Dusko Valentic, Dusko Gruborovic, Mladen Vasary, Ljudevit Galic

331. *Hound of Silver Creek*

The new schoolmistress Molly White (Gloria Grey) is saved by Dynamite, Jack Brooks' (Edmund Cobb) police dog. Molly and Jack become friends. The dog witnesses a shooting and runs off with some valuable papers while saving a boy. The dog protects Molly from the advances of the shooter. When the dog goes to retrieve the documents, he is discovered by the shooter but stops the villain until his owner arrives.

Universal. US. 1927. B&W. *Producer:* Carl Laemmle *Director:* Stuart Paton *Writer:* Paul M. Bryan *Cast:* Dynamite (dog), Edmund Cobb, Gloria Grey, Gladden James, Billy Red Jones, Frank Rice, Frank Clark

The House see Húsið: Trúnaðarmál

House with an Attic see Dom s Mezoninom

The Householder see Gharbar

332. Housemaster

Charles Donkin (Otto Kruger), beloved headmaster at a private boys' school, is well respected and admired by the boys because of his fairness. A new headmaster, Mr. Ovington (Kynaston Reeves), is the opposite of Charles: rigid, rule-bound, and extremely strict. Into the mix come three young ladies and their guardian from Paris. Mr. Ovington wants Charles transferred.

ABPC. Great Britain. 1938. 95m. B&W. *Producer:* Walter Mycroft *Director:* Herbert Brenon *Writers:* Dudley Leslie, Elizabeth Meehan *Cast:* Otto Kruger, Diana Churchill, Phillips Holmes, Joyce Barbour, Kynaston Reeves, Rene Ray, Walter Hudd, John Wood, Cecil Parker, Michael Shepley, Jimmy Hanley, Henry Hepworth

333. How Green Was My Valley

Huw Morgan (Roddy McDowall) recounts the story of his family the Morgans, a Welsh mining clan. Minister Mr. Gruffydd (Walter Pidgeon) tries to help this coal-mining community and gives Huw with a thirst for knowledge. The townspeople think of the clergy as stiff, so during a party they hide their drinking when Gruffydd arrives; he surprises them by taking a drink. They realize this is not your typical minister when he tells them he thinks that they should form a labor union. Gruffydd loves Angharad (Maureen O'Hara) but she marries the mine owner's son. With the help of the minister, Huw passes the exams for the national school and begins attending classes in the next valley, where he must deal with local bully and the English Mr. Jonas, a cruel teacher who hates the Welsh. Jonas believes his job is to curb Welshness in his pupils. "There is no wonder that civilized men look down upon Welshmen as savages. However, I shall endeavor to do my utmost for you." He calls Huw a "dirty little sweep." Jonas catches Huw fighting in the playground and beats him until his cane breaks. It is his way of teaching manners. When Dai Bando sees Huw's back, he decides to teach Jonas manners by thrashing him at school. Eventually Huw stands up to Jonas. The head of the school demotes Jonas to teaching infants. In 1975, the BBC presented a six-hour television version starring Stanley Baker.

TCF. US. 1941. 118m. B&W. *Producer:* Darryl F. Zanuck *Director:* John Ford *Writers:* Philip Dunne, Richard Llewellyn (novel) *Cast:* Walter Pidgeon, Maureen O'Hara, Donald Crisp, Anna Lee, Roddy McDowall, John Loder, Sara Allgood, Barry Fitzgerald, Patric Knowles, Arthur Shields, The Welsh Singers, Ann Todd, Morton Lowry

334. Hurry Sundown

In post–World War II Georgia, a canning plant wants to take over a large tract of farmland. Holdouts include Rad McDowell (John Phillip Law), a combat veteran with a wife and family; Reeve Scott (Robert Hooks), a young African American. Draft dodger Henry Warren (Michael Caine) wants the deal to go through, and plans to charge Reeve with illegal ownership. Schoolteacher Vivian Thurlow (Diahann Carroll), granddaughter of the most respected member of the local African

American community, finds proof of Reeve's legal ownership. Henry is so desperate that he dynamites the dam above the farms.

Paramount. US. 1967. 146m. C. *Producer-Director:* Otto Preminger *Writers:* Thomas C. Ryan, Horton Foote, K.B. Gilden (novel) *Cast:* Michael Caine, Jane Fonda, John Phillip Law, Diahann Carroll, Robert Hooks, Faye Dunaway, Burgess Meredith, Robert Reed, George Kennedy, Frank Converse, Loring Smith, Beah Richards, Madeleine Sherwood, Rex Ingram, Steve Sanders, John Mark, Doro Merande, Luke Askew, Donna Danton, Jim Backus, Peter Goff, William Elder, Dawn Barcelona, David Sanders, Michael Henry Roth, Gladys Newman, Joan Parks, Robert C. Bloodwell, Charles Keel, Gene Rutherford, Bill Hart, Dean Smith, Kelly Ross, Ada Hall

335. *Húsið: Trúnaðarmál (The House)*

Bjorgg (Lilja Thorisdottir), a teacher of deaf children, and her composer husband Petur (Johann Sigurdarson) move into an old house. Left alone for a few days, Bjorgg is menaced by visions. Is it the house or are they just from her mind?

Iceland. 1983. 101m. C. *Producers:* Jon Thor Hannesson, Snorri Pórisson *Director:* Egill Eovarosson *Writer:* Björn Björnsson, Egill Eovarosson, Snorri Pórisson *Cast:* Róbert Arnfinnsson, Póra Borg, Helgi Skúlason, Lilja Thorisdottir, Árni Tryggvason

I Am a Cat see **Wagahai wa Neko de Aru**

I Have a New Master see **L'École Buissonnière**

I Like Money see **Mr. Topaze**

The Ideal Schoolmaster see **Kantor ideál**

336. *I'll Wait for You*

In an effort to renew himself, a gangster goes to the country where there is fresh air and barnyard animals. He places himself under the influence of a country schoolmarm.

MGM. US. 1941. 73m. B&W. *Producer:* Edwin Knopf *Director:* Robert B. Sinclair *Writer:* Guy Trosper *Cast:* Robert Sterling, Marsha Hunt, Virginia Weidler, Paul Kelly, Fay Holden, Henry Travers, Don Costello, Carol Hughes, Reed Hadley, Ben Welden, Theodore Von Eltz, Leon Belasco, Mitchell Lewis, Joe Yule, Eddie Hart, Jerry Jerome, Steve Darrell, William Tannen

337. *Iluzija (Mirage)*

Tortured by a tumultuous family life and school bullies, twelve-year-old Marko (Marko Kovacevic) finds hope when his teacher (Mustafa Nadarevic) encourages him to enter a poetry competition in Paris. When the teacher cowers before the bullies and dashes Marko's hopes, Marko turns to another man for guidance. His teacher, fighting his own demons, does little to control the going-ons in his classroom.

Picture This. Republic of Macedonia. 2004. 107m. C. *Director:* Svetozar Ristovski *Writers:* Svetozar Ristovksi, Grace Lea Troje *Cast:* Marko Kovacevic, Mustafa Nadarevic, Vlado Jovanoyski, Nikola Djuricko, Degan Acimovic, Elena Mosevska, Slavica Manaskove Nikola Heijko

338. *The Impersonator*

The townspeople of Northbridge, England, are outraged by a series of attacks on single women and suspect someone at a nearby American base. Sgt. Jimmy Bradford (John Crawford) invites the town children to a Mother Goose play but the school board declines. Teacher Ann Loring (Jane Griffiths) accepts his invitation to an airbase dance. She goes on without him when his bus breaks down. At the local diner he has to get rid of an unwanted customer. Later that night, a woman is murdered by the ejected customer. Jimmy is blamed but the real killer is Mother Goose, female impersonator.

Continental Motion Pictures. Great Britain. 1960. 64m. B&W. *Producer:* Anthony Perry *Director:* Alfred Shaughnessy *Writers:* Alfred Shaughnessy, Kenneth Cavander *Cast:* John Crawford, Jane Griffiths, Patricia Burke, John Salew, John Dare, Yvonne Ball, John Arnatt, Edmund Glover

In a Strange City see *Zai moshengoe chengshi*

339. *In Old Oklahoma*

Cowboy Dan Somers (John Wayne) and oilman Hunk Gardner (Albert Dekker) are rivals for schoolteacher Catherine Elizabeth Allen (Martha Scott) and oil leasing rights on Native American lands.

Republic. US. 1943.102m. B&W. *Director:* Albert S. Rogell *Writer:* Thomson Burtis *Cast:* John Wayne, Martha Scott, Albert Dekker, George "Gabby" Hayes, Marjorie Rambeau, Dale Evans

340. *In the Wake of a Stranger*

A schoolmarm helps a sailor prove that he did not kill a man while drunk.

Crest. Great Britain. 1959. 64m. B&W. *Producers:* Jacques de Lane Lea, Jon Pennington *Director:* David Eady *Writers:* John Tully, Ian Stuart Black (novel) *Cast:* Tony Wright, Shirley Eaton, Danny Green, Willoughby Goddard, Harry H. Corbett, Peter Sinclair, Tom Bowman, Alun Owen

341. *Indictment: The McMartin Trial*

The McMartins are devastated when they are accused of child molestation at their small family-owned pre-school. Seven McMartin teachers were indicted in

1984 on 115 charges. Charges against five of the teachers were ultimately dropped. Raymond Buckey and his mother, school co-owner Peggy McMartin Buckey, were acquitted in trials portrayed in this film. The children told stories of outrageous abuse.

HBO. US. 1995. 135m. C. *Director:* Mick Jackson *Writers:* Abby Mann, Myra Mann *Cast:* James Woods, Mercedes Ruehl, Lolita Davidovich, Sada Thompson, Henry Thomas, Shirley Knight, Mark Blum, Alison Elliott, Chelsea Field, Joe Urla, Scott Waara, Valerie Wildman, Richard Bradford, Scott Armstrong, Roberta Bassin

342. *The Infamous Miss Revell*

Twin sisters Julien and Paula Revell hit hard times with their musical act. After their father dies, they are determined to support their younger brothers and sisters. Julien accepts the protection of a rich man. Underpaid teacher Max Hildreth (Cullen Landis) is hired to teach the Revell children. Max falls in love with Julien but her past stands in the way until it is revealed that he is actually in love with Paula.

Metro Pictures. 1921. B&W. *Director:* Dallas M. Fitzgerald *Writer:* Arthur J. Zellner *Cast:* Alice Lake, Cullen Landis, Jackie Saunders, Lydia Knott, Herbert Standing, Alfred Hollingsworth, Stanley Goethals, Francis Carpenter, May Giraci, Geraldine Condon

343. *Inferno*

When a solar anomaly causes the temperature to rise in Los Angeles, a doctor who had lost his license and a city schoolteacher rise to the occasion by helping in the ensuing emergency.

Viacom. US. 1998. 100m. C. *Writer-Producers:* Bruce A. Taylor, Roderick Taylor *Director:* Ian Barry *Cast:* James Remar, Jonathan LaPaglia, Stephanie Niznik, Anthony Starke, Kathryn Morris, Daniel von Bargen, Antwon Tanner

344. *Inherit the Wind*

This film tells the thinly disguised story of the 1925 Scopes Monkey Trial. Teacher Bertram T. Cates (Dick York) is arrested for teaching Darwin's theory of evolution (forbidden by state law). Attorneys Harry Drummon (Spencer Tracy) and Matthew Harrison Brady (Fredric March) battle it out in the courtroom.

UA. US. 1960. 127m. B&W. *Producer-Director:* Stanley Kramer *Writer:* Nathan E. Douglas, Harold Jacob Smith *Cast:* Spencer Tracy, Fredric March, Florence Eldridge, Gene Kelly, Dick York, Donna Anderson, Harry Morgan, Elliott Reid, Claude Akins, Philip Coolidge, Paul Hartman, Jimmy Boyd, Noah Beery, Jr., Gordon Polk, Ray Teal, Norman Fell, Hope Summers, Renee Godfrey

345. *Innocence*

When retired organist-music teacher Andreas Borg discovers that his first love Claire, a woman he has not seen for almost 50 years, lives nearby, he decides to write her a letter. Through flashbacks we see their relationship develop.

IDP Distribution. Australia/Belgium. 2000. 94m. C. *Producers:* Paul Cox, Mark Patterson *Writer-Director:* Paul Cox *Cast:* Charles "Bud" Tingwell, Julia Blake, Robert Menzies, Chris Haywood, Marta Dusseldorp, Terry Norris, Norman Kaye.

346. An Innocent Thief

A governess is accused of theft after her charges hide a necklace.
A&C. Great Britain. 1914. B&W. *Writer:* C.J. Cutcliffe-Hyne

347. The Innocents

A spinster governess Miss Giddens (Deborah Kerr) battles evil spirits for the souls of her two charges. Based on the novel *The Turn of the Screw.*
TCF. Great Britain. 1961. 99m. B&W. *Producers:* Albert Fennell, Jack Clayton *Director:* Jack Clayton *Writers:* William Archibald, Truman Capote, John Mortimer, Henry James (novel) *Cast:* Deborah Kerr, Megs Jenkins, Pamela Franklin, Martin Stephens, Michael Redgrave, Peter Wyngarde, Clytie Jessop, Isla Cameron

Inspection of the Scene of a Crime 1901 see *Wizia Lokalna 1901*

348. Inspector Hornleigh Goes to It

Detectives pose as teachers, mailmen, and soldiers to catch spies.
TCF. Great Britain. 1941. 87m. B&W. *Producer:* Edward Black *Director:* Walter Forde *Writers:* Frank Launder, Val Guest, J.O.C. Orton *Cast:* Gordon Harker, Alastair Sim, Phyllis Calvert, Edward Chapman, Raymond Huntley, Charles Oliver, Percy Walsh, David Horne, Peter Gawthorne, Wally Patch, Betty Jardine, O.B. Clarence

349. Intermezzo

Anna Hoffman (Ingrid Bergman), a promising young pianist, is hired to give lessons to the daughter of a famous violinist. The violinist and Anna fall and he forsakes his family for her, but then realizes that it cannot last.
A.B. Svensk. Sweden. 1937. 88m. B&W. *Director:* Gustaf Molander *Writer:* Gustaf Molander, Gösta Stevens *Cast:* Ingrid Bergman, Gösta Ekman, Inge Tidblad, Britt Hagman, Hans Ekman

350. Internado para Señoritas (Girls' Boarding School)

In this Mexican musical, an impressionable schoolgirl falls in love with her handsome teacher (Emilio Tuero). He doesn't realize her love until she is almost expelled for some infraction.
Clasa Studios. Mexico. 1944. 94m. B&W. *Producer:* Mauricio de la Serna *Director:* Gilberto Martínez Solares *Writers:* Adolfo Fernández Bustamante, Eduardo

Ugarte, Ladisla Fodor (novel) *Cast:* Mapy Cortés, Emilio Tuero, Fernando Cortés, María Luisa Zea, Delia Magaña, Esther Luquín, Katy Jurado, Rafael Banquells, Mercedes Soler, Enrique Uthoff, María Luisa Elio

351. *Inugami*

A young teacher from Tokyo, Akira (Atsuro Watabe), accepts a position in a remote Japanese village. He soon falls in love with Miki (Yuki Amami), a papermaker whose family is associated with the evil inugami spirits "Dog Gods." Akira brushes off the curse as superstition, but mysterious deaths start to occur.

Stomp Visual. Japan. 2001. 106m. B&W/C. *Director:* Masato Harada *Writers:* Masato Harada, Masako Bando (novel) *Cast:* Yuki Amami, Atsuro Watabe, Eugene Harada, Shiho Fujimura, Kazuhiro Yamaji, Kanako Fukaura, Shion Machida, Kenichi Yajima, Masato Irie, Makoto Togashi, Torahiko Hamada, Muy Watase, Keiko Awaji, Koichi Sato

The Invisible Army see *Back to Bataan*

352. *The Invisible Power*

Ex-convict Sid Chambers (House Peters) meets schoolteacher Laura Chadwick (Irene Rich), who believes in him in spite of his record. They are married and move to the city. When Chambers is sent to prison on a false charge by detective Shadwell, Laura gives her baby up for adoption fearing that it will develop criminal instincts. Chambers is released, vowing to kill Shadwell. When Laura tries to warn the detective, she finds her baby in his house. Everyone is happily reunited at the end.

Goldwyn Pictures. 1921. B&W. *Producer-Director:* Frank Lloyd *Writer:* Charles Kenyon *Cast:* House Peters, Irene Rich, DeWitt Jennings, Sydney Ainsworth, Jessie De Jainette, William Friend, Gertrude Claire, Lydia Yeamans Titus

353. *Io Speriamo Che Me la Cava (Ciao, Professore!)*

Because of a computer glitch, teacher Marco Sperelli (Paolo Villaggio) is assigned not to the refined northern town of Corsano but sent to the crime-ridden south and a tough third-grade class. In this town, children help in the family businesses and do not attend school. Marco sees the janitor selling chalk and toilet paper to the children and the principal knows better than to try to change things for the better. Marco's first task is to drag the kids to school. During his short time there, he changes the lives of the streetwise students and discovers things about himself.

Miramax Films. Italy. 1991. 91m. C. *Producers:* Ciro Ippolito, Mario and Vittorio Cecchi Gori *Director:* Lina Wertmuller *Writers:* Alessandro Bencivenni, Leonardo Benvenuti, Piero De Bernardi, Domenico Saverni, Lina Wertmüller, Marcello D'Orta (novel) *Cast:* Paolo Bonacelli, Pier Francesco Borruto, Esterina Carloni, Isa Danieli, Ciro Esposito, Gigio Morra, Sergio Solli, Marco Troncone, Paolo Villaggio

Iron Island see *Jazireh ahani*

354. Istgah-Matrouk (The Deserted Station)

Feizollah (Mehran Rajabi) is a good-hearted teacher, mechanic, and father of two girls. He cares for the abandoned children in his remote desert village. Feizollah founded the one-room school and uses his own money to pay for supplies. While driving from Tehran to Mashad, a couple gets lost and has car trouble. With his motorbike, Feizollah helps the husband obtain an auto part while the wife substitutes as teacher. The wife is ashamed that she has had two miscarriages and is profoundly moved by her interactions with the children.

First Run Features. Iran. 2002. 88m. C. *Producer:* Hossein Zandof *Director:* Ali Reza Raisian *Writer:* Kambozia Partov *Cast:* Leila Hatami, Nezam Manouchehri, Mehran Rajabi, Mahmoud Pak Neeyat

It All Starts Today see *Ça Commence Aujourd'hui*

It Rains in My Village see *Bice Skoro Propast Sveta*

The Italian see *Italianetz*

355. Italianetz (The Italian)

Six-year-old stray Vanya (Kolya Spiridonov) lives in an orphanage right out of a Dickens novel, only it is 2002 Russia. Two Italians have come to adopt him, but he has his own idea of going home. A corrupt adoption broker, Madam (Mariya Kuznetsova), arranges for foreigners to adopt Russian children. Sometimes children are adopted by an organ purveyor. The headmaster (Yuri Itskov) drinks most of the money away and doesn't care about the children at all. The children, led by the Fagin-like Kolyan (Denis Moiseenko), must fend for themselves.

Sony Pictures. Russia. 2005. 90m. C. *Director:* Andrei Kravchuk *Writer:* Andrei Romanov *Cast:* Kolya Spiridonov, Denis Moiseenko, Sasha Sirotkin, Andrei Yelizarov, Vladimir Shipov, Polina Vorobbieva, Olga Shuvalova, Dima Zemlyanko, Mariya Kuznetsova, Nikolai Reutov, Yuri Itskov, Dariya Lesnikova, Rudolf Kuld

356. It's a Big Country: An American Anthology

In this anthology of what makes up America, the eighth episode takes place in a San Francisco elementary school. The teacher Mrs. Colman (Nancy Davis) calls on Joseph Esposito (Bobby Hyatt) to do a division problem but the boy has trouble seeing the numbers. Mrs. Colman sends a letter home with Joey suggesting he have an eye exam. Joey's proud Italian American papa is outraged and goes to see the teacher. He feels glasses will make Joey different. His mother takes him for glasses when he starts getting headaches. Joey is playing one afternoon and when he sees his papa coming he removes the glasses. He falls into a pile of bricks and is injured. Mrs. Coleman tutors him at night at home. One night Papa pulls out his glasses, as does Joey.

MGM. US. 1952. 89m. B&W. *Producer:* Robert Sisk *Directors:* Richard Thorpe, John Sturges, Charles Vidor, Don Weis, Clarence Brown, William A. Wellman, Don Hartman *Writers:* William Ludwig, Helen Deutsch, Ray Chordes, Isobel Lennart, Allen Rivkin, Dorothy Kingsley, George Wells, Edgar Brooke, Claudia Cranston, William Ludwig, John McNulty, Charles Palmer, Joseph Petracca, Dore Schary, Lucille Schlossberg *Cast:* Ethel Barrymore, Keefe Brasselle, Gary Cooper, Nancy Davis, Van Johnson, Gene Kelly, Janet Leigh, Marjorie Main, Fredric March, George Murphy, William Powell, S.Z. Sakall, Lewis Stone, Keenan Wynn, Angela Clarke, Bobby Hyatt, Sharon McManus, Angela Clarke, Bill Baldwin, June Hedin, Luana Mehlberg, Jeralyn Alton, Jacqueline Kenley, George Economides, Don Fields, Jerry Hunter, Don Gordon, Lucile Curtis, Dolly Arriaga, Elena Savanarola, Rhea Mitchell

357. *It's Great to Be Young*

Mr. Dingle (John Mills) is the popular music teacher at an English school. The new headmaster, Frome (Cecil Parker), fires Dingle for standing up for the students. The students come to Mr. Dingle's aid.

AB-Pathé. Great Britain. 1956. 93m. C. *Producer:* Victor Skutezky *Director:* Cyril Frankel *Writer:* Ted Willis *Cast:* John Mills, Cecil Parker, Jeremy Spencer, Dorothy Bromiley, John Salew, Derek Blomfield, Eleanor Summerfield, Bryan Forbes, Brian Smith, Carole Shelley, Richard O'Sullivan, Mary Merrall, Derek Blomfield, Marjorie Rhodes, Eddie Byrne

358. *Jack*

Due to an unusual disorder that has aged him four times faster than a normal human being, Jack Charles Powell (Robin Williams) enters the fifth grade with the body of a 40-year-old man. As he goes to public school for the first time, Miss Marquez (Jennifer Lopez) is his teacher.

Buena Vista. US. 1996. 113m. C. *Director:* Francis Ford Coppola *Writers:* James DeMonaco, Gary Nadeau *Cast:* Robin Williams, Diane Lane, Brian Kerwin, Jennifer Lopez, Bill Cosby, Fran Drescher, Adam Zolotin, Todd Bosley, Seth Smith, Mario Yedidia, Jeremy Lilliott, Jurnee Smollett, Dani Faith, Hugo Hernandez, Rickey D'Shon Collins

359. *Jakten (Manhunt)*

A policeman and his teacher friend search for a killer on the run. The three must survive brutal, near-Arctic conditions, especially when the killer refuses to go back to base camp.

Europa Film. Sweden. 1966. 94m. C. *Director:* Yngve Gamlin *Writer:* Per Olaf Sundman *Cast:* Halvar Bjork, Leif Hedberg, Lars Passgard

360. *Jane Eyre*

The classic tale of an orphan girl, Jane (Mabel Ballin), who is hired by Mr. Rochester (Norman Trevor) as a governess to his young ward Adele. Clergyman St. John Rivers (Crauford Kent) falls in love with Jane. After much turmoil, Jane and Rochester are reunited at the end.

W.W. Hodkinson. US. 1921. B&W. *Producer-Director:* Hugo Ballin *Writers:* Hugo Ballin, Charlotte Bronte (novel) *Cast:* Norman Trevor, Mabel Ballin, Crauford Kent, Emily Fitzroy, John Webb Dillon, Louis Grisel, Stephen Carr, Vernie Atherton, Elizabeth Aeriens, Harlan Knight, Helen Miles, Julia Hurley, Sadie Mullen, June Ellen Terry, Florence Flagler, Bertha Kent, Marie Schaefer

361. *Jane Eyre*

Orphan Jane Eyre (Joan Fontaine) secures a position as governess to the ward of Edward Rochester (Orson Welles). Eventually Jane and Rochester fall in love, but at their wedding, disturbing news arrives: Edward is still married, but to an insane woman.

TCF. US. 1943. 96m. B&W. *Producer:* William Goetz *Director:* Robert Stevenson *Writers:* Aldous Huxley, Robert Stevenson, John Houseman, Charlotte Bronté (novel) *Cast:* Joan Fontaine, Orson Welles, Margaret O'Brien, Henry Daniell, John Sutton, Agnes Moorehead, Peggy Ann Garner, Sara Allgood, Aubrey Mather, Hillary Brooke, Edith Barrett, Ethel Griffies, Barbara Everest, John Abbott

362. *Jane Eyre*

Another telling of the story of orphan Jane Eyre and her position as governess for the ward of Mr. Rochester.

British Lion. Great Britain. 1970. 110m. C. *Producer:* Frederick H. Bogger *Director:* Delbert Mann *Writers:* Jack Pulman, Charlotte Bronte (novel) *Cast:* George C. Scott, Susannah York, Ian Bannon, Jack Hawkins, Nyree Dawn Porter, Rachel Kempson, Kenneth Griffith, Peter Copley, Michele Dotrice, Clive Morton, Constance Cummings, Kara Wilson, Sarah Gibson, Clive Morton, Hugh Latimer, Stella Tanner

363. *Jane Eyre*

A moving telling of Jane Eyre (Ruth Wilson) from her rejection by an evil aunt, to life at a harsh orphanage, to governess to Edward Rochester's (Toby Stephens) ward, to schoolteacher at a small country school, and her reunion with Rochester.

BBC. Great Britain. 2005. C. *Producer:* Diederick Santer *Directors:* Susanna White, M. Pink Christofalo *Writers:* Sandy Welch, Charlotte Bronte (novel) *Cast:* Ruth Wilson, Toby Stephens, Francesca Annis, Alisa Arnah, Lorraine Ashbourne, Christopher Bowen, Andrew Buchan, Christina Cole, Arthur Cox, Maisie Dimbleby, Pam Ferris, Tara Fitzgerald, Bethany Gill, Jeanne Golding, Tim Goodman, Georgie Henley, Cara Horgan, Georgia King, Cosima Littlewood, Emma Lowndes, Aidan McArdle, Richard McCabe, Elso Mollien

The Jar see Khomreh

364. *Jazireh ahani (Iron Island)*

A community of squatters makes their home on an abandoned oil freighter in the Persian Gulf. Captain Nemat (Ali Nassirian) runs the ship as a benevolent dictator: Children attend school on board, men salvage scrap metal and oil, women keep house and the captain maintains order and discipline. The idealistic but frustrated schoolteacher uses the Islamic style of repetitive memorization, which is difficult with only old newspapers about mysterious wars to study as texts. The captain's young assistant has fallen in love with a young woman already promised to another. The schoolteacher is convinced that the ship is sinking.

Kino International. Iran. 2005. 90m. C. *Producers:* Mohammad Rasoulof, Abolhasan Davoodi *Writer-Director:* Mohammad Rasoulof *Cast:* Ali Nassirian, Hossein Farzi-Zadeh, Neda Pakdaman

365. *Jersey Girl*

A New Jersey schoolteacher crashes her Volkswagen into a Mercedes that belongs to a handsome and successful Manhattan man. True love wins out in the end.

Entertainment/Electric/Interscope. US. 1992. 95m. C. *Director:* David Burton Morris *Writer:* Gina Wendkos *Cast:* Jami Gertz, Dylan McDermott, Molly Price, Aida Turturro, Star Jasper, Sheryl Lee, Joseph Bologna, Joseph Mazzello, Philip Casnoff

366. *Jhor (The Storm)*

A village school founded on western rationalism comes into conflicts with orthodox ideas. European ideas are introduced to the students by a Portuguese Indian teacher. His students save a woman from being sent to the funeral pyre of her husband. This leads to run-ins with authorities.

India. 1979. 100m. C. *Director:* Utpal Dutt *Cast:* Utpal Dutt, Ujjal Sengupta

367. *Joe the King*

The son of an alcoholic school janitor, 14-year-old delinquent Joe Henry (Noah Fleiss) is very troubled and steals everything in sight. Setting the tone, in the prologue we see nine-year-old Joe being spanked by an ogre-like teacher. Joe is always late for school, abused by his teachers and yelled at by family and employer.

Trimark Pictures. US. 1999. 100m. C. *Producers:* Robin O'Hara, Scott Macaulay, Jennifer Dewis, Lindsay Marx *Writer-Director:* Frank Whaley *Cast:* Noah Fleiss, Val Kilmer, Karen Young, Ethan Hawke

368. *Johnny Tiger*

Schoolteacher George Dean (Robert Taylor) and his three children move to Florida when he takes a teaching position at a Seminole Indian reservation. Johnny

(Chad Everett), the chief's grandson, falls in love with George's daughter (Brenda Scott), causing turmoil. George is attracted to a pretty doctor (Geraldine Brooks) who is dedicated to healing the poor.

Nova Hook. US. 1966. 102m. C. *Producer:* John Hugh *Director:* Paul Wendkos *Writers:* Paul Crabtree, John Hugh *Cast:* Robert Taylor, Geraldine Brooks, Chad Everett, Brenda Scott, Marc Lawrence

369. The Jucklins

Bill Hawes (Monte Blue), a young farmer, travels to a small North Carolina community to teach school. He stays at the home of the Jucklins and falls in love with their daughter Guinea (Mabel Julienne Scott). Guinea is promised to a man whose father paid for her education. Alf Jucklin (Zell Covington) is accused of murdering his rival in love but Bill fights for his innocence by having the body exhumed and proving that death was caused by a heart attack. True love flourishes.

Famous Players-Lasky Corp./Paramount. US. 1921. B&W. *Producer:* Jesse L. Lasky *Director:* George Melford *Writer:* Frank Condon *Cast:* Winter Hall, Mabel Julienne Scott, Monte Blue, Ruth Renick, Fannie Midgely, Zell Covington, J.M. Dumont, Clarence Burton, Guy Oliver, Robert Brower, Jack Herbert, Jack Hull, Walter Scott, Frank Weatherwax, William Boyd, Charles Ogle, Jack Byron

370. Judgment of the Hills

Tad Dennison (Frankie Darro), a Kentucky Hills child, worships his big brother, alcoholic Brant (Orville Caldwell). Schoolteacher Margaret Dix (Virginia Valli) persuades Brant to allow Tad to attend school. Margaret tells Brant he is unworthy because he refuses to join the army after receiving a draft summons. Brant hides but is found and sent to join the army. He returns a decorated hero and reforms for Margaret and Tad.

Film Booking Offices of America. US. 1927. B&W. *Producer:* Joseph P. Kennedy *Director:* James Leo Meehan *Writer:* Dorothy Yost *Cast:* Virginia Valli, Frankie Darro, Orville Caldwell, Frank McGlynn, Jr., Johnny Gough

371. Judy Berlin

A lonely elementary schoolteacher, Sue Berlin (Barbara Barrie), enjoys flirting with her married principal Arthur Gold (Bob Dishy). He is prevented from acting on his own feelings by a high-strung wife and a loser son. Sue has an aspiring actress (Edie Falco) for a daughter. In one scene Sue is showing her pupils how to view an imminent solar eclipse without harming their eyes when a retired teacher with Alzheimer's disease wanders into the classroom and causes a stir. The confrontation has Arthur interceding and Sue in tears. As he comforts her, their unexpressed feelings come out.

Shooting Gallery. US. 1999. 93m. C. *Writer-Director:* Eric Mendelsohn *Cast:* Barbara Barrie, Bob Dishy, Edie Falco, Carlin Glynn, Aaron Harnick, Bette Henritze, Madeline Kahn, Julie Kavner, Anne Meara, Novella Nelson, Peter Appel, Marcia DeBonis, Glenn Fitzgerald, Marcus Giamatti, Judy Graubart

372. Jukemyeon salrira (Die to Live)

A teacher at a girls' middle school goes to the national assembly to plead her right to worship Christianity. She is arrested and sentenced to death.

South Korea. 1982. 100m. C. *Producer:* Dong-hwan Jeong *Director:* Dae-jin Kang *Writers:* In-suk Ahn, Se-ho Kim *Cast:* Bok-hie Yun, Am Park, Seong-Kwan Choi, Min-gyu Kim, Eun-jin Han, Hae-suk Kim, Yeong-a Oh, A-ra Ko, Dyeong-hie Lee, In-su Seok

373. Der Junge Törless (Young Törless)

At a semi-military boarding school, an intelligent student witnesses the brutal beating and bullying of his friend by two people. By the time he realizes his moral obligation, it is too late. He is left with the unsatisfactory answers to his questions of his teachers.

Franz Seitz/Nouvelles Éditions De Film. West Germany. 1966. 85m. B&W. *Writer-Director:* Volker Schlöndorff *Cast:* Matthieu Carrière, Bernd Fiscer, Marian Seidowsky, Alfred Dietz, Barbara Steele

374. Just My Luck

A shy music teacher tries to become more outgoing by taking a "How to Succeed" course. His girlfriend's father puts him in charge of a hotel. He is accused of embezzling but proves his innocence when he catches the accountant in the act.

B&D. Great Britain. 1933. B&W. *Producer:* Herbert Wilcox *Director:* Jack Raymond *Writer:* Ben Travers *Cast:* Ralph Lynn, Winifred Shotter, Davy Burnaby, Robertson Hare, Vera Pearce, Frederick Burtwell, Phyllis Clare

375. Kådisbellan (Slingshot)

Young Roland lives with his socialist father, Jewish mother and boxing brother in 1920s Stockholm. At his school, Roland learns to defy the soft-spoken masters, who are sadistic anti-Semites in frock coats.

Sony Pictures Classics. Denmark/Sweden. 1993. 102m. C. *Producer:* Waldemar Bergendahl *Director:* Ake Sandgren *Writers:* Ake Sandgren, Roland Schutt (novel) *Cast:* Jesper Salen, Stellan Skarsgard, Niclas Olund, Basia Frydman

376. Kan shang qu hen mei (Little Red Flowers)

In late-1940s Beijing, four-year-old rebel Qiang finds himself in a residential kindergarten because his parents are often away. The kindergarten seems colorful, but it is meant to train these children to be good citizens. Qiang tries to fit in but fails to conform to the teachers' model. He yearns to win the little red flowers awarded each day as tokens for good behavior. He talks back to the strict teacher Li and Principal Kong. Eventually he wins the other kids over and convinces them that Li is a child-eating monster in disguise. Will he be able to live by his own rules?

Fortissimo Films. China/Italy. 2006. 92m. C. *Director:* Yuan Zhang *Writers:* Dai Ning, Shuo Wang (novel) *Cast:* Ning Yuanyuan, Zhao Rui, Li Xiaofeng, Dong Bowen, Chen Manyuan, Ning Yuayuan

377. *Kantor Ideál (The Ideal Schoolmaster)*

Based on a book. No description available.

Czechoslovakia. 1932. B&W. *Director:* Martin Fric *Writers:* Martin Fric, Václav Wasserman *Cast:* Carl Lamac, Anny Ondra, Oscar Marion, Theodor Pistek, Svetla Svozilová, Antonie Nedosinská, Valentin Sindler, Cenek Slégl, Jaroslav Marvan

378. *Karla (Carla)*

An idealistic young teacher starts her career in East German schools. She discovers that her students hide their true thoughts and only say what is expected of them. She tries to make changes and break down walls but her superiors intervene. The film was labeled hostile by the Unity Party of Germany and only in 1990 was it shown in cinemas.

DEFA. East Germany. 1965. 128m. B&W. *Producer:* Gert Golde *Director:* Herrmann Zschoche *Writers:* Ulrich Plenzodorf, Herrmann Zschoche *Cast:* Fred Delmare, Herwart Grosse, Hans Hardt-Hardtloff, Jürgen Hentsch, Jutta Hoffmann, Rolf Hoppe, Inge Keller, Jörg Knoche, Jürgen Krumrey, Gisela Morgen, Klaus-Peter PleBow, Heidemarie Schneider, Dieter Wien

379. *The Katzenjammer Kids in School*

When the teacher steps away from her country schoolroom, the youngsters have fun and two kids tie a string across the aisle. When the teacher returns, she trips and falls and the children throw books at her.

American Mutoscope Co. US. 1898. B&W.

380. *Keepers of Youth*

This film tells the story of attempts to seduce an assistant school matron.

BIP. Great Britain. 1931. 70m. B&W. *Producer:* John Maxwell *Director:* Thomas Bentley *Writers:* Frank Launder, Thomas Bentley, Walter Mycroft *Cast:* Garry Marsh, Ann Todd, Robin Irvine, John Turnbull, O.B. Clarence, Mary Clare, Herbert Ross, John Hunt, Ethel Warwick, Rene Ray

381. *Keita, l'Héritage du Griot (Keita! The Voice of the Griot)*

Mabo, a young boy, lives in Sindou, in the west of Burkina Fasso. He finds himself torn between Djéliba, who represents Africa of yesterday, and his schoolteacher, who is anxious to instruct him with modern knowledge. Djéliba shares epic tales of old days.

Burkina Faso (Upper Volta). France. 1995. 94m. C. *Writer-Director:* Dani

Kouyate *Cast:* Sotigul Kouyaté, Hamed Dicko, Seydou Rouamba, Seydou Boro, Abdoulaye Komboudri

382. *Kes*

A non-achieving boy, Billy (David Bradley), lives with a bully of an older brother and their tired mother, who was abandoned by her husband. In one scene Billy and a group of friends, all smokers, are called into the headmaster's office and end up spanking an innocent boy. The headmaster calls him a regular tobacco factory. With tears, the boy accepts this injustice. Billy raises a kestrel and names it Kes. He works at training the bird, and when he shows his class what he has accomplished, the teacher Mr. Farthing (Colin Welland) sees the boy's potential. Billy's brutal stepbrother kills Kes out of revenge.

UA. Great Britain. 1969. 113m. C. *Producer:* Tony Garnett *Director:* Kenneth Loach *Writers:* Barry Hines, Kenneth Loach, Tony Garnett *Cast:* David Bradley, Lynne Perrie, Freddie Fletcher, Colin Welland, Brian Glover, Bob Bowes, Robert Naylor, Trevor Hesketh, Geoffrey Banks, Eric Bolderson, Joey Kaye

383. *Khomreh (The Jar)*

In a school in a poor desert village, the teacher is a sensitive and sensible young man. Every day the schoolchildren walk into the yard and dip a metal cup into a jar. One day they discover a leak and hear from their new teacher that it will take time for the government to send another. This causes a real crisis in the village and we get a glimpse of the life and attitudes of the villagers. One boy's father agrees to patch the jar, but the job will require scarce items (ashes, lime and eggs). Somehow the teacher manages to stumble his way through the crisis.

Artistic License Films. Iran. 1992. 86m. C. *Producer:* Alirenza Zarrin *Writer-Director:* Ebrahim Forouzesh *Cast:* Behzad Khodaveisi, Fatemeh Azrah, Abbas Khavaninzadeh, Hassein Balai, Alireza Haji-Ghasemi, Sakineh Mehrizi, Ramazan Moila-Abbasi, A.R. Vaziri

384. *Kindergarten Cop*

Tough detective John Kimble (Arnold Schwarzenegger) is a fish out of water when he goes undercover as a kindergarten teacher at Astoria Elementary School. John and his partner Phoebe O'Hara (Pamela Reed) are trying to identify the ex-wife and son of bad guy-drug dealer Cullen Crisp. The family changed their name and fled to Astoria, Oregon. John and Phoebe need to find them before Crisp does. This no-nonsense cop turns out to be a warm and wonderful teacher. The film ends on a violent note with lots of gunfire.

Universal. US. 1990. 111m. C. *Producers:* Brian Grazer, Ivan Reitman *Director:* Ivan Reitman *Writers:* Murray Salem, Herschel Weingrod, Timothy Harris *Cast:* Arnold Schwarzenegger, Penelope Ann Miller, Pamela Reed, Linda Hunt, Richard Tyson, Carroll Baker, Cathy Moriarty, Joseph Cousins, Christian Cousins, Park Overall, Jayne Brook

385. The King and I

This is the musical version of the story of English schoolteacher Anna Leonowens (Deborah Kerr) and her son Louis (Rex Thompson), who arrive in Siam where she has been hired to teach English to the children of the royal household of King Mongkut (Yul Brynner). Their customs are so different that there is conflict between Anna and the king. The two fall in love, but her British background prevents her from acting on it. She is about to leave Siam when she hears of the king's imminent death and returns to help his son, her favorite pupil, rule his people.

TCF. US. 1956. 133m. C. *Producer:* Charles Brackett *Director:* Walter Lang *Writer:* Ernest Lehman *Cast:* Deborah Kerr, Yul Brynner, Rita Moreno, Martin Benson, Alan Mowbray, Geoffrey Toone, Terry Saunders

King of the Children see *Hai Zi Wang*

386. King Spruce

John Barrett (Melbourne MacDowell) doesn't approve of a romance between his daughter Elva and schoolteacher Dwight Wade (Mitchell Lewis). John also wants to burn out squatters in his forests. Kate, his own daughter by the wife of a lumberjack, ties him up in the burning forest. Wade rescues John and confronts him with his lies, forcing him to recognize Kate and give him Elva's hand in marriage.

W.W. Hodkinson Corp. US. 1920. B&W. *Director:* Roy Clements *Cast:* Mitchell Lewis, Melbourne MacDowell, Mignon Anderson, Arthur Millet, James O'Neill, Betty Wales, Joe Ray, Gus Soville, Frederick Herzog

387. The Knack

Young schoolteacher Colin (Michael Crawford) owns a boardinghouse in London. His tenant Tolen (Ray Brooks) has the ability to attract women — a knack which Colin tries to learn.

UA. Great Britain. 1965. 84m. B&W. *Producer:* Oscar Lewenstein *Director:* Richard Lester *Writers:* Charles Wood, Richard Lester *Cast:* Michael Crawford, Ray Brooks, Rita Tushingham, Donal Donnelly, John Bluthal, Wensley Pithey, Charles Dyer, Peter Copley, Dandy Nichols, Timothy Bateson, George Chisholm, Bruce Lacey, Charles Wood

388. Kohayagawa-ke no aki (The End of Summer)

Elderly widower Manbei Kohayagawa (Ganjiro Nakamura) has given the family business to the husband of one of his daughters. Another daughter is engaged to someone selected for her but she has fallen in love with a schoolteacher.

New Yorker Films/Toho Co. Japan. 1962. 103m. C-B&W. *Producer:* Sanezumi Fujimoto, Masakatsu Kaneko, Tadahiro Teramoto *Director:* Yasujiro Ozu *Writers:* Kogo Noda, Yasujiro Ozu *Cast:* Ganjiro Nakamura, Setsuko Hara, Yoko Tsukasa, Michiyo Aratama, Yumi Shirakawa, Reiko Dan, Keiju Kobayashi, Daisuke Kato, Chieko Naniwa, Haruko Togo, Haruko Sugimura, Hisaya Morrishige, Chishu Ryu, Yuko Mochizuk

389. *Konopielka*

Peasant Kaziuk (Krzysztof Majchrzak) and his pregnant wife live in a small village which is visited by a couple of strangers and then by the new schoolteacher Nauczycielka (Joanna Sienkiewicz) arrives. Her presence generates erotic fantasies in Kaziuk. In frustration he cuts down a family tree and cuts the grass with a scythe, causing outrage in the village.

Poland. 1982. 92m. B&W. *Director:* Witold Leszczynski *Writers:* Witold Leszczynski, Edward Redlinski (novel) *Cast:* Krzysztof Majchrzak, Anna Seniuk, Joanna Sienkiewicz, Jerzy Block, Tomasz Jarosinski, Franciszek Pieczka, Anna Milewska, Arkadiusz Bazak, Aleksander Fogiel, Jan Jurewicz, Zbigniew Kaczmarek, Jacel Kalucki, Marek Kepinski, Jan Pawel Kruk, Tadeusz Wojtych, Wojciech Zagóski, Sylwester Maciejewski

390. *La bi xiao xiao sheng (Trouble Maker)*

A meek, middle-aged schoolteacher in charge of a class of troublemakers runs off to a Shaolin temple where he studies martial arts. He returns with his new skills to whip the students into shape.

Hong Kong/Taiwan. 1995. C. *Director:* Yin-Ping Chu *Cast:* Siu-Man Fok, Man Tat Ng, Athena Chu, Wai Man Baak, Lai Yuen, Takeshi Kanesbiro

391. *Ladies*

In this adaptation of an Anton Chekhov story, veteran schoolteacher Vremensky (N. Nikitich) is fired when he loses his voice. The school director is pressured by the women to hire a "ladies man."

Artkino Pictures. Soviet Union. 1955. 20m. *Writer-Directors:* G. Oganesyan, L.Kuliijamov *Cast:* N. Nikitich, N. Shaternikova, K. Bartashevich, O. Zhizneva, A. Peselev

392. *The Lady from Cheyenne*

In the railroad town of Laraville in the Wyoming Territory of 1869, villainous Jim Cork (Edward Arnold) intends to buy up town lots to get complete control. Naïve and earnest Quaker schoolmarm Annie Morgan (Loretta Young) buys a piece of land, so Cork sends his attorney Steve Lewis (Robert Preston) to woo her and get back the lot. Annie happens to be a liberated woman and a strong advocate for women's suffrage.

Universal. US. 1941. 87m. B&W. *Producer-Director:* Frank Lloyd *Writers:* Kathryn Scola, Warren Duff *Cast:* Loretta Young, Robert Preston, Gladys George, Edward Arnold, Frank Craven, Jessie Ralph, Spencer Charters, Alan Bridge

The Lady Is Fickle see *La Donna È Mobile*

393. *The Lady Pays Off*

Vacationing in Las Vegas, *Time* magazine's "Schoolteacher of the Year" Evelyn Warren (Linda Darnell) $7000 in debt to casino owner Matt Braddock (Stephen

McNally). He will forgive the debt if Evelyn agrees to tutor his young daughter Diana (Gigi Perreau). Evelyn is hoping to make Matt fall in love with her and then dump him for revenge. Diana likes Evelyn and works to get Matt and Evelyn together.

Universal. US. 1951. 80m. B&W. *Director:* Douglas Sirk *Writers:* Frank Gill, Jr., Albert J. Cohen *Cast:* Linda Darnell, Stephen McNally, Gigi Perreau, Virginia Field, Ann Codee

394. Ladybug Ladybug

At a rural elementary school, a civil defense alarm box flashes a warning that a nuclear attack is imminent. Principal Calkins (William Daniels) assumes there is a problem with the alarm, but after checking it out he realizes that the alert is real. The children are divided into groups and one group is under the supervision of sixth grade teacher Mrs. Andrews (Nancy Marchand). Mrs. Andrews is unable to ease the children's fears because of her own anxiety. Unaware that it is a false alarm, twelve-year-old Harriet (Alice Playten) invites some of the children into her family's bomb shelter. She and the others go about organizing themselves when another child knocks. When Harriet won't let her in, the terrified child runs to find a hiding place. An older boy leaves to find her but she has sealed herself in an old refrigerator.

UA. US. 1963. 84m. *Producer-Director:* Frank Perry *Writers:* Eleanor Perry, S. Lois Dickert *Cast:* Jane Connell, William Daniels, James Frawley, Richard Hamilton, Kathryn Hays, Jane Hofffman, Ele Karam, Judith Lowry, Nancy Marchand, Estelle Parsons, Doug Chapin, Miles Chapin, Bozo Dell, Dianne Higgins, Alan Howard, Christopher Howard, David Komoroff, Donnie Melvin, Susan Melvin, Linda Meyer, Alice Playten, Marilyn Rogers, Jennifer Stones

395. Lågor i dunklet

After his mother's death, Latin schoolmaster Sjögren (Stig Järrel) teaches at Ringsala, a new boarding school. In this forerunner to *Hets*, this teacher is mentally disturbed! There has been a series of mysterious fires around the school and one of the students has seen Sjögren setting fire to a barn. Will anyone believe the student? The student wants to confide in a trusted teacher, schoolmaster Nordmark (Edvin Adolphson).

Sweden. 1942. 94m. B&W. *Producer:* Lorens Marmstedt *Director:* Hasse Ekman *Writers:* Dagmar Edqvist, Hasse Ekman *Cast:* Edvin Adolphson, Stig Järrel, Inga Tidblad, Huggo Björne, Linnéa Hillberg, Hasse Ekman, Agneta Lagerfeldt, Hilda Borgström, Axel Högel

396. Lamb

Michael Lamb (Liam Neeson), a member of the Christian Brotherhood, teaches at a private special education school in Ireland. Lamb befriends a fatherless epileptic, Owen Kane (Hugh O'Conor). Brother Superior Benedict's (Ian Bannen) evil and unscrupulous behavior forces Lamb to go to London with Owen. As an indirect result of Lamb's concern, Owen loses his life.

Cannon. Great Britain. 1986. 110m. C. *Producer:* Neil Zeiger *Director:* Colin Gregg *Writer:* Bernard MacLaverty *Cast:* Liam Neeson, Hugh O'Connor, Harry Towb, Frances Tomelty, Ian Bannen

397. Land of Fury

Philip Wayne (Jack Hawkins), a disgraced gentleman, decides to go to the New Zealand wild country to make his home. He takes pretty schoolteacher Marion Southey (Glynis Johns) to be his wife. They wage a losing battle with a tribe of unfriendly Maori and die with honor. Their baby is the sole survivor.

Universal. Great Britain. 1954. 90m. C. *Producer:* George Brown *Director:* Ken Annakin *Writer:* William Fairchild *Cast:* Jack Hawkins, Glynis Johns, Noel Purcell, Laya Raki, Inia Te Wiata, Patrick Warbrick, Kenneth Williams, Tony Erstich, Edward Baker

398. The Last Round-Up

Denver, foreman of Bar D Ranch, fights with hand Hardy for driving recklessly with passenger Lucy Graves, the new schoolmistress. Hardy quits, rustles cattle and kidnaps Lucy. Denver saves the day.

Syndicate Pictures. US. 1929. B&W. *Director:* J.P. McGowan *Writer:* Sally Winters *Cast:* Bob Custer, Hazel Mills, Bud Osborne, Cliff Lyons, Hank Bell, J.P. McGowan, Adabelle Driver

The Last Village see Akhareen Abadeh

399. The Late Edwina Black (Obsessed)

A Scotland Yard Inspector (Roland Culver) is investigating the mysterious death of a village schoolteacher's domineering wife. He has three suspects: schoolteacher Gregory (David Farrar), his mistress Elizabeth (Geraldine Fitzgerald) and housekeeper Ellen (Jean Cadell).

IFD. Great Britain. 1951. 78m. B&W. *Producer:* Ernest Gartside *Director:* Maurice Elvey *Writers:* Charles Frank, David Evans *Cast:* Geraldine Fitzgerald, David Farrar, Roland Culver, Jean Cadell, Mary Merrall, Harcourt Williams, Charles Heslop, Ronald Adam

400. The Learnin' of Jim Benton

Jim Benton (Roy Stewart) was too busy ranching to learn how to read and write so he hires schoolteacher Evelyn (Fritzie Ridgeway) to start a school on his ranch. Jim becomes her number one pupil. Evelyn makes Jim promise to shoot only in self-defense. When Jim is falsely accused of shooting a sheep rancher, Evelyn is there to save him from the gallows.

Triangle Film Corp. US. 1917. B&W. *Director:* Cliff Smith *Writer:* Alvin J. Neitz *Cast:* Roy Stewart, Fritzie Ridgeway, Walter Perry, Edward Brady, Thornton Edwards, William Ellingford, John P. Wild, Harry Rattenberry

401. *Lease of Life*

A country village vicar, Reverend William Thorne (Robert Donat), learns he only has one year to live. Even with this knowledge, he finds real happiness and gives a controversial sermon. His one dilemma: raising money for his daughter's music school tuition. His wife gives in to temptation and steals some money for the tuition. A teacher friend (Denholm Elliott) tries to help.

GFD. UK. 1954. 94m. C. *Producer:* Jack Rix *Director:* Charles Frend *Writer:* Eric Ambler *Cast:* Robert Donat, Kay Walsh, Denholm Elliott, Adrienne Corri, Walter Fitzgerald, Reginald Beckwith, Vida Hope, Cyril Raymond, Jean Anderson, Mark Daly, Russell Waters, Richard Wattis, Beckett Bould, Frank Atkinson, Frederick Piper, John Salew

402. *The Legend of Sleepy Hollow*

The story of Ichabod Crane and the Headless Horseman.
Kalem. US. 1908. B&W.

403. *La Lengua de las Mariposas (Butterfly)*

The film takes place in a picturesque Spanish village during the 1930s, with the Spanish Civil War on the horizon. Moncho (Manuel Lozano) has not been allowed to start school due to health reasons until now. He arrives at school terrified because his older brother regularly comes home beaten by the teacher. Fortunately, Don Gregorio (Fernando Feman Gomez), a man of warmth and wisdom, has Moncho accepted by the others and he assumes a grandfatherly role, showing him the wonders of nature. Don Gregorio is an enlightened man who does believe in the traditional hellfire-and-damnation view of religion. At the time of his retirement he states, "If we allow just one generation to grow up in freedom, they will never allow liberty to be taken from us."

Miramax. Spain. 1999. 96m. C. *Director:* José Luis Cuerda *Writers:* Rafael Azcona, José Luis Cuerda, Manuel Rivas *Cast:* Fernando Fernan Gomez, Manuel Lozano, Alexis de los Santos, Uxia Blanco, Elena Fernandez, Gonzalo Uriarte

Leper see *Tredowata*

404. *Let's Make Music*

An elderly schoolmarm, Malvina Adams (Elisabeth Risdon), teaches music to students who prefer swing to Mozart. School principal Mr. Stevens (Louis Jean Heydt) feels that she doesn't connect with her students. Malvina writes a song for the school band which the students call too corny. Malvina's niece Abby Adams

(Jean Rogers) mails it to a music publisher. The song leads to a nightclub singing career for Malvina. Malvina's popularity eventually fades, but Abby's love for a band leader grows. He helps Malvina with one more song and she returns to the classroom a celebrity. Even though this is set in a high school, it was included because the teacher is older and the center of the film.

RKO. US. 1940. 85m. B&W. *Producer:* Howard Benedict *Director:* Leslie Goodwins *Writers:* Nathanael West, Helen Phillips, Bernard Dougall *Cast:* Bob Crosby, Jean Rogers, Elisabeth Risdon, Joseph Buloff, Joyce Compton, Bennie Bartlett, Louis Jean Heydt, Frank Orth, Walter Tetley, Bob Crosby's Orchestra

405. *La Lettera*

A class of eighteen elementary students and their young teacher fight for the life of George Middletown, a Native American on Death Row in Austin, Texas.

Minerva Pictures. Italy. 2004. 110m. C. *Producer:* Pietro Balpedio *Director:* Luciano Cannito *Writers:* Massimiliano Durante, Carmelo Pennisi *Cast:* Dino Abbrescia, Raffaella Appià, Salvo Arena, Vittoria Belvedere, Gianni Federico, Timothy Martin, Marco Pannella, Marcello Perracchio, Giorgia Pieretti, Antonio Sapone

406. *Liam*

Told from the point of view of Liam (Anthony Borrows), a seven-year-old boy, the film depicts the trials and tribulations of a working-class Catholic family during tight financial times. At Catholic school, his teacher, Mrs. Abernathy (Anne Reid), and Father Ryan (Russell Dixon) prepare him for his first communion. The priest and the teacher continually drum into the kids how filthy their souls will become if they sin. His father (Ian Hart) is unable to get work after the shipyard closes. Growing very bitter, he turns to fascism which ultimately leads to violence.

Lions Gate. Great Britain/Germany/France. 2000. 90m. C. *Producers:* Colin McKeown, Martin Tempia *Director:* Stephen Frears *Writer:* Jimmy McGovern *Cast:* Ian Hart, Claire Hackett, Anthony Borrows, David Hart, Megan Burns, Anne Reid, Russell Dixon, Julia Deakin, Andrew Sehofield, Bernadette Shortt

Life and Nothing But see *La Vie et Rien d'Autre*

Life Is a Bed of Roses see *La Vie Est un Roman*

Life Is a Dream see *Mémoire des Apparences*

Life Is Beautiful see *La Vita È Bella*

407. *The Life of Jimmy Dolan*

Champion light heavyweight prizefighter Jimmy Dolan (Douglas Fairbanks, Jr.) accidentally kills a newspaper man at a party. His manager and girlfriend steal his money and watch, then leave him. They die in an auto accident and the police think Jimmy Dolan is dead. Jimmy hides out at a health farm for ill children run by dedicated Mrs. Moore (Aline MacMahon) and Peggy (Loretta Young). He is won over by seeing their devotion to the children.

Warner. US. 1933. 89m. B&W. *Director:* Archie Mayo *Cast:* Douglas Fairbanks, Jr., Loretta Young, Aline MacMahon, Guy Kibbee, Lyle Talbot, Fifi Dorsay, Harold Huber, Shirley Grey, George Meeker, David Durand, Farina, Mickey Rooney, Dawn O'Day, Arthur Hohl

408. *Little Man Tate*

Single working mom Dede Tate (Jodie Foster) discovers that her eight-year-old son Fred (Adam Hann-Byrd) is a genius. Fred is enrolled in a program for gifted children run by Dr. Jane Grierson (Dianne Wiest). The director happens to be an adult genius. Dede and Dr. Grierson conflict over Fred's emotional and intellectual needs.

Orion Pictures. US. 1991. 99m. C. *Producesr:* Peggy Rajski, Scott Rudin *Director:* Jodie Foster *Writer:* Scott Frank *Cast:* Jodie Foster, Dianne Wiest, Adam Hann-Byrd, Harry Connick, Jr., David Hyde Pierce, Debi Mazar, P.J. Ochlan, Alex Lee, Michael Shulman, Nathan Lee, Celia Weston, Danitra Vance, Richard Fredette, George Plimpton, Jennifer Trier

409. *Little Men*

At New England's Plumfield School for Boys, Prof. Bhaer (Ralph Morgan) and his wife Jo (Erin O'Brien-Moore) love and care for the boys. Thanks to Jo's persistence, street orphans become part of the farmhouse school. There are numerous incidents with the boys but everything is resolved.

Mascot. US. 1934. 77m. B&W. *Director:* Phil Rosen *Writers:* Gertrude Orr, Louisa M. Alcott (novel) *Cast:* Ralph Morgan, Erin O'Brien-Moore, Junior Durkin, Cora Sue Collins, Frankie Darro, Dickie Moore, Phyllis Fraser, Robert Carlton, Finis Barton, David Durand, Dickie Moore, Tad Alexander, Buster Phelps, Ronnie Crosby, Tommy Bupp, Bobby Cox, Dickie Jones, Richard Quine, Donald Buck, George Ernest, Hattie McDaniel, Margaret Mann, Jacqueline Taylor, Gustav von Seyffertitz, Billy Johnson

The Little Nuns see Le Monachine

410. *The Little Princess*

In Queen Victoria's England, little Sara Crewe (Shirley Temple) is sent to an exclusive school for girls, Michin Seminary, while her father Captain Crewe (Ian Hunter) is off to war in Africa. Amanda Michin (Mary Nash) rules the school with a strict hand. Sara becomes friends with young teacher Rose Hamilton (Anita Louise) and the riding instructor Geoffrey (Richard Greene). When Sara's father is apparently killed, Sara's money is gone but she is allowed to stay at the school as a servant. She suffers terribly until her shell-shocked father returns. Other film versions of this story have been made.

TCF. US. 1939. 93m. C. *Producer:* Gene Markey *Director:* Walter Lang *Writers:* Ethel Hill, Walter Ferris, Frances Hodgson (novel) *Cast:* Shirley Temple, Richard Greene, Anita Louise, Ian Hunter, Cesar Romero, Arthur Treacher, Mary Nash, Sybil Jason, Miles Mander, Marcia Mae Jones, Beryl Mercer, E.E. Clive

Little Red Flowers see Kan shang qu hen mei

411. *The Little Red Schoolhouse*

Bootleggers secretly operate in the basement of the school where Mercy Brent (Martha Mansfield) teaches. Her fiancé John Hale (E.K. Lincoln) breaks up the illegal activities and solves a murder.

Arrow Film Corp. US. 1923. B&W. *Director:* John G. Adolfi *Writer:* James Shelley Hamilton *Cast:* Martha Mansfield, Harlan Knight, Sheldon Lewis, E.K. Lincoln, Edmund Breese, Florida Kingsley, Paul Everton

412. *The Little Red Schoolhouse*

Orphans Frankie and Dickie are cared by their older sister Mary (Ann Doran), a teacher at Hilldale Public School in Ohio. Mary's fiancé Owen Rogers (Lloyd Hughes) falsely accuses Frankie of starting a fight. Frankie runs away and gets into trouble with the law. Owen jeopardizes his career to help Frankie. All is resolved when Mary and Owen marry, and Frankie learns the importance of an education.

Chesterfield Motion Pictures Corp. US. 1936. 66m. B&W. *Producer:* George R. Batcheller *Director:* Charles Lamont *Writer:* Paul Perez *Cast:* Frank Coghlan, Jr., Lloyd Hughes, Dickie Moore, Ann Doran, Richard Carle, Ralf Harolde, Frank Sheridan, Mathew Betz, Sidney Miller, Kenneth Howell, Gloria Brown, Don Brodie, Lou Davis, Fred A. Kelsey, Henry Otho, Sherry Hall, Jack Shutta

413. *The Little School Ma'am*

Narrow-minded town officials are outraged when schoolmistress Nan (Dorothy Gish) goes out one night with her sweetheart. She is fired when they don't believe her explanation. Her beau rescues her from a rape attack and they marry.

Triangle Film Corp. US. 1916. 50m. B&W. *Directors:* Chester M. Franklin, Sidney Franklin *Writers:* Bernard McConville, Frank E. Woods *Cast:* Dorothy Gish, Elmer Clifton, George C. Pierce, Jack Brammall, Howard Gaye, Josephine Crowell, Luray Huntley, Millard Webb, Hal Wilson, George Stone

The Little School Mistress see La Maestrina

414. *Little Secrets*

While her girlfriends are at camp, 14-year-old Emily Lindstrom (Evan Rachel Wood), an aspiring concert violinist, spends the summer practicing with her music teacher Pauline (Vivica A. Fox) for a big audition. One of her activities is a "secret keeper" booth in her backyard where she draws long lines of kids eager to confide some secret they have for 50 cents.

Columbia Tristar. US. 2001. 96m. C. *Director:* Blair Treu *Writer:* Jessica Barondes *Cast:* Evan Rachel Wood, Michael Angarano, David Gallagher, Vivica A. Fox, Jan Broberg Felt, Rick Macy, Paul Kiernan, Tayva Patch, Micah Schow, Caitlin E.J. Meyer, Landon Kunzelman, Danielle Chuchran, Haley McCormick, RuDee Lipscomb, Erica Angarano

415. *The Little Teacher*

The Little Teacher has a rebellion against her led by a school bully who is beyond any teacher's control. She goes home crying when a surveyor asks her what is wrong. She tells him and he beats up the bully. The bully becomes interested in the teacher, but she has eyes on her defender. Unfortunately the surveyor is married and the Little Teacher accepts the bully.

Biograph Co. US. 1909. 11m. B&W. *Director:* D.W. Griffith *Writer:* Mary Pickford *Cast:* Mary Pickford, Arthur Johnson, Edward Dillon, Kate Bruce

416. *Ljubica (Violet)*

Thirtyish, attractive Ljubica works with deaf children. She is separated from her husband (who works abroad) and her son (who lives with her in-laws). A much younger man enters her life but she decides to live with her son and do her work.

Yugoslavia. 1978. 92m. C. *Director:* Kresimir Golik *Writer:* Goran Massot *Cast:* Relja Basic, Husein Cokic, Vanja Drach, Bozidarka Frajt, Jana Kasper, Miodrag Krivokapic, Franjo Majetic, Lela Margetic, Jadranka Matkovic, Mia Oremovic, Ivan Stancic, Zvonimir Torjanac

417. *The Lonely Passion of Judith Hearne*

Judith Hearne (Maggie Smith), a middle-aged "maiden lady" piano teacher living in a Dublin boarding house, yearns for her new neighbor. When he thinks she has money, he returns her affections. She is shattered when the truth comes out.

HandMade. Great Britain. 1987. 116m. C. *Producers:* George Harrison, Denis O'Brien *Director:* Jack Clayton *Writers:* Peter Nelson, Brian Moore (novel) *Cast:* Maggie Smith, Bob Hoskins, Wendy Hiller, Marie Kean, Prunella Scales

418. *The Long Hot Summer*

Drifter Ben Quick (Paul Newman) arrives back in his hometown after being kicked out of another town for allegedly burning a barn for revenge. Will Varner (Orson Welles) hates Ben's father because he was an arsonist. Will owns just about everything in town and runs the show. Initially, Will hates Ben but gains a respect for him after seeing him work. Will views his own son Jody (Anthony Franciosa) as weak and lacking in ambition, and begins to think of Ben as a potential husband for his schoolteacher daughter Clara (Joanne Woodward), who he thinks will never marry even though she has a weak-willed boyfriend. Jody becomes jealous of Ben, sets a fire and blames Ben.

TCF. US. 1958. 115m. C. *Producer:* Jerry Wald *Director:* Martin Ritt *Writers:* Irving Ravetch, Harriet Frank, Jr., William Faulkner (story) *Cast:* Paul Newman, Joanne Woodward, Anthony Franciosa, Orson Welles, Lee Remick, Angela Lansbury, Richard Anderson, Sarah Marshall, Mabel Anderson

419. *Looking for Mr. Goodbar*

Theresa Dunn (Diane Keaton), a dedicated teacher of deaf children, starts cruising bars at night after an unhappy relationship. She is obsessed with sex and then drugs, but during the days is committed to the children. Theresa has a kind and reassuring demeanor with the children and sits down on their level to interact with them.

Paramount. US. 1977. 136m. C. *Producer:* Freddie Fields *Director:* Richard Brooks *Writers:* Richard Brooks, Judith Rossner (novel) *Cast:* Diane Keaton, Tuesday Weld, William Atherton, Richard Kiley

Louise see *Chère Louise*

420. *Love Lessons*

Fourth grade teacher Jonah Stein (Jon Stahl) falls for the woman his mother has set him up with. Then he is suddenly attracted to a fellow teacher. He begins to question his ideas about family, faith and love.

US. 2005. 99m. C. *Producers:* Jon Stahl, Marcia T. Mohiuddin *Writer-Director:* Jon Stahl *Cast:* Louise Gallanda, Sam Greenfield, Jennifer Kalison, Brent Katz, Joe Lima, William Mahoney, Eric Milano, Kit Paquin, Jon Stahl, Marissa Tiamfook

Love Me Once Again '80 see *Miwodo dashi hanbeon '80*

421. *Love That Brute*

Soft-hearted gangster "Big Ed" Hanley (Paul Douglas) falls in love with pretty recreation director of parks Ruth Manning (Jean Peters). "Big Ed" hires Ruth as the governess for his child — but the problem is that he *has* no child. He sends Bugs (Keenan Wynn) to find him a child. When Ruth discovers that "Big Ed" is a gangster, she almost leaves, but then learns about his made-up killer image. A remake of the 1941 comedy *Tall, Dark and Handsome*.

TCF. US. 1950. 85m. B&W. *Producer:* Fred Kohlmar *Director:* Alexander Hall *Writers:* Darrell Ware, John Lee Mahin, Karl Tunberg *Cast:* Paul Douglas, Jean Peters, Cesar Romero, Joan Davis, Arthur Treacher

422. *Love's Enduring Promise*

In frontier days, headstrong young schoolteacher Missie Davis (January Jones) is torn between a handsome young stranger (Logen Arens) and a railroad magnate (Mackenzie Astin).

Hallmark. US. 2004. 88m. C. *Producers:* Lincoln Lageson, Randy Pope *Director:* Michael Landon, Jr. *Writers:* Cindy Kelley, Michael Landon, Jr., Janette Oke (novel) *Cast:* Logan Arens, Mackenzie Astin, Michael Bartel, Logan Bartholomew, E.J. Callahan, Katia Coe, Cara DelLizia, Cliff De Young, Douglas Fisher, Katerine Heigl, January Jones, Dominic Scott Kay, Joshua Michael Kwiat, Robert Lyons, Dale Midkiff, Blaine Pate, Matthew Peters, K'Sun Ray

423. *Lubinghua (Dull Ice Flower)*

Kuo, a young fine-arts teacher, is assigned to a small farming village. He discovers Ah-Ming, an eight-year-old painting genius in his class. Ah-Ming's poverty prevents him from painting freely. Kuo wants Ah-Ming's work to be entered in a painting competition but the other teachers want the governor's son entered instead. Kuo leaves the school in protest and Ah-Ming is upset. Ah-Ming gets an illness and dies. The school learns that Kuo sent in Ah-Ming's work to an international competition and it won, and realizes too late how talented he was.

Taiwan. 1989. C. *Producers:* Nai Chung Chow, Y.L. Tu *Director:* Li Kao Yang *Writers:* Nien-Jen Wu, J.J. Chong (novel) *Cast:* Sung Young Chen, C. Chen Li, Kwan Yuen Wong

424. *Lucia*

Three stories about women named Lucia. In the third story, set in 1969, agricultural worker Lucia meets a teacher who wants to instruct her to read and write, but her truck-driving husband doesn't want her to learn.

Cuban Institute of Art and Cinema. Cuba. 1969. 155m. B&W. *Director:* Humberto Solas *Writers:* Humberto Solas, Julio Garcia Espinosa, Nelson Rodriguez *Cast:* Raquel Revuelta, Eslinda Nuñez, Adela Legra, Adolfo Liaurado, Ramon Brito

425. *Lucie Aubrac*

Aubrac was the Resistance code name for Raymond Samuel (Daniel Auteuil), a Jewish schoolteacher. This is the story of Raymond and his wife Lucie Bernard (Carole Bouquet) and their daring wartime missions. Lucie is a dedicated grade school teacher concerned that her pupils understand the importance of learning from the past and look to the future. Luci stops at nothing to save her husband's life and the lives of his imprisoned colleagues.

USA Films. France. 1997. 116m. C. *Writer-Producer-Director:* Claude Berri *Cast:* Carole Bouquet, Daniel Auteuil, Patrice Chereau, Heino Ferch

426. *The Luck of the Irish*

Plumber William Grogan (James Kirkwood) falls in love with the feet of pretty schoolteacher Ruth Warren (Anna Q. Nilsson).

Realart Pictures Corp. US. 1920. B&W. *Producer-Director:* Allan Dwan *Cast:* James Kirkwood, Anna Q. Nilsson, Harry Northrup, Ward Crane, Ernest Butterworth, Gertrude Messenger, Madame Deione, Louise Lester

427. Lust for a Vampire

Vampire Count Karnstein (Mike Raven) relies on feedings by vampire Mircalla (Yutte Stensgaard) for his life blood. She finds a good supply at a girls' finishing school. Teacher Richard Lestrange (Michael Johnson) and the headmaster begin to investigate the strange going-ons.

Hammer. Great Britain. 1970. 95m. C. *Producers:* Harry Fine, Michael Style *Director:* Jimmy Sangster *Writer:* Tudor Gates *Cast:* Ralph Bates, Michael Johnson, Barbara Jefford, Suzanna Leigh, Yutte Stensgaard, Mike Raven, Helen Christie, David Healy, Michael Brennan, Pippa Steel, Jack Melford, Erik Chitty

428. Macskajaték (Cats' Play)

Mrs. Orbán, an elderly, widowed music teacher living in Budapest, devotes her life to her wealthy paralyzed sister in Germany, communicating via letter and phone. She also dines every Thursday with a retired opera singer.

Hunnia Studio. Hungary. 1974. 115m. C. *Director:* Károly Makk *Writers:* Károly Makk, János Tóth *Cast:* Margit Dayka, Elma Bulla, Margit Makay, Samu Balász

Mad Little Island see Rockets Galore

Madame Rosa see La Vie Devant Soi

429. Madame Sousatzka

The Sen family—Sushila, her husband, and her son Manek—immigrates to London. The father dies suddenly and Sushila must struggle to survive. Manek is so talented that his schoolteacher refers him to Russian immigrant Madame Yuline Sousatzka (Shirley MacLaine). Manek learns about life and the piano. When his mother loses her job, Manek is under pressure to use his skills to make money.

Curzon. Great Britain. 1988. 122m. C. *Producer:* Robin Dalton *Director:* John Schlesinger *Writers:* Ruth Prawer Jhabvala, John Schlesinger *Cast:* Shirley MacLaine, Peggy Ashcroft, Twiggy, Shabana Azmi, Leigh Lawson, Geoffrey Bayldon, Lee Montague, Robert Rietty, Navin Chowdhry

430. Mädchen in Uniform (Girls in Uniform)

When her mother dies, Manuela von Meinhardis (Hertha Thiele), a spirited and sensitive student, is sent to an girls' boarding school. The principal (Emilia Unda) feels that discipline is good for the girls and rules with an iron fist. Manuela develops a romantic attraction to young teacher Frälein Elizabeth von Bernburg (Dorothea Wieck), who believes trust is most important. Manuela makes the mistake of announcing her love. The movie was initially banned in the United States. It wasn't until Eleanor Roosevelt saw the importance of the movie that the ban was lifted.

Deutsch Film. Germany. 1931. 90m. B&W. *Director:* Leontine Sagan *Writer:*

Freidrich Dammann *Cast:* Emilia Unda, Dorothea Wieck, Hedwig Schlichter, Ellen Schwannecke, Hertha Thiele

431. *Mädchen in Uniform (Girls in Uniform)*

After the death of her parents, Manuela von Meinhardis (Romy Schneider) is sent to a strict all-girl boarding school. Manuela is attracted to the sensitive and loving teacher Fräulein von Bernburg (Lilli Palmer). When word gets out, von Bernburg is forced to leave the school even though she did not return the love and Manuela is severely punished.

Filmkunst. West Germany. 1958. 91m. C. *Director:* Géza von Radványi *Writers:* Friedrich Dammann, Franz Höllering *Cast:* Lilli Palmer, Romy Schneider, Thérèse Giehse, Margaret Jahnen, Blandine Ebinger, Adelheid Seeck, Gina Albert, Sabine Sinjen, Christine Kaufmann, Danik Patisson, Genette Pigeon, Marthe Mercadier, Regine Burghardt, Ulla Moritz, Lou Seitz

432. *Madeline*

A film based on Ludwig Bemelman's books about a spunky redheaded nine-year-old named Madeline. Miss Clavel (Frances McDormand) is the nun and headmistress of the Parisian girls' school that Madeline attends. Madeline befriends a young boy and has some adventures. Miss Clavel is kind and beloved by the girls. Trouble erupts when Lord Covington decides to sell the school.

Tristar. US/France. 88m. 1998. C. *Producers*: Saul Cooper, Allyn Stewart, Pancho Kohner *Director*: Daisy von Scherler Mayer *Writers*: Mark Levin, Jennifer Flackett, Malia Scotch Marmo *Cast*: Frances McDormand, Nigel Hawthorne, Hatty Jones, Kristian de la Osa, Stéphane Audran, Chantal Neuwirth, Ben Daniels, Julien Maurel, Clare Thomas, Bianca Strohmann, Alix Ponchon, Jessica Mason, Christina Mangani, Alice Lavaud, Emilie Jessula, Pilar Garrard, Morgane Farcat, Eloise Eonnet

433. *Mademoiselle*

Mademoiselle (Jeanne Moreau), the new town schoolmarm, is admired by the villagers. She is sexually repressed and is attracted to Manou (Ettore Manni), a virile Italian logger. Mademoiselle accidentally sets a fire and shirtless Manou comes to the rescue. She starts fires and a flood in order to see Manou in action. Villagers blame Manou for the events.

Lopert Pictures. France/Great Britain. 1966. 103m. B&W. *Producer:* Oscar Lewenstein *Director:* Tony Richardson *Writers:* Marguerite Duras, Jean Genet *Cast:* Jeanne Moreau, Ettore Manni, Umberto Orsini, Keith Skinner, Georges Aubert, Jean Gras, Jane Beretta, Gabriel Gobin, Paul Barge, Rosine Luguet

434. *La Maestrina (The Little School Mistress)*

In a small Italian village, a teacher is still in pain at the thought of how she almost lost her baby. The local political chief protects her from the wrath of the female school director.

Cinés-Pittaluga. Italy. 1933. 60m. B&W. *Producer:* Giuseppe Amato *Director:* Guido Brignone *Cast:* Andreina Pagnani, Renato Cialente, Jone Frigerio, Egisto Oliveri, Mario Ferari, Enzo Gainotti, Giuseppe Galeati, Olga Vittoria Gentilli, Gina Grappasonni, Cesare Zoppetti

435. *Il Maestro (The Teacher and the Miracle)*

A beloved teacher, widower Giovanni Merino (Aldo Fabrizi), is crushed by the death of his young and talented pupil son. Into his life and classroom comes enters Antonio (Eduardo Nevola), the son of a carpenter. Antonio comforts him with words of wisdom and rejuvenates his love of teaching before abruptly disappearing. The teacher realizes that the child was a heavenly apparition.

President Films. Spain/Italy. *Producer-Director:* Aldo Fabrizi *Writers:* L. Lucas, J. Gallardo, Aldo Fabrizi, M. Amendola *Cast:* Aldo Fabrizi, Eduardo Nevola, Marco Paoletti, Alfred Mayo, Mary Lamar

436. *Il Maestro di Vigevano (The Teacher from Vigevano)*

Mr. Mombelli, a contented primary schoolteacher, is driven by his wife to resign and set up a shoe factory. The factory fails and his wife starts to be unfaithful.

President Films. Spain/Italy. 1963. 90m. B&W. *Producer:* Dino De Laurentis *Director:* Elio Petri *Writers:* Agenore Incrocci, Furio Scarpelli, Lucio Mastronardi (novel) *Cast:* Alberto Sordi, Claire Bloom, Anna Carena, Egidio Casolari, Agniello Coastabile, Gustavo D'Arpe, Bruno De Cerce, Vito De Taranto, Ya Doucheskaya, Lilla Ferrante, Gaetano Fusari, Ignazio Gilbilisco, Eva Magni, Piero Mazzarella, Tullio Scavazzi, Guido Spadea, Adrianna Tocchio

437. *The Magus*

British schoolteacher Nicholas Urfe (Michael Caine) arrives on a sleepy Greek island to take a vacant teaching post (the previous teacher committed suicide). He is soon drawn into a game created by reclusive mystic-magician (magus) Maurice Conchis (Anthony Quinn).

TCF. Great Britain. 1968. 116m. C. *Producers:* John Kohn, Jud Kinberg *Director:* Guy Green *Writer:* John Fowles *Cast:* Michael Caine, Anthony Quinn, Candice Bergen, Anna Karina, Paul Stassino, Julian Glover, George Pastell

438. *Le Maître de Musique (The Music Teacher)*

Aging opera singer Joachim Fallayrac (José van Dam) retires and moves to the countryside to teach two young singers. The training is rigorous, training but they develop a good relationship. The students are invited to participate in a singing contest.

Orion. Belgium/France. 1988. 95m. C. *Director:* Gérard Corbiau *Writers:* Andrée Corbiau, Gérard Corbiau *Cast:* José van Dam, Anne Roussel, Philippe Volter, Sylvie Fennec, Patrick Bauchau

439. The Making of O'Malley

Lucille Thayer (Dorothy Mackaill), a society schoolteacher, asks a New York precinct captain to have a policeman watch the traffic when the children leave school. O'Malley is assigned the task and Lucille gives him his instructions. While on duty, O'Malley notices a poor crippled girl and arranges for an operation to cure her. Besides his school duty, he tangles with bootleggers. A society crook, "Dandy the Dude," is engaged to Lucille.

First National Pictures. US. 1925. B&W. *Producer:* Joseph Plunkett *Director:* Lambert Hillyer *Cast:* Milton Sills, Dorothy Mackaill, Helen Rowland, Warner Richmond, Thomas G. Carrigan, Claude King, Allen Brander, Charles Graham, Jack DeLacey, Julia Hurley

440. Making the Grade

At the urging of his father, Eddie Romson (David Butler) accompanies an expedition to Russia. He wins the heart of peasant schoolmarm Sophie Semenoff (Helen Ferguson) and takes her for his wife. Eddie's mother disapproves but she helps save Sophie from kidnappers. It turns out Sophie is a princess with family jewels.

Western Pictures Exploitation Co. US. 1921. B&W. *Director:* Fred J. Butler *Writer:* A.P. Younger *Cast:* David Butler, Helen Ferguson, William Walling, Lillian Lawrence, Jack Cosgrove, Alice Wilson, Otto Lederer, Jack Rollins

441. Malou

A young German schoolteacher, in the midst of a personal crisis, tries to come to terms with the memory of her dead mother, Malou. She decides to travel to Argentina where Malou lived a tragic life.

Regina Ziegler. West Germany. 1980. 93m. C. *Writer-Director:* Jeanine Meerapfel *Cast:* Ingrid Cavin, Grische Huber, Helmut Griem, Ivan Desny, Marie Colbin, Peter Chatel, Margarita Calahorra

442. The Man Above the Law

Duke Chalmers (Jack Richardson) renounces civilization and moves to New Mexico to become a whiskey trader. He marries a Navaho woman who bears him a daughter. Esther Brown (Josie Sedgwick) arrives from the east to open a school but Duke refuses to let his daughter attend. Esther grows to love the daughter. Duke rescues Esther from a pair of drunks and falls in love with her. Esther reminds him of his family duty and Duke and his family move farther west.

Triangle Film Corp. US. 1918. B&W. *Director:* Raymond Wells *Cast:* Jack Richardson, Josie Sedgwick, Claire McDowell, May Giraci

Man on the Train see *L'Homme du Train*

443. Man Rustlin'

Schoolteacher Mary Wilson (Florence Lee) urges her sweetheart Buck Hayden (Bob Custer) to become a reporter for the local newspaper. He gets the big story and the girl.

Independent Pictures. US. 1926. B&W. *Director:* Del Andrews *Writer:* William Branch *Cast:* Bob Custer, Florence Lee, Jules Cowles, Sam Allen, James Kelly, Pat Beggs, Howard Fay, Skeeter Bill Robbins

444. Man-Thing

Kyle Williams (Mathew Le Nevez) thought taking the job of sheriff in a small town would be the change he wanted. The sleepy town is not what it seems with a series of gruesome murders. Secrets are hidden and his only help comes from feisty young schoolteacher Terri (Richael Taylor). They must face an evil oil tycoon and Man-Thing, a swamp-monster.

Artisan. US/Australia. 2005. 97m. C. *Director:* Brett Leonard *Writers:* Steve Gerber, Hans Rodionoff *Cast:* Mathew Le Nevez, Richael Taylor, Jack Thompson, Rawiri Paratene, Alex O'Loughlin, Steve Bastoni, Robert Mammone, Patrick Thompson, William Zappa, John Batchelor, Ian Bliss, Brett Leonard, Imogen Bailey, James Coyne, Cheryl Craig

445. *The Man Who Played God (The Silent Voice)*

A musician goes deaf but finds salvation in teaching music to a young student.

Warner. US. 1932. 81m. B&W. *Director:* John G. Adolfi *Writers:* Julian Josephson, Maude Howell *Cast:* George Arliss, Violet Heming, Ivan Simpson, Bette Davis, Louise Closser Hale, Donald Cook, Ray Milland

The Man Who Stole the Sun see *Taiyo o nusunda otoko*

446. *The Man Without a Face*

Once a teacher, Justin McLeod (Mel Gibson) is now a disfigured recluse. He tutors a young boy, Chuck (Nick Stahl), so that Chuck can go to the same military academy his deceased father attended. Ten years earlier, Justin's face was disfigured in an automobile accident and fire in which a boy was incinerated and for which Justin was convicted of involuntary manslaughter, even though he had done nothing wrong. He is also suspected of being a pedophile. The friendship of Justin and Chuck causes gossip, but Justin is able to help the boy achieve his dream.

Entertainment/Icon. US. 1993. 115m. C. *Producer:* Bruce Davey *Director:* Mel Gibson *Writers:* Malcolm MacRury, Isabelle Holland (novel) *Cast:* Mel Gibson, Margaret Whitton, Fay Masterson, Gaby Hoffman, Geoffrey Lewis, Richard Masur, Nick Stahl, Viva

447. *Mandy (The Crash of Silence)*

A little girl born deaf is sent to a special school.

Ealing. Great Britain. 1952. 93m. B&W. *Producer:* Leslie Norman *Director:* Alexander Mackendrick *Writers:* Nigel Balchin, Jack Whittingham, Hilda Lewis (novel) *Cast:* Jack Hawkins, Terence Morgan, Phyllis Calvert, Mandy Miller, Godfrey Tearle, Dorothy Alison, Nancy Price, Edward Chapman, Marjorie Fielding, Patricia Plunkett, Eleanor Summerfield, Colin Gordon, Julian Amyes, Jane Asher

Manhunt see *Jakten*

448. *Mara of the Wilderness*

After her parents are killed, Mara is left alone in the forest with two wolf pups. The wolves are very protective of her as she grows up. She saves the life of an anthropologist when he is caught in a trap. Mara is captured by a brutal trapper, but aided by her wolves she escapes. The anthropologist tracks down the trapper and finds Mara. He starts to teach Mara about civilization.

Allied Artists. US. 1965. 90m. C. *Producer:* Brice Mack *Director:* Frank McDonald *Writer:* Tom Blackburn *Cast:* Adam West, Linda Saunders, Theo Marcuse, Denver Pyle, Sean McClory, Eve Brent, Roberto Contreras, Ed Kemmer, Stuart Walsh, Lelia Walsh

449. *Marry Me*

Attractive schoolteacher Hetty Gandy (Florence Vidor) falls in love with chicken farmer John Smith, who proposes marriage. Hetty is called away, but leaves her answer on an egg. The egg is to be given to John for breakfast but it is put into cold storage instead. Hetty waits for five years. More complications ensue.

Paramount. US. 1925. B&W. *Producers:* Adolph Zukor, Jesse L. Lasky, *Director:* James Cruze *Writer:* Anthony Coldeway, Walter Woods *Cast:* Florence Vidor, Edward Everett Horton, John Roche, Helen Jerome Eddy, Fanny Midgley, Ed Brady, Z. Wall Covington, Anne Schaefer, Erwin Connelly

450. *Marty*

A 34-year-old Bronx butcher, Marty (Ernest Borgnine), meets an unattractive schoolteacher named Clara (Betsy Blair). They hit it off but his family and friends don't want the romance to blossom.

UA. US. 1955. 91m. B&W. *Producer:* Harold Hecht *Director:* Delbert Mann *Writer:* Paddy Chayefsky *Cast:* Ernest Borgnine, Betsy Blair, Esther Minciotti, Joe Mantell, Karen Steele, Jerry Paris, Augusta Ciolli, Frank Sutton, Walter Kelley

The Martyrdom of St. John see *Szentjános Fejevétele*

451. *Mary Had a Lovely Voice*

A spurned man wins the girl by posing as music teacher.
Clarendon. Great Britain. 1910. B&W. *Director:* Percy Stow

452. Mary Kay Letourneau Story: All-American Girl

The true story of married 35-year-old Seattle teacher Mary Kay Letourneau (Penelope Ann Miller), who is arrested and jailed for raping a 13-year-old student. She becomes the mother of two of his children. In 2000, another movie on Letourneau was directed by Jack Perez

USA Network. US. 2000. C. *Director:* Lloyd Kramer *Writer:* Julie Hébert *Cast:* Penelope Ann Miller, Omar Anguiano, Mercedes Ruehl, Rena Owen, Greg Spottiswood, Christopher Bondy, Janet-Laine Green, Gary Hudson, Robert Clark, Lori Hallier, Julie Khaner

453. Mary Poppins

A musical tale with some animation about a magical nanny who changes everyone's lives. Mary Poppins (Julie Andrews) cares for two children who have a very stern London banker as a father. At one point they enter a picture drawn by Bert, Mary's friend. In the animated land they are served by dancing penguins, ride carousel horses, and join a fox hunt. A "supercalifragilisticexpialidocious" film.

Buena Vista. US. 1964. 148m. C. Live and Animated. *Producers:* Walt Disney, Bill Walsh *Director:* Robert Stevenson *Writers:* Bill Walsh, Don DaGradi, P. L. Travers (novel) *Cast:* Julie Andrews, Dick Van Dyke, David Tomlinson, Glynis Johns, Ed Wynn, Hermione Baddeley, Karen Dotrice, Matthew Garber, Elsa Lanchester, Arthur Treacher, Reginald Owen, Reta Shaw, Arthur Malet, Jane Darwell, Cyril Delevanti, Lester Matthews, Clive l. Halliday, Don Barclay, Marjorie Bennett, Alma Lawton, Majorie Eaton *Voices:* J. Pat O'Malley, Jim Macdonald

Master of the House see Du Sjak Aere Din Hustru

The Masters see Gente di Rispetto

454. La Maternelle

When Rose's (Madeleine Renaud) father files for bankkruptcy and suddenly dies, and she is jilted by her fiancé, she takes a job as a maid in a kindergarten with poor children. She is particularly dedicated to a little girl abandoned by her prostitute mother.

Photosonor. France. 1932. 89m. B&W. *Directors:* Jean Benoît-Lévy, Marie Epstein *Writer:* Jean Benoît-Lévy *Cast:* Madeleine Renaud, Paulette Elambert, Alice Tissot, Mady Berry, Sylvette Fillacier, Henri Debain, Alex Bernard, Edmond Van Daële

455. Matilda

Matilda Wormwood (Mara Wilson) has the worst parents in the world, the worst principal (Pam Ferris) at her school, but a good teacher, Jennifer "Jenny" Honey (Embeth Davidtz). Matilda has special powers and is extremely smart. After taking care of the evil principal, she also rids herself of her parents and gets to live with Miss Honey.

Sony/Tristar/Universal. US. 1996. 102m. C. *Producers:* Liccy Dahl, Danny DeVito, Michael Shamberg, Stacey Sher *Director:* Danny DeVito *Writers:* Nicholas Kazan, Robin Swicord, Roald Dahl (book) *Cast:* Mara Wilson, Danny DeVito, Rhea Perlman, Embeth Davidtz, Pam Ferris, Paul Reubens, Tracey Walter, Brian Levinson, Jacqueline Steiger

456. *Matir moina (The Clay Bird)*

Anu (Nural Islam Bablu) is sent to a religious school by his devout Islamic father in 1960s Bangladesh. One teacher, Ibrahim, recognizes Anu's decency. Anu takes an interest in Rokon (Russell Farazi), an awkward student.

Milestone Film. France/Pakistan/Bangladesh. 2002. 95m. C. *Director:* Tareque Masud *Writers:* Catherine Masud, Tareque Masud *Cast:* Nurul Islam Bablu, Russell Farazi, Jayanto Chattopadhyay, Rokeya Prachy, Soaeb Islam, Lamees R. Reemjheem, Moin Ahmed, Md. Moslemuddin, Abdul Karim, Shah Adam Dewan, Golam Mahmud, Pradip Mittra Mithun, Auyon Chowdhury, Masud Ali Khan, Manjila Begum

457. *Les Mauvais Coups (Naked Autumn)*

Into a loveless marriage of ten years steps a young sweet schoolteacher, Helene (Alexandra Stewart). The wife, a drinker and a gambler, introduces Helene to her husband Milan (Reginald Kernan), a girl-chasing race car driver.

United Motion Picture. 1961. 98m. B&W. *Producer:* Jean Thullier *Director:* Francois Leterrier *Writer:* Roger Vailland *Cast:* Simone Signoret, Reginald Kernan, Alexandra Stewart, Serge Rosseau, Marcelle Ranson, Dorian Leigh Parker, Nicole Chollet, Maria Claude-Poirier, Serge Sauvion, Antoine Roblot, Marcel Pagliero, Jose Luis de Villalonga

458. *Max Keeble's Big Move*

Twelve-year-old Max Keeble (Alex D. Linz) gets harassed by school bullies Troy McGinty and Dobbs (Noel Fisher and Orlando Brown) and evil principal Elliot T. Jindraike (Larry Miller). Max learns from his parents (Nora Dunn and Robert Carradine) that he's moving to Chicago. He starts to get revenge on the people who harassed him and soon finds out that he's not moving.

Buena Vista. US. 2001. 86m. C. *Producer:* Mike Karz *Director:* Tim Hill *Writers:* David L. Watts, Jonathan Bernstein *Cast:* Alex D. Linz, Larry Miller, Jamie Kennedy, Zena Grey, Josh Peck

The Meaning of Life see *Monty Python's The Meaning of Life*

459. *Meet the Parents*

Pretty kindergarten teacher Pam (Teri Polo) and her live-in boyfriend Greg (Ben Stiller) head off for a weekend with her parents and family. Greg's attempts to ingratiate himself with her family go badly. He then learns that her father is a former C.I.A. profiler.

Universal/Dreamworks Pictures. US. 2000. 108m. C. *Producers:* Nancy Tenenbaum, Jane Rosenthal, Robert De Niro, Jay Roach *Director:* Jay Roach *Writers:* Jim Herzfeld, John Hamburg *Cast:* Robert De Niro, Ben Stiller, Blythe Danner, Teri Polo, James Rebhorn, Jon Abrahams, Owen Wilson, Kali Rocha

460. *Megáll az Idö (Time Stands Still)*

In the 1960s, two boys, sons of political refugees in Vienna, attend a boys' school in Hungary. We learn about the school's political hierarchy through scenes such as a classroom being searched for contraband and a biology teacher forced out of his job. The new female teacher is more political and has a husband who must be locked up when guests visit. The principal gives a speech about the triumph of the 1956 Soviet takeover. In another scene we see a boy and his teacher embracing in a bathroom with the camera looking down through the blades of the fan. All the boys want is to listen to American rock'n'roll.

Libra Films. Hungary. 1982. 99m. C. *Director:* Peter Gothar *Writers:* Geza Beremenyi, Pether Gothar *Cast:* István Znamenak, Henrik Pauer, Sándor Söth, Péter Gálfy, Pál Hetényi, Lajos Szabo, Ádám Rajhona, Jozef Króner, Mária Ronyecz, Tamás Jordán

461. *Meili de dajiao (For the Children)*

After the death of her husband and young son, Zhang Meili founds a school in the deserts of northwest China. She is determined to give her students a better life. Zhang befriends a new teacher, Xia, a cultured woman sent to help teach. Even though they come from very different backgrounds, they share the same goal of educating the disadvantaged children.

Ardustry Home Entertainment. China. 2002. 103m. C. *Director:* Yarzhou Yang *Writer:* Wei Li *Cast:* Ping Ni, Quan Yuan, Haiyin Sun, Yajun Xu, Zhijun Ge

462. *La Meilleure Façon de Marcher (The Best Way to Walk)*

At a summer camp for boys, instructor-counselor Marc accidently discovers counselor Philippe, son of the camp owner, in drag. Marc bullies him endlessly.

Specialty Films. France. 1976. 82m. C. *Director:* Claude Miller *Writers:* Claude Miller, Luc Béraud *Cast:* Patrick Dewaere, Patrick Bouchitey, Christine Pascal, Claude Piéplu

463. *O Melissokomos (The Beekeeper)*

Visiting beehives around Greece, a retired and solemn schoolteacher (Marcello Mastroianni) picks up a female hitchhiker (Nadia Mourouzi). He has left his family to follow in the footsteps of his father and grandfather, setting up hives around the countryside.

Greek Film Centre. Greece/France. 1986. 122m. C. *Director:* Theodorus

Angelopoulos *Writers:* Theodorus Angelopoulos, Dimitris Nollas, Tonino Guerra *Cast:* Marcello Mastroianni, Nadia Mourouzi, Serge Reggiani, Jenny Roussea, Dinos Illipoulos, Vassia Panagopolou, Dimitris Poulikakos

464. *Melody for Three*

Dr. Christian (Jean Hersholt) reunites a music-teacher mother and an orchestra-conductor father for the sake of their son, a violin prodigy.

RKO. US. 1941. 67m. B&W. *Director:* Erle C. Kenton *Writers:* Lee Loeb, Walter Ferris *Cast:* Jean Hersholt, Fay Wray, Walter Woolf King, Astrid Allwyn, Schuyler Standish, Andrew Tombes, Maude Eburne, Patsy Parsons, Toscha Seidel, Irene Ryan, Eliva Allman, Irene Shirley, Donnie Allen, Leon Tyler, Cliff Nazarro

Melody for Youth see *They Shall Have Music*

465. *Mémoire des Apparences (Life Is a Dream)*

A teacher uses Pedro Calderon's classic 17th century play as a mnemonic device to remember the names of over 5,000 Chilean members of an anti-Junta movement. The teacher sits inside a theater watching old movies, trying to remember and dodging Junta terrorist bullets. Ten years later, at the same theater, the man recalls his experience.

International Film Circuit. France. 1986. 100m. C. *Writer-Director:* Raoul Ruiz *Cast:* Sylvain Thirolle, Roch Leibovici, Bénédicte Sire, Jean-Bernard Guillard, Jean-Pierre Agazar, Alain Halle-Halle, Jean-François Lapalus, Alain Rimoux, Laurence Cortadellas

466. *Men of Boys Town*

In this sequel to *Boys Town*, the kindly and understanding Father Edward J. "Eddie" Flanagan (Spencer Tracy) brings to Boys Town Ted Martley (Larry Nunn), a crippled boy who is bitter and never laughs. Ted had his back broken by a guard at a reformatory. He never told the true story of how a guard was killed. Ted doesn't respond to anyone until Whitey (Mickey Rooney) gives him a dog, Beau Hunk. The dog belongs to the Maitlands, members of the parole board. The Maitlands are persuaded to let the dog remain with Ted. The dog brings the child much happiness it dog is accidentally killed. After an operation, Ted is able to walk to the dog's grave. At the conclusion, all problems at Boys Town are resolved. It was reported that this sequel was made after donations to the real Boys Town dropped because people thought that Boys Town no longer had financial problems. Sequel to *Boys Town*.

MGM. US. 1941. 106m. B&W. *Producer:* John Considine, Jr. *Director:* Norman Taurog *Writer:* James Kevin McGuinness *Cast:* Spencer Tracy, Mickey Rooney, Bobs Watson, Larry Nunn, Darryl Hickman, Henry O'Neill, Mary Nash, Lee J. Cobb, Sidney Miller, Addison Richards, Lloyd Corrigan, George Lessey, Robert Emmett Keane, Arthur Hohl, Bem Welden, Anne Revere

467. *Merlusse*

Schoolteacher Merlusse (Henri Poupon) is hated by his pupils. During the Christmas break he shows warmth to those students left behind. We learn that the teacher frightens the boys because he is afraid himself.

Les Films Marcel Pagnol. France. 1935. 75m. B&W. *Writer-Director:* Marcel Pagnol *Cast:* Henri Poupon, André Pollack, Thommeray, André Robert, Rellys

468. *Merry Andrew*

A stiff, meek schoolteacher from a family of schoolteachers is searching for a buried Roman statue. He cannot marry his longtime fiancée until he finds the statue and then he will be made a headmaster. On the spot where he wants to dig sits a traveling Italian family circus. While digging he becomes attracted to the impulsive niece of the circus owner. He claims he is a teacher, not a performer, but steps in when the ringmaster loses his voice.

MGM. US. 1958. 103m. C. *Producer:* Sol C. Siegel *Director:* Michael Kidd *Writers:* Isobel Lennart, I.A.L. Diamond *Cast:* Danny Kaye, Pier Angeli, Baccaloni, Noel Purcell, Robert Coote, Patricia Cutts, Rex Evans, Walter Kingsford, Tommy Rall, Rhys Williams

469. *Mery per Sempre (Forever Mary)*

Good teacher Marco Terzi (Michele Placido) has returned from Milan to his native Sicily to teach at a Palermo reformatory. The title character is a teenage transvestite prostitute formerly known as Mario. The boys are instantly against Marco but he does not physically confront or fight them, but lets them test the limits of their own selves. For example, when the ringleader insists on making phallic references during classtime, Marco reads a poem containing metaphors on the same subject.

Cinevista. Italy. 1989. 100m. C. *Producer:* Claudio Bonivento *Director:* Marco Risi *Writers:* Sandro Petraglia, Stefano Rulli, Aurelio Grimaldi (novel) *Cast:* Michele Placido, Alessandro di Sanzo, Claudio Amendola, Francesco Benigno

470. *The Meteor Man*

When a meteor hits schoolteacher Jefferson Reed (Robert Townsend), he develops superhuman powers. His family and friends want him to protect their community. Unfortunately, he is afraid of heights.

MGM. US. 1993. 99m. C. *Producer:* Loretha C. Jones *Writer-Director:* Robert Townsend *Cast:* Robert Townsend, Marla Gibbs, Eddie Griffin, Robert Guillaume, James Earl Jones, Bill Cosby, Frank Gorshin

Middle of Nowhere see *The Webster Boy*

471. *The Mighty*

Maxwell Kane (Elden Henson) is a big hulking kid who lives near disabled Kevin Dillon (Kieran Culkin), a wisecracking kid who can't walk. Kevin has a degenerative condition that will end his life early. Both boys are interested in the knights of King Arthur. An article by Charles Duncan about physical education teachers in motion pictures refers to the "confusing scene" in which "[t]he mother of a child with a disability wants him to participate in physical education." Kevin's mother goes to a school administrator who explains that children with disabilities cannot participate in "athletics." (It is clear that the mother is talking about physical education class, yet the administrator apparently does not understand the difference.) The article writer also says that physical educators will wince as they watch this movie's phys ed teacher.

Miramax. US. 1998. 100m. C. *Producers:* Jane Startz, Simon Fields *Director:* Peter Chelson *Writers:* Charles Leavitt, Rodman Philbrick (novel) *Cast:* Sharon Stone, Gena Rowlands, Harry Dean Stanton, Gillian Anderson, James Gandolfini, Kieran Culkin, Elden Henson, Meat Loaf

472. *A Militant School Ma'am*

No description available.

General Film Co. US. 1915. B&W. *Director:* Tom Mix *Writer:* Edwin R. Coffin *Cast:* Leo D. Maloney, Goldie Colwell, Sid Jordan

473. *Milk and Honey*

A Jamaican woman leaves her family to work as a nanny in Canada.

Zenith/JA Film. Canada. 1988. 95m. C. *Producer:* Peter O'Brian *Directors:* Rebecca Yates, Glen Salzman *Writers:* Glen Salzman, Trevor Rhone *Cast:* Josette Simon, Lyman Ward, Djanet Sears, Fiona Reid, Leonie Forbes, Richard Mills

474. *Le Mioche (Forty Little Mothers)*

A deserted mother (Madeline Robinson) is forced to abandon her infant on the doorstep of Prosper Martin (Lucien Baroux), an honest teacher. Instead of notifying an orphanage, he takes the child with him to his new school assignment. He will be teaching at a posh finishing school for girls with high moral standards. When the girls discover his secret, they initially want to expose him. Prosper pleads the child's case, makes an appeal to the girls' maternal instincts and wins them over.

National Pictures. France. 1938. 83m. B&W. *Director:* Leonide Moguy *Writer:* Jean Guitton *Cast:* Lucien Baroux, Little Phillipe, Madeleine Robinson, Gabrielle Dorziat, Pauline Carton, Jean Perier

475. *Miracle at Moreaux*

In December 1943, three Jewish children flee Nazi-occupied France and find refuge in a Catholic school run by Sister Gabrielle (Loretta Swit). At first the other children are frightened but soon they risk their own lives to devise a plan for the Jewish children to reach freedom.

Wonder Works. US. 1986. 58m. C. *Producer:* Janice Platt *Director:* Paul Shapiro *Writers:* Jeffrey Cohen, Paul Shapiro *Cast:* Loretta Swit, Geneviéve Appleton, Milan

Cheylov, Simon Craig, Thomas Hellman, Robert Joy, Robert Kosoy, Bonfield Marcoux, Marsha Moreau, Carla Napier

476. *The Miracle Worker*

The moving real-life story of Helen Keller (Patty Duke) and her teacher Annie Sullivan (Anne Brancroft). Helen was left blind and deaf following an illness as an infant. Her tantrums disrupt her family members' lives because she has no other way to communicate. Helen's father hires Annie to live with the family and teach Helen. Annie's teaching approach involves firmness, persistence, and consistency. Annie will not let her young pupil retreat from her rigorous learning demands and challenges to help Helen fight the darkness and silence of her world.

UA. US. 1962. 106m. B&W. *Producer:* Fred Coe *Director:* Arthur Penn *Writer:* William Gibson *Cast:* Anne Bancroft, Patty Duke, Victor Jory, Inga Swenson, Andrew Prine, Beah Richards

Mirage see *Iluzija*

477. *Le Miroir A Deux Faces (The Mirror Has Two Faces)*

An unambitious schoolmaster living with his mother marries a plain woman. After six dull years together, the wife has plastic surgery to become beautiful. His indifference turns to jealousy.

Paris/Union. France. 1958. 98m. B&W. *Director:* André Cayatte *Writers:* André Cayatte, Gérard Oury *Cast:* Michèle Morgan, Bourvil, Ivan Desny, Elisabeth Manet, Gérard Oury, Sandra Milo, Sylvie, Jane Marken

The Mirror Has Two Faces see *La Miroir A Deux Faces*

478. *Miss Crusoe*

Dorothy Evans (Virginia Hammond) instructs at her aunt's girls' school. Dorothy has a yen for adventure, travels to an island in the Chesapeake Bay for vacation, helps capture a gang of crooks and falls in love.

World Film Corp. 1919. B&W. *Director:* Frank Crane *Writers:* J. Clarkson Miller, Roy S. Sensabaugh *Cast:* Virginia Hammond, Rod La Rocque, Nora Cecil

479. *Miss Mary*

A young British woman is hired as governess by a wealthy Argentine family. She sees how the upper class is crumbling and a fascist movement is preparing to take over.

New World. Argentina/US. 1986.100m. C. *Producer:* Lita Stantic *Director:* María Luisa Bemberg *Writers:* María Luisa Bemberg, Beda Docampo Feijóo, Jorge Goldenberg, Juan Bautista Stagnaro *Cast:* Julie Christie, Nacha Guevara, Eduardo Pavlovsky, Gerardo Romano, Iris Marga, Guillermo Battaglia, Barbara Bunge, Donald McIntire, Sofía Viruboff, Luisina Brando, Nora Zinsky

480. Mr. Nanny

Former wrestling star Sean Armstrong (Hulk Hogan) agrees to be a bodyguard for two spoiled children whose father is being threatened. The children scared away their previous nanny.

Entertainment. US. 1992. 84m. C. *Producer:* Bob Engelman *Director:* Michael Gottlieb *Writers:* Edward Rugoff, Michael Gottlieb *Cast:* Terry "Hulk" Hogan, Sherman Hemsley, Austin Pendelton, Robert Gorman, Madeline Zima, Raymond O'Connor, David Johansen

481. Mr. Perrin and Mr. Traill

At a stuffy British school, a handsome new master becomes very popular with the boys, creating jealousy in an older schoolmaster.

GFD/Two Cities. Great Britain. 1948. 92m. B&W. *Producer:* Alexander Galperson *Director:* Lawrence Huntington *Writers:* L.A.G. Strong, T.J. Morrison, Hugh Walpole (novel) *Cast:* Marius Goring, David Farrar, Greta Gynt, Edward Chapman, Raymond Huntley, Mary Jerrold, Finlay Currie, Ralph Truman, Lloyd Pearson, Archie Harradine, Viola Lyel, Maurice Jones, Pat Nye, Howard Douglas, Roddy Hughes

482. Mr. Topaze (I Like Money)

Schoolmaster Topaze (Peter Sellers) loses his job at a boys' school after he gave a low grade to the grandson of a baroness. He becomes involved with illegal money schemes and learns not to look at rules too hard.

TCF. Great Britain. 1961. 84m. C. *Producers:* Pierre Rouve, Dimitri de Grunwald *Director:* Peter Sellers *Writer:* Pierre Rouve *Cast:* Peter Sellers, Herbert Lom, Leo McKern, Nadia Gray, Martita Hunt, John Neville, Billie Whitelaw, Michael Gough, Joan Sims, John Le Mesurier, Michael Sellers, Pauline Shepherd

Mistress of the Mountains see *Gente Così*

483. Miwodo dashi hanbeon '80 (Love Me Once Again '80)

Kindergarten teacher Jeon Hye-yeong brings her son to the child's father, Shin-ho, to be raised. The child is unhappy at his father's house and dreams about living with his mother. Shin-ho's frustration with the boy turns to violence.

South Korea. 1980. 90m. *Director:* Jang-ho Byeon *Writer:* Bong-seung Shin *Cast:* Il-bong Yun, Yeong-ran Kim, Yun-kyeong Kim, Min-hie Kim, Jun-jae Lee

484. M'Liss

Wild and unruly M'Liss Smith (Mary Pickford) decides to get an education when handsome young schoolteacher Charles Gray (Thomas Meighan) comes to Red Gulch in 1849. Bummer Smith, M'Liss's father, is to inherit a fortune but others plot to get the money. When Bummer is murdered, a woman impersonates his widow and Charles is falsely accused of the murder. The real murderers are exposed and M'Liss gets the teacher.

Artcraft Pictures. US. 1918. B&W. *Director:* Marshall Neilan *Writers:* Frances Marion, Bret Harte (novel) *Cast:* Mary Pickford, Theodore Roberts, Thomas Meighan, Tully Marshall, Charles Ogle, Monte Blue, Winifred Greenwood, Helen Kelly, Val Paul, W.H. Brown, John Burton, Bud Post, Guy Oliver

485. *M'Liss*

The story of the small-town romance between meek and uneducated M'Liss Smith (Anne Shirley) and young schoolteacher Stephen Thorne (John Beal). Also in town are gamblers, rivals, and meddling families.

RKO. US. 1936. B&W. *Producer:* Robert Sisk *Director:* George Nicholls Jr *Writers:* Dorothy Yost, Bret Harte (novel) *Cast:* Anne Shirley, John Beal, Guy Kibbee, Douglass Dumbrille, Moroni Olsen, Frank M. Thomas, Arthur Hoyt, Barbara Pepper, Margaret Armstrong, Esther Howard, James Bush

486. *Le Monachine (The Little Nuns)*

Sister Celeste (Catherine Spaak) and Mother Rachele (Didi Perego) travel to Rome to convince the authorities to change the route of airplanes which pass directly over their convent-school (the sound wave vibrations are destroying the convent's ancient fresco of Saint Domitilla and disturbing the children).

Embassy Pictures. Italy. 1963. 100m. B&W. *Producer:* Ferruccio Brusarosco *Director:* Luciano Salce *Writers:* Franco Castellano, Giuseppe Moccia *Cast:* Catherine Spaak, Sylva Koscina, Amedeo Nazzari, Didi Perego, Umberto D'Orsi, Sandro Bruni, Annie Gorassini, Alberto Bonucci, Lando Buzzanca

487. *The Monolith Monsters*

Geologist Dave Miller (Grant Williams) and his schoolteacher-girlfriend Cathy Barrett (Lola Albright) investigate why people in their desert town are turning to stone. During a desert field trip, Ginny (Linda Scheley), one of Cathy's students, finds a black rock to take home and starts turning to stone.

Universal. US. 1957. 77m. B&W. *Producer:* Howard Christie *Director:* John Sherwood *Writers:* Norman Jolley, Robert M. Fresco *Cast:* Grant Williams, Lola Albright, Les Tremayne, Trevor Bardette, Linda Scheley, Phil Harvey, William Flaherty, Harry Jackson, Richard Cutting

488. *A Montana Schoolmarm*

In this frontier town, all the cowboys try to win the pretty schoolteacher. However, she only has eyes for the local intellectual (called Schoolboy by his rivals). When he is killed by the town bully, the males vengefully track down and lynch the murderer.

Selig Polyscope Co. US. 1908. B&W.

489. *Monte Carlo*

Three small town girls — schoolteacher Sally Roxford (Gertrude Olmsted), seamstress Hope Durant (ZaSu Pitts) and Flossie Payne (Trixie Friganza) — win a trip to Monte Carlo. Star reporter Bancroft (Arthur Hoyt) acts as their guide. While evading detectives, Tony Townsend (Lew Cody) dresses as a prince and bumps into Sally. After more mistaken identities, everything turns out well.

MGM. US. 1926. B&W. *Director:* Christy Cabanne *Writers:* Alice D.G. Miller, Carey Wilson *Cast:* Lew Cody, Gertrude Olmsted, Roy D'Arcy, Karl Dane, ZaSu Pitts, Trixie Friganza, Margaret Campbell, André Lanoy, Max Barwyn, Barbara Shears, Harry Myers, Cesare Gravina, Antonio D'Algy, Arthur Hoyt

490. *Monty Python's The Meaning of Life*

A movie composed of skits within skits. One segment involves a group of religious schoolboys who get live sex education demonstrations from the teacher and his wife.

Universal. Great Britain. 1983. 90m. C. *Producer:* John Goldstone *Director:* Terry Jones *Writers:* Graham Chapman, John Cleese, Terry Gilliam, Eric Idle, Terry Jones, Michael Palin *Cast:* Graham Chapman, John Cleese, Terry Gilliam, Eric Idle, Terry Jones, Michael Palin

491. *Moonrise*

Young Danny Hawkins (Dane Clark) accidentally kills one of his persecutors. He has been tormented since childhood because his father was hanged for murder. Danny tries hard to keep his crime hidden. Schoolteacher Gilly Johnson (Gail Russell) is in love with Danny but is troubled by his dark moody side. Theirs is an unhappy romance.

Republic. US. 1948. 90m. B&W. *Producers:* Charles F. Haas, Marshall Grant *Director:* Frank Borzage *Writer:* Charles Haas *Cast:* Dane Clark, Gail Russell, Ethel Barrymore, Allyn Joslyn, Rex Ingram, Henry Morgan, David Street, Selena Royle, Harry Carey, Jr., Irving Bacon, Lloyd Bridges, Houseley Stevenson, Phil Brown, Harry V. Cheshire, Lila Leeds

492. *The Mountain Eagle (Fear o' God)*

A young schoolteacher, fleeing to the mountains to escape the attentions of a businessman, ends up marrying a loner.

Gainsborough-Emelka. Great Britain. 1926. B&W. *Producer:* Michael Balcon *Director:* Alfred Hitchcock *Writer:* Eliot Lapworth *Cast:* Nita Naldi, Malcolm Keen, John Hamilton, Bernhard Goetzke

493. *Mrs. Doubtfire*

In San Francisco, Daniel Hillard (Robin Williams) becomes an out-of-work actor when he walks out of his job dubbing a cartoon character. His ex-wife doesn't want him to see his children because he is so unreliable. In order to be close to his children, he disguises himself as lovable Euphegenia Doubtfire, a 65-year-old nanny who speaks with a soft Scottish accent.

TCF. US. 1993. 125m. C. *Producers:* Marcia Garces Williams, Robin Williams, Mark Radcliffe *Director:* Chris Columbus *Writers:* Randi Mayem Singer, Leslie Dixon, Anne Fine (novel) *Cast:* Robin Williams, Sally Field, Pierce Brosnan, Harvey Fierstein, Polly Holiday, Lisa Jakub, Matthew Lawrence, Mara Wilson, Robert Prosky

494. *Munting tinig, Mga (Small Voices)*

Melinda (Alessandra de Rossi), an idealistic new schoolteacher and recent graduate of the University of Manilla, arrives in the poor Philippines village of Malawig to teach. She is shocked to find a corrupt school administration, unprepared, apathetic teachers, and a shortage of books and materials. The students are eager to learn but are pulled out of class to work in the fields. Facing hostility, anger and suspicion, Melinda sets out to change things. She enters her class in a regional singing contest to motivate students and their parents.

Sky Island Films. Philippines. 2002. 109m. C. *Producers:* Ray Cuerdo, Gil Portes *Director:* Gil Portes *Writers:* Adolfo Alix, Jr., Gil Portes, Senedy Que *Cast:* Alessandra de Rossi, Dexter Doria, Gina Alajar, Amy Austria, Bryan Homecillo, Pierro Rodriguez, Irma Adlawan, Keno Agaro, Sining Blanco, Noni Buencamino, Mhalouh Crisologo, Christian Galindo, Nanding Josef, Tony Mabesa, Lailani Navarro

495. *Murder on a Bridle Path*

The body of equestrienne Violet is discovered in Central Park. Police Inspector Oscar Piper (James Gleason) considers it an accidental death and is about to close the case when schoolteacher-amateur detective Hildegarde Withers (Helen Broderick) finds blood on Violet's horse. The coroner now declares it murder by blunt instrument to the head. There are many suspects and twists in this murder investigation.

RKO. US. 1936. 66m. B&W. *Directors:* William Hamilton, Edward Killy *Writers:* Dorothy Yost, Thomas Lennon, Edmund H. North, James Gow, Stuart Palmer (novel) *Cast:* James Gleason, Helen Broderick, Louise Latimer, Owen Davis, Jr., John Arledge, John Carroll, Leslie Fenton, Christian Rub, Sheila Terry, Willie Best, John Miltern, Spencer Charters, James Donlan, Gustav von Seyffertitz, Frank Reicher

496. *Murder on a Honeymoon*

While on vacation on Catalina Island, busybody schoolteacher-detective Hildegarde Withers (Edna May Oliver) becomes interested in the mysterious death of another passenger on her flight. The locals see it as death by natural causes but Miss Withers suspects murder and has Inspector Oscar Piper (James Gleason) take over the investigation.

RKO. US. 1935. 74m. B&W. *Producer:* Kenneth Macgowan *Director:* Lloyd

Corrigan *Writers:* Robert Benchley, Seton I. Miller, Stuart Palmer (novel) *Cast:* Edna May Oliver, James Gleason, Lola Lane, George Meeker, Dorothy Libaire, Harry Ellerbe, Chick Chandler, Willie Best, Leo G. Carroll, DeWitt Jennings, Spencer Charters, Arthur Hoyt, Matt McHugh, Morgan Wallace, Brooks Benedict

497. *Murder on the Blackboard*

Schoolteacher-amateur detective Hildegarde Withers (Edna May Oliver) discovers the body of music teacher Louise Halloran and informs Inspector Oscar Piper (James Gleason). By the time he arrives at the school, the body has disappeared. As suspects accumulate, someone tries to kill Hildegarde with a hatchet. They also learn that Louise was slowly poisoned.

RKO. US. 1934. 80m. B&W. *Director:* George Archainbaud *Writers:* Willis Goldbeck, Stuart Palmer (novel) *Cast:* James Gleason, Edna May Oliver, Bruce Cabot, Gertrude Michael, Tully Marshall, Frederik Vogeding, Regis Toomey, Jackie Searle, Barbara Fritchie, Gustav von Seyffertitz

498. *Music of the Heart*

Feeling worthless after being dumped by her husband, Roberta Guaspari (Meryl Streep) is encouraged to teach at an East Harlem school. At first Principal Janet Williams (Angela Bassett) is not receptive to Roberta's plan to start a violin program. Roberta is a demanding teacher who gets results. This true story follows the students' progress until the big event, a benefit concert at Carnegie Hall.

Mirimax. US. 110m. C. *Producers:* Marianne Maddalena, Walter Scheuer, Allan Miller, Susan Kaplan *Director:* Wes Craven *Writer:* Pamela Gray *Cast:* Meryl Streep, Aidan Quinn, Gloria Estefan, Angela Bassett, Jane Leeves, Cloris Leachman, Kieran Culkin, Charlie Hofheimer, Josh Pais

499. *Music Teacher*

No description available.
Pathé Frères. France. 1908. B&W.

500. *The Music Teacher*

No description available.
Motion Picture Distributors and Sales Co. US. 1910. B&W. *Cast:* Stuart Holmes

The Music Teacher see *Le Maître de Musique*

501. *Must Love Dogs*

After her husband runs off with a younger woman, forty-something pre-school teacher Sarah (Diane Lane) looks to the Internet for love. Jake, one of her first responders, is a boat builder; their meeting doesn't go well. Another is Bobby, a suave divorced father whose child attends Sarah's pre-school.

Warner. US. 2005. 98m. C. *Director:* Gary David Goldberg *Writers:* Gary David Goldberg, Claire Cook (novel) *Cast:* Diane Lane, John Cusack, Elizabeth Perkins, Christopher Plummer, Dermot Mulroney, Stockard Channing, Ali Hillis, Brad William Henke, Julie Gonzalo

502. *My Dear Miss Aldrich*

When the owner of a New York newspaper dies without a will, his only living relative, old-maid schoolteacher Martha Aldrich (Maureen O'Sullivan), inherits the paper. She turns out *not* to look like an old schoolmarm. Martha and her Aunt Lou (Edna May Oliver) head for New York where they meet Ken Morley (Walter Pidgeon), managing editor of the paper. His attitude towards women infuriates Martha and she takes a job as a reporter to prove him wrong.

MGM. US. 1937. 74m. B&W. *Director:* George B. Seitz *Writer:* Herman J. Mankiewicz *Cast:* Edna May Oliver, Maureen O'Sullivan, Walter Pidgeon, Rita Johnson, Janet Beecher

503. *My Girl*

Motherless 11-year-old Vada Sultenfuss (Anna Chlumsky) and her father Harry (Dan Aykroyd), a playful mortician, are happy. When a new assistant cosmetologist, Shelly DeVoto (Jamie Lee Curtis), is hired, she and Harry are attracted to each other and Vada becomes jealous. Vada's best friend Thomas J. (Macaulay Culkin) dies. Vade develops a crush on her new creative-writing teacher Mr. Bixler (Griffin Dunne). Harry and Shelly's relationship grows and they get married.

Columbia. US. 1991. 102m. C. *Producer:* Brian Grazer *Director:* Howard Zieff *Writer:* Laurice Elehwany *Cast:* Dan Aykroyd, Jamie Lee Curtis, Macaulay Culkin, Anna Chlumsky, Richard Mazur, Griffin Dunne, Ann Nelson, Peter Michael Goetz, Jane Hallaren

My Love Has Been Burning see *Waga koi wa moenu*

504. *My Pal Gus*

Rich businessman Dave Jennings (Richard Widmark) neglects his five-year-old son Gus. Dave's secretary enrolls Gus in the Playtime School and Dave must meet with the teacher, Lydia Marble (Joanne Dru). She explains that parents are required to participate in their child's education. Gus responds to Lydia's instruction and Dave keeps him in the school. As time passes, Dave becomes a devoted father, and his romance with Lydia becomes an engagement. Dave's ex-wife shows up claiming there was no divorce. Dave, Lydia and Gus must spend the night at his beach house. Joyce charges Dave with adultery and names Lydia as the co-respondent. The resulting bad press forces Lydia to close her school. Dave is willing to give Joyce everything to keep Gus.

TCF. US. 1952. 84m. B&W. *Producer:* Stanley Rubin *Director:* Robert Parrish *Writers:* Fay and Michael Kanin *Cast:* Richard Widmark, Joanne Dru, Audrey Totter,

George Winslow, Joan Banks, Regis Toomey, Ludwig Donath, Ann Morrison, Lisa Golm, Christopher Olsen, Robert Foulk, Mimi Gibson, Sandy Descher, Marie M. Brown, Gordon Nelson, Mabel Albertson, Jerrilyn Flannery, William Cottrell, Jay Adler, Frank Marlowe, William Dyer, Jr., Otto Forrest, James Flavin, Jonathan Hole, Frank Kruger, George Riley, Carl Betz

My Sweet Little Village see Vesnickó Má Stredisková

505. *Mystère Alexina (The Mystery of Alexina)*

In 1858, Alexina goes from a convent to teaching in a small boarding school, and becomes friends with the owner's daughter. Sexual tensions grow until they discover that Alexina is really a young man. The daughter renames him Camille and they want to wed.

Les Cinéastes Associés. France. 1985. 90m. C. *Director:* René Feret *Writers:* Jean Gruault, René Feret *Cast:* Vuillemin, Valérie Stroh, Véronique Silver, Bernard Freyd, Pierre Vial

506. *La Mystérieuse Mademoiselle C (The Mysterious Miss C)*

Eccentric Mademoiselle Charlotte is the teacher of the 6D, the worst class of St. Cécile Elementary School. With her great imagination she transforms her class and the school.

Christal Films. Canada. 2002. 108m. C. *Producers:* Jaques Bonin, Claude Veillet *Director:* Richard Ciupka *Writer:* Dominique Demers (novels) *Cast:* Marie-Chantal Perron, Gildor Roy, Éve Lemieux, Félex-Antoine Despatie, Maxime Dumontier, Émilie Cyrenne-Parent, Amélie Richer, Serge-Olivier Paquette, Jean-Philippe Beaudry Graham, Marie-Éve Ferland-Miron, Patrick Labbé, Marilyse Bourke, Dominique Pétin, Maria Verdi, Claudine Paquette, Annette Garant, Anick Lemay, Alexandra Danyluk

The Mysterious Miss C see La Mystérieuse Mademoiselle C

The Mystery of Alexina see Mystère Alexina

Naked Autumn see Les Mauvais Coups

507. *The Nanny*

Nanny (Bette Davis) has always taken care of Virgie Fane (Wendy Craig) and is now looking after her two children. Joey (William Dix), the older of the two, has been in a home for two years because he may have been involved with his sister's drowning. Joey has always claimed that Nanny was responsible. Virgie becomes ill and Aunt Pen (Jill Bennett) comes to help. Aunt Pen begins to believe Joey's story. When Aunt Pen has a heart attack, Nanny withholds her medication. Nanny, now mad, tries to kill Joey also.

ABP/Hammer. Great Britain. 1965. 93m. B&W. *Producer:* Jimmy Sangster *Director:* Seth Holt *Writers:* Jimmy Sangster, Evelyn Piper (novel) *Cast:* Bette Davis, Jill Bennett, William Dix, James Villiers, Wendy Craig, Pamela Franklin, Maurice Denham, Jack Watling, Maurice Denham, Alfred Burke, Nora Gordon, Harry Fowler

The Nanny see *La Balia*

508. *Nanny McPhee*

Nanny McPhee (Emma Thompson) comes to the rescue of widowed Mr. Brown (Colin Firth) and his seven unruly children. Nanny uses magic to control and change the children's behavior. Initially she appears as a very ugly woman, but as the children learn a lesson she becomes better looking.

Universal. US/Great Britain/France. 2005. 97m. C. *Producer:* Tim Bevan *Director:* Kirk Jones *Writer:* Emma Thompson *Cast:* Emma Thompson, Colin Firth, Kelly Macdonald, Thomas Sangster, Eliza Bennett, Jennifer Rae Daykin, Raphaël Coleman, Samuel Honywood, Holly Gibbs, Hebe Barnes, Zinnia Barnes, Angela Lansbury, Celia Imrie, Imelda Staunton, Elizabeth Berrington, Derek Jacobi, Patrick Barlow, Adam Godley, Claire Downes, Phillida Law, Freya Fumic

509. *När Seklet Var Ungt (Turn of the Century)*

Squire Munthe (Edvard Persson) heads a sugar beet farm where he deals with the problems of farm workers and imported laborers. The squire is a good man and tries to be tolerant and understanding. His daughter Hillevi (Marianne Gyllenhammar) loves schoolteacher Yngve Sjöö (Claes Thelander), who champions the farm workers.

Scandia Films. Sweden. 1944. 114m. B&W *Director:* Gunnar Olsson *Writers:* Henry Richter, Erik Zetterström, Karl Gustav Ossiannilsson (novel) *Cast:* Edvard Persson, Stina Hedberg, Marianne Gyllenhammar, Claes Thelander, Walter Sarmell, Mim Persson, Fritiof Billquist, Ivar Käge, John Norrman, Nils Nordståhl, Erik Rosén, Axel Högel, Bullan Weijden, Karl Erik Flens, Karl Nygren-Kloster

The Nasty Girl see *Das Schreckliche Mädchen*

510. *Natsukashiki fue ya taiko (Eyes, the Sea and a Ball)*

When Toru Ieda refuses to loan a friend money, the friend commits suicide. Feeling guilty, Toru takes a teaching position on a remote island where he can care for his friend's son. On the island there is no respect for education by the fisherman and their families. Toru introduces the children to volleyball and, after some resistance, everyone becomes energized by the sport. The ragtag team goes on to win the national tournament. Toru decides to stay and teach even though he promised his fiancée he would leave.

Toho Co. Japan. 1968. 115m. C. *Writer-Director:* Keisuke Kinoshita *Cast:*

Yosuke Natsuki, Mayumi Ozora, Kumeko Urabe, Kamatari Fujiwara, Yoichiro Takahashi

511. *Nattvardsgästerna (Winter Light)*

Widowed village pastor Tomas Ericsson (Gunnar Björnstrand) is devoid of faith and unloved. On a wintry Sunday, he reveals his bitter failures to his flock. After services, he attempts to help others but can only talk about his troubled relationship with God. A schoolteacher offers her love but he resists. *Nattvardsgästerna* is part of a film trilogy dealing with man's relationship with God.

Janus Films. Sweden. 1963. 81m. B&W. *Producer:* Allan Ekelund *Writer-Director:* Ingmar Bergman *Cast:* Ingrid Thulin, Gunnar Björnstrand, Max von Sydow, Allan Edwall, Kolbjörn Knudsen, Olof Thunberg, Elsa Ebbesen

Navy Heroes see *The Blue Peter*

512. *Nearer My God to Thee*

A hunchbacked schoolmaster falls for a pretty teacher. Unaware of his love, she marries a stranger who has come to the village; she is mistreated, and must raise a child by herself. Eventually the husband is shot and the schoolmaster can finally live in happiness with his love.

Hepworth. Great Britain. 1917. B&W. *Director:* Cecil M. Hepworth *Writer:* Herbert Pemberton *Cast:* Henry Edwards, Alma Taylor, A.V. Bramble, Teddy Taylor, Beryl Rhodes

513. *The Nearsighted Schoolteacher*

A schoolmaster is so engrossed with work that the children are out of control. One youngster ties a fake spider to a ruler and scares the teacher.

American Mutoscope Co. US. 1898. B&W.

514. *Neighbors*

Ruth is loved by Paul Harding, but because she is only a schoolteacher, Paul's mother forbids their marriage. The mother also disapproves of the friendship between her young daughter Effie and Ruth's sister Clarissa. After Clarissa saves Effie from drowning, Mrs. Hardy allows the marriage between Paul and Ruth.

World Film Corp. US. 1918. B&W. *Director:* Frank Crane *Writers:* Harry O. Hoyt, Hamilton Smith, Maravene Thompson *Cast:* Madge Evans, Johnny Hines, Violet Palmer, J.A. Furey, Maxine Elliott Hicks, Mathilde Brundage, Herbert Pattee, Kitty Johnson, Frank Beamish, Charles Hartley, Anthony Merlo

515. *Neokonchennaya Pyesa dlya Mekhanicheskogo Pianin (Unfinished Piece for Mechanical Piano)*

Schoolteacher Platanov is married to simple Sasha; complications ensue.

Mosfilm. Soviet Union. 1977. 100m. C. *Director:* Nikita Mikhalkov *Writers:* Aleksander Adabashyan, Nikita Mikhalkov *Cast:* Alexander Kalyagin, Elena Solovel, Eugenia Glushenko, Antonina Shuranova, Yuri Bogatyrev, Nikita Mikhalkov

516. *Never Take Sweets from a Stranger*

Jean Carter (Janina Faye) is the nine-year-old daughter of the town's newly-appointed school principal, Peter Carter (Patrick Allen). She and her friend Lucille are asked to dance nude for candy. Peter is outraged and files a complaint but is told that the accused family has more standing in the community and that their lawyer will show Jean no mercy. The man is acquitted and Peter attacks him. The decision forces the family to move out of town, but Jean meets the accused man once again.

Hammer. Great Britain. 1960. 81m. B&W. *Producer:* Anthony Hinds *Director:* Cyril Frankel *Writer:* John Hunter *Cast:* Gwen Watford, Patrick Allen, Felix Aylmer, Niall MacGinnis, Bill Nagy, Janina Faye, Macdonald Parke, Michael Gwynn, Frances Green, Alison Leggatt, Robert Arden, Cal McCord, Estelle Brody

517. *Never Trust a Gambler*

Virtuous schoolmarm Virginia (Cathy O'Donnell) loyally protects her ex-husband, a gambler turned murderer, until a police detective rescues her.

Columbia. US. 1951. 79m. B&W. *Producers:* Louis B. Appleton, Jr., Monty Shaff *Director:* Ralph Murphy *Writers:* Jesse L. Lasky, Jr., Jerome Odlum *Cast:* Dane Clark, Cathy O'Donnell, Tom Drake, Jeff Corey, Myrna Dell, Rhys Williams

518. *The New Boy*

A schoolboy tricks his tormentors.
DFSA. Great Britain. 1914. B&W. *Director:* Dave Aylott

519. *The New Schoolmarm of Green River*

No description available.
General Film/Essanay Film. US. 1913. B&W. *Director:* Gilbert M. "Broncho Billy" Anderson *Cast:* Fred Church, Eleanor Blevins, Harry Keenan, Gilbert M. "Broncho Billy" Anderson

520. *The New Schoolteacher*

The pupils of country schoolteacher Professor Fibble (Charles "Chic" Sale) play pranks on him until he wins their admiration by rescuing one from the burning schoolhouse. He also wins over the girl.

C.C. Burr Pictures. US. 1924. B&W. *Producer:* C.C. Burr *Director:* Gregory La Cava *Cast:* Doris Kenyon, Charles "Chic" Sale, Mickey Bennett, Russell Griffin, Freddy Strange, Kent Raymond, Henry O'Connor, Edward Weisman, Edward Quinn, Billy Quinn, Buddy Raynor, Paul Jachia, Fred Gorman, Bert Gorman,

Warren Gorman, Polly Archer, Robert Bentley, May Kitson, Harlan Knight, Helen Gerould, Leslie King

521. The New Teacher

Society girl Constance Bailey (Shirley Mason) becomes a schoolteacher on New York's Lower East Side. Her fiancé Bruce (Allan Forrest) thinks she is in Europe. When he learns the truth, he joins the police force to be near her. Bruce keeps rescuing her and finally convinces her that she needs a husband.

Fox Film Corp. US. 1922. B&W. *Producer:* William Fox *Director:* Joseph Franz *Writers:* Dorothy Yost, Margaret Elizabeth Sangster (novel) *Cast:* Shirley Mason, Allan Forrest, Earl Metcalf, Otto Hoffman, Ola Norman, Pat Moore, Kate Price

The New Teacher see Uchitel

522. Nicholas Nickleby

In this Dickens tale, young teacher Nicholas Nickleby (Derek Bond) is hounded by his evil uncle. Nicholas goes from adventure to adventure. The story has been filmed many times.

GFD. Great Britain. 1947. 105m. B&W. *Producer:* Michael Balcon *Director:* Alberto Cavalcanti *Writers:* John Dighton, Charles Dickens (novel) *Cast:* Derek Bond, Cedric Hardwicke, Alfred Drayton, Sybil Thorndike, Stanley Holloway, James Hayter, Sally Ann Howes, Jill Balcon, Cyril Fletcher, Fay Compton, Bernard Miles, Mary Merrall, Cathleen Nesbitt, Vera Pearce, Athene Seyler, Cecil Ramage, George Relph, Emrys Jones, Aubrey Woods, James Hayter, Vida Hope, Roddy Hughes, Timothy Bateson, Frederick Burtwell, Laurence Hanray, Michael Shepley, Drusilla Willis, Guy Rolfe, Eliot Makeham, Hattie Jacques, John Salew

523. The Night Has Eyes (Terror House)

Two schoolteachers, British Marian Ives (Joyce Howard) and man-hungry American Doris (Tucker McGuire), go to the Yorkshire moors on holiday. They lose their way on the path when it starts raining hard. This is the same area where, in the previous year, another schoolteacher had gotten lost. They end up at the isolated cottage of musician Stephen Deremid (James Mason), shell-shocked since World War I. Doris disappears and Marian starts having feelings for Stephen. But could he be responsible for the disappearances?

ABPC. Great Britain. 1942. 79m. B&W. *Producer:* John Argyle *Director:* Leslie Arliss *Writers:* John Argyle, Alan Kennington *Cast:* James Mason, Joyce Howard, Wilfred Lawson, Mary Clare, Tucker McGuire, John Fernald

524. The Night of the Iguana

T. Lawrence Shannon (Richard Burton), a defrocked clergyman, is now a bus guide on Mexican cheap tours. His new group consists of complaining female American teachers. He is pursued by a young vixen, the man-hungry hotel owner, and another spinster. The leader of the schoolteachers, Judith Fellowes (Grayson Hall), is bent on making his life difficult because of the vixen's interest in him.

MGM. US. 1964. 125m. B&W. *Producers*: Ray Stark, John Huston *Director*: John Huston *Writers:* Anthony Veiller, John Huston, Tennesse Williams (play) *Cast*: Richard Burton, Ava Gardner, Deborah Kerr, Sue Lyon, Grayson Hall, Cyril Delevanti, Mary Boylan, Gladys Hill, Billie Matticks, Fidelmar Duran, Roberto Leyva, C. G. Kim, Eloise Hardt, James Ward

525. *The Nightcomers*

The sado-masochistic affair between governess Miss Jessel (Stephanie Beacham) and gardener Peter Quint (Marlon Brando) has a very negative effect on orphans Flora and Miles, and causes the children to murder them. A prequel to the film *The Innocents*.

Avco-Embassy. Great Britain. 1971. 96m. C. *Producer-Director:* Michael Winner *Writer:* Michael Hastings *Cast:* Marlon Brando, Stephanie Beacham, Thora Hird, Harry Andrews, Verna Harvey, Christopher Ellis, Anna Palk

526. *Nighthawks*

London schoolteacher Jim (Ken Robertson) cruises bars by night and teaches during the daytime. He makes no attempt to conceal his gay lifestyle from his colleagues nor does he announce it. A few punks in Jim's class taunt him with rumors that he is gay. Jim handles the situation calmly and well.

Washburgh/Four Corner. Great Britain. 1979. 113m. C. *Director:* Ron Peck *Writer-Producers:* Ron Peck, Paul Hallam *Cast:* Ken Robertson, Tony Westrope, Rachel Nicholas James, Maureen Dolan, Stuart Craig Turton, Clive Peters, Robert Merrick, Frank Dilbert, Peter Radnall, Derek Jarman, Susan Lloyd

527. *Nije Nego*

Students get a chance to tell their side of things during a television show being filmed at their school. The girls are interested in themselves and boys are involved with sports and girls. In one scene, a teacher is depicted as a lothario on the blackboard, and there is great concern about finding the culprit.

Yugoslavia. 1978. 97m. C. *Producer:* Petar Sobajic *Director:* Mica Milosevic *Writers:* Mica Milosevic, Sinisa Pavic *Cast:* Velimir "Bata" Zivojinovic, Nikola Simic, Marko Todorovic, Ljiljana Krstic, Pavle Vujisic, Ruzica Sokic, Danilo "Bata" Stojkovic, Mirjana Kodzic, Radmila Radovanovic, Roberta Ataide

528. *Nijushi no hitomi (Twenty-Four Eyes)*

The film follows the lives of a teacher and her students over a twenty-year period, from 1928 to just after World War II in Japan. A very modern, free-thinking teacher, Hisako Oishi (Hideko Takamine), takes a position in a poor island village elementary school. At first her students don't know what to think about Miss Oishi but they soon love her. As the years pass, everything is ruined by war, poverty and tradition. After World War II ends, teacher and students reminisce about those who died in the war.

Shochiku Kinema. Japan. 1954. 154m. B&W. *Director:* Keisuke Kinoshita *Writers:* Keisuke Kinoshita, Sakae Tsuboi (novel) *Cast:* Hideki Goko, Hideko Takamine, Yukio Watanabe, Makoto Miyagawa, Takero Terashita, Kunio Sato, Hiroko Ishii, Yasuko Koike, Setsuko Kusano, Kaoko Kase, Yumiko Tanabe, Ikuko Kambara, Hiroko Uehara, Hitobumi Goko, Shirô Watanabe

529. *Nijushi no hitomi (Children on the Island)*

This is almost a scene-by-scene re-filming of the 1954 *Nijushi no hitomi*. The 1954 and the 1987 films are known by different American titles.

Shochiku Kinema Kenkyû-jo Japan. 1987. 129m. C. *Director:* Yoshitaka Asama *Writers:* Keisuke Kinoshita, Sakae Tsuboi (novel) *Cast:* Yûko Tanaka, Tetsuya Takeda, Sumie Saski, Misako Konno, Taro Kawano, Naoko Nozawa, Miho Takagi, Tatsuo Matsumura, Kiyoshi Atsumi

530. *No Kidding*

David (Leslie Phillips) and Catherine (Geraldine McEwan) inherit Chartham Place, a large country home, and convert it into a camp for the deprived children of the rich.

GHW Productions. Great Britain. 1960. 86m. B&W. *Producer:* Peter Rogers *Director:* Gerald Thomas *Writers:* Norman Hudis, Robin Estridge, Verily Anderson (novel) *Cast:* Leslie Phillips, Geraldine McEwan, Julia Lockwood, Noel Purcell, Irene Handl, Joan Hickson, June Jago, Cyril Raymond, Esma Cannon, Alan Gifford, Sydney Tafler, Eric Pohlmann, Patricia Jessel, Joy Shelton, Christopher Witty, Martin Stephens, Francesca Annis, Mike Sarne, Earl Cameron

No Life King see No Raifu Kingh

No More Sorrow see Seulpeumeun ije geuman

531. *No Raifu Kingh (No Life King)*

Japanese schoolboys are addicted to their favorite video game, "No Life King." These children are estranged from the world, and their technological society allowed it to occur. The colorless regimented school life is compared with the bright and non-structured computer game. School administrators are aware of the game's addictive quality but they are susceptible to it themselves. When the students have questions in class, they are to communicate electronically by using computers.

Kitty Video. Japan. 1989. 106m. C. *Producers:* Taketo Niitsu, Yutaka Okada *Director:* Jun Ichikawa *Writers:* Hiroaki Jinno, Seikou Ito (novel) *Cast:* Ryo Takayama, Neko Saito, Nobuo Nakamura, Issei Ogata, Saeko Suzuki

532. None Shall Escape

Father Warecki (Henry Travers) is the first witness to tell the story of Wilhelm Grimm (Alexander Knox) before a Tribunal of War Crimes after World War II. He recalls the spring of 1919 when Wilhelm, a crippled German soldier, returned from World War I and resumed teaching in a small Polish village. Bitter, he turned to the Nazi ideology. Wilhelm was forced to leave the village after he violated a student. He rose in the Nazi party and returned to the village as a commandant. His reign was marked by terror. For example, Rabbi Levin (Richard Hale) died for his convictions rather than suffer under Nazis. Wilhelm ordered Jewish people to be herded into cattle cars for deportation to concentration camps; the rabbi urged them to resist but was shot and killed. Person after person testifies, telling Wilhelm's whole evil story.

Columbia. US. 1944. 85m. B&W. *Producer*: Samuel Bischoff *Director*: André De Toth *Writer*: Lester Cole *Cast*: Marsha Hunt, Alexander Knox, Henry Travers, Erik Rolf, Richard Crane, Dorothy Morris, Richard Hale, Ruth Nelson, Kurt Kreuger, Shirley Mills, Frank Jaquet

Not One Less see *Yi ge dou bun eng shao*

533. *Notes of a Scandal*

Middle-aged teacher Barbara (Judi Dench) discovers that the new teacher (Cate Blanchett) at St. George's Sheba is having an affair with one of her 15-year-old pupils. And the friendship between the two women turns out to be not what it seems.

TCF. Great Britain. 2006. 92m. C. *Producers*: Scott Rudin, Robert Fox *Director:* Richard Eyre *Writers:* Patrick Marber, Zoë Heller (novel) *Cast:* Judi Dench, Cate Blanchett, Bill Nighy, Andrew Simpson

534. *The Nun and the Sergeant*

During the Korean War, Sergeant McGrath (Robert Webber) takes men from the brig on a dangerous mission. Behind enemy lines they meet a nun teacher (Anna Sten) and a group of Korean schoolgirls whose bus has been destroyed by a bomb. When it becomes apparent that the nun will die of her leg wound, McGrath permits the schoolgirls to take her to a nearby village.

UA. US. 1962. 74m. B&W. *Producer*: Eugene Frenke *Director*: Franklin Adreon *Writer*: Don Cerveris *Cast*: Robert Webber, Anna Sten, Leo Gordon, Hari Rhodes, Robert Easton, Dale Ishimoto, Linda Wong, Linda Ho, Tod Windsor, Valentin de Vargas

The Oak see *Balanta*

535. Obecná Skola (Elementary School)

In 1945 Czechoslovakia, ten-year-old Eda goes to school with devilish boys who caused their previous teacher to have a nervous breakdown. The new teacher is a tough disciplinarian who doesn't mind using corporal punishment. Eda brags that he played a role in the resistance to the Nazis. The other boys like him but he does have one problem in that he is a ladies' man.

José Esteban Alenda Dist. Czechoslovakia. 1991. 100m. C. *Director:* Jan Sverák *Writer:* Zdenek Sverák *Cast:* Jan Triska, Zdenek Sverák, Libuse Safránková, Daniela Kolárová, Václay Jakoubek, Radoslav Budác, Eva Holubová

536. The Object of My Affection

We first see George Hanson (Paul Rudd) at a posh private school in Manhattan, directing a musical adaptation of *The Little Mermaid* performed by first graders. The few scenes with George as a teacher show him to be gentle, creative and engaging with the children. Pregnant Nina's (Jennifer Aniston) daughter attends the school. Nina and George are good friends who go dancing, converse, and share ice cream. After George is jilted, Nina offers him a place to live.

TCF. US. 1998. 110m. C. *Producer:* Laurence Mark *Director:* Nicholas Hytner *Writers:* Wendy Wasserstein, Stephen McCauley (novel) *Cast:* Paul Rudd, Jennifer Aniston, Alan Alda, Allison Janney, Tim Daly, John Pankow, Nigel Hawthorne, Steve Zahn

Obsessed see The Late Edwina Black

537. Odna (Alone)

A schoolteacher (Yelena Kuzmina) in love with a young man in Moscow is sent to a village in the far north. She feels that she must accept what is offered to her even if she doesn't want to go. The Soviet village chairman is indifferent to her and the corrupt medicine man does not care for her. When she takes sides against the medicine man and declares she is going to report him, he has her abandoned in the white cold wilderness. Miraculously she is rescued and flown out.

Amkino Corporation. Soviet Union. 1931. 80m. B&W. *Producer:* Soyuzkino *Writer-Director:* Grigori Kozintsev, Leonid Trauberg *Cast:* Yelena Kuzmina, Pyotr Sobolevsky, Sergei Gerasimov, Yanina Zhejmo, Boris Chirkov, Mariya Babanova, Liu-Sian Van

The Official Story see La Historia Oficial

The Official Version see La Historia Oficial

538. Old Bones of the River

Professor Benjamin Tibbetts (Will Hay), representative of the Teaching and Welfare Institution for the Reformation of Pagans, is to bring education to the

African natives. But someone has beaten him to it: The students know more about math and geography than their teacher! Tibbetts takes it on himself to collect taxes from the villages. He meets two men operating an old paddle-steamer and they all find themselves heading straight into a native uprising.

GFD/Gainsborough. Great Britain. 1938. 90m. B&W. *Producer:* Edward Black *Director:* Marcel Varnel *Writers:* Marriott Edgar, Val Guest, J.O.C. Orton *Cast:* Will Hay, Moore Marriott, Graham Moffatt, Robert Adams, Jack Livesey, Jack London, Wyndham Goldie, Western Brothers

539. *Old Gringo*

Cross paths in Chihuahua are Harriet Winslow (Jane Fonda), a prim, repressed schoolteacher fleeing her lonesome past; Tomas Arroyo (Jimmy Smits), a handsome young general in Pancho Villa's Mexican army; and old gringo (Gregory Peck), an American writer who has cut all ties with his family. Harriet is sexually awakened by her two suitors, who develop a friendship between themselves. The old gringo is writer Ambrose Bierce.

Columbia Tristar. US. 1989. 120m. C. *Producer:* Lois Bonfiglio *Director:* Luis Puenzo *Writers:* Aida Bortnik, Luis Puenzo, Carlos Fuentes (novel) *Cast:* Jane Fonda, Gregory Peck, Jimmy Smits, Patricio Contreras, Jenny Gago, Gabriela Roel, Sergio Calderon

540. *Old Mother Riley, Headmistress*

Tart-tongued Irish washerwoman Mother Riley (Arthur Lucan) is appointed the headmistress of a girls' school.

Renown. Great Britain. 1950. 75m. B&W. *Producer:* Harry Reynolds *Director:* John Harlow *Writers:* John Harlow, Ted Kavanagh *Cast:* Arthur Lucan, Kitty McShane, Willer Neal, Cyril Smith, C. Denier Warren, Enid Hewitt, Paul Sheridan, Harry Herbert, Ossie Waller, Jenny Mathot, Myrette Morven, Ethel Royale, Bill Stephens, Patricia Owens

541. *Ole Dole Doff (Eeny Meeny Miny Moe)*

Teacher Martensson (Per Oscarsson) struggles in vain to have a rapport with his students. He has qualms about his love-hate relationship with his pupils, over whom he has lost all control. He is harassed and as a teacher he is forced to carry out the rules of society while secretly siding with the kids against himself.

Svensk Filmindustri. Sweden. 1968. 116m. B&W. *Director:* Jan Troseil *Writers:* Jan Troseil, Bengt Forslund, C'as Engstrom *Cast:* Per Oscarsson, Kerstin Tidelius, Ann-Marie Gyllenspetz, Harriet Forsseli, Psort Ebersol, Georg Oddner, Psort Sjostrand, Catharina Edleidt, Bo Malmqvist

542. *Olivia (Pit of Loneliness)*

In the 1880s, Olivia, an English girl, attends a French boarding school run by two sisters, Mademoiselle Julie (Edwige Feuillère) and Mademoiselle Cara (Simone

Simon). In this fashionable finishing school there is rivalry among several for the attention of the handsome headmistress, Julie. Olivia is drawn to Julie, creating problems.

Arthur Davis Assoc. France. 1950. 88m. B&W. *Director:* Jacqueline Audry *Writers:* Colette Audry, Pierre Laroche *Cast:* Edwige Feuillère, Simone Simon, Claire Olivia, Yvonne De Bray, Suzanne Dehelly, Lesly Meynard, Rita Roanda, Marie-Claire Olivia, Marina De Berg, Lesly Meynard, Danielle Delorme

The Omniscient see *Sarvasakshi*

543. *One Big Affair*

American schoolteachers Jean Harper (Evelyn Keyes), Hilda Bowers (Mary Anderson) and Miss Marple (Connie Gilchrist) are on a bus tour of Mexico. Jean is looking for adventure and love and finds both. She runs into American lawyer Jimmy Donovan (Dennis O'Keefe) and after all the chaos is cleared up, Jimmy and Jean intend to marry.

UA. US. 1952. 80m. B&W. *Producer:* Benedict Bogeaus *Director:* Peter Godfrey *Writers:* Leo Townsend, Francis Swann, George Bricker *Cast:* Evelyn Keyes, Dennis O'Keefe, Mary Anderson, Connie Gilchrist, Gus Schilling, José Torvay, Andrew Veláquez, Thurston Hall

One Way or Another see *De Cierta Manera*

544. *The Opposite of Sex*

The story revolves around gay schoolteacher Bill (Martin Donovan) and his half-sister, the selfish, wicked Dedee (Christina Ricci). Bill is the kind of schoolteacher who, when finding rude graffiti about himself on a bathroom wall, corrects the grammar. Another important character is lonely spinster-schoolteacher Lucia (Lisa Kudrow), sister of Bill's previous lover (who died from AIDS). Dedee is rotten to the core and steals Bill's money and boyfriend. A student's false accusations cause Bill to lose his teaching position.

Sony Pictures Classics. US. 1998. 100m. C. *Producers:* David Kirkpatrick, Michael Besman *Writer-Director:* Don Roos *Cast:* Christina Ricci, Martin Donovan, Lisa Kudrow, Lyle Lovett, Johnny Galecki, Ivan Sergei, William Scott Lee

545. *Osenny Marafon (Autumn Marathon)*

In Leningrad, a mild-mannered English language teacher (Oleg Basilashvili) must deal with his wife, his mistress, students and snoopy neighbors.

Mosfilm. Soviet Union. 1979. 90m. C. *Director:* Georgy Danelia *Writer:* Alexander Volodin *Cast:* Oleg Basilashvili, Natalia Gundareva, Marina Neyelova, Evgeni Leonov

546. Oss Emellan (Close to the Wind)

An unsuccessful artist with three children devotes his life to nonconformity, while his schoolteacher-wife supports the family.

Omega Film. Sweden. 1969. 110m. C. *Director:* Stellan Olsson *Writers:* Stellan Olsson, Per Oscarsson *Cast:* Per Oscarsson, Bärbel Oscarsson, Lina Oscarsson, Boman Oscarsson, Maria Oscarsson, Beppe Wolgers, Christina Johansson

547. Otkradnati Ochi (Stolen Eyes)

This story of the impossible love between Muslim Bulgarian-Turk schoolteacher Ayten (Vesela Kazakova) and a non-Muslim Bulgarian man, Ivan (Valeri Yordanov). Ivan is responsible for the official seals, which are used when forcibly changing ethnic Turk names to Bulgarian ones. Ayten tries to steal the seals thinking that she can slow down the ethnic genocide. He must rename her or face the consequences. They later meet again when Ayten's small child is killed by a special force team led by Ivan. Ivan and Ayten end up in the same hospital and accept their differences.

Bulgaria/Turkey. 2005. 110m. C. *Producers:* Kerem Altug, Kiril Kinlov, Galina Toneva, Atilla Yucer *Director:* Radoslav Spassov *Writers:* Radoslav Spassov, Neri Terzieva *Cast:* Vesela Kazakova, Valeri Yordanov, Nejat Isler, Itzhak Finzi, Iliana Kitanova, Stoyan Aleksiev, Maria Kavardjikova, Maria Statoulova, Deyan Donokov, Djoko Rosic, AnaniYavashev, Veliko Stoianov, Nikolai Urumow, Veselin Rankov, Regel Vulchanov

Our Twisted Hero see *Urideului ilgeuleojin yeongung*

Out in the Open see *Aire Libre*

548. Outback

A naïve young Australian teacher (Gary Bond) is poorly prepared for his new position in the outback. The community is composed of amoral, primitive people who care nothing about education or propriety.

NIT/Group W. Australia. 1970. 109m. C. *Producer:* George Willoughby *Director:* Ted Kotcheff *Writers:* Evan Jones, Kenneth Cook (novel) *Cast:* Gary Bond, Donald Pleasence, Chips Rafferty

549. The Outcasts of Poker Flat

In 1850 California, physician-turned-gambler John Oakhurst (Preston Foster) delivers a baby girl whose mother dies. He keeps the girl, Luck, and raises her with his partner, the Duchess (Margaret Irving). Eight years later, Poker Flat is growing and soon a reform-minded Reverend Sam Woods (Van Heflin) and schoolteacher Helen Colby (Jean Muir) arrive. John sends tomboy Luck (Virginia Weidler) to live with Helen and attend school. John forces outlaws to contribute money to the church building fund to slow down the reform movement. John is shot and seriously wounded after arguing with Helen about Luck. Helen agrees to marry Woods but changes her mind when Luck tells her that John loves her. After recovering from his wound, John romances Helen. The Duchess is upset about John's pacifism and confronts him. John shoots two outlaws and is driven out of town by a vigilante group. Helen joins John and the Duchess in exile. When their horses are stolen, they end up in a deserted cabin. Luck and Woods arrive to find the Duchess frozen to death, Helen unconscious and John's corpse with a suicide note.

RKO. US. 1937. 72m. B&W. *Producer:* Robert Sisk *Director:* Christy Cabanne *Writers:* John Twist, Harry Segall *Cast:* Preston Foster, Jean Muir, Van Heflin, Virginia Weidler, Margaret Irving, Frank M. Thomas, Si Jenks, Dick Elliott, Al St. John, Bradley Page, Richard Lane, Monte Blue, Billy Gilbert, Dudley Clements

The Outsider see *The Guinea Pig*

550. *The Pacifier*

Navy SEAL Shane Wolf's (Vin Diesel) new assignment has him protecting five children from enemies of their deceased father, a government scientist. This tough guy is now a nanny. He becomes acquainted with school principal Claire Fletcher (Lauren Graham) and vice principal Murney (Brad Garrett). Shane finds himself attracted to Claire.

Buena Vista Pictures. Canada/US. 2005. 95m. C. *Producers:* Gary Barber, Roger Birnbaum, Jonathan Glickman *Director:* Adam Shankman *Writers:* Thomas Lennon, Ben Garant *Cast:* Vin Diesel, Lauren Graham, Faith Ford, Brittany Snow, Max Thieriot, Chris Potter, Carol Kane, Brad Garrett, Morgan York

551. *Pagan Love Song*

The story of the romance of an ex-teacher, in Tahiti to collect property left him, and a local girl.

MGM. US. 1950. 76m. C. *Producer:* Arthur Freed *Director:* Robert Alton *Writers:* Robert Nathan, Jerry Davis *Cast:* Esther Williams, Howard Keel, Rita Moreno, Minna Gombell

552. *Pagine Chiuse (Closed Pages)*

When a child's parents get a divorce, he is sent to a parochial school. Reserved, silent and stubborn, he incurs the wrath of a priest-teacher who refuses communion to the boy. The boy's family and teachers at the school fail him.

Italy. 1969. 90m. B&W. *Writer-Director:* Gianni Da Campo *Cast:* Giorgio Da Ros, Silvano De Munari, Matrina Gazziola, Duilio Laurenti, Luigi Nadali

553. *Paolo Barca, Maestro Elementare, Praticamente Nudista (Schoolteacher and Weekend Nudist)*

A sophisticated mama's boy from Milan goes to teach in an elementary school in Sicily.

Italy. 1974. 112m. C. *Director:* Flavio Mogherini *Cast:* Renato Pozzetto, Magali Noël, Janet Agren, Stefano Satta Flores, Liana Trouche, Miranda Martino

554. Paper Tiger

A meek English schoolmaster (David Niven) hires himself out as the tutor to the son of the Japanese ambassador (Toshiro Mifune) to a southeastern Asian country. When the boy and the tutor are kidnapped by terrorists, the tutor must become a hero.

Fox-Rank. Great Britain. 1975. 99m. C. *Producer:* David Anderson *Director:* Ken Annakin *Writer:* Jack Davies *Cast:* David Niven, Toshiro Mifune, Hardy Kruger, Ando, Ivan Desny, Irene Tsu, Ronald Fraser, Miko Taka, Jeff Corey, Patricia Donahue, Kurt Christian, Jeanine Siniscal, Gatz Shariff

555. Pardon My French

Boston schoolteacher Elizabeth Rockwell (Merle Oberon) sails to the French Riviera to claim her inheritance, her grandfather's castle. She has decided to live in the castle and is expecting to lead an exciting life, quite different from that of a schoolteacher. She quickly learns that squatters have moved into the castle.

On behalf of the many other squatters, Paul Rencourt (Paul Henreid) welcomes her to her own castle. Paul then introduces a few of the residents. After various complications, Elizabeth realizes that she has become attached to the residents and tells everyone they can stay, as she does with Paul.

UA. US/France. 1952. 82m. B&W. *Producers:* Peter Cusick, André Sarrut *Director:* Bernard Vorhaus *Cast:* Paul Henreid, Merle Oberon, Paul Bonifas, Dora Doll, Maximilienne, Lauria Daryl, Jim Gérald, Lucien Callamand, Alexandre Rignault, Victor Mérenda, Martial Rèbe, Gilberte Defoucault, Marina, Gérard Rosset, Albert Culazz, Nicole Monnin, André Aversa

Pardon My Trunk see *Buongiorno, Elefante!*

Passion for Life see *L'École Buissonnière*

556. Passionate Summer

In a Jamaican school, a dedicated teacher tries to inspire his students, especially one troubled young girl. His tumultuous personal life involves a flight attendant and the headmaster's wife. When the girl sees the teacher and the headmaster's wife, she runs into a hurricane and her death.

Briar. Great Britain. 1958. 104m. C. *Producers:* Kenneth Harper, George Willoughby *Director:* Rudolph Cartier *Writers:* Joan Henry, Richard Mason (novel) *Cast:* Virginia McKenna, Bill Travers, Yvonne Mitchell, Alexander Knox, Ellen Barrie, Carl Mohner, Guy Middleton, Bruce Pitt, Martin Stephens

The Patriot see *Die Patriotin*

557. Die Patriotin (The Patriot)

Gabi Teichert (Hannelore Hoger), a Frankfurt history teacher, tries new ways to present Germany's past to the new generation.

The Other Cinema. West Germany. 1979. 120m. B&W/C. *Writer-Producer-Director:* Alexander Kluge *Cast:* Hannelore Hoger, Alfred Edel, Alexander von Eschwege, Hans Heckel, Beate Holle, Kurt Jürgens, Dieter Mainka, Willi Münch

558. Pay It Forward

Seventh grader Trevor McKinney (Haley Joel Osment) is given an assignment by his teacher Eugene Simonet (Kevin Spacey). Eugene, a man with a burn-scarred face, is a mental wreck. The assignment is to think of something that will change the world. Trevor comes up with pyramidal good deeds. When one of Trevor's good deeds brings a homeless man into the house, Trevor's alcoholic mother Arlene (Helen Hunt) storms to the school to confront Mr. Simonet.

Warner. US. 2000. 122m. C. *Director:* Mimi Leder *Writers:* Leslie Dixon, Catherine Ryan Hyde (novel) *Cast:* Kevin Spacey, Helen Hunt, Haley Joel Osment, Jay Mohr, Jon Bon Jovi, James Caviezel, Angie Dickinson, David Ramsey, Gary Werntz

559. The Penguin Pool Murder

Stockbroker Gerald Parker's body is found in the penguin tank at the local aquarium. Inspector Oscar Piper (James Gleason) is on the case with two suspects: the man's wife and her boyfriend. Schoolteacher Hildegarde Withers (Edna May Oliver) takes an interest in the case. A memorable quote from Miss Withers: "I'm a schoolteacher, and I might have done wonders with you if I'd caught you young enough."

RKO. US. 1932. 69m. B&W. *Director:* George Archainbaud *Writers:* Willis Goldbeck, Stuart Palmer (novel) *Cast:* Edna May Oliver, James Gleason, Mae Clarke, Robert Armstrong, Donald Cook, Edgar Kennedy, Clarence H. Wilson, James Donlan, Gustav Von Seyffertitz, Mary Mason, Rochelle Hudson, Guy Usher, Joe Hermano, William Le Maire

Peppermint Soda see *Diabolo Menthe*

560. The Perfect Nanny

Fresh from a mental institution where she was recovering from a suicide attempt, Andrea McBride (Tracy Nelson) is hired as a nanny by widower James Lewis (Bruce Boxleitner), a wealthy, handsome surgeon. Could this "perfect nanny" be responsible for the series of mysterious deaths that start soon after her hiring?

York Entertainment. US. 2000. 90m. C. *Producers:* Pierre David, Noël A. Zanitsch *Director:* Rob Malenfant *Cast:* Dana Barron, Scott Terra, Katherine Helmond, Darren Gray Ward, Cindy Guyer, Bruce Boxleitner

561. *Péril en la Demeure (Death in a French Garden)*

Music teacher David (Christphe Malavoy) is seduced by a pupil's mother and drawn into murder, deception, and voyeurism.

Artificial Eye/Gaumont. France. 1985. 101m. C. *Producer:* Emmanuel Schlumberger *Director:* Michel Deville *Writers:* Michel Deville, Rosalind Damamme, Rene Belletto (novel) *Cast:* Michel Piccoli, Nicole Garcia, Anemone, Christophe Malavoy, Richard Bohringer, Anaïs Jeanneret, Jean-Claude Jay

562. *Pervyy Uchitel (The First Teacher)*

In 1923, an ex-Red Army officer opens a new school in a small village. Gradually he wins over the hostile community but he falls in love with a beautiful 16-year-old girl.

Kirghizfilm/Mosfilm. Soviet Union. 1965. 98m. B&W. *Director:* Andrei Mikhalkov-Konchalovsky *Writers:* Chingiz Aytmatov, Boris Dobrodeyev *Cast:* Bolot Beishenaliev, Natalia Arinbasarova, Idris Nogaibayev, D. Kouioukova, M. Kychtobaiev

563. *Peter Pan*

The story of Peter Pan, who never grows up and lives in Never Never Land. The three Darling children go to the land, encountering the villainous Captain Hook. The children's nanny is Nana the dog. There is also a hungry crocodile that scares the captain.

Walt Disney. US. 1953. 76m. C. Animated. *Producer:* Walt Disney *Directors:* Hamilton Luske, Clyde Geronimi, Wilfred Jackson *Writers:* Ted Sears, Bill Peet, Joe Rinaldi, Erdman Penner, Winston Hibler, Milt Banta, Ralph Wright, Sir James Barrie (play) *Voices:* Bobby Driscoll, Kathryn Beaumont, Hans Conried, Bill Thompson, Heather Angel, Paul Collins, Tommy Luske, Candy Candido, Tom Conway

564. *Les Petits (The Children)*

In a French middle-class boarding school reside two seven-year-old sweethearts. When the romance is discovered the heads of the school expel the sinners, making a mountain out of a molehill. The little boy learns that his widowed father (who rarely visits) is to remarry. The boy wanders toward the river.

France. 1937. B&W. *Directors:* Constant Remy, Alfred Machard *Cast:* Constant Remy, E. Roncier, Jeanne Boitel, C. Borelli, Saturnin Fabre, Teddy Dargy, Alice Tissot, M. Donnio

565. *Phyllis and the Foreigner*

A schoolgirl suspects the new French teacher of being a German spy.

Hepworth. Great Britain. 1915. B&W. *Director:* Frank Wilson *Cast:* Chrissie White, Johnny Butt

566. *Physical Culture*

Two men start school to teach gymnastics to girls.
Hepworth. 1911. B&W. *Director:* Frank Wilson

567. *The Piano Teacher*

No description available.
Kleine Optical Co. 1909. B&W.

568. *Piatka z Ulicy Barskiej (Five from Barska Street)*

Five boys from Barska Street, on parole for juvenile crimes, become involved with a gang. The boys eventually turn on the gang. Hanka (Alecksandra Slaska), an attractive teacher, is drawn to one of the youths.
Artkine. Poland. 1955. 109m. C. *Director:* Aleksander Ford *Writer:* Kazinlerz Keyniewski *Cast:* Alecksandra Slaska, Tadeusz Janezar, Andryzcj Kozak, Tadeusz, Marian Rulka, Wlozzimerz Skocylas, Mieczyslaw Sloof

569. *Picnic*

Drifter Hal Carter (William Holden) comes to a sleepy Kansas town over Labor Day to look up an old college pal. His visit stirs up a variety of emotional responses. Rosemary Sydney (Rosalind Russell), a middle-aged spinster schoolteacher, lusts after Hal and marriage but also pretends indifference to men and is scary in her drunken rage toward Hal. Restless town beauty Madge Owens (Kim Novak) dumps her beau Alan (Cliff Robertson) to run off with Hal. *Picnic* was remade for television in 1986 with Gregory Harrison, Jennifer Jason Leigh, and Michael Learned. It was again remade for television in 2000 with Bonnie Bedelia, Josh Brolin, and Gretchen Mol.
Columbia. US. 1955. 115m. *Director:* Joshua Logan *Writer:* Daniel Taradash *Cast:* Willam Holden, Kim Novak, Betty Field, Rosalind Russell, Cliff Robertson

570. *Picnic at Hanging Rock*

Headmistress Mrs. Appleyard (Rachel Roberts) runs a tight ship at a girls' boarding school where sexual longings abound. There is the innocence of girlhood and unexplored sexuality on Valentine's Day in 1900 Australia. Many of the young women explore and picnic at a rock outcropping named Hanging Rock. Three of them disappear without a trace. One girl, who also went with the others, turns up but remembers nothing.
Picnic Productions/Australia Film Corporation. Australia. 1975. 115m. C. *Producers:* Hal and Jim McElroy *Director:* Peter Weir *Writers:* Cliff Green, Joan Lindsay (novel) *Cast:* Rachel Roberts, Dominic Guard, Helen Morse, Jacki Weaver, Vivean Gray, Kirsty Child

571. *Pieniä Eroja*

Thirteen-year-old Salla (Vilma Vuorio) has a crush on her ex-teacher Tarsala (Jari Nissinen). She dreams about him and eventually they become friends.

FS Film Oy. Finland. 2002. 58m. C. *Director:* Mari Rantasila *Writer:* Seija Ahava *Cast:* Vilma Vuorio, Jari Nissinen, Sara Malmberg, Lina Schiffer, Kirsti Väänäinen, Mikko Vanhala, Timo Tikka, Milla Kaitalahti, Emma Kiukkonen, Riikka Räsänen, Elma Reinikka, Elina Kanerva, Esa Illi

Pierino Against the World see *Pierino contro tutti*

572. *Pierino Contro Tutti (Pierino Against the World)*

A forty-year-old man has failed so many times, he is still in the third grade. In this elementary school we also find an ugly old-maid schoolteacher, an unbelievable sexy substitute and a macho gym teacher.

Medusa. Italy. 1981. 92m. C. *Director:* Marino Girolami *Writer:* Gianfranco Clerici *Cast:* Alvaro Vitali, Michela Miti, Enzo Liberti, Michele Gammino, Riccardo Billi, Marisa Merlini, Vincenzo Crocitti, Ennio Antonelli, Salvatore Baccaro, Francesca Romana Coluzzi, Enzo Robutti, Enzo Garinei, Gioia Scola, Attilio Dottesio

573. *Pioneer's Gold*

Once powerful, now old and sick, rancher Bob Hartley (Spottiswood Aitken) writes to his only relatives, schoolteacher Mary Marsden (Kathryn McGuire) and his nephew Jim Hartley (Pete Morrison), to come marry each other and inherit the ranch. Imposters attempt to step in, but Jim and Mary stop them. Bob is content to finally have his kin close by for the rest of his life.

Grapevine. US. 1924. 64m. B&W. *Director:* Denver Dixon *Writer:* William Lester *Cast:* Kathryn McGuire, Pete Morrison, Virginia Warwick, Spottiswood Aitken, Louis Emmons, Merrill McCormick, Les Bates, George King, William McCormick

Pit of Loneliness see *Olivia*

574. *Playthings of Destiny*

In Canada, country schoolteacher Julie Leneau (Anita Stewart) marries Geoffrey Arnold (Herbert Stewart). A woman shows up and convinces Julie that she is Geoffrey's lawful wife. Julie flees and almost dies in a blizzard before being found by Hubert Randolph (Walter McGrail). In order to give a name to her baby, she marries Hubert. When Geoffrey visits, Julie learns that he had not been unfaithful. Randolph gives up his wife and her child.

Associated First National Pictures. US. 1921. B&W. *Director:* Edwin Carewe *Writer:* Anthony Paul Kelly *Cast:* Anita Stewart, Herbert Rawlinson, Walter McGrail, Grace Morse, William V. Mong, Richard Headrick

575. Please, Sir

Sensitive teacher Bernard Hedges (John Alderton) takes a position teaching London slum children. The film was based on the then-popular British television series.

Rank. Great Britain. 1971. 101m. C. *Producer:* Andrew Mitchell *Director:* Mark Stuart *Writers:* John Esmonde, Bob Larbey *Cast:* John Alderton, Deryck Guyler, Joan Sanderson, Noel Howlett, Eric Chitty, Richard Davies, Patsy Rowlands, Peter Cleall, Carol Hawkins, Liz Gebhardt, David Barry, Peter Denyer, Malcolm McFee, Ariz Resham, Brinsley Forde, Jill Kernan, Norman Bird, Barbara Mitchell, Peter Bayliss, Jack Smethurst, Brenda Cowling, Richard Everett

576. Please, Teacher

An unemployed man, recovering from a hangover, learns he has inherited his aunt's fortune, hidden within a bust of Napoleon in her house. He rushes there and finds that it has become a girls' school with no men allowed. He poses as the brother of a girl to gain access. He isn't the only one searching, though.

ABPC. Great Britain. 1937. 76m. B&W. *Producer:* Walter C. Mycroft *Writer-Director:* Stafford Dickens *Cast:* Bert Lee, Bobby Howes, René Ray, Wylie Watson, Bertha Belmore, Vera Pearce, Lyn Harding, Aubrey Dexter, Arthur Chesney

577. The Plot Thickens

Inspector Oscar Piper (James Gleason) and schoolmarm Hildegarde Withers (ZaSu Pitts) investigate the case of John Carter, who was murdered in his car and moved to his library. Piper sees it as a simple romantic triangle but Hildegard stumbles on a clue leading to international jewel thieves.

RKO. US. 1936. 69m. B&W. *Producer:* William Sistrom *Director:* Ben Holmes *Writers:* Clarence Upson Young, Jack Townley, Stuart Palmer (novel) *Cast:* James Gleason, ZaSu Pitts, Owen Davis, Jr., Louise Latimer

578. Polly Ann

When Jud Simpkins (John Lockney) needs slave labor at his inn, he gets indentured servant Polly Ann (Bessie Love). A troupe of actors comes to town and Polly Ann falls for one of them. Meanwhile, in Boston, Howard Straightlan (Rowland Lee) is in trouble for his wild ways so his father sends him to a small country town to be a schoolteacher. Howard saves Polly Ann from the actor. Polly Ann learns she is a niece of Howard's father and that he wants her to come to Boston. The father forgives his son, because he has fallen in love with Polly Ann.

Triangle. US. 1917. B&W. *Director:* Charles F. Miller *Writers:* J. Hawks, Cecil Smith *Cast:* John Plockney, Bessie Love, Rowland Lee, William Ellingford, David Foss, Alfred Hollingsworth, Josephine Headley

579. Pontiac Moon

In 1969, eccentric teacher Washington Bellamy (Ted Danson) turns the men-to-the-Moon trip into a science project for his son Andy (Ryan Todd). They leave behind wife and mother Katherine (Mary Steenburgen), an agoraphobic, to travel across the country so the car's odometer will match the mileage traveled by Apollo XI. They encounter many different people on their trip.

Paramount. US. 1994. 107m. C. *Producers:* Ted Danson, Youssef Vahabzadeh, Robert Schaffel *Director:* Peter Medak *Writers:* Jeffrey Brown, Finn Taylor *Cast:* Ten Danson, Mary Steenburgen, Ryan Todd, Eric Schweig, Cathy Moriarty, Tamara Wilcox-Smith, Arthur Senzy, Don Swayze, Gene Borkan, J.C. Quinn, James Oscar Lee, John Scluck, Keith MacKechnic, Leslie Ryan, Ron Burke

Portrait of a Life see *Ekti Jiban*

580. *The Pretender*

Cowboy Bob Baldwin (William Desmond) meets injured Percival Longstreet (Joseph J. Franz), who is to be the town's new schoolmaster but is too hurt to teach. Longstreet convinces the cowboy to impersonate him. "Schoolmaster" Bob is liked by the town and by Dolly (Ethel Fleming), Percival's sister, but is uncomfortable in the classroom. He is found out as an imposter but becomes sheriff.

Triangle Film Corp. US. 1918. B&W. *Director:* Cliff Smith *Writer:* Alvin J. Neitz *Cast:* William Desmond, Ethel Fleming, Eugene Burr, Joseph J. Franz, C.E. Thurston, Graham Pettie, Percy Challenger, Walter Perkins, Joe Singleton

581. *Prima della Rivoluzione (Before the Revolution)*

Fabrizio (Francesco Barilli) rejects his middle-class values and his fiancée Clelia (Cristina Pariset). His friends Cesare (Morando Morandini), a schoolteacher, and Agostino (Allen Midgette), son of a wealthy manufacturer, encourage him to adopt a Marxist ideology. His parents, upset, ask Fabrizio's young aunt Gina (Adriana Asti) to talk some sense into him. Fabrizio secretly falls in love with Gina but breaks it off when he sees her with another man. He returns to his old life and marries Clelia. Cesare preaches revolution to another generation.

New Yorker Films. Italy. 1964. 112m. B&W. *Writer-Director:* Bernardo Bertolucci *Cast:* Adriana Asti, Francesco Barilli, Allen Midgette, Morando Morandini, Domenico Alpi, Giuseppe Maghenzani, Cecrope Barilli, Cristina Pariset, Emilia Borghi, Iole Lundardi, Evelina Alpi, Gianni Amico, Goliardo Padova, Guido Fanti, Salvatore Enrico, Ida Pellegri

582. *The Prime of Miss Jean Brodie*

At an Edinburgh girls' school, liberated and very unorthodox Jean Brodie (Maggie Smith) instructs her students in the ways of life. She teaches love, politics and art but not algebra or science. Her affairs with two male teachers become known and she finds herself fighting to keep her job. She believes that she can always count on the 100 percent support of her favorite pupils, but one of them is starting to learn about life herself.

TCF. Great Britain. 1969. 116m. C. *Producer:* Robert Fryer *Director:* Ronald Neame *Writers:* Jay Presson Allen, Muriel Spark (novel) *Cast:* Maggie Smith, Robert

Stephens, Pamela Franklin, Celia Johnson, Gordon Jackson, Jane Carr, Diane Grayson, Shirley Steedman, Margo Cunningham, Isla Cameron, Rona Anderson, Molly Weir

583. *The Private War of Major Benson*

Major Bernard Benson (Charlton Heston), a tough career army officer, is assigned to a post at Sheraton Military Academy in Santa Barbara. To his horror, it turns out to be a Catholic institution run by nuns, and his "troops" range in age six to fifteen. Mother Redempta (Nana Bryant), the very wise Mother Superior, and school doctor Kay Lambert (Julie Adams) help soften his approach.

Universal. US. 1955. 105m. C. *Producer:* Howard Pine *Director:* Jerry Hopper *Writers:* Richard Alan Simmons, Joe Connelly, Bob Mosher, William Roberts *Cast:* Charlton Heston, Julie Adams, William Demarest, Tim Hovey, Nana Bryant, Tim Considine, Sal Mineo, Milburn Stone, Mary Field

584. *P'Tang Yang Kipperbang*

At a British school, both adults and children have romantic hurdles to overcome. English teacher (Alison Steadman) is in love with the gardener (Garry Cooper). Young Alan (John Albasiny) is in love with Ann (Abigail Cruttenden) and is nervous because he must kiss her in the school play.

MGM/UA. Great Britain. 1984. 81m. C. *Producer:* Chris Griffin *Director:* Michael Apted *Writer:* Jack Rosenthal *Cast:* John Albasiny, Abigail Cruttenden, Maurice Dee, Alison Steadman, Mark Brailsford, Chris Karallis, Frances Ruffelle, Robert Urquhart, Garry Cooper, Maurice O'Connell, Tim Seeley, Richenda Carey, Peter Dean, Nicola Prince, John Arlott

585. *The Pure Hell of St. Trinian's*

St. Trinian's school has been burnt to the ground by some terrible young girls. A shyster posing as a teacher takes the girls on a tour of Greece and then forces them to marry the sons of an Arab shiek.

Hallmark/Tudor. Great Britain. 1960. 94m. B&W. *Producers:* Frank Launder, Sidney Gilliat *Director:* Frank Launder *Writers:* Frank Launder, Sidney Gilliat, Val Valentine *Cast:* Cecil Parker, Joyce Grenfell, George Cole, Thorley Walters, Irene Handl, Eric Barker, Dennis Price, Raymond Huntley, Julie Alexander, Sidney James, Julie Alexander, Lloyd Lamble, Nicholas Phipps, Liz Fraser, John Le Mesurier, George Benson, Elwyn Brook-Jones, Lisa Lee

586. *Qingchun Ji (Sacrificed Youth)*

Li Chun is a repressed 17-year-old student sent from Beijing to work with the peasants in the rice fields. She finds it difficult but strikes up a friendship. An argument and jealousy cause her to leave and become a teacher in another village.

Youth Film Studio of the Beijing Film Academy. China. 1985. 96m. C. *Writer-Director:* Zhang Nuanxin *Cast:* Li Fengxu, Feng Yuanzcheng, Song Tao, Guo Jianguo, Yu Da, Yu Shuai

587. Les Quatre Cents Coups (The Four Hundred Blows)

The moving story of a troubled 12-year-old boy, Antoine Doinel (Jean Pierre Léaud). The teacher (Guy Decomble) is a stupid and uninspired man who does wrong to bright boys. This Truffaut film, said to be autobiographical, shows stages of the boy's disintegration at home and school.

Films du Carrosse/SEDIF. France. 1959. 94m. B&W. *Producer:* Georges Charlot *Writer-Director:* François Truffaut *Cast:* Jean Pierre Léaud, Guy Decomble, Claire Maurier, Albert Rémy, Patrick Auffray, Robert Beauvais

588. The Quiller Memorandum

When two British Intelligence agents are murdered in Berlin, American agent Quiller (George Segal) is assigned to find the leader of a neo-Nazi movement trying to corrupt German thinking. During his investigating, Quiller visits the school where a teacher convicted of Nazi war crimes recently hanged himself. There Quiller is attracted to a teacher, Inge Lindt (Senta Berger). She is drawn into the identification and capture of the neo-Nazi leader when Quiller asks for her help. She gives him her contact, who is the headmistress at the school. Quiller is beaten, tortured, etc., while on the hunt. Quiller goes to check on Inge and finds her back at her school. As Quiller leaves, Inge returns to teaching the young of Berlin.

RFD. Great Britain. 1966. 103m. C. *Producers:* Ivan Foxwell, Sydney Streeter *Director:* Michael Anderson *Writers:* Harold Pinter, Elleston Trevor (novel) *Cast:* George Segal, Alec Guinness, Max von Sydow, Senta Berger, George Sanders, Robert Helpmann, Robert Flemyng, Peter Carsten, Edith Schneider, Gunter Meisner

589. Rabbit-Proof Fence

Three Australian Aborigines mixed-race children—14-year-old Molly (Everlyn Sampi), her eight-year-old sister Daisy (Tianna Sansbury) and their ten-year-old cousin Gracia (Laura Monoghan)—are forcibly taken from their home. They are sent 1500 miles to a settlement where they are forbidden to speak their language and indoctrinated into white culture. Eventually they will become domestic servants. The settlement resembles a poor rural orphanage with dormitory housing and strict rules. A.O. Neville (Kenneth Branagh) oversees Australia's policy of getting rid of natives. The girls escape and set out on a long journey home.

Hanway Films. Australia. 2002. 94m. C. *Producers:* Phillip Noyce, Christina Olsen, John Winter *Director:* Phillip Noyce *Writers:* Christine Olsen, Doris Pilkington (novel) *Cast:* Everlyn Sampi, Tianna Sansbury, Laura Monoghan, Kenneth Branagh, David Gulpilil, Ningali Lawford, Myarn Lawford, Deborah Mailman, Jason Clarke

590. Rachel, Rachel

Thirty-five-year-old, sexually repressed schoolteacher Rachel Cameron (Joanne Woodward) believes that unless a major change happens, she will soon become an old maid. Fellow teacher Calla (Estelle Parsons) makes a pass at her and a shallow childhood friend, Nick (James Olson), offers her a romantic option. She has a relationship with Nick and thinks she may be pregnant with his child. The "pregnancy" turns out to be a cyst and Rachel moves to Oregon to start a new life. As a teacher, Rachel is playful and tender with the children in the classroom.

Warner/Kayos. US. 1968. 101m. C. *Producer-Director:* Paul Newman *Writers:* Stewart Stern, Margaret Laurence (novel) *Cast:* Joanne Woodward, Estelle Parsons, James Olson, Kate Harrington, Donald Moffat, Geraldine Fitzgerald, Bernard Barrow

591. *Rachida*

Pretty young Rachida (Ibtissem Djouadi) lives and teaches in an old neighborhood in Algeria. She feels far removed from the bloody conflict until one day she is attacked and then asked by terrorists to plant a bomb in her school. When she refuses, they shoot her. She survives and seeks refuge in a neighboring village.

Esse Ci Cinematografica/Les Films du Paradoxe. Algeria/France. 2002. 100m. C. *Producer:* Margarita Seguy *Writer-Director:* Yamina Bachir *Cast:* Ibtissem Djouadi, Bahia Rachedi, Rachida Messaoui En, Hamid Remas, Zaki Boulenafed, Amel Choukh, Abdelkader Belmokadem, Azzedine Bougherra

Radio Stories see *Historias de la Radio*

592. *Ragbar (Rainstorm and Downpour)*

The story of the life of an idealistic new teacher in a slum school.

Iran. 1971. 126m. C. *Producer:* Barbod Taheri *Director:* Bahram Beyzai *Cast:* Rogheyed Chehreh-Azad, Mohamad Ali Keshavarz, Jamshid Layegh, Parvis Fanizadeh, Parvaneh Masumi, Manuchehr Farid

Ragtime Summer see *Age of Innocence*

593. *The Rainbow*

Ursula Brankgwen (Sammi Davis) has a lesbian affair with her schoolteacher, Winifred (Amanda Donohoe). Ursula then works as a teacher in an elementary school which is like something out of Dickens, overseen by a brutal headmaster. She sees her idealism disappear as she violently canes a student who has kicked her. She finds the love of her life in dashing soldier Anton Skrbensky (Paul McGann). She decides to never marry. This is the prequel to *Women in Love*.

Vestron Pictures. Great Britain. 1989. 113m. C. *Producer-Director:* Ken Russell *Writers:* Ken Russell, Vivian Russell, D.H. Lawrence (novel) *Cast:* Sammi Davis, Paul McGann, Amanda Donohoe, Christopher Gable, David Hemmings, Glenda Jackson, Dudley Sutton, Jim Carter

Rainbow see *Wo xin fei xiang*

594. *Rainbow Over the Range*

While investigating horse rustling, U.S. Marshal Tex Reed (Tex Ritter) and his sidekick Slim Chance (Slim Andrews) discover that the only school in town is in danger of closing, leaving Mary Manners (Dorothy Fay) with no job. Tex knows that Mary and her brother Jeff hold contracts for horses for the military. Tex and Jeff team up to expose the rustling ringleader.

Monogram Pictures Corp. US. 1940. 58m. B&W. *Producer:* Edward Finney *Director:* Al Herman *Writers:* Rolland Lynch, Robert Emmett, Roger Merton *Cast:* Tex Ritter, Slim Andrews, Dorothy Fay, Warner Richmond, Jim Pierce, Chuck Morrison, Dennis Moore, Steve Lorber, Art Wilcox, Gene Alsace

Rainstorm see *Ragbar*

595. *Raintree County*

During the Civil War, Southern belle Susanna Drake (Elizabeth Taylor) gets the man she thinks she wants—John Wickliff Shawnessy (Montgomery Clift). But finds life as a schoolmaster's wife proves boring. Susanna has inherited her family's curse of insanity. John enlists in the Northern army to escape his marriage.

MGM. US. 1957. 166m. C. *Producer:* David Lewis *Director:* Edward Dmytryk *Writers:* Millard Kaufman, Ross Lockridge (novel) *Cast:* Montgomery Clift, Elizabeth Taylor, Eva Marie Saint, Nigel Patrick, Lee Marvin, Rod Taylor, Agnes Moorehead, Walter Abel, Jarma Lewis, Tom Drake, Gardner McKay, Rhys Williams

596. *Rascal*

In the summer of 1918 11-year-old Wisconsin boy Sterling North (Bill Mumy) saves a raccoon from a lynx. He names it Rascal and they become buddies. Sterling's widowed father spends most of his time on the road. Three neighbors look out for Sterling: his teacher Miss Whalen (Bettye Ackerman), the new minister Mr. Thurman (Herbert Anderson) and merchant Mr. Pringle (Herbert Anderson). Sterling and Rascal have many adventures. Sterling's sister returns home to find a mess and forces the father to take a job in town. Sterling releases Rascal in the company of a female raccoon.

Buena Vista. US. 1969. 85m. C. *Producer:* James Algar *Director:* Norman Tokar *Writers:* Harold Swanton, Sterling North (novel) *Cast:* Steve Forrest, Bill Mumy, Pamela Toll, Elsa Lanchester, Henry Jones, Bettye Ackerman, Jonathan Daly, John Fiedler, Richard Erdman, Herbert Anderson, Robert Emhardt, Steve Carlson, Maudie Pickett, Walter Pidgeon

597. *Recess: School's Out*

TJ and his buddies have finished the fourth grade and are ready to spend the summer vacation at various camps. Alone one day, TJ notices a weird glow emanating from the school and sees strangers going in and out. The police aren't interested. TJ must go to the boys for help.

Buena Vista/Walt Disney. US. 2001. 82m. Animated. C *Director:* Chuck Sheetz *Writers:* Paul Germain, Joe Ansolabehere *Voices:* Andrew Lawrence, Rickey D'Shon Collins, Paul Willson, Jason Davis

598. *Reckless Riding Bill*

The hero runs a legitimate gambling establishment. When a schoolteacher arrives, he rescues her from a runaway stagecoach. In the end, he gives away the gambling establishment and reforms, getting the girl.

Sanford Productions. US. 1924. B&W. *Director:* Frank Morrow *Cast:* Dick Carter, Alys Morrell

599. *The Re-creation of Brian Kent*

Under the eyes of schoolteacher Auntie Sue (Mary Carr), bank clerk embezzler Brian Kent (Kenneth Harlan) reforms and writes a book. Auntie Sue persuades the bank president (a former pupil of hers) not to prosecute Brian. Brian's demanding wife drowns, and Brian finds happiness with another.

Principal Pictures. US. 1925. B&W. *Producer:* Sol Lesser *Director:* Sam Wood *Writers:* Arthur Statter, Mary Alice Scully *Cast:* Kenneth Harlan, Helene Chadwick, Mary Carr, ZaSu Pitts, Rosemary Theby, T. Roy Barnes, Ralph Lewis, Russell Simpson, DeWitt Jennings, Russell Powell

600. *Red Love*

Thunder Cloud (John Lowell), a Sioux and a graduate of Carlisle, becomes an outcast when he believes he has killed the evil Bill Mosher (Wallace Jones), a white man. He steals horses and cattle but always leaves money or an IOU for what he takes. He falls in love with teacher Starlight (Evangeline Russell), the half-breed daughter of the sheriff (Willima Calhoun). Thundercloud kidnaps her but everything is cleared up when it is revealed that Mosher was not killed and that it was a plot against Thundercloud. Starlight gives up teaching to be with Thundercloud.

Davis Distributing. US. 1925. B&W. *Director:* Edgar Lewis *Writer:* L. Case Russell. *Cast:* John Lowell, Evangeline Russell, F. Serrano Keating, William Calhoun, Ann Brody, William Cavanaugh, Wallace Jones, Charles W. Kinney, Frank Montgomery, Dexter McReynolds, Chick Chandler

601. *Remember the Day*

Aging schoolteacher Nora Trinell (Claudette Colbert) is waiting to meet presidential candidate Dewey Roberts (Shepperd Strudwick). As Nora bides her time, she reflects on her past and that of young Dewey (Douglas Croft), then one of Nora's pupils. He had a schoolboy crush on her and she inspired him to pursue his dreams. Dewey is upset when she secretly weds fellow teacher Dan Hopkins (John Payne). Dan joins the Canadian Army during World War I.

TCF. US. 1941. 86m. B&W. *Producer:* William Perlberg *Director:* Henry King *Writers:* Tess Schlesinger, Frank Davis, Allan Scott *Cast:* Claudette Colbert, John

Payne, Shepperd Strudwick, Jane Seymour, Anne Revere, Frieda Inescort, Douglas Croft

602. *La Residencia (The Boarding School)*

Sinister happenings abound in a French boarding school around 1900. Mme. Fourneau (Lilli Palmer) runs the boarding school and her strict discipline have fostered torture, lesbianism and sexual desire among the girls. Mme. Fourneau tries to keep her adolescent son, who may be a killer, isolated from the girls.

JF Films de Regia-Arturo. Spain. 1969. 99m. C. *Producer:* Arturo Ganzález *Writer-Director:* Narciso Ibáñez Serrador *Cast:* Lilli Palmer, Cristina Galbó, John Moulder-Brown, Mary Maude, Cándida Losada, Tomás Blanco, Pauline Challoner

603. *The Return of Count Yorga*

Vampire Count Yorga (Robert Quarry) and his cohorts move into a mansion next door to an orphanage. Yorga falls in love with and kidnaps Cynthia (Mariette Hartley), a young orphanage worker.

AIP. US. 1971. 97m. C. *Producer:* Michael Macready *Director:* Bob Kelljan *Writers:* Bob Kelljan, Yvonne Wilder *Cast:* Robert Quarry, Mariette Hartley, Roger Perry, Yvonne Wilder, Tom Toner, Rudy De Luca, Philip Frame, George Macready, Walter Brooke, Edward Walsh, Craig T. Nelson, David Lampson, Karen Ericson, Helen Baron, Jesse Wells, Michael Pataki, Corinne Conley, Allen Joseph, Peg Shirley, Liz Rogers, Paul Hansen, Marilyn Lovell

604. *Rhythm Serenade*

During World War II, a schoolteacher runs a day nursery so that mothers can work in the factories. She falls in love with a soldier recovering from a nervous breakdown.

Columbia British. Great Britain. 1943. 87m. B&W. *Producer:* Ben Henry *Director:* Gordon Wellesley *Writers:* Basil Woon, Marjorie Deans *Cast:* Vera Lynn, Peter Murray-Hill, Julien Mitchell, Charles Victor, Jimmie Jewel, Ben Warris, Irene Handl, Jimmy Clitheroe, Joan Kemp Welch

605. *The Right of the Strongest*

District schoolteacher Mary Elizabeth Dale (Helen Ferguson) is drawn into engineer's John Marshall's (E.K. Lincoln) mysterious mission. He is there to take over the land so a dam to provide power can be built. Mary Elizabeth convinces him to pay well and helps him when a mob wants to lynch him. After the death of an innocent boy, peace comes to the valley.

Selznick Distributing Corp. US. 1924. B&W. *Director:* Edgar Lewis *Writers:* Doty Hobart, Frances Nimmo Greene *Cast:* E.K. Lincoln, Helen Ferguson, George Siegmann, Tom Santschi, Robert Milasch, F. B. Phillips, Tully Marshall, James Gibson, Coy Watson, Gertrude Norman, Milla Davenport, June Elvidge, Winter Hall, Niles Welch, Beth Kosick, Leonard Clapham

606. *Río Escondido (Hidden River)*

In spite of a heart condition, courageous young teacher Rosaura Salazar (María Félix) travels to the Mexican desert town of Rio Escondido to educate its poverty-stricken illiterates. Rosaura must battle an evil landlord in order to answer her patriotic call to educate the poorest people in Mexico.

Case-Mohme. Mexico. 1948. 110m. B&W/C. *Director:* Emilio Fernández *Writers:* Emilio Fernández, Mauricio Magdaleno *Cast:* María Félix, Domingo Soler, Carlos López Moctezuma, Arturo Soto Rangel, Fernando Fernández, Columba Domínguez, Juan García, Mauel Dondé, Carlos Múzquiz, Agustín Isunza, Roberto Cañedo, Lupe del Castillo, María Germán Valdéz, Jaime Jiménez Pons

The Road Home see *Wode fu qin mu qin*

The Road to Happiness see *Saluti e Baci*

607. *The Rocket from Calabuch (Calabuch)*

A wanderer, Professor George Hamilton (Edmund Gwenn), finds sanctuary in a small village perched high on a cliff above a calm Spanish seacoast. He turns out to be a famed atomic scientist. He is identified when he makes a rocket that wins at a competition. Donna Sofia (Valentina Cortesa) is the local schoolteacher who yearns for love and an escape from Calabuch. Other community members include the teacher's love Franco Fabrizi, a jack-of-all-trades, and the police chief.

Trans-Lux. Spain/Italy. 1956. 90m. B&W. *Producers:* José Luis, Jerez Aloza *Director:* Senor Berlanga *Writer:* Leonardo Martin *Cast:* Edmund Gwenn, Valentina Cortesa, Franco Fabrizi, Juan Calvo, Felix Fernandez, Lolita Isbert, Jose Lois Ozores, Francisco Bernal

608. *Rockets Galore (Mad Little Island)*

The Isle of Todday is chosen as the site for a rocket base. The villagers do not want it. The schoolmistress, Janet Maclead (Jeannie Carson), appeals to people's feelings about birds.

Rank. Great Britain. 1958. 94m. C. *Producer:* Basil Dearden *Director:* Michael Relph *Writer:* Monja Danischewsky *Cast:* Jeannie Carson, Donald Sinden, Roland Culver, Catherine Lacey, Noel Purcell, Ian Hunter, Duncan Macrae, Jean Cadell, Gordon Jackson, Alex Mackenzie, Carl Jaffe, Nicholas Phipps, Cameron Clark

609. *Romance*

Marie (Caroline Ducey), an elementary school teacher, has a self-centered boyfriend (Sagamore Stévenin) who after only three months is no longer attracted to her. Marie tries to energize their relationship through sexual jealousy.

Trimark. France. 1999. 99m. C. *Producer:* Jean-François Lepetit *Writer-Director:* Catherine Breillat *Cast:* Caroline Ducey, Sagamore Stévenin, François

Berléand, Rocco Siffredi, Ashley Wanninger, Emma Colberti, Fabien de Jomaron, Hervé P. Gustave, Alain L'Yle, Oliver Buchette

610. *Romance of a Schoolteacher*

No description available.
Kleine Optical Co. Italy. 1908. B&W

611. *The Romance of Rosy Ridge*

Post-Civil War Missouri serves as the backdrop for this tale of young love. Veteran Henry Carson (Van Johnson) is a wandering, banjo-playing schoolteacher who comes to the Missouri hills. Young love blossoms, but is threatened by the simple fact that the girl's father suspects Henry of being a Unionist.

MGM. US. 1947. 103m. B&W. *Producer*: Jack Cummings *Director*: Roy Rowland *Writers*: Lester Cole, MacKinlay Kantor (novel) *Cast*: Van Johnson, Thomas Mitchell, Janet Leigh, Marshall Thompson, Selena Royle, Charles Dingle, Dean Stockwell, Guy Kibbee, Elisabeth Risdon, Jim Davis, Russell Simpson, O.Z. Whitehead, James Bell, Joyce Arling, William Bishop, Selena Royle

612. *Romantic Comedy*

Schoolteacher Phoebe (Mary Steenburgen) and Jason (Dudley Moore) are playwright-partners. Phoebe is from the Northwoods and Jason is getting married when they meet. Their first effort is a failure and then they have a list of successes. After nine years, will they partner in love?

MGM/UA. US. 1983. 102m. C. *Producers:* Walter Mirisch, Morton Gottlieb *Director:* Arthur Hiller *Writer:* Bernard Slade *Cast:* Dudley Moore, Mary Steenburgen, Frances Sternhagen, Janet Eilber, Robyn Douglass, Ron Leibman

613. *The Ron Clark Story*

Ron Clark (Matthew Perry) was a schoolteacher in a small town in North Carolina. His classes did very well on their standardized test so he moved to New York to find a school where he was really needed. He drove to New York, moved into a room and used the phonebook to look up the names of Harlem elementary schools. To make a living until he finds a teaching job, he works as a waiter at a themed restaurant. He lands his teaching job where he happens to be caught in a confrontation among the principal, a difficult teacher and a teacher who quits. Principal Turner (Ernie Hudson) doesn't know why Ron wants to take on the most unruly, lowest-scoring sixth-grade class, but he hires him. The children disobey his rules and sleep in class until Ron gets their attention by drinking chocolate milk.

TNT. US. 2006. 120m. C. *Producers:* Tox Cox, Craig McNeil, Murray Ord, Jordy Randall *Director:* Randa Haines *Writers:* Annie deYoung, Max Enscoe *Cast:* Matthew Perry, Judith Buchan, Hannah Hodson, Jerry Callaghan, Melissa De Sousa, Micah Williams, C.J. Jackman-Zigante, Brandon Smith, Ernie Hudson

614. *Room 6*

A young elementary school teacher and her fiancé are in a car accident. He is taken to a very strange hospital and she has strange delusional visions. We see her as a caring teacher who is very worried about one of her pupils. She must sacrifice her life to save her fiancé from a horrible fate in this haunted hospital.

Imagine Entertainment. US. 2006. 94m. C. *Director:* Michael Hurst *Writers:* Mark A. Altman, Michael Hurst *Cast:* Christine Taylor, Shane Brolly, Chloe Moretz, Jerry O'Connell, Ellie Cornell, Jimmy Shubert, Lisa Ann Walter, Marshall Bell, John Billingsley, Jack Riley, Andrew Davoli, Marissa N. Blanchard, Stacy Fuson, Katie Lohmann, Cheryl Tsai

615. *Rosewood*

In 1920s Florida, Rosewood is a close-knit African American community where families own their own land and businesses. Music teacher Sylvester Carrier (Don Cheadle) is willing to risk standing up to white people so that things can be different. Stranger Mann (Ving Rhames) catches the eye of winsome schoolteacher Scrappy (Elise Neal) and thinks about staying. A white woman falsely claims that she was raped by a black man. This sets up a massacre at Rosewood.

Warner. US. 1997. 135m. C. *Producer:* Jon Peters *Director:* John Singleton *Writer:* Gregory Poirier *Cast:* John Voight, Ving Rhames, Don Cheadle, Bruce McGill, Loren Dean, Esther Rolle, Elise Neal, Michael Rooker, Catherine Kellner

616. *The Rotters*

A headmistress recognizes a married man as her ex-lover and stops him from sentencing a man.

Ideal. Great Britain. 1921. B&W. *Director:* A.V. Bramble *Writer:* Arthur Q. Walton *Cast:* Joe Nightingale, Sydney Fairbrother, Sydney Paxton, Margery Meadows, Roger Treville, Ernest English, Cynthia Murtagh, Clarel Greet, Stanley Holloway, Margaret Shelley

617. *Ruby Bridges*

The true story of Ruby Bridges (Chaz Monet), an African American girl who, in 1960 at age six, helped to integrate an all-white elementary school in New Orleans. Her best friend Jill begins going to a Catholic school and, according to her father, this school makes her better than public school children. Ruby reasons that her new school must be better because she has a teacher, a classroom and the whole school to herself— it is a real private school. Miss Woodmere (Diana Scarwid) is Ruby's teacher and Dr. Robert Coles (Kevin Pollak) is the psychiatrist studying Ruby as a child under stress.

US. 1998. *Director:* Euzhan Palcy *Writer:* Toni Ann Johnson *Cast:* Chaz Monet, Penelope Ann Miller, Kevin Pollak, Michael Beach, Lela Rochon, Jean Louisa Kelly, Peter Francis James, Diana Scarwid, Patrika Darbo

618. *Runaway Romany*

Showgirl Anitra St. Clair (Ormi Hawley) is convinced to paint a birthmark on her shoulder and pose as millionaire mine owner Theodore True's long-lost daughter. The impersonation works and she meets Bud Haskell (Matt Moore), schoolmaster to a gypsy tribe. The beautiful gypsy Romany (Marion Davies) ran away to escape marrying the chief's son Zinga. Bud and Romany meet on her first outing from boarding school and fall in love. After a few episodes of trouble, all ends well.

Pathé Special Distribution Co. US. 1917. B&W. *Director:* George W. Lederer *Writer:* Marion Davies *Cast:* Marion Davies, Joseph Kilgour, Matt Moore, Ormi Hawley, Gladden James, Boyce Combe, W.W. Bittner, Pedro de Cordoba

619. *The Runner Stumbles*

A priest is accused of murdering the nun-teacher he has fallen in love with. The story is told in three parts: Father Rivard (Dick Van Dyke) in jail; the story of the relationship between Rivard and Sister Rita (Kathleen Quinlan), who arrives to teach and befriends the lonely priest; and then the trial. Rivard is a lonely and depressed priest stuck in a poor mining town. With the arrival of young, perky Sister Rita, he cheers up and soon falls in love. Based on an actual 1927 murder case.

TCF. US. 1979. 109m. C. *Producer-Director:* Stanley Kramer *Writer:* Milan Stitt (play) *Cast:* Dick Van Dyke, Kathleen Quinlan, Maureen Stapleton, Ray Bolger, Tammy Grimes, Beau Bridges, Allen Nause, John Procaccino, Sister Marguerite Morrissey, Zoaunne LeRoy, Jock Dove

620. *Rushmore*

Precocious tenth-grade scholarship student Max (Jason Schwartzman) attends Rushmore, a private school where he is not doing well. When he is forced to attend the local high school, he meets recently widowed pre-school teacher Rosemary Cross (Olivia Williams). He falls madly in love with her but he has a rival in wealthy industrialist Herman Blume (Bill Murray), who becomes a mentor to him.

Buena Vista. US. 1998. 93m. C. *Producers:* Barry Mendel, Paul Schiff *Director:* Wes Anderson *Writers:* Wes Anderson, Owen Wilson *Cast:* Jason Schwartzman, Bill Murray, Olivia Williams, Seymour Cassel, Brian Cox, Mason Gamble, Sara Tanaka, Stephen McCole, Connie Nielsen

621. *Rustling for Cupid*

When Bradley Blatchford (George O'Brien) returns to his father's ranch from college, he meets Sybil Hamilton (Anita Stewart), who is coming to the ranch town as a schoolteacher. Bradley and Sybil fall in love but not before some rustling and gunfights occur and family secrets are revealed.

Fox Film Corp. US. 1926. B&W. *Producer:* William Fox *Director:* Irving Cummings *Writer:* L. G. Rigby *Cast:* George O'Brien, Anita Stewart, Russell Simpson, Edith Yorke, Herbert Prior, Frank McGlynn, Jr., Sid Jordan

622. Ryan's Daughter

In 1916 Ireland, Rosy (Sarah Miles), the immature young wife of village schoolmaster Charles (Robert Mitchum), falls in love with a shell-shocked soldier, Randolph (Christopher Jones). An affair develops. A subplot involves rebel gun running and betrayal. Father Collins (Trevor Howard) is the knowing village priest.

MGM. Great Britain. 1970. 206m. C. *Producer*: Anthony Havelock-Allan *Director*: David Lean *Writer*: Robert Bolt *Cast*: Robert Mitchum, Trevor Howard, Sarah Miles, Christopher Jones, John Mills, Leo McKern, Barry Foster, Archie O'Sullivan, Marie Kean, Barry Jackson

Sacrificed Youth see *Qingchun Ji*

623. The Sagebrush Trail

Sheriff Larry Reid (Roy Stewart) pursues a stranger Neil (Johnny Walker) found with a gun, which is forbidden in Silvertown. He tracks Neil to the home of pretty schoolmistress Mary Gray (Marjorie Daw), but she claims not to know Neil. Larry is attracted to Mary but is concerned about Neil. When Larry captures Neil, he discovers that Neil is Mary's brother and innocent. Larry arrives in time to save Mary from the unwanted advances of a bandit.

Exploitation Co. US. 1922. B&W. *Director:* Robert T. Thornby *Writer:* H.H. Van Loan *Cast:* Roy Stewart, Marjorie Daw, Johnny Walker, Wallace Beery

624. Saint Ralph

Fatherless 14-year-old Ralph (Adam Butcher) believes that winning the 1954 Boston Marathon will bring his mother out of a coma. He comes to this conclusion when he is put on the cross-country team as penance for an act of self-abuse. Teachers Father George Hibbert (Campbell Scott) and Father Fitzpatrick (Gordon Pinsent) have opposing views on Ralph's quest.

Samuel Goldwyn Films. Canada. 2004. 98m. C. *Producers:* Teza Lawrence, Andrea Mann, Seaton McLean, Michael Souther *Writer-Director:* Michael McGowan *Cast:* Adam Butcher, Campbell Scott, Gordon Pinsent, Jennifer Tilly, Shauna MacDonald, Tamara Hope, Frank Crudele, Michael Kaney, Chris Ploszczansky, Paulette Sinclair, Lubica Kucerova, Ben Gans, Jock McLeod, Jeff Baxter, Daniel Karasik

625. Saluti e Baci (The Road to Happiness)

Radio man Carlo Mastelli (Philippe Lemaire) is out of ideas for his radio show until he meets a young schoolteacher, Marina (Catherine Erard). She persuades him to broadcast an appeal for an underprivileged pupil, while recording a singing contest. She asks listeners to send in postcards to cheer up the little boy. Carlo's ratings increase and lots of mail arrives. Eventually Carlo marries Marina.

Athena Cinematografica. Italy/France. 1953. 92m. B&W. *Producers:* Silvio Clementelli, Clément Duhour *Directors:* Maurice Labro, Giorgio Simonelli *Writer:*

Age, Edorado Anton, Jacques Emmanuel, Furio Scarpelli *Cast:* Philippe Lemaire, Catherine Erard, Clément Duhour, Christian Duvalex, Auturo Bragaglia

626. *The Sandpiper*

Single would-be artist Laura Reynolds (Elizabeth Taylor) and a married Episcopalian minister, Dr. Edward Hewitt (Richard Burton) are having an affair. Hewitt is headmaster of a private school for boys attended by her nine-year-old son.

MGM. US. 1965. 117m. C. *Producer:* John Calley *Director:* Vincente Minnelli *Writers:* Dalton Trumbo, Michael Wilson *Cast:* Elizabeth Taylor, Richard Burton, Eva Marie Saint, Charles Bronson, Robert Webber, James Edwards, Torin Thatcher, Tom Drake, Douglas Henderson, Morgan Mason

627. *Sango Malo*

Malo (Jérome Bolo) is an idealistic teacher in a Cameroonian village whose ideas of education clash with those of the school's colonialist administrators. He insists that the students be taught modern subjects and is met with resistance.

Les Films Terre Africaine. Cameroon/Burkina Faso. 1990. 92m. C. *Producer:* Emmanuel Toko *Writer-Director:* Bassek Ba Kobhio *Cast:* Jérome Bolo, Marcel Mvondo II, Edwige Ntongon è Zock, Jean Minguele, Jimmy Biong, Henriette Fenda

628. *Sarvasakshi (The Omniscient)*

A progressive schoolteacher in a small village helps fight a local epidemic by getting the children inoculated. The local bhagat (witch doctor) is angry about this intervention. The teacher's wife goes to the bhagat when she is pregnant because she has lost a child. To her horror, he demands a human sacrifice. She later dies in childbirth. The teacher is falsely accused of superstitious activity but is eventually cleared.

Giriraj Pictures Production Co. India. 1978. 135m.B&W. *Writer-Producer-Director:* Ramdas Phutane *Cast:* Smita Patil, Jairam Hardikar, Anjali Paigankar, Vihay Joshi

629. *The Scamp*

A schoolmaster and his doctor-wife befriend and take in a neglected child whose father, an alcoholic vaudeville actor, deserted him to go on a tour. When the child thinks he has killed his father, he runs back to the schoolmaster and his wife.

Renown. Great Britain. 1957. 88m. B&W. *Producer:* James Lawrie *Writer-Director:* Wolf Rilla *Cast:* Richard Attenborough, Dorothy Alison, Colin Petersen, Terence Morgan, Jill Adams, Maureen Delany, Margaretta Scott, David Franks, Geoffrey Keen, Charles Lloyd Pack, June Cunningham, Sam Kydd, Victor Brooks

630. *The Scandalous Boys and the Fire Chute*

A teacher follows boys down a fire chute and ends up in a tub of water.
Clarendon. Great Britain. 1908. B&W. *Director:* Percy Stow *Writer:* Langford Reed

631. *The Scapegoat*

French Count Jacques DeGue (Alec Guinness) schemes to kill his wife and implicate John Barratt (Alec Guinness), a mild-mannered English schoolteacher whom he resembles.

MGM. Great Britain. 1959. 92m. B&W. *Producer:* Michael Balcon *Director:* Robert Hamer *Writers:* Gore Vidal, Robert Hamer, Daphne du Maurier (novel) *Cast:* Alec Guinness, Bette Davis, Nicole Maurey, Irene Worth, Pamela Brown, Annabel Bartlett, Geoffrey Keen, Leslie French, Noel Howlett, Peter Bull

632. *Scattergood Baines*

Despite his questionable past, Scattergood Baines (Guy Kibbee) has become a leading citizen of Coldriver, a small New England town. As chair of the school board he accepts the decision to hire prim Helen Parker (Carol Hughes). When Scattergood goes to pick up Helen, he is surprised to find a beauty. To make the school board members happy, he has her wear glasses and wear her hair in an unflattering style. The town gossip peers through Helen's window and sees her with a man and also notices that she is beautiful. The school board demands that she resign.

RKO. US. 1941. 69m. B&W. *Producer:* Jerrold T. Brandt *Director:* Christy Cabanne *Writers:* Michael L. Simmons, Edward T. Lowe *Cast:* Guy Kibbee, Carol Hughes, John Archer, Francis Trouth, Emma Dunn, Willie Best, Fern Emmett, Lee Lasses White, Joseph Crehan, Edward Earle, Bradley Page, Paul White, Earl Hodgins

633. *Schlussakkord (Final Chord)*

When her embezzler husband commits suicide, Hanna returns to Germany to find her young son. To be near the boy, she becomes the governess in the home of an orchestral conductor and his faithless wife where her son lives.

UFA. Germany. 1936. 100m. B&W. *Director:* Detlef Sierck *Writers:* Kurt Heuser, Detlef Sierck *Cast:* Willy Birgel, Lil Dagover, Maria Von Tasnady, Theodor Loos, Maria Koppenhöfer, Albert Lippert, Kurt Meisel

634. *School Days*

A look at rural America and the one-room schoolhouse. Country boy Speck Brown (Wesley Barry) is reared by cruel Deacon Jones (George Lessey), who makes Speck attend school. Speck is fond of his kindly schoolteacher (Margaret Seddon), his friends and dog Hippy. When Speck's teacher defends him against the Deacon, the Deacon forces her to resign. A wealthy stranger arranges for Speck to attend a private school in New York City. He finds city life not to his liking and returns to his hometown.

Warner. US. 1921. B&W. *Producer:* Harry Rapf *Director:* William Nigh *Writers:* Walter De Leon, William Nigh *Cast:* Wesley Barry, George Lessey, Nellie P. Spaulding, Margaret Seddon, Arline Blackbum, J.H. Gilmore, John Galsworthy, Jerome Patrick, Evelyn Sherman, Arnold Lucy, Hippy the Dog

635. *School for Randle*

The janitor at a girls' school discovers that his estranged daughter is one of the students.

Film Studios Manchester. Great Britain. 1949. 89m. B&W. *Producer-Director:* John E. Blakeley *Writer:* Harry Jackson *Cast:* Frank Randal, Dan Young, Terry Randal, John Singer, Alec Pleon, Maudie Edwards, Hilda Bayley, Ian Fleming, Jimmy Clitheroe, Elisa Tee

636. *School of Life*

New history teacher "Mr. D" D'Angelo (Ryan Reynolds) has a hip approach to teaching the students. His passion for the subject catches on with his students, who thought they were in for another boring year. The kids and the faculty love "Mr. D" and this threatens stuffy biology teacher Matt Warner's (David Paymer) chance of winning the Teacher of the Year award. He is the son of wildly popular educator Stormin' Norman Warner (John Astin), a man who won Teacher of the Year award for 43 years in a row. Matt is desperate get that award.

ABC Family. Canada/US. 2005. 111m. C. *Producer:* Rosanna Milliken *Director:* William Dear *Writer:* Jonathan Kahn *Cast:* David Paymer, Ryan Reynolds, John Astin, Andrew Robb, Kate Vernon, Don McKay, Brenda McDonald, Paul Jarrett, Leila Johnson, Chris Gauthier, Shylo Sharity

637. *School of Rock*

Would-be rocker Dewey Finn (Jack Black) hits bottom when he is dumped by his own band and is in financial trouble. His landlord and friend Ned Schneebly (Mike White) earns a living as a substitute teacher. Dewey impersonates Ned and applies to Horace Green Prep School. Stiff, mousy Principal Rosalie Mullins (Joan Cusack) hires him to teach at the elementary school. Initially he has no intention of doing anything in the classroom but decides to shape the kids into a rock band named School of Rock using non-performers as roadies. They gear up for a Battle of the Bands competition, all the prep work done secretly during school hours.

Paramount. US. 2003. 108m. C. *Producer:* Scott Rudin *Director:* Richard Linklater *Writer:* Mike White *Cast:* Jack Black, Joan Cusack, Mike White, Sarah Silverman, Joey Gaydos, Jr., Robert Tsai, Maryam Hassan, Kevin Clark

638. Schoolgirl Rebels

A schoolgirl irritates her new teacher by getting her schoolmates to answer an inspector incorrectly.

Hepworth. Great Britain. 1915. B&W. *Director:* Frank Wilson *Cast:* Chrissie White, Stewart Rome, Violet Hopson

639. The Schoolmarm's Ride for Life

No description available.

Motion Picture Distributors and Sales Co. US. 1910. B&W.

640. The Schoolmarm's Shooting Match

No description available.

Sekig Pollyscope/Geberal Film. US. 1913. B&W. *Writer-Director:* William Duncan *Cast:* William Duncan, Myrtle Stedman, Lester Cuneo, Rex De Rosselli, Tom Mix, Hugh Mosher, William Jones

641. Schoolmaster Matsumoto

In a 1920 review of this film, it is noted that the film is extremely popular and has been running in Japan for more than a year and still drawing crowds. Postcards and songs were generated by the film. *Schoolmaster Matsumoto* shows the bravery of a schoolteacher at Nagata Common School in Tokyo. It was based on a true-life incident when teacher Matsumoto died trying to save a drowning boy. At one point in the movie, one of three boys steals a pen and the teacher asks for a confession. The teacher tells the story of George Washington and the cherry tree. He still gets no confession and lets the boy leave. Blaming himself, he takes a stick and beats his hand until it bleeds.

Japan. B&W.

642. The Schoolmaster of Mariposa

No description available.

General Film Company. US. 1910. B&W. *Director:* Francis Boggs *Writer:* Lanier Bartlett *Cast:* Betty Harte, Tom Mix

643. The Schoolmaster's Portrait

A boy draws a caricature of his teacher on the blackboard and is caned by the teacher.

Bamforth Films/Riley Bothers. Great Britain. 1898. B&W.

644. The Schoolmaster's Surprise

Two bad boys fill a lamp chimney with flour, and the schoolmaster is fooled.
American Mutoscope Company. US. 1898. B&W.

645. The Schoolteacher and the Waif

No description available.
General Film Company. US. 1912. 17m. B&W. *Director:* D.W. Griffith *Cast:* Edwin August, Mary Pickford, Charles Hill Mailes, Bert Hendler, Claire McDowell, William A. Carroll

Schoolteacher and Weekend Nudist see *Paolo Barca, Maestro Elementare, Praticamente Nudista*

646. Das Schreckliche Mädchen (The Nasty Girl)

Sonja is an admired schoolgirl in a small town when she wins an essay competition. With her next essay (on her home town during the Third Reich), no one is willing to help. When she marries a schoolteacher, she continues to uncover the truth even when in danger.
Sentana. West Germany. 1989. 92m. C. *Producer:* Michael Senftleben *Writer-Director:* Michael Verhoeven *Cast:* Lena Stoltze, Monika Baumgautner, Michael Gahr, Fred Stillkrauth, Elisabeth Bertram, Robert Giggenbach, Hans Richard Müller

647. Scuola Elementare

Dante Trilli teaches school in southern Italy but takes another position in Milan. His childhood friend Pilade Mucci also works in Milan and the two are reunited. Dante falls for beautiful Laura, a substitute teacher. She soon quits and becomes a high-paid model. Dante, upset, helps Pilade sell a patent and takes charge of public relations for the new company. Dante realizes that he wants to remain a teacher during the school's award ceremony.
Italy. 1954. 97m. B&W. *Director:* Alberto Lattuada *Cast:* Maria Teresa Albani, Riccardo Billi, Lise Bourdin, Mario Carotenuto, Nadia Catani, René Clermont, Diana Dei, Dario Fo, Floriana Joannucci, Laura Nucci, Patrizia Polvere, Mario Riva

648. Searching for Bobby Fischer

Josh Waitzkin (Max Pomeranc) is a gifted eight-year-old chess player. His parents are torn between a chess hustler (Laurence Fishburne), fast-talking Vinnie and Bruce Pandolfini (Ben Kingsley), a teacher who claims to remember every game Bobby Fischer ever played. Vinnie relies on speed and instinct while Bruce takes an elitist and mystical view of chess. The two teachers ultimately unite in support of the chess prodigy.
Paramount. US. 1993. 110m. C. *Producer:* Scott Rudin, William Wahrman *Director:* Steven Zaillian *Writers* Steven Zaillian, Fred Waitzkin (book) *Cast:* Max Pomeranc, Joe Mantegna, Joan Allen, Ben Kingsley, Laurence Fishburne, Michael Nirenberg, Robert Stephens, David Paymer, Hal Scardino, Vasek Simek, William H. Macy

The Second Awakening of Christa Klages see *Das Zweite Erwachen der Christa Klages*

649. Second Fiddle

A public relations expert (Tyronne Power) is sent in search of an unknown star for the studio's production *Girl of the North*. He finds Minnesota schoolmarm Trudy Hovland (Sonja Henie). Romantic complications ensue.

TCF. US. 1939. 86m. B&W. *Producer:* Gene Markey *Director:* Sidney Lanfield *Writer:* Harry Tugend *Cast:* Sonja Henie, Tyrone Power, Edna May Oliver, Rudy Vallee, Mary Healy, Lyle Talbot, Alan Dinehart

650. The Secret of Black Mountain

Miriam Vale (Vola Vale) travels to California to research her grandfather, gold prospector Jim Vale. To pay for the trip, she has been teaching school. Miriam learns that Jim was robbed and killed but there is no proof of who did it. She is ready to go back home to Vermont when a strange man forces her to his cabin where a woman lays injured by her husband's hand. The woman tells Miriam to look under a stone in the fireplace for a map. Miriam learns the truth about her grandfather and sets out to find his gold.

General Film Co. US. 1917. B&W. *Producers:* H.M. Horkheimer, E.D. Horkheimer *Director:* Otto Hoffman *Cast:* Vola Vale, Philo McCullough, Charles Dudley, George Austin, Henry Crawford, Mignon LeBrun, James Warner, Lewis King, Jack McLaughlin, H.C. Russell

Seeking Asylum see *Chiedo Asilo*

651. Selskaya Uchitelnitsa (A Village Schoolteacher and The Teacher from Shatryj and The Village Teacher)

The story of Russia's political evolution told through the life of a pretty schoolteacher sent to a village in Siberia. It shows her aging over a period of 35 years. She informs the children that better days will come, and she is proven right, in this not-so-subtle propaganda film.

Soviet Union. 1947. 100m. B&W. *Director:* Mark Donskoy *Writer:* Mariya Smirnova *Cast:* Vera Maretskaya, Pavel Oleney, Daniil Sagal, Vladimir Maruta, Vladimir Belokurov, Anatoli Gonichev

652. Une Semaine de Vacances (A Week's Holiday)

Dissatisfied with life, Laurence Cuers (Nathalie Baye), a young schoolteacher from Lyons, takes a week off to think, see old friends, make new friends, visit relatives and wander the town. She re-examines her work, family and love, and her reflections lead her to better understand her life.

Biograph International. France. 1980. 102m. C. *Director:* Bertrand Tavernier

Writers: Marie François Hans, Bertrand Tavernier, Colo Tavernier *Cast:* Nathalie Baye, Gérard Lanvin, Flore Fitzgerald, Michel Galabru, Jean Dasté, Marie-Louise Ebeli, Philippe Delaigue, Geneviève Vauzeilles, Philippe Léotard, Philippe Noiret, Jean-Claude Durand, Catherine Anne Duperray, Jean Soubier, André Mortamais, Thierry Herbivo

653. *Sensei the Teacher*

Twenty-seven years after the atomic bomb was dropped on Nagasaki, a popular schoolteacher is diagnosed with aplastic anemia. Before her death she shares with students her memories of the day of the bombing. Her medical treatment is chillingly portrayed.

Elizo Kikaku Co. Japan. 1983. 100m. C. *Director:* Yutaka Ohsawa *Writer:* Kou Seki *Cast:* Megumi Igarashi, Yasumasa Miyazaki, Aya Shikaya, Tomoko Salto, Kei Yamamoto

654. *Seongnan cosmos (The Angry Cosmos)*

In a rural village school, a young, modern-thinking schoolteacher dedicates herself to the students in her care. She finds herself in conflict with parents and school administration who dislike her liberal views.

Hu Ban-ki Productions. South Korea. 1963. C. *Producer-Director:* Bong-rae Lee *Writer:* Kyeong-ok Kim *Cast:* Aeng-ran Eom, Hie-gab Kim, Jin Kyu Kim, Jong-hwa Park

655. *Seonsaeng Kim Bong-du (Teacher Kim-Bong-du)*

A teacher tries to lure a handful of his students from a small rural school to Seoul in the hopes that he can move on to a better school. His efforts backfire and his school becomes among the highest ranked in the nation.

South Korea. 2003. 117m. C. *Producer:* Mi-hee Kim *Director:* Gyu-seong Jang *Cast:* Seung-won Cha, Hie-bong Byeon, Ji-ru Sung, Jae-eung Lee

656. *Separate Tables*

It's the off-season at the lonely Beauregard Hotel in Bournemoth, and only the long-term tenants are still in residence. Life at the Beauregard is stirred up, however, when the beautiful Ann Shankland (Rita Hayward) arrives to see her alcoholic ex-husband, John Malcolm (Burt Lancaster), who is secretly engaged to Pat Cooper (Wendy Hiller), the woman who runs the hotel. Meanwhile, overbearing and snobbish Mrs. Railton-Bell (Gladys Cooper) discovers that the kindly if rather reserved Major Pollock (David Niven) is not what he appears to be. The news is particularly shocking for her frail daughter, Sibyl (Deborah Kerr), who is secretly in love with the major. Then there's an unmarried young couple hiding out, and several elderly characters (including a retired schoolteacher played by Felix Aylmer) sitting out the ends of their lives.

UA/Hecht-Hill-Lancaster. US. 1958. 98m. B&W. *Producer:* Harold Hecht

Director: Delbert Mann *Writers:* Terrence Rattigan, John Gay *Cast:* Burt Lancaster, Rita Hayworth, David Niven, Deborah Kerr, Wendy Hiller, Gladys Cooper, Cathleen Nesbitt, Felix Aylmer, Rod Taylor, Audrey Dalton, May Hallatt

657. *SER (Freedom in Paradise)*

Thirteen-year-old Sasha is at a residential school for troubled children. His mother is dead and his father is a political prisoner. He is always trying to escape but he is also always caught.

Mosfilm. Soviet Union. 1989. 75m. C. *Writer-Director:* Sergei Bodrov *Cast:* Volodya Kozyrev, Alexander Bureyev, Svetlana Gaitan, Vitautas Tomkus

658. *Seulpeumeneun ije geuman (No More Sorrow)*

Third grader Mi-na seems cheerful in class but at home she is often in tears. She alone cares for her infant brother and invalid father. Sometimes she must miss school to search for herbs to ease her father's pain. When the new teacher learns her secret, she comes up with a plan to improve Mi-na's life.

Woosung Productions. South Korea. 1978. 95m. C. *Producer:* Yong-deok Kim *Director:* Jun-shik Kim *Writers:* Mi-na Park, Sam-yuk Yoon *Cast:* Soo-yeon Kang, Geun-hyeong Park, Hye-suk Han, Hun Jang, Seung-nam Kim, Seung-yeol Lee, Il-ju Yun, Dae-hyeon Kim, Sun-cheol Kim, Jeon Son

659. *Seven Faces of Dr. Lao*

Elderly Dr. Lao, a Chinese showman, rides into the desert town of Abalone. While placing an ad in the local newspaper, he meets Ed Cunningham, the editor. Ed is romancing Angela Benedict, the prim and proper schoolteacher, librarian and widowed mother of an eight-year-old boy. Ed is also battling the town bully Clint Stark. During his show, Dr. Lao disguises himself to show how weak and small-minded the townspeople are. In this fantasy, a pet fish becomes a huge serpent after two thugs break its bowl. Dr. Lao's Pan unleashes the inner woman of Angela.

MGM. US. 1964. 100m. C. *Producer-Director:* George Pal *Writers:* Charles Beaumont, Charles G. Finney (novel) *Cast:* Tony Randall, Arthur O'Connell, John Ericson, Barbara Eden, Noah Beery, Jr., Lee Patrick, Minerva Urecal, John Qualen, Frank Kreig, Peggy Rea, Eddie Little Sky, Royal Dano, Argentina Brunetti, John Doucette, Dal McKennon, Frank Cady, Chubby Johnson, Douglas Fowley, Kevin Tate

660. *Shadow Zone: My Teacher Ate My Homework*

A child purchases a stuffed bear that looks like his teacher Mrs. Fink (Shelley Duvall). Soon the bear looks even more like Mrs. Fink and it acts like a voodoo doll.

Ardustry Home Entertainment. Canada. 1997. C. *Director:* Stephen Williams *Writers:* Garfield Reeves-Stevens, Judith Reeves-Stevens *Cast:* Shelley Duvall, Gregory Smith, Sheila McCarthy, Edwin Hodge, Diana Theodore, Dara Perlmutter,

Tim Progosh, John Neville, Margot Kidder, Mackenzie Gray, Dan Warry-Smith, Karen Robinson, Damon D'okiveira

661. *Shao nian 15/16 shi (They Don't Care About Us)*

An idealistic young architect agrees to take a substitute teaching job at an inner city junior high school after the job drives her friend to a nervous breakdown. She faces apathetic teachers and budding criminals but takes on the system to help give the students hope.

Hong Kong. 1996. C. *Director:* Kim Wah Lo *Writer:* Sharon Hui *Cast:* Hoi Ying Chang, Woody Chan, Vincent Kok, Jerry Lamb, Annabelle Lau, Siu-Kei Lee, Theresa Lee, Tang Chi Lin, Carlo Ng, Fong Fong Poon, Kwan Yuen Wong, Yut Fei Wong

662. *She Stood Alone*

In 1832 Connecticut, Prudence Crandall (Mare Winningham), an ex-Quaker and teacher, opens the Canterbury Boarding School for Young Ladies. After she allows an African American girl to sit in the back of the class, Prudence begins accepting other non-white students. Outraged, the local people forbid their daughters to go to the school. There is a trial and eventually the school becomes an all-black girls' school.

US. 1991. 95m. C. *Producer:* Barry Bernardi *Director:* Jack Gold *Writer:* Bruce Franklin Singer *Cast:* Mare Winningham, Ben Cross, Taurean Blacque, Robert Desiderio, Daniel Davis

663. *The Sheriff*

The sheriff is inspired to deeds of heroism after seeing a Douglas Fairbanks movie. A desperado comes into town and causes turmoil for the local schoolteacher, with whom the sheriff is in love. The desperado captures the teacher and threatens her with death. The sheriff's dog gets into the cabin and unties the teacher just as the villain is shot.

Paramount. US. 1918. 18m. B&W. *Writer-Director:* Roscoe "Fatty" Arbuckle *Cast:* Roscoe "Fatty" Arbuckle, Betty Compson, Monty Banks, Glen Cavender

664. *Sheriff's Girl*

The sheriff loves the schoolteacher but she wants to travel before marrying him. The bank is robbed and a fugitive hides in the schoolhouse, aided by the teacher. The sheriff discovers them together en route to New York. It turns out that the fugitive is her brother and the brother was framed for the bank robbery.

Rayart Pictures. US. 1926. B&W. *Director:* Ben Wilson *Cast:* Ben Wilson, Fang (dog)

665. *Shiloh 2: Shiloh Season*

In this sequel set in Friendly, West Virginia, the hard-working Preston family includes seventh-grader Marty and his adopted dog Shiloh. The town has a kindly country doctor and the new schoolteacher is too sweet to be true. At school the teacher discusses the important difference between truth and gossip.

Legacy Releasing. US. 1999. 96m. C. *Producers:* Carl Borack, Dale Rosenbloom *Director:* Sandy Tung *Writers:* Dale Rosenbloom, Phyllis Reynolds Naylor (novel) *Cast:* Michael Moriarty, Scott Wilson, Zachary Browne, Ann Dowd, Caitlin Wachs, Joe Pichler, Rachel David, Marissa Leigh, Bonnie Bartlett, Rod Steiger

666. Ships That Pass in the Night

An architect and a suffragist schoolteacher fall in love at a tuberculosis sanatorium.

Screen Plays. Great Britain. 1921. B&W. *Director:* Percy Nash *Writers:* Percy Nash, Beatrice Marraden (novel) *Cast:* Filippi Sowson, Francis Roberts, Daisy Markham, Arthur Vezin, Irene Rooke

667. Shunko

The tale of a city schoolteacher struggling to establish a school in a primitive region of Argentina.

Argentina. 1960. 76m. *Producer:* Leo Kanaf *Director:* Lautaro Murua *Writers:* Jorge Washington Abalos, Augusto Roa Bastos *Cast:* Carlos Garay, Ángel Greco, Oscar Llompart, Raúl Parini

668. Siberia

Imperial Russian Army officer Petroff (Edmund Lowe) is in love with schoolteacher Sonia Vronsky (Alma Rubens), who is involved with revolutionaries. Sonia and her brother are exiled to Siberia. Petroff is sent to Siberia through his position and their romance is continued. During the revolution, Sonia saves Petroff and they escape across the frozen wasteland pursued by wolves and Egor, a revolutionary leader.

Fox Film Corp. US. 1926. B&W. *Producer:* William Fox *Director:* Victor Schertzinger *Writers:* Eve Unsell, A. Dunaev *Cast:* Alma Rubens, Edmund Lowe, Lou Tellegen, Tom Santschi, Paul Panzer, Vadim Uraneff, Lilyan Tashman, Helen D'Algy, James Marcus, Daniel Makarenko, Harry Gripp, Samuel Blum

*The Silent Voice see **The Man Who Played God***

669. Silk Hat Kid

Pale-faced killer Eddie Howard (Lew Ayres) is brought from Albany to protect Tim Martin's (Paul Kelly) casino from a rival mob. Tim runs a legitimate business and is a great friend of Father Joe (William Harrigan), the priest who runs a place for the poor. In his quiet way Father Joe makes a change in Tim when he takes Tim's gun away from him and puts him to work as a boxing instructor at the institution. Trouble begins when Eddie falls in love with schoolteacher Laura Grant

(Mae Clarke), who is desired by Tim. To complicate matters, Laura is caring for a baby which is actually Tim's. When the rivals decide to fight it out, Father Joe makes them throw away their guns and settle the argument with their fists. Tim gets the baby and Eddie gets Laura.

Fox. US. 1935. 70m. B&W. *Producer:* Joseph Engel *Director:* H. Bruce Humberstone *Writers:* Edward Eliscu, Lou Breslow, Dore Schary *Cast:* Lew Ayres, Mae Clarke, Paul Kelly, Ralf Harolde, William Harrigan, Billy Lee, John Qualen, Warren Hymer, Vince Barnett, William Benedict, James Flavin

670. *Simon Birch*

Joe Wenteworth (Joseph Mazzello) is a normal kid living with his mother at grandma's house. His best friend Simon Birch (Ian Michael Smith), a bright kid with dwarfish features, is neglected by his parents. Mr. Baker is portrayed as a compassionate physical education teacher who includes Simon in the phys ed class. Simon doesn't mind speaking up to the minister or the Sunday school teacher (Jan Hooks). His mother's new suitor is local drama teacher Ben Goodrich (Oliver Platt). Tragedy hits during a baseball game when Simon hits a ball that strikes Joe's mother in the head, killing her. She was like a mother to Simon and now Joe doesn't know who his father is. Joe and Simon were estranged after the accident, but have become friends again as they search for Joe's father.

Buena Vista Pictures.US. 1998 110m. C. *Producers:* Laurence Mark, Roger Birnbaum *Director:* Mark Steven Johnson *Writers:* Mark Steven Johnson, John Irving (novel) *Cast:* Ian Michael Smith, Joseph Mazzello, Ashley Judd, Oliver Platt, David Strathairn, Dana Ivey, Jim Carrey, Jan Hooks

The Sin see *Hakai*

671. *The Singing Nun*

Belgian Dominican nun Sister Ann (Debbie Reynolds) becomes involved with helping little Dominic (Ricky Cordell) and his sister Nicole (Katharine Ross). Father Clementi (Ricardo Montalban) hears Sister Ann singing and, against the wishes of Mother Prioress (Greer Garson), enters her into a talent contest. A record deal comes Sister Ann's way as well as an old boyfriend. Unprepared for her newfound fame, she does not immediately embrace a musical career. After a series of actions that alienate the local people, she realizes that perhaps music is her way to make a contribution and share God's gift with others. Soon she finds herself on TV's *The Ed Sullivan Show*. A crisis develops when Dominic is hit by a car. The experience shocks Sister Ann into the realization that she really wants to be a missionary nun rather than a singer. At the conclusion, she becomes a missionary in Africa. This film is based on a real-life nun turned recording artist. She gave up her habit to pursue a singing career which didn't take off. She then failed at running a school for autistic children. She eventually committed suicide.

MGM. US. 1966. 98m. C. *Producer:* John Beck *Director:* Henry Koster *Writers:* John Furia, Sally Benson *Cast:* Debbie Reynolds, Ricardo Montalban, Greer

Garson, Agnes Moorehead, Chad Everett, Katharine Ross, Ed Sullivan, Juanita Moore, Ricky Cordell, Michael Pate, Tom Drake

672. *Sinner's Parade*

To support her sister and her sister's child, Mary Tracy (Dorothy Revier) teaches by day and dances by night. Caught in a raid on the club, she is fired from her teaching position. Mary has two admirers: Morton, the cabaret owner, and Bill, who seems to be good on the outside but runs a crime syndicate. Mary saves Morton's life and finds love and marriage.

Columbia. US. 1928. B&W. *Producer:* Harry Cohn *Director:* John G. Adolfi *Writers:* Beatrice Van, David Lewis *Cast:* Victor Varconi, Dorothy Revier, John Patrick, Edna Marion, Marjorie Bonner, Clarissa Selwynne, Jack Mower

673. *Sister Act*

Lounge singer Deloris Van Cartier (Whoopi Goldberg) sees her Mafia boyfriend kill someone and winds up in the witness protection program. The police hide her in a place where the boyfriend would never look: a convent-school. Soon she becomes Sister Mary Clarence. Against the wishes of Mother Superior (Maggie Smith), Sister Mary Clarence is assigned to the convent's choir. She makes friends with Sister Mary Robert (Wendy Makkena), Sister Mary Lazuras (Mary Wickes), and Sister Mary Patrick (Kathy Najimy). She ends up coaching the choir and making it a big success. Followed by *Sister Act 2: Back in the Habit.*

Buena Vista. US. 1992. 100m. C. *Producer:* Teri Schwartz *Director*: Emile Ardolino *Writer:* Joseph Howard *Cast:* Whoopi Goldberg, Maggie Smith, Kathy Najimy, Wendy Makkena, Mary Wickes, Harvey Keitel, Bill Nunn, Robert Miranda, Ellen Albertini Dow, Carman Zapata, Pat Crawford Brown

674. *Sister Act 2: Back in the Habit*

The sisters ask Deloris Van Cartier/Sister Mary Clarence (Whoopi Goldberg) to once again don the nun's habit to teach music in their parochial school, presided over by Mother Superior (Maggie Smith). Unfortunately the school is slated to be closed. The choir has made it to the state championship, but the mother of the most talented girl has forbidden her to sing.

Buena Vista. US. 1993. 107m. C. *Producers*: Scott Rudin, Dawn Steel *Director*: Bill Duke *Writers:* Joseph Howard, James Orr, Jim Cruickshank, Judi Ann Mason *Cast*: Whoopi Goldberg, Kathy Najimy, Maggie Smith, Barnard Hughes, Mary Wickes, James Coburn, Michael Jeter, Wendy Makkena, Sheryl Lee Ralph, Robert Pastorelli, Thomas Gottschalk, Maggie Smith

675. *The Sixth Sense*

A young boy, Cole, sees dead people and a child psychologist (Bruce Willis) attempts to treat him. Cole attends a private school and even though we initially don't see teachers we can envision him in the classroom. In one scene, he describes his drawing of a man stabbed in the neck with a screwdriver. During class, Cole confronts the teacher who keeps telling Cole to not look at him. Cole shouts out that when the teacher was a little boy he was a stutterer. In fear and anger, the teacher calls Cole a freak. Cole continues seeing dead people but he learns to cope. At the end of the film, the psychologist discovers that he is dead.

Buena Vista. US. 1999. 107m. C. *Producers:* Kathleen Kennedy, Frank Marshall, Barry Mendel *Writer-Director:* M. Night Shyamalan *Cast:* Bruce Willis, Haley Joel Osment, Toni Collett, Olivia Williams, Donnie Wahlbert, Peter Anthony Tambakis, Jeffrey Zubernis, Bruce Norris, Glenn Fitzgerald, Greg Wood, Mischa Barton, Trevor Morgan, Angelica Torn, Firdous Bamji

676. *Skandal um Eva*

Cheery young schoolteacher Eva adopts a little boy. The villagers and school officials are surprised when one day the child runs up to Eva and calls her mother. Gossip runs rampant and her dismissal is demanded. At first the principal and teachers welcome the investigation, but then they learn that all connected with the school will undergo an investigation. They visit Eva and beg her to resign. Everything changes when Eva's fiancé Kurt, the minister of education, turns out to be the father of the child in question.

Foreign Film Exchange. Germany. 1930. 96m. B&W. *Producer:* Henny Porten *Director:* G.W. Pabst *Writers:* Friedrich Raff, Julius Urgiss *Cast:* Henry Porten, Adele Sandrock, Paul Henckels, Kart Ettlinger, Ludwig Stossel, Oscar Sima, Claus Clausen, Fritz Odemar, Käthe Haack, Frigga Braut

677. *Skeezer*

A therapeutic dog belonging to Carrie Jessup (Karen Valentine) works wonders in a home for emotionally disturbed children. The film is based on *Skeezer, Dog with a Mission* by Elizabeth Yates.

ITC Entertainment. US. 1982. 96m. C. *Producer:* Lee Levinson *Director:* Peter Hunt *Writer:* Robert Hamilton *Cast:* Karen Valentine, Dee Wallace, Tom Atkins, Mariclare Costello, Leighton Greer, Justin Lord, Jeremy Licht, Jack De Mave

678. *The Skipper's Wooing*

Schoolteacher Annie Getting (Cynthia Murtagh) sends rivals for her affections to find her missing father, who is hiding because he thinks that he killed someone. Her father is found and Annie gets her true love.

Artistic. Great Britain. 1922. B&W. *Producer:* George Redman *Director:* Manning Haynes *Writers:* Lydia Hayward, W.W. Jacobs (novel) *Cast:* Gordon Hopkirk, Cynthia Murtagh, Johnny Butt, Thomas Marriott, Bobbie Rudd, Jeff Barlow, Charles Levey, Mary Price, J.T. Macmillan, Roy Travers

679. *Sky-High Saunders*

Sky-High Saunders (Al Wilson) saves schoolteacher Helen Leland (Elsie Tarron)

from the unwanted attention of airplane smuggler Delatour (Bud Osborne). Saunders exposes the crooks and gets the girl.
Universal. US. 1927. B&W. *Producer:* Carl Laemmle *Writer-Director:* Bruce Mitchell *Cast:* Al Wilson, Elsie Tarron, Frank Rice, Bud Osborne

680. Sleepers

Four boys growing up in New York's Hell's Kitchen during the 1960s are sent to Wilkinson Home for the Boys when a prank goes deadly. There they are raped repeatedly and tortured by the guards. A caring teacher encourages one boy's dreams and takes notice of his interest in class. She gives the boy a copy of *The Count of Monte Cristo*. Later, as adults, they are connected by that shame. When two of the men see one of their old tormentors, they shoot him. One of the boys is now an assistant DA. Father Bobby (Robert De Niro) is a tough-guy priest who drinks, smokes and threatens. He knew the men as kids and lies on the stand to help them.
Warner. US. 1996. 147m. C. *Producers:* Steve Golin, Barry Levinson *Director:* Barry Levinson *Writers:* Barry Levinson, Lorenzo Carcaterra (book) *Cast:* Brad Pitt, Jason Patric, Joseph Perrino, Brad Renfro, Geoffrey Wigdor, Jonathan Tucker, Robert De Niro, Kevin Bacon, Billy Crudup, Ron Eldard, Dustin Hoffman, Terry Kinney, Minnie Driver, Vittorio Gassman, Bruno Kirby

The Slingshot see Kådisbellan

Small Change see L'Argent de Poche

Small Voices see Munting tinig, Mga

681. The Snob

Nancy Claxton (Norma Shearer) disappears when her wealthy father is involved in a scandal. Nancy becomes a teacher in a small Pennsylvania town where she meets Eugene Curry (John Gilbert), also a teacher. Eugene wants to be someone of social importance and is willing to do anything to climb the ladder. Eugene marries Nancy but continues his affair with wealthy Dorothy Rensheimer (Phyllis Haver). Nancy loses her baby after learning of the affair. When Nancy reveals her wealth, Eugene wants another chance but Nancy is going with her childhood sweetheart.
MGM. US. 1924. B&W. *Producer:* Louis B. Mayer *Director:* Monta Bell *Writer:* Monta Bell *Cast:* John Gilbert, Norma Shearer, Conrad Nagel, Phyllis Haver, Hedda Hopper, Margaret Seddon, Aileen Manning, Hazel Kennedy, Gordon Sackville, Roy Laidlaw, Nellie Bly Baker

682. So Big

Rich girl Selina (Jane Wyman) comes to a small Dutch community outside of Chicago to teach. Selina falls in love with farmer Pervus DeJong (Sterling Hayden).

When Pervus dies, she is left a single mother with no money. Selina raises the boy, who grows up to be a creative architect. There have been several other versions of this movie.

Warner. US. 1953. 101m. B&W. *Producer:* Henry Blanke *Director:* Robert Wise *Writer:* John Twist, Edna Ferber (novel) *Cast:* Jane Wyman, Sterling Hayden, Nancy Olson, Steve Forrest, Elisabeth Fraser, Richard Beymer, Martha Hyer

683. *Solntse Svetit Vsem (The Sun Shines for All)*

Schoolteacher turned Soviet soldier Nikolay Savelyev (Valentin Zubkov) is seriously wounded and blinded during World War II. His nurse Svetlana (Liliya Aleshnikova) is in love with him, and takes him home to his wife and family in the town where he had been a schoolteacher before the war. His return to normal life is troubled. He has an unhappy marriage and, although he resumes his teaching job, he is very upset when a student takes advantage of his blindness to cheat. Nikolay then discovers that Koren (Yevgeniy Burenkov), the new school principal, who calls for his dismissal, is the cowardly deserter responsible for his wartime disability. Even though things are rough, he feels a new sense of responsibility towards his students. He leaves his wife and reunites with Svetlana.

Artkino Pictures. Soviet Union. 1959. 92min. B&W. *Director:* Konstantin Voinov *Writer:* Semyon Freylikh *Cast:* Valentin Zubkov, Liliya Aleshnikova, Tatyana Konyukhova, Yevgeniy Burenkov, Nikolay Sergeyev, Yelena Maksimova, Viktor Koltsov, Olya Narovchatova, Vitya Lobzov, Lyudmila Ovchinnikova, R. Rakitin, A. Lebedev, I. Ryabinin, O. Dolgova, M. Zharova, N. Pogodin, N. Smirnov, V. Seleznyov, S. Korenev, V. Pitsek, L. Chubarov, S. Gorokhova, N. Burenkova, P. Dolzhanov

684. *Song for a Raggy Boy*

After returning to Ireland in 1939, William Franklin (Aidan Quinn) takes a teaching job. The only non-cleric on staff at St. Jude's, an Irish Catholic reform school for boys, he disagrees with Brother John's (Iain Glen) strict disciplinarian style and befriends students like Liam Mercier (John Travers). He intervenes to stop Brother John's vicious punishment and tries to instill a sense of achievement and self-worth in the boys. One boy claims to have been raped by Brother Mac (Marc Warren). The film was based on Patrick Galvin's life at an Irish Catholic reform school.

Lolafilms/Subotica Entertainment. Ireland/Denmark/Great Britain/Spain. 2003. 100m. C. *Producers*: Tristan Lynch, Dominic Wright, John McDonnell, Kevin Byron Murphy *Director*: Aisling Walsh *Writers*: Patrick Galvin, Aisling Walsh, Kevin Byron Murphy *Cast*: Aidan Quinn, Iain Glen, Marc Warren, Dudley Sutton, Alan Devlin, Stuart Graham, John Travers, Chris Newman

685. *Songcatcher*

After being denied a promotion at the university where she teaches music, Lily Penleric (Janet McTeer) goes up an Appalachia mountainside to visit her sister Elna

(Jane Adams), who, with a partner, Harriet Tolliver (E. Katherine Kerr), has established a struggling rustic school in the North Carolina woods. There Lily stumbles upon the discovery of her life: ancient ballads handed down from generation to generation. Two of the locals glimpse Elna and Harriet kissing passionately in the woods and take devastating action against these "whores of Babylon," as the local preacher calls them.

Lions Gate Films. US. 2000. 109m. C. *Producers:* Richard Miller, Ellen Rigas-Venetis *Writer-Director:* Maggie Greenwald *Cast:* Janet McTeer, Michael Davis, Michael Goodwin, Greg Russell Cook, Jane Adams, E. Katherine Kerr, Emmy Rossum, Pat Carroll, Stephanie Roth Haberle, Aidan Quinn, Bart Hansard, Erin Blake Clanton, David Patrick Kelly, Kristin Hall, Michael Harding

686. *Songs and Bullets*

Guitar-playing partners Melody Smith (Fred Scott) and Fuzzy (Al St. John) are mistaken for rustlers but freed in time to perform. Melody meets the new schoolteacher Jeanette Du Mont (Alice Ardell). While the townsmen greet Jeanette in her classroom, a gang robs the hotel safe. The sheriff is part of the gang. Jeanette asks the sheriff to arrest the man that killed her father, a local rancher. The sheriff plots to have her killed as well, but Melody and Fuzzy save her.

Spectrum Pictures Corp. US. 1938. 58m. B&W. *Producer:* Jed Buell *Director:* Sam Newfield *Writer:* George Plympton *Cast:* Fred Scott, Al St. John, Alice Ardell, Charles King, Carl Hackett, Frank La Rue, Richard Cramer, Budd Buster, Jimmy Aubrey, Lew Porter, Sherry Tansey

687. *Sonia*

A student makes a fortune in Mexico, is blinded in war, becomes a teacher and weds a reformed flirt.

Screen Plays. Great Britain. 1921. B&W. *Director:* Denison Clift *Writer:* Denison Clift, Stephen McKenna (novel) *Cast:* Evelyn Brent, Clive Brook, Cyril Raymond, Olaf Hytten, Henry Vibart, M. Gray Murray, Hetta Bartlett, Leo Stormont, Gladys Hamilton, George Travers, Julie Hartley-Milburn

688. *The Sound of Music*

A musical adaptation of the life of Maria von Trapp, set in the 1930s when the Nazis are just beginning to occupy Austria. Maria (Julie Andrews) is a novice at the abbey in Salzburg, and governess to the seven motherless von Trapp children. Mother Abbess (Peggy Wood) is very understanding and supportive of Maria. At first Maria finds the children's father, a retired naval officer, to be a strong disciplinarian and the children to be hostile, but she eventually wins them all over. After she and the father marry, the sisters at the abbey help the von Trapp family escape from the Nazis, who want the captain to serve in their navy.

TCF. US. 1965. 174m. C. *Producer-Director*: Robert Wise *Writers*: Ernest Lehman, Maria Augusta Trapp (book) *Cast*: Julie Andrews, Christopher Plummer, Eleanor Parker, Richard Haydn, Peggy Wood, Charmian Carr, Heather Menzies,

Nicholas Hammond, Duane Chase, Angela Cartwright, Debbie Turner, Kym Karath, Anna Lee, Portia Nelson, Ben Wright, Daniel Truhitte, Norma Varden, Gilchrist Stuart, Marni Nixon, Evadne Baker

689. *Sounder*

The Morgans are a strong, loving family of Louisiana sharecroppers. While searching for his father, who is in a prison camp, David (Kevin Hooks) and his dog Sounder meet Camille Johnson, the black supervisor of a small country school. She shows him many books and introduces him to some black writers. He spends his time in class listening and learning. She encourages him to keep searching for his father and tells him that he did not fail when he couldn't find him. She gives him some books to take home. In the fall, Ms. Johnson wants him to stay with her and continue going to school.

TCF. US. 1972. 105m. C. *Producer:* Robert B. Radnitz *Director:* Martin Ritt *Writer:* Lonnie Elder III, William H. Armstrong (novel) *Cast:* Paul Winfield, Cicely Tyson, Kevin Hooks, Carmen Mathews, James Best, Taj Mahal, Eric Hooks, Yvonne Jarrell, Sylvia Kuumba Williams, Teddy Airhart, Richard Durham, Myrl Sharkey, Inez Durham, William T. Bennett, Janet MacLachlan

690. *Sounder*

A remake of 1972's *Sounder* directed by Kevin Hooks, who played young David in the original. In this version, the teacher is a man.

ABC. Canada/US. 2003. 96m. C. *Director:* Kevin Hooks *Writers:* Bill Cain, William H. Armstrong (novel) *Cast:* Carl Lumbly, Suzzanne Douglass, Daniel Lee Robertson III, Peter MacNeill, Bill Lake, Paul Winfield, Marcus Johnson, Ashley Archer, Joshua Watkis, Eugene Clark, Neil Girvan, Patrick Stevenson, Lili Francks, Bruce McFee, Conrad Coates

691. *Sounder, Part 2*

David is set on getting a school for his area. His father and neighbors work day and night to build the schoolhouse so the local teacher will stay instead of traveling north.

Gamma III. US. 1976. 98m. C. *Director:* William A. Graham *Writers:* Lonne Elder III, William H. Armstrong (novel) *Cast:* Teddy Airhart, Raymond Armelino, Earl Billings, Ronald Bolden, Walter Breaux, Don Bynum, Annazette Chase, Harry Franklin, Emanual Jarrell, Warren Kenner, Kuumba, Taj Mahal, Irene Nofles, Carol Sutten, Harold Sylvester, Ebony Wright, Darryl Young, Erika Young

692. *South Riding*

The story of six people working for a typical local government council. Beneath the surface of public servants' lives runs a personal story. A country squire whose wife is in a mental hospital becomes attracted to a crusading local schoolmistress.

London Films. Great Britain. 1937. 91m. B&W. *Producers:* Alexander Korda,

Victor Saville *Director:* Victor Saville *Writers:* Ian Dalrymple, Donald Bull, Winifred Holtby (novel) *Cast:* Ralph Richardson, Edna Best, Edmund Gwenn, Ann Todd, Glynis Johns, John Clements, Marie Lohr, Milton Rosmer, Edward Lexy, Joan Ellum, Josephine Wilson, Peggy Novak, Gus McNaughton, Lewis Casson, Felix Aylmer, Jean Cadell, Skelton Knaggs

693. *Spare the Rod*

Just out of school and new to teaching, John Saunders (Max Bygraves) is assigned to a tough East End inner city school and a class of rude and hostile kids. The general rule amongst the teachers is to enforce discipline with physical pain but Saunders wants to win their hearts and minds. He must also win over the administration.

British Lion. Great Britain. 1961. 93m. B&W. *Producers:* Victor Lyndon, Jock Jacobson *Director:* Leslie Norman *Writers:* John Cresswell, Michael Croft (novel) *Cast:* Max Bygraves, Geoffrey Keen, Donald Pleasence, Richard O'Sullivan, Betty McDowall, Eleanor Summerfield, Mary Merrall, Peter Reynolds, Jean Anderson, Claire Marshall, Jeremy Bulloch, Aubrey Woods

Spinster see *Two Loves*

694. *Spoorloos (The Vanishing)*

When a Dutch couple on a motor trip stop for a rest, the woman disappears, never to be seen again. Three years later the man is still obsessed about what happened to her. We learn about the monster who took her–a happily married schoolteacher with two children. They meet and the monster agrees to let him know her fate.

Golden Egg Film/Ingrid Productions. Netherlands/France. 1988. 106m. C. *Director:* George Sluizer *Writer:* Tim Krabbé *Cast:* Bernard-Pierre, Donnadieu, Gene Bervoets, Johanna Ter Steege, Gwen Eckhaus

Spring River Flows East see *Yijiang Chunshul Xiang Dong Liu*

695. *The Spy in Black (U-Boat 29)*

Captain Hardt (Conrad Veidt), a World War I German submarine commander, is leading a mission to attack the British Fleet. When he puts ashore on a Scottish island to meet his contacts, he meets the local schoolmistress (Valerie Hobson).

Harefield. Great Britain. 1939. 82m. B&W. *Producers:* Irving Asher, Alexander Korda *Director:* Michael Powell *Writers:* Emeric Pressburger, Roland Pertwee, J. Storer Clouston (novel) *Cast:* Conrad Veidt, Valerie Hobson, Sebastian Shaw, Marius Goring, June Duprez, Athole Stewart, Agnes Lauchlan, Helen Haye, Cyril Raymond, Grant Sutherland, Robert Rendel, Torin Thatcher, Skelton Knaggs

696. *Star Kid*

Insecure 12-year-old Spencer attends Waverly Street Elementary School, fears the class bully, can't talk to girls and trembles when his teacher asks him to hold a big spider. However Spencer also encounters evil aliens, cyborsuits, and crashed spaceships. The pretty science teacher proves she's just one of the gang by using the slang term for "passing air" in science class. Spencer's widowed father is very taken with her.

Trimark Pictures. US. 1997. 101m. C. *Producer:* Jennie Lew Tugend *Writer-Director:* Manny Coto *Cast:* Joseph Mazzello, Ashlee Levitch, Joey Simmrin, Richard Gilliland, Corinne Bohrer, Jack McGee

697. *The Stars Look Down*

Davey Fenwick (Michael Redgrave) leaves his mining village on a university scholarship, intending to return to better support the miners against the owners. He comes back as a schoolteacher before finishing his degree because he has fallen in love and married cheap busybody Jenny (Margaret Lockwood). Jenny still loves her old boyfriend. Davey tries to become a spokesman for the miners. Nothing seems to change as the miners continue to face death in the pits.

MGM. Great Britain. 1940. 110m. B&W. *Producers:* Isadore Goldsmith, Maurice J. Wilson *Director:* Carol Reed *Writers:* A. Coppel, A.J. Cronin (novel) *Cast:* Michael Redgrave, Margaret Lockwood, Emlyn Williams, Nancy Price, Allan Jeayes, Edward Rigby, Linden Travers, Cecil Parker, Milton Rosmer

698. *Starting Over*

Phil Potter (Burt Reynolds), a divorced man, is torn between his singer ex-wife Jessica (Candice Bergen) and a meek nursery schoolteacher, Marilyn Holmberg (Jill Clayburgh). In a furniture store, his psychiatrist brother counsels him through a premarital crisis.

Paramount. US. 1979. 106m. C. *Producers:* Alan J. Pakula, James Brooks *Director:* Alan J. Pakula *Writer:* James Brooks *Cast:* Burt Reynolds, Jill Clayburgh, Candice Bergen, Charles Durning, Austin Pendleton, Frances Sternhagen, Mary Kay Place, MacIntyre Dixon, Jay O. Sanders, Charles Kimbrough

699. *Station Jim*

Bob, a railroad station porter, discovers a dog hiding in some crates and adopts it as the station mascot in order to impress Harriet, the new teacher at the local orphanage. The mascot, "Station Jim," chases moles out of the stationmaster's garden, alerts Bob to a fire at the orphanage, and befriends young orphan Henry. With Queen Victoria arriving soon, Station Jim must save the day.

Pathé Frères. Great Britain. 2000. 87m. C. *Producer:* Ann Scott *Director:* John Roberts *Writer:* Mark Wallington *Cast:* George Cole, Charlie Creed-Miles, Frank Finlay, Laura Fraser

Stolen Eyes see *Otkradnati Ochi*

700. Stop, Look, and Listen

Luther Meek (Larry Semon), a subdued and frugal young man, is in love with schoolteacher Dorothy (Dorothy Dwan), who wants to try her luck as an actress before consenting to marriage. Luther is tricked into financing a musical play with Dorothy as the lead. Troubles occur but Dorothy gets her fill of acting and is now ready for marriage.

Pathé Exchange. US. 1926. B&W. *Producer:* John Adams *Director:* Larry Semon *Writers:* Harry B. Smith, Larry Semon *Cast:* Larry Semon, Dorothy Dwan, Mary Carr, William Gillespie, Lionel Belmore, Bull Montana, Oliver Hardy, Curtis McHenry, Joseph Swickard

701. La Storia (History)

Ida (Claudia Cardinale), a half-Jewish schoolteacher, lives in fear of persecution and feels guilt for hiding her background. Ida is the mother of a teenage boy and an epileptic son sired through rape by a German soldier. Terrible things keep happening to Ida and her two sons.

Worldwide Distribution. Italy. 1986. 150m. C. *Producer:* Paolo Infascelli *Director:* Luigi Comencini *Writers:* Suso Cecchi D'Amico, Cristina Comencini, Ligi Comencini, Elsa Morante (novel) *Cast:* Claudia Cardinale, Francisco Rabal, Andrea Spada, Antonio Degli Fiorenzo Fiorentini, Tobias Hoesl, Lambert Wilson

The Storm see *Jhor*

Stranded see *Valley of Mystery*

Strange Gods see *Los Dioses Ajenos*

Strayed see *Les Égarés*

702. Sudden Terror: The Hijacking of School Bus 17

A movie based on actual events. In debt to the IRS, Harry Kee (Michael Paul Chan) hijacks a school bus to draw attention to the unfairness he has to suffer. In the bus are special needs kids who start to panic, but bus driver Marta Caldwell (Maria Conchita Alonso) is calm under pressure. Kee becomes more and more deranged and the police who surround the bus are ready to shoot. The teachers and other involved parties are very concerned.

Sony Pictures. US. 1996. 91m. C. *Producers:* Laurie Hannon-Anton, S. Bryan Hickox, Diane Jacques, Jonathan Rintels *Director:* Paul Schneider *Writer:* Jonathan Rintels *Cast:* Maria Conchita Alonso, Marcy Walker, Michael Paul Chan, Dennis Boutsikaris, Bruce Weitz, Elizabeth Omilami, Christina Karman, Avis-Marie

Barnes, Brett Rice, Rus Blackwell, Jim R. Coleman, John Archie, Emiliano Díaz, Leesa Halstead, Mark Conlon

703. *The Suffragette*

The uncle of a disowned schoolmistress destroys her father's amended will.

Pathe. Great Britain. 1913. B&W. *Cast:* Agnes Glynne, James Carew, Evangeline Hilliard

704. *Suffragettes in the Bud*

Schoolgirls play trick on their schoolmistress.

Clarendon. Great Britain. 1913. B&W. *Director:* Percy Stow *Cast:* Maude Derby

The Summer of Bobby Charlton see *L'Estate di Bobby Charlton*

705. *Summerfield*

A young schoolteacher goes to a small fishing town in Victoria to replace a teacher who disappeared. She is fascinated by the townspeople and by the teacher's mysterious disappearance. He discovers that one of his students has a rare blood disease.

Roadshow. Australia. 1977. 95m. C. *Producer:* Patricia Lovell *Director:* Ken Hannam *Cast:* Nick Tate, John Waters, Elizabeth Alexander, Michelle Jarman, Charles "Bud" Tingwell, Geraldine Turner, Max Cullen

The Sun Shines for All see *Solntse Svetit Vsem*

706. *Sunstruck*

A Welsh schoolteacher emigrates to the Australian outback and starts a school choir.

MGM-EMI. Great Britain. 1972. 92m. C. *Producers:* Jack Neary, James Grafton *Director:* James Gilbert *Writers:* Stan Mars, James Gilbert, James Grafton, Elwyn Jones *Cast:* Harry Secombe, Maggie Fitzgibbon, John Meillon, Dawn Lake, Peter Whittle, Bobby Limb, Norman Erskine, Jack Allen, Lornal Wilde, Roger Cox, Tommy Mack, John Armstrong, Stuart Wagstaff, Jeff Ashby, Max Brougy, Dennis Jordan

707. *Sur: The Melody of Life*

Middle-aged composer-singer Vikramaditya Singh (Lucky Ali) runs a small music school. He hopes to find a great talented student and shape that person. When he hears Tina Marie (Gauri Karnik) singing in a choir, he knows he has found his future star. Tina begins learning to read music and play the violin. Soon her music is praised, but jealousy sets in for Vikramaditya. He steals her melody and releases it under his name. Tina is so upset that she leaves the school. He realizes his mistake and does make her a star, then returns to teaching music.

Media Patters. India. 2002. C. *Producers:* Pooja Bhatt, Rangita Pritish Nandy *Director:* Tanuja Chandra *Writers:* Tanuja Chandra, Vibba Singh *Cast:* Lucky Ali, Simone Singh, Achint Kanur, Ehsan Khan, Harsh Vasisht, Yashodhan Bal, Gauri Karnik, Divya Dutta, Baby Gazala, Parinaaz, Pravesh Kumar, Zafar Sanjari, Vishal Kapoor, Anil Yadav, Gautam Saugat

Sweet Emma, Dear Böbe see *Édes Emma, Dróga Böbe*

708. *Sweet Inniscarra*

In 1930s Ireland, a millionaire impersonates a simple schoolteacher to win the love of a pretty young woman.

Emmett More. Great Britain. 1934. B&W. *Writer-Director:* Emmett Moore *Cast:* Sean Rogers, Mae Ryan

709. *Sylvia*

Young Sylvia Henderson (Eleanor David), her husband Keith (Tom Wilkinson) and their children arrive at their new post in 1940s New Zealand. Keith will be headmaster of the small remote schoolhouse and Sylvia will be a teacher. Still recovering from a nervous breakdown, Sylvia cautiously starts to teach. Initially the Maori children have no interest in learning European history and the English language. Sylvia encourages the children to become involved. This film is a portrait of real-life teacher Sylvia Ashton-Warner, whose work with Maori children became the basis of her pioneering educational theories.

Southern Light/Cinepro. New Zealand. 1985. 98m. C. *Producers:* Don Reynolds, Michael Firth *Director:* Michael Firth *Writers:* Michael Quill, F. Fairfax, Michael Firth, Sylvia Ashton (books) *Cast:* Eleanor David, Nigel Terry, Tom Wilkinson, Mary Regan, Martyn Sanderson, Terence Cooper, David Letch, Sarah Peirce

710. *Szentjános Fejevétele (The Martyrdom of St. John)*

The story of a young schoolteacher and her struggles in a village school.

Mafilm-Budapest Studio. Hungary. 1966. 87m. *Director:* Márk Novák *Writer* Lajos Galambos (novel) *Cast:* Ilona Béres, Islván Sztankay, Margit Dayka, Ádám Szirtes, János Görbe, Ilona Agárdy, Károly Kovács, József Fonyó, Kornélia Sallay, Bertalan Solti, András Bálint, Tibor Molnár

711. *Taiyo o nusunda otoko (The Man Who Stole the Sun)*

Hip, long-haired science teacher Makato Kido (Kenji Sawada) wants to build a homemade atomic bomb and use it to demand a Rolling Stones concert in Tokyo. He steals some plutonium and, while he is building the bomb, his pet cat licks the plutonium and dies — possibly the teacher's fate also.

Kitty Film. Japan. 1979. 147m. C. *Director:* Kazuhiko Hasegawa *Writers:* Leonard Schrader, Kazuhiko Hasegawa *Cast:* Kenji Sawada, Bunta Sugawara, Kimiko Ikegami, Yutaka Mizutani, To-shiyuki Nishida

712. *Takhté siah (Blackboards)*

The story of the plight of a group of nomadic teachers who travel the mountainous Kurdistan region of Iran, blackboards strapped to their backs, in search of students. They offer education for food, but are turned down. Two teachers, Said and Reeboir, break from the group and take separate paths. Said meets a tribe of 100 nomads who have gotten lost searching for their homeland. The group has one lone woman, her ailing father and a little boy. Said marries the woman. Reeboir travels with a group of boys acting as mules carrying contraband. He helps one boy write his name. Both groups are approaching the Iraqi border with fear.

Leisure TimeFeatures/Kimstim Iran/Italy/Japan. 2000. 85m. C. *Producer:* Mohamad Ahmadi *Director:* Samira Makhmalbaf *Writers:* Mohsen Makhmalbaf, Samira Makhmalbaf *Cast:* Said Mohamadi, Behnaz Jafari, Bahman Ghobadi, Mohamad Karim Rahmati, Rafat Moradi, Mayas Rostami, Saman Akbari, Ahmad Bahrami, Mohamad Moradi, Karim Moradi, Hassan Mohamadi, Somaye Veisee

713. *Tamahine*

A lovely South Seas island girl travels to England when her father dies and becomes the ward of her kindly cousin, headmaster of a boys' school. She doesn't realize her beauty and power over men. She marries the son of her cousin, who eventually becomes head of the school. His father moves to the island where she came from.

ABP. Great Britain. 1963. 95m. C. *Producer:* John Bryan *Director:* Philip Leacock *Writers:* Denis Cannan, Thelma Nicklaus (novel) *Cast:* John Fraser, Nancy Kwan, Dennis Price, Derek Nimmo, Justine Lord, James Fox, Coral Browne, Michael Gough, Allan Cuthbertson, Dick Bentley, Howard Marion Crawford

714. *Tänk, om jag gifter mig med prästen*

Eva Oern (Viveca Lindfors) gets a schoolteaching position in rural Vikarlunda. She does not quite live up to the townspeople's idea of the ideal female teacher. She has an affair with the local priest, but they must keep their love a secret.

Sweden. 1941. *Producers:* Stellan Claësson, Per Lindberg *Director:* Ivar Johansson *Writers:* Evar Johansson, Ester Lindin (book) *Cast:* Viveca Lindfors, Torsten Bergström, Greta Forsgren, Anna-Lisa Fröberg, Linnéa Hillberg, Torsten Hillberg, Axel Högel, Anna Lindahl, Nils Lundell, Helge Mauritz, Barbro Ribbing, Erik Rosén, Georg Rydeberg, Viran Rydkvist, Ruth Stevens

715. *The Tao of Steve*

Dex (Donal Logue), an underachieving, overweight kindergarten teacher, believes in a life celebrating the lax and lazy. He preaches the virtues of irresponsibility combining that concept with the worship of cool celebrities. His new girlfriend encourages him to change his ways.

Sony Pictures. US. 2000. 87m. C. *Producer:* Anthony Bregman *Director:* Jenniphr Goodman *Writers:* Jenniphr Goodman, Duncan North, Green Goodman *Cast:* Donal Logue, Greer Goodman, James "Kimo" Wills, Ayelet Kaznelson, David Aaron Baker, Nina Jaroslaw, John Hines, John Harrington Blad

716. *Tattoo, a Love Story*

Uptight elementary schoolteacher Sara (Megan Edwards) is horrified when one of her students brings in Virgil, a biker and tattoo artist, for show and tell. She finds herself wanting to know more about his lifestyle which differs from her well-ordered life.

Ardustry. US. 2002. C. *Producers:* Stephen F. Davies, Mike Vukas *Director:* Richard W. Bean *Writers:* Richard W. Bean, Gregg Sacon *Cast:* Megan Edwards, Virgil Mignanelli, Benjamin Burdick, Kathryn Cherasaro, Gordon Reinhart, Stitch Marker, Stacey Bean, Stephen F. Davies

717. *Tavalod-E Parvaneh (Birth of a Butterfly)*

The film consists of three tales in which faith is tested. In one parable, the main character is an energetic schoolteacher who has left civilization for the wilderness to teach the children of a remote village. He advises the people about lost cows and sons, and word spreads that he is a prophet. When a flood threatens the village, the people plead with him for help. When he admits that he has no powers, the people do not believe him.

Cima Film. Iran. 1998. 98m. C. *Director:* Mojtaba Raei *Writer:* Saeid Shapouri *Cast:* Rahim Jahani, Mahmud Nazar Alian, Mohammad M. Faqih, Zahra Farhadi, Seyed Sayeed Musavi, Hamid Nahrain

Taxi to the John see *Taxi zum Klo*

718. *Taxi zum Klo (Taxi to the John)*

This sexually explicit film about a gay grade school teacher details his daily routine and his evening sexual affairs. Eventually he loses his job.

Promovision International Films. West Germany. 1981. 92m. C. *Producers:* Laurens Straub, Frank Ripploh, Horst Schier *Writer-Director:* Frank Ripploh *Cast:* Frank Ripploh, Bernd Broaderup, Orpha Termin, Peter Fahrni, Dieter Godde, Gitte Lederer, Hans-Gerd Mertens, Franco Papadou, Hans Jurgen Moller

The Teacher see *Sensei the Teacher*

719. *The Teacher*

In early 1961, a 15-year-old Havana boy, student teacher Mario, goes into remote Cuban swamps as a member of Castro's Conrado Benitez Brigade to eliminate illiteracy. He teaches the peasants to read as well as overcoming his own fears.

El Brigadista. Cuba. 1977. 113m.C. *Director:* Octavio Cortazar *Writer:* Luis R. Noguera *Cast:* Patricio Wood, Salvador Wood, Rene de la Cruz, Luis Alberto Ramirez, Luis Rielo, Mario Balmaseda

The Teacher and the Miracle see *Il Maestro*

The Teacher from Shatryj see *Sleskaya uchitelnitsa*

The Teacher from Vigevano see *Il Maestro di Vigevano*

Teacher Kim Bong-du see *Seonsaeng Kim Bong-du*

720. *Teacher, Teacher*

Hamilton Cade (David McCallum), an alcoholic teacher trying to put his life back together, accepts a job tutoring an exceptional child, Freddie (Billy Schulman). Hamilton soon learns that Freddie is mentally challenged. Charles Carter (Ossie Davis), who works for Freddie's father, also takes an interest in Freddie learning.

US. 1969. C. *Producer:* George Lefferts *Director:* Fielder Cook *Writer:* Ian Sloane *Cast:* Ossie Davis, George Grizzard, David McCallum, Billy Schulman

721. *Teacher's Pet*

Leonard is a fourth grader whose mother Mary Lou Helperman is his teacher. She has been nominated for a teaching award. Unbeknownst to Mrs. Helperman, Leonard's dog Spot has been impersonating a boy, Scott, who happens to be her star pupil. Spot wants nothing more than to be a real boy, and sees a method when mad scientist Ivan Krank appears on television. Krank thinks he can turn animals into humans. Spot is turned into a boy but it isn't like he thought it would be.

Buena Vista. US. 2004. 74m. Animated. C. *Producer:* Stephen Swofford *Director:* Timothy Bjorklund *Writers:* Bill and Cheri Steinkellner *Voices:* Nathan Lane, Shaun Flemming, Kesley Grammer, Paul Reubens, Megan Mullally, David Ogden Stiers

722. *The Teacher's Unexpected Bath*

Small boys watch in glee as a schoolteacher is drenched by a bucket of water placed over the door.

American Mutoscope Co. US. 1898. B&W.

723. *The Teacher's Unexpected Ducking*

Two mischievous youths place a pail of water over a door and then knock. When the female schoolteacher opens the door, she is drenched.

American Mutoscope and Biograph Co. US. 1903. B&W.

724. Term of Trial

Graham Weir (Laurence Olivier) is a dedicated schoolteacher in a poor area of England. He drinks to escape the taunting of his wife, who thinks he is spineless. His students don't care about learning until one student asks for extra tutoring. She falls in love with him but he refuses to have sex. She is so upset that she accuses him of sexual assault. Graham is tried and convicted, but the girl breaks down and he is cleared. He and his wife reunite after he lies and tells her that they did have an affair.

Romulus. Great Britain. 1962. 130m. B&W. *Producer:* James Woolf *Director:* Peter Glenville *Writers:* Peter Glenville, James Barlow (novel) *Cast:* Laurence Olivier, Sarah Miles, Simone Signoret, Hugh Griffith, Terence Stamp, Roland Culver, Frank Pettingell, Thora Hird, Dudley Foster, Norman Bird, Newton Blick, Allan Cuthbertson, Nicholas Hannen, Lloyd Lamble, Vanda Godsell, Earl Cameron

Terror House see *The Night Has Eyes*

A Test of Love see *Annie's Coming Out*

725. Texas Jack

After a medicine show is run out of town, entertainer Texas Jack Carroll (Jack Perrin) and his horse Starlight meet Ann Hall (Jayne Regan). Ann has been hired by saloon owner Don Corey (Robert Walker) as schoolteacher in the rough town of Escondido. During a fight to help a friend get the money owed him, Jack loses a locket with a picture of his sister Helen, who committed suicide. He notices that Corey recognized the photo, thus confirming Jack's idea that he was the man who hired Helen to be a schoolteacher but forced her into working in a dance hall. Corey kidnaps Ann to put her in a dance hall, but Jack comes to the rescue. Jack and Ann will marry and continue in the medicine show.

State Rights William Steiner. US. 1935. 62m. B&W. *Director:* B.B. Ray *Writer:* Carl Krusada *Cast:* Jack Perrin, Jayne Regan, Nelson McDowell, Robert Walker, Cope Borden, Lew Meehan, Blackie Whiteford, Budd Buster, Oscar Gahan, Jim Oates, Starlight

There Was a Father see *Chichi Ariki*

726. There's Hair

A girl stops a governess from marrying her widowed father.
Bamforth. Great Britain. 1915. B&W. *Director:* Cecil Birch *Cast:* Baby Langley

727. These Three

At an exclusive girl's school, founded and run by friends Martha Dobie (Miriam Hopkins) and Karen Wright (Merle Oberon), Mary Tilford (Bonita Granville)

falsely accuses the two women of being involved in a romantic triangle with a male friend, Dr. Joe Cardin (Joel McCrea). Even though the girl recants, the school is ruined by the scandal.

UA. US. 1936. 93m. B&W. *Producer:* Samuel Goldwyn *Director:* William Wyler *Writer:* Lillian Hellman *Cast:* Merle Oberon, Miriam Hopkins, Joel McCrea, Bonita Granville, Catherine Doucet, Alma Kruger, Marcia Mae Jones, Margaret Hamilton, Walter Brennan

They Don't Care About Us see *Shao nian 15/16 shi*

728. *They Shall Have Music (Melody of Youth)*

In New York, street urchin Frankie (Gene Reynolds) finds tickets to a Jascha Heifetz concert, which renews his interest in the violin. He runs away from home and comes across a music school for children. Kindly Professor Lawson (Walter Brennan) takes him in. The school is facing foreclosure but the kids and Frankie get Heifetz to perform and support the school

UA. US. 1939. 105m. B&W. *Producer:* Samuel Goldwyn *Director:* Archie Mayo *Writers:* John Howard Lawson, Irmgard von Cube *Cast:* Joel McCrea, Jascha Heifetz, Andrea Leeds, Gene Reynolds, Walter Brennan, Porter Hall, Terry Kilburn, Diana Lynn

729. *Things Are Looking Up*

Prim and proper schoolteacher Bertha Fytte (Cicely Courtneidge), not liked by her students, secretly elopes with a wrestler. Her twin sister, circus performer Cicely (Cicely Courtneidge), helps her conceal the wedding by taking her place at the school. Cicely does quite well and is in the running to replace the retiring headmistress.

Gaumont. Great Britain. 1935. 78m. B&W. *Producer:* Michael Balcon *Director:* Albert de Courville *Writers:* Stafford Davies, Con West *Cast:* Cicely Courtneidge, William Gargan, Max Miller, Mary Lawson, Dick Henderson, Dick Henderson, Jr., Judy Kelly, Suzanne Lenglen, Vivien Leigh, Mark Lester, Henrietta Watson, Cicely Oates, Judy Kelly, Danny Green, Wyn Weaver, Alma Taylor

This Age Without Pity see *Anthracite — Cet Âge Est Sans Pitié*

730. *This Could Be the Night*

Virtuous schoolteacher Anne Leeds (Jean Simmons) answers an ad for a part-time secretarial job during the night shift at the Tonic nightclub.

MGM. US. 1957. 104m. B&W. *Producer:* Joe Pasternak *Director:* Robert Wise *Writer:* Isobel Lennart *Cast:* Jean Simmons, Paul Douglas, Anthony Franciosa, Julie Wilson, Joan Blondell, Neile Adams, William Ogden Joyce, Ray Anthony, J. Carrol Naish, Rafael Campos, ZaSu Pitts, Tom Helmore, Murvyn Vye, Vaughn Taylor, Frank Ferguson, James Todd, John Harding

731. This Is My Father

Irish-American schoolteacher Kieran Johnson (James Caan) and Jack (Jacob Tierney) arrive in their Irish homeland. Kieran is searching for clues to his father's identity, armed with a snapshot of his mother and an unknown beau.

Sony Pictures Classics. US. 1998. 120m C. *Producers:* Nicolas Clermont, Phillip King *Writer-Director:* Paul Quinn *Cast:* James Caan, Jacob Tierney, Colm Meaney, Moira Deady, Aidan Quinn, Moya Farrelly, Gina Moxley, Stephen Rea, John Cusack, Brendan Gleeson

732. This Land Is Mine

A French town occupied by Nazis is the home of meek schoolteacher Albert Lory (Charles Laughton), his overbearing and possessive mother Emma (Una O'Connor), their next door neighbor and fellow teacher Louise Martin (Maureen O'Hara) and her brother Paul (Kent Smith). Albert secretly loves Louise. The mayor has ordered the head of the school, Professor Sorel (Philip Merivale), to destroy the works of Plato and Aristotle. Albert complies but Louise vows that one day she will paste the pages back. During a bombing, Louise cheers while Albert cringes in a cellar. Paul bombs a group of German troops and is hunted. The Germans round up hostages and when Albert is taken, his mother informs on Paul. Paul is shot down by German soldiers and Albert is released. Albert is later arrested for murdering Lambert, Louise's boyfriendl who actually committed suicide. The Nazis try to bribe him to keep his mouth shut in court. Albert sees Sorel and others murdered and then he decides that the courtroom is his only place to freely speak and to glorify Paul. Albert shows courage when he delivers an impassioned speech on liberty, impressing his students. He is freed and his final act is to read from a book to his students before being taken away.

RKO. US. 1943. 103m. B&W *Producers:* Jean Renoir, Dudley Nichols *Director:* Jean Renoir *Writer:* Dudley Nichols *Cast:* Charles Laughton, Maureen O'Hara, George Sanders, Walter Slezak, Kent Smith, Una O'Connor, Philip Merivale, Thurston Hall, George Coulouris, Nancy Gates, Ivan Simpson, John Donat, Frank Alten, Wheaton Chambers, Cecil Weston

This Special Friendships see Les Amitiés Particulières

Three Brothers see Tre Fratelli

The Three Sisters see Tri Sestry

733. Three Who Paid

Riley Sinclair sets out to avenge the death of his brother by the three who left him to die in the desert. One commits suicide, another is killed in self defense, and the third is killed by someone else. A young schoolmaster, who is actually a woman trying to escape her cruel husband, is accused of murder but Riley proves her innocence.

Fox Film Corp. US. 1923. B&W. *Director:* Colin Campbell *Writer:* Joseph Franklin Poland *Cast:* Dustin Farnum, Fred Kohler, Bessie Love, Frank Campeau, Robert Daly, William Conklin, Robert Agnew

734. *Thung lung hoang vang (The Deserted Valley)*

The film deals with love and sexual politics in rural northern Vietnam. The three main characters are two women schoolteachers and the school principal.

Vietnam. 2000. 90m. C. *Director:* Pham Nhue Giang *Writer:* Quang Lap Nguyen *Cast:* Hâu Nguyen Duy, Anh Hong, Hanh Tuyet, Trang Thu, Dung Trung, A Phai Giang

Time of Miracles see *Vrema Cudo*

Time Stands Still see *Megall az Ido*

Tito and Me see *Tito i Ja*

735. *Tito i Ja (Tito and Me)*

Ten-year-old plaster-eating Zoran (Dimitrie Vojnov) lives in Belgrade with his father, a musician; his mother, a ballet dancer; his aunt and uncle and their daughter; and his grandmother. Zoran is the black sheep of this bourgeois family because of his admiration for Marshal Tito. He is so obsessed with Tito that he keeps scrapbooks on Tito and imitates his gestures. Zoran's composition "Why I like the President" is the best one submitted by the Belgrade schoolchildren and he wins a week's camping trip with other privileged children and a reception at Tito's palace. The trip is led by Raja (Lazar Ristovski), a vain, dimwitted young teacher. Zoran learns about totalitarianism and the dangers of one-man rule from the idiocies of the teacher.

Kino International. Yugoslavia. 1992. 104m. C. *Writer-Producer-Director:* Goran Markovic *Cast:* Dimitrie Vojnov, Lazar Ristovski, Anica Dobra, Predrag Manojlovic, Ljiljana Dragutinovic, Bogdan Diklic, Olivera Markovic, Rade Markovic, Vesna Trivalic, Vojislav Brajovic, Ilija Basic, Olja Beckovic, Branimir Brstina, Milutin Dapcevic, Bogdan Diklic, Nebojsa Dugalic, Dusan Jaksic, Miki Manojlovic, Jelena Mrdak, Dragan Nikolic, Uros Nikolic, Kazar Ristovski, Goran Smigic, Milivoje Tomic, Miodrag Tomovic, Vesna Trivalic, Tamara Vuckovic, Milena Vukosav, Jelena Zivkovic

736. *To Serve Them All My Days*

David Powlett-Jones (John Duttine) returns to England injured and shell-shocked after serving in World War I. He takes a teaching post in a boys' boarding school. Being from the Welsh valleys, he is not sure he can do the job but the headmaster has confidence in him.

BBC. Great Britain. 1980. 673m. C. *Producer:* Ken Riddington *Directors:* Terence Dudley, Peter Jeffries, Ronal Wilson *Writers:* Andrew Davies, R.F. Delderfield (novel) *Cast:* John Duttine, Frank Middlemass, Alan MacNaughton, Neil Stacy, David King, Charles Kay, Belinda Lang, Kim Braden, Susan Jameson

Together see He ni Zai Yi Qi

737. Tokyo Monogatari (Tokyo Story)

An old couple living in southern Japan takes a trip to Tokyo to visit their married children. The children are a little put out by the visit. After a few days, the parents leave for home. On the return train trip, the mother becomes ill, and later dies. The youngest daughter is an unmarried schoolteacher who lives at home. She asks, "Isn't life disappointing?"

Shochiku. Japan. 1953. 136m. B&W. *Director:* Yasujiro Ozu *Writers:* Yasujireo Ozu, Kogo Noda *Cast:* Chishu Ryu, Chiyeko Higashiyama, Setsuko Hara, Satoshi Yamamura, Haruko Sugimura

Tokyo Story see Tokyo Monogatari

738. Tom Brown's Schooldays

A boy remembers his favorite teacher and his school days.

International Exhibitors. Great Britain. 1916. B&W. *Writer-Director:* Rex Wilson, Thomas Hughes (novel) *Cast:* Joyce Templeton, Jack Coleman, Jack Hobbs, Evelyn Boucher, Wilfred Benson, Mr. Daniels, Mr. Johnson, Laurie Leslie, C. Arundell, Mona Damt, Eric Barker, Rolf Leslie, Miss Marley, H. Dobell, Mr. Morley, Mr. Canielli

739. Tom Brown's Schooldays

At the grave of Dr. Thomas Arnold (Cedric Hardwicke), the beloved headmaster of Rugby, Tom Brown (Jimmy Lydon) meets his old classmate East (Freddie Bartholomew). The two remember when Tom's father asked tutor Arnold to run for headmaster at Rugby. Arnold is convinced by his wife that it would be a way of implementing his educational theories. He arrives to find chaos at the school and his new methods win him no friends. Tom's family supports Arnold by enrolling Tom as a student. Tom and East become friends but are estranged when Tom challenges a tyrannical student and is accused by being a tattletale.

RKO. US. 1940. 86m. B&W. *Producers:* Gene Towne, Graham Baker *Director:* Robert Stevenson *Writers:* Walter Ferris, Frank Cavett, Thomas Hughes (novel) *Cast:* Jimmy Lydon, Sir Cedric Hardwicke, Billy Halop, Freddie Bartholomew, Gale Storm, Josephine Hutchinson, Polly Moran, Hughie Green, Ernest Cossart, Alec Craig, Barlowe Borland, Forrester Harvey, Leonard Willey, Ian Fulton, Charles Smith, Dick Chandler, Harry Duff, Paul Matthews, John Collum

740. Tom Brown's Schooldays

A boy remembers his favorite teacher and his school days.
Talisman. Great Britain. 1951. 96m. B&W. *Producers:* Brian Desmond Hurst, George Minter *Director:* Gordon Parry *Writers:* Noel Langley, Thomas Hughes (novel) *Cast:* Robert Newton, John Howard Davies, Diana Wynyard, Francis de Wolff, Kathleen Byron, Hermione Baddeley, James Hayter, Rachel Gurney, Amy Veness, Max Bygraves, Michael Hordern, John Charlesworth, John Forrest, Brian Worth, Michael Brennan

Tomorrow Is Too Late see Domani È Troppo Tardi

741. Top of the Form

In trouble because of his gambling, bookmaker Ronnie Fortescue (Ronald Shiner) is forced to impersonate a teacher and hide out in a boys' school. When the lazy boys need to pass, cheating isn't a problem with their teacher. Ronnie discovers that boys have a natural aptitude for gambling and takes them on a tour of European casinos. Along the way they get ensnarled in a plot to steal the Mona Lisa.
BFM. Great Britain. 1953. 75m. B&W. *Producer:* Paul Soskin *Director:* John Paddy Carstairs *Writers:* John Paddy Carstairs, Patrick Kirwan, Ted Willis *Cast:* Ronald Shiner, Harry Fowler, Alfie Bass, Jacqueline Pierreux, Anthony Newley, Mary Jerrold, Richard Wattis, Howard Marion-Crawford, Roland Curram, Terence Mitchell, Gerald Campion, Oscar Quitak, Kynaston Reeves, Martin Benson

742. Topaze

Honest and naïve schoolteacher Professor Auguste Topaze (John Barrymore) gets a lesson in how the world works outside the classroom.
RKO. US. 1933. 78m. B&W. *Producer:* David O. Selznick *Director:* Harry d'Abbabie d'Arrast *Writer:* Ben Hecht *Cast:* John Barrymore, Myrna Loy, Jobyna Howland, Jackie Searl, Reginald Mason, Albert Conti, Frank Reicher, Luis Alberni

743. Topaze

Topaze (Louis Jouvet), a very honest teacher, is fired from his job at a boys' school when he refuses to please a boy's mother by lying about her son's conduct. He becomes a tutor and then a pawn in a scheme to sell trash trucks to the city for inflated prices. Topaze becomes rich and declines an offer of presidency of the school. He decides this life is better than that of a teacher.
Paramount. France. 1933. 103m. B&W. *Producer:* Marcel Pagnol *Director:* Louis Gasnier *Writer:* Marcel Pagnol *Cast:* Louis Jouvet, Paul Pauley, Simone Héliard, Marcel Vallée, Jane Loury, Maurice Vallée, Maurice Rémy, Pierre Larquey, Edwige Feuillère, Camille Beuve, Henri Vilbert, Micheline Bernard, Jacqueline Delubac, Raymonde Debrennes

744. Topaze

Naive schoolmaster Topaze (Arnaudy) discovers he is being manipulated and quits.

Films Marcel Pagnol. France. 1936. 110m. B&W. *Writer-Director:* Marcel Pagnol *Cast:* Arnaudy, André Pollack, Sylvie Bataille, Pierre Asso, Jean Arbuleau, Henri Poupon

745. Topaze

Idealistic schoolteacher Topaze (Fernandel) learns from his boss that there are more profitable and less legal ways of making money.

Les Films Marcel Pagnol. France. 1951. 135m. B&W. *Writer-Director:* Marcel Pagnol *Cast:* Fernandel, Marcel Vallée, Jacqueline Pagnol, Pierre Larquey, Jacques Morel

Tormet see Hets

746. Torzók (Abandoned)

Áron is a happy child until his mother falls ill and he is displaced to an orphanage. After finally being accepted by the other children, he faces a bigger obstacle: The teachers treat him cruelly and this leads to horrible consequences.

Budapest Film Stúdió. Hungary. 2001. 100m. C. *Producers:* László Kántor, Ferenc Kardos *Writer-Director:* Árpád Sopits *Cast:* Tamás Mészáos, Szabolcs Csizmadia, Attila Zsilák, Péter Müller, Imre Thúri, Krisztián Tóth, Zoltán Nádházi, Pál Mácsai, Lásló, Dóra Létay, Tamás Fodor, Sándor Gáspár, Krisztina Somogyi, Lajos Kovács, László Szabó

747. The Trap (A Woman's Law)

Jean Carson (Olive Tell), an Eastern girl, teaches school in the Yukon. She marries gambler Steve Fallon (Earl Schenck) after her father and Ned (Jere Austin), Steve's brother, go prospecting, but leaves her new husband when he boasts of having another wife. Ned proposes upon his return. Jean goes to New York to visit her sick sister Helen (Tallulah Bankhead). When she hears that Steve has died, she marries Bruce Graham (Sidney Mason) and is happy for five years. Then an old acquaintance shows up and blackmails Jean. There is a murder but all ends well with Ned marrying Helen.

Universal Film Mfg. US. 1919. B&W. *Director:* Frank Reicher *Writer:* Eve Unsell *Cast:* Olive Tell, Sidney Mason, Jere Austin, Rod La Rocque, Tallulah Bankhead, Joseph Burke, Earl Schenck

748. Die Trapp Familie (The Trapp Family)

Adapted from the memoirs of Baroness Maria Trapp, this film tells of Maria's (Ruth Leuwerik) life as a young novice, leaving the convent to teach seven motherless children. Soon she falls in love with their father Baron Trapp and they marry. Another film version of the story, *The Sound of Music*, is very well known.

Hispano Foxfilms. West Germany. 1956. 106m. C. *Producers:* Wolfgang Reinhardt, Utz Utermann *Director:* Wolfgang Liebeneiner *Writer:* George Hurdalek *Cast:* Ruth Leuwerik, Hans Holt, Maria Holst, Josef Meinard, Agnes Windeck, Friedrich Domin, Hilde von Stolz, Liesl Karlstadt, Alfred Balthoff, Hans Schumm, Gretl Theimer

The Trapp Family see *Die Trapp Familie*

749. Tre Fratelli (Three Brothers)

Three brothers — a judge from Rome, a teacher of maladjusted children from Naples, and a factory worker from Turin — return to their rural childhood home to attend their mother's funeral and to be with their aged father. Each brother represents a different social class and geographical area in Italian culture.

Iter/Gaumont. Italy. 1981. 111m. C. *Director:* Francesco Rosi *Writers:* Francesco Rosi, Tonino Guerra *Cast:* Phillippe Noiret, Vittorio Mezzagiorno, Michele Placio, Charles Vanel, Andréa Ferréol

The Treasure of Cantenae see *Le Tresor De Cantenac*

750. Tredowata (Leper)

At a high society school, young teacher Stefcia Rudecka (Elzbieta Starostecka) falls in love with nobleman Waldemar Michorowski (Leszek Teleszynski). His family is against the marriage since Stefcia is from a lower social class and they do everything to make her life miserable. She dies before her wedding day in the arms of her beloved.

Film Polski. Poland. 1976. 91m. C. *Director:* Jerzy Hoffman *Writers:* Stanislaw Dygat, Helena Mniszek (novel) *Cast:* Elzbieta Starostecka, Leszek Teleszynski, Gabriela Kownacka, Czeslaw Wollejko, Anna Dymna

751. Le Tresor de Cantenac (The Treasure of Cantenae)

In a rundown French village where everyone is related to everyone else, a woman lives with her husband and her lover, the town drunk, and a pair of twins are the priest and the mayor of the town. They hate each other. The priest has no parishioners and the mayor is the history teacher but only covers history as far as the French Revolution. The baron of the town is in dire financial straits and on the verge of suicide when he finds out about a secret treasure. There is a rebirth of the town: The priest gets a flock and the teacher adds Napoleon to the curriculum.

Continental. France. 1950. 100m. B&W. *Producer:* Boris Morros *Writer-Director:* Sacha Guitry *Cast:* Sacha Guitry, Lana Marconi, Marcel Simon, Pauline Carton

752. Tri Sestry (The Three Sisters)

In the 1890s, the three Prozorov sisters — Olga (Lyubov Sokolova), the spinster schoolteacher; Marsha (Margarita Volodina), unhappily married to the local schoolmaster; and Irina (Tatyana Malchenko), who was forced to take a dull job — live in a provincial Russian town. Many years have passed since moving from Moscow with their army officer father, who has since died. Their brother leaves his university studies and marries a scheming and unfaithful woman, who takes over the household. Then the suffering begins.

Artkino Pictures. Soviet Union. 1964. 112m. B&W. *Writer-Director:* Samson Samsonov *Cast:* Lyubov Sokolova, Margarita Volodina, Tatyana Malchenko, Leonid Gubanov, Alla Larionova, Lev Ivanov, Leonid Gallis, Konstantin Sorokin, Oleg Strizhenov, Vladimir Druzhnikov, L. Konstantinova, V. Stepanov, N. Lubko

The Trials of a Schoolmaster see *L'École Infernale*

753. Tribulations of a Country Schoolmarm

The schoolmarm puts a naughty boy on the dunce's chair and then goes to speak to another student. The naughty student pulls her wig off with a pointer and a bent pin.

American Mutoscope Co. US. 1898. B&W.

754. Das Tripas Coração (Heart and Guts)

A government administrator arrives at a girls' boarding school to investigate and possibly close the failing school. Among the personnel are two sexually frustrated headmistresses, lustful janitors and an assortment of visitors.

Embrafilme. Brazil. 1982. 101m. C. *Producers:* Uéze Zahpan, Jacques Eluf, Snibal Massini *Writer-Director:* Ana Carolina *Cast:* Antônio Fagundes, Xuxa Lopes, Ana Maria Abreu, Solange Alfane, Nair Belo, Isadora DeFarias, Clotilde Borgas, Denise Franco, Stela Freitas, Jobelsina Gomes, Mira Haar, Margareth Lemos, Maria Padilha, Ivete Rocha, Dina Sfat

Trouble Maker see *La bi xiao xiao sheng*

755. The Trouble with Angels

At the all-girl's Catholic boarding school St. Francis' Academy, Mother Superior (Rosalind Russell) battles two juvenile pranksters, extrovert Mary Clancy (Hayley Mills) and sensitive Rachel Devery (June Harding). Their pranks include smoking cigars in the boiler room and secretly entering the cloister. In one touching scene, Mother Superior stays up all night helping Rachel finish her sewing project while recalling her own dream of being a fashion designer. The film treats the nuns with respect and very positively. In fact, Mary Clancy decides to remain and join the order herself. Followed by *Where Angels Go Trouble Follows*.

Columbia. US. 1966. 112m. C. *Producer:* William Frye *Director:* Ida Lupino *Writers:* Blanche Hanalis, Jane Trahey (novel) *Cast:* Rosalind Russell, Binnie Barnes, Camilla Sparv, Mary Wickes, Marge Redmond, Dolores Sutton, Margalo Gillmore, Portia Nelson, Marjorie Eaton, Barbara Bell Wright, Judith Lowry, Hayley Mills, June Harding, Gypsy Rose Lee, Barbara Hunter

756. *The Troubles of the Pretty School Marm*

No description available.
Chicago Film Exchange. US. 1909. B&W

Turn of the Century see *När Seklet Var Ungt*

Twenty-Four Eyes see *Nijushi no hitomi*

The Twenty-Four Hour Lover see *Bengelchen Liebt Kreuz und Quer*

The Twilight Story see *Bokuto kidan*

757. *Twilight Zone: The Movie*

In the third segment, schoolteacher Helen Foley (Kathleen Quinlan) meets strange young Anthony (Jeremy Licht) and his family. The family lives in terror of Anthony because of his supernatural ability to make things happen his way.

Warner. US. 1983. 101m. C. *Producers:* Steven Spielberg, John Landis *Directors:* John Landis, Steven Spielberg, Joe Dante, George Miller *Writers:* John Landis, George Clayton Johnson, Richard Matheson, Josh Rogan, Rod Serling *Cast:* Dan Aykroyd, Vic Morrow, Scatman Crothers, Bill Quinn, Kathleen Quinlan, Kevin McCarthy, John Lithgow, Jeremy Licht

758. *Two Loves (Spinster)*

American Anna Vorontosov (Shirley MacLaine) teaches school in a remote section of New Zealand. She has earned the love of her pupils and their parents with her teaching style. The unhappily married school inspector W.W.J. Abercrombie (Jack Hawkins) admires her. Her personal life is full of insecurity, fear of love, and sexual inhibitions. Fellow teacher Paul Lathrop (Laurence Harvey), an immature man who wants to be a singer, is eager to begin a relationship but Anna is not. Anna learns that one of her helpers, a 15-year-old unmarried Maori girl, is pregnant. Anna is surprised by how everyone is so calm about the situation. The baby dies at birth and Paul is killed in a motorcycle accident that was possibly a suicide. Anna learns that Paul was the father of the baby and she feels responsible. Abercrombie assures her that she wasn't guilty of anything and offers her love.

MGM. US. 1961. 100m. C. *Producer:* Julian Blaustein *Director:* Charles Walters

Writers: Ben Maddow, Sylvie Ashton Warner (novel) *Cast:* Shirley MacLaine, Jack Hawkins, Laurence Harvey, Nobu McCarthy, Ronald Long, Norah Howard, Juano Hernandez, Edmund Vargas, Neil Woodward, Lisa Sitjar, Alan Roberts

759. *Two Wise Maids*

Schoolteacher "Old Lady Ironsides" Agatha Stanton (Alison Skipworth) and her roommate, fellow teacher Prudence Matthews (Polly Moran), help get a favorite student out of jail for stealing roller skates. Agatha is expecting to be made principal but that day she finds out that newcomer Bruce Arnold (Donald Cook) is getting the job. Other teachers, including Ellen Southard (Hope Manning), are upset but Agatha decides to keep teaching. When a child is almost hit by a car, Agatha and Prudence organize the mothers into blocking the street so children can play. A misunderstanding with a lying boy almost costs Agatha her job, but her loyal students and prominent citizens speak up for her at the hearing.

Republic. US. 1937. 70m. B&W. *Producer:* Nat Levine *Director:* Phil Rosen *Writer:* Sam Ornitz *Cast:* Alison Skipworth, Polly Moran, Hope Manning, Donald Cook, Jackie Searl, Lila Lee, Luis Alberni, Maxie Rosenbloom, Marcia Mae Jones, Harry Burns, Clarence Wilson, Selmer Jackson, John Hamilton, Theresa Conover, Raymond Brown, James C. Morton, Stanley Blystone, Bob McClung

U-Boat 29 see *The Spy in Black*

760. *Uchitel (The New Teacher)*

On April 7, 1941, *The New York Times* reviewed this film. "Emancipated women giggle behind their veils whenever a stalwart Stahkanovite casts an inquiring look in their direction, the men behave like overgrown boys . . . But it's a pleasant admission that love makes the world go round. We wonder if Marx thought of that."

Artkino Pictures. Soviet Union. 1939. B&W. *Writer-Director:* Sergei Gerasimov *Cast:* Boris Chirkov, Tamara Makarova, Lyudmila Shabalina, Pavel Volkov, Valentina Telegina, Vera Pomerants, Ivan Nazarov, Mikhail Yekaterininsky, N. Sunozok, Anna Matveyeva, S. Shinkevich, V. Zamyatin, O. Korovatskii

761. *Under Western Skies*

The stagecoach carrying Willie Well's Variety Show, a musical revue, is attacked by a bandit gang. They don't want money, just a performance. Later the show people arrive in town but the ladies' social club has them banned from performing at the opera house. Katie Wells (Martha O'Driscoll) convinces the saloon to let them perform there. Katie meets schoolteacher Tod Howell (Noah Beery, Jr.), who doesn't approve of variety shows. That night he sneaks into the show and rescues Katie when a melee breaks out. They go on a moonlight carriage ride. The gang causes more trouble and kidnaps Katie, but near-sighted sheriff captures the gang and rescues Katie. Katie and Todd are married.

Universal. US. 1945. 57m. B&W. *Producer:* Warren Wilson *Director:* Jean

Yarbrough *Writers:* Stanley Roberts, Clyde Bruckman *Cast:* Martha O'Driscoll, Noah Beery, Jr., Leo Carrillo, Leon Errol, Irving Bacon, Ian Keith, Jennifer Holt, Edna May Wonacott, Earle Hodgins, Dorothy Granger, Jack Rice, Gladys Blake, George Lloyd, Claire Whitney, Frank Lackteen, Jack Ingram, Patsy O'Byrne, Nan Leslie, Ed Waller, Perc Launders, Donald Kerr, Warren Jackson, Charles Sherlock

762. *The Unexpected Advent of the Schoolteacher*

No description available.
American Mutoscope Co. US. 1898. B&W.

Unfinished Piece for Mechanical Piano see *Neokonchennaya Pyesa dlya Mekhanicheskogo Pianin*

763. *Unman Wittering and Zigo*

A new schoolteacher, John Ebony (David Hemmings), learns that the previous teacher may have been killed by his pupils. Just after calling roll (Unman, Wittering, and Zigo are the last names), his students threateningly tell him that he had better leave them alone to do as they wish.

Paramount. Great Britain. 1971. 102m. C. *Producer:* Gareth Wigan *Director:* John Mackenzie *Writer:* Simon Raven *Cast:* David Hemmings, Douglas Wilmer, Anthony Haygarth, Carolyn Seymour, Hamilton Dyce, Barbara Lott, Donald Gee, David Jackson, Hubert Rees, David Auker, Tom Morris, Richard Gill, Michael Kitchen, Nicholas Hoye, Tom Owen, Toby Simpson, James Wardroper, Clive Gray, Rodney Paulden, Keith Janess, Michael Howe, Colin Barrie

764. *The Unseen*

Widower Davie Fielding (Joel McCrea), who is suspected of causing his wife's death, hires Elizabeth Howard (Gail Russell) as governess to his children. Elizabeth is obsessed with learning the truth.

Paramount. US. 1945. 82m. B&W. *Director:* Lewis Allen *Writer:* Hagar Wilde, Raymond Chandler *Cast:* Joel McCrea, Gail Russell, Herbert Marshall, Richard Lyon, Nona Griffith

Until Monday see *Dozhivyom do Ponedelnika*

765. *Up in the Air*

Victorian schoolboy Freddie (Gary Smith) is sent away to boarding school where he is mistreated and miserable. He tries to escape.

Fanfare (CFF). Great Britain. 1969. 55m. C. *Producer:* George H. Brown *Director:* Jan Darnley Smith *Writers:* Wally Bosco, Jan Darnley Smith *Cast:* Gary Smith, Jon Pertwee, Felix Felton, Mark Colleano, Susan Payne, Gary Warren, Julian Close, Earl Younger, Brenda Cowling, Leslie Dwyer

766. Urideului ilgeuleojin yeongung (Our Twisted Hero)

The family of 12-year-old Han Byung Yae (Ko Jungll) moves from Seoul to the provinces in 1959. At school Han discovers that the teacher has abdicated many disciplinary duties to the class student monitor, Um Suk Dae (Hong Kyuhgh). Um is larger than the other boys and has set up a police state with himself as the dictator. He and his henchmen beat up any dissenters. Han tries to fight back but eventually he gives in to Um. Um's reign of terror ends with the arrival of a new teacher. The film paints a picture of South Korea's public education system in the 1950s, which was far sterner and harsher than in the U.S.

South Korea. 1992. 119m. C. *Producer:* Do Dong Hwan *Director:* Chong Won Park *Writers:* Mun-yeol Lee, Yi Mum Yol (novel) *Cast:* Min-sik Choi, Kyoun-In Hong, Goo Shin, Ko Jungll, Hong Kyuhgh

767. The Utah Kid

Hunted outlaw Cal Reynolds (Rex Lease) finds Butch (Tom Santschi), leader of his gang, making advances to teacher Jennie Lee (Dorothy Sebastian) in the local saloon. Jennie is not there by choice and Cal is forced to marry her. She was engaged to Sheriff Bentley (Walter Miller). Cal decides to turn over a new leaf but the gang doesn't see it that way. After a few shootouts, Jennie decides that Cal is her man.

Tiffany Productions. US. 1930. 57m. B&W. *Director:* Richard Thorpe *Writer:* Frank Howard *Cast:* Rex Lease, Dorothy Sebastian, Tom Santschi, Mary Carr, Walter Miller, Lafe McKee, Boris Karloff, Bud Osborne

768. Vacanze in America (Vacation in America)

Students from a parochial boys' academy are on a trip across the United States for vacation. A picky young cleric teacher, Don Burro (Christian De Sica), supervises the journey. Also helping out is Signora De Romanis (Edwige Fenech), the beautiful mother of one of the boys. She and Don almost end up in bed together but the priest remains chaste.

Columbia. Italy. 1984. 98m. C. *Producers*: Mario and Vittorio Cecchi Gori *Director*: Carlo Vanzina *Writers*: Enrico and Carlo Vanzina *Cast*: Jerry Calà, Christian De Sica, Claudio Amendola, Antonella Interlenghi, Edwige Fenech, Fabio Ferrari, Giacomo Rosselli, Gianmarco Tognazzi

Vacation in America see *Vacanze America*

769. Vakonesh panjom (Fifth Reaction)

When her conservative father-in-law refuses to take her and her two children in after her husband's tragic death, teacher-mother (Niki Karimi) risks everything to keep her family together. The father-in-law fights her for custody of the two children so she must overcome a society of patriarchal traditions.

Facets. Iran. 2003. 106m. C. *Writer-Director*: Tahmineh Milani *Cast:* Jamshid

Hashempur, Seyd-Ali Hosseini, Shahib Hosseini, Niki Karimi, Gohar Kheirandish, Marila Zarei

770. *Valley of Mystery (Stranded)*

An international jetliner is blown off course during a typhoon and forced to land in the jungles of equatorial South America. The passengers include Ben Barstow (Peter Graves), a writer-explorer in search of his lost sister; Rita Brown (Lois Nettleton), an attractive liquor saleswoman; Joan Simon (Julie Adams), a neurotic schoolteacher; Pete Patton (Joby Baker), a pop singer; Danny O'Neill (Harry Guardino), an alcoholic comedian; and Francisco Rivera (Fernando Lamas), a convicted murderer. Ben realizes that they have crash-landed near where his sister disappeared so he and Rita set out to look around. They come across Dr. Weatherly (Alfred Ryder), who wishes to sacrifice them to the gods.

Universal. US. 1967. 94m. C. *Producer:* Harry Tatelman *Director:* Josef Leytes *Writers:* Richard Neal, Lowell Barrington *Cast*: Richard Egan, Peter Graves, Joby Baker, Lois Nettleton, Harry Guardino, Julie Adams, Fernando Lamas, Alfred Ryder, Karen Sharpe, Barbara Werle, Lee Patterson, Rodolfo Acosta, Douglas Kennedy, Don Stewart, Leonard Nimoy, Tony Patino, Otis Young, Lisa Gaye, George Tyne

771. *The Vanishing*

Remake of *Spoorloos* but with a happy ending this time. When a mild-mannered schoolteacher kidnaps a woman, her boyfriend attempts to find her.

TCF. US. 1993. 110m. C. *Producers:* Larry Brezner, Paul Schiff *Director:* George Slulzer *Writers:* Todd Graff, Tim Krabbé (novel) *Cast:* Jeff Bridges, Kiefer Sutherland, Nancy Travis, Sandra Bullock, Park Overall, Lisa Eichhorn, Maggie Linderman

The Vanishing see *Spoorloos*

772. *Vernico Cruz*

Vernico is a young boy brought up by his grandmother in loneliness and despair in the remote mountains in Argentina. When a schoolteacher (Juan José Camero) arrives with comic books and a radio, the outside world comes to life for Vernico. The teacher befriends and educates Vernico and becomes a surrogate father to him. The teacher is an idealist but a new official warns him to get rid of all political books.

Mainframe Film. Argentina/Great Britain. 1987. 96m. C. *Producers:* Julio Lencina, Sasha Menocki *Director:* Miguel Pereira *Writers:* Eduardo Leiva Mueller, Miguel Pereira *Cast:* Juan José Camero, Gonzalo Morales, René Olaguivel, Guillermo Delgado, Don Leopoldo Abán, Ana Maria Gonzales, Fortunato Ramos

773. *A Very Missing Person*

Schoolteacher-sleuth Hildegarde Withers (Eve Arden) and detective Oscar Piper (James Gregory) are on the case of a missing heiress.

ABC. US. 1972. 90m. C. *Producer:* Edward Montagne *Director:* Russ Mayberry *Writers:* Philip H. Reisman, Jr., Fletcher Flora (novel), Stuart Palmer (novel) *Cast:* Eve Arden, James Gregory, Julie Newmar, Ray Danton, Skye Aubrey, Dennis Rucker, Robert Easton, Woodrow Parfrey, Bob Hastings, Pat Morita, Ezra Stone, Linda Gillen, Dwan Smith, Peter Morrison Jacobs, Savannah Benthley

774. *A Very Young Lady*

Tomboy Kitty Russell (Jane Withers) would rather ride horses and dream of owning a motorcycle than pay attention to her classes at the Spring Valley School for Girls, much to the despair of her teachers. The handsome school principal, Dr. Franklin Meredith (John Sutton), listens to the advice of teacher Alice Carter (Nancy Kelly), who urges him to induce Kitty to attend one of the school's tea dances. Complications ensue.

TCF. US. 1941. 80m. B&W. *Producer:* Robert Kane *Director:* Harold Schuster *Writers:* Ladislas Fodor, Elaine Ryan *Cast:* Jane Withers, Nancy Kelly, John Sutton, Janet Beecher, Richard Clayton, June Carlson, Charles Halton, Cecil Kellaway, Marilyn Kinsley, JoAnn Ransom, Catherine Henderson, June Horne, Dorothy Moore

775. *Vesnickó Má Stredisková (My Sweet Little Village)*

In a picturesque Czechoslovakian village lives a middle-aged, common-sensible doctor who has an accident every time he drives. Other characters in the village are a pretty young wife, her lover and her jealous older husband; a farmboy painfully in love with the village schoolmarm, a sweet-tempered, mentally challenged man and his boss.

Circle Releasing Corporation. Czechoslovakia. 1985. 100m. C. *Director:* Jirí Menzel *Writer:* Zdanek Sverák *Cast:* János Bán, Marián Labuda, Rudolf Hrusínsky, Milena Dvorska, Ladislav Zupanic, Petr Cepek, Libuse Safránková, Jan Hartl, Evzen Jegorov, Oldrich Vlach, Petr Cepek, Miloslav Stibich, Oldrich Vlach, Stanislav Aubrecht, Zdenek Sverák, Magda Sebestová, Július Satinsky, Josef Somr, Frantisek Vlácil

776. *Vice Versa*

A boy and his father switch bodies and minds. This switch wreaks havoc in the schoolroom. This story has been filmed numerous times; the father in the boy's body creates many scenes in all the versions.

Jury. Great Britain. 1916. B&W. *Director:* Maurice Elvey *Writer:* F. Anstey (novel) *Cast:* Charles Rock, Douglas Munro, Edward O'Neill, Guy Newall

777. *Vice Versa*

The son (Anthony Newley) of a stuffy stockbroker (Roger Livesey) comes into possession of a magic stone and wishes on it. He gets his father's brain and personality and vice versa. A feet-of-clay schoolmaster (James Robertson Justice) gets involved in this supernatural situation.

Two Cities. Great Britain. 1948. 111m. B&W. *Producers:* Peter Ustinov, George H. Brown *Director* Peter Ustinov *Writers:* Peter Ustinov, F. Anstey (novel) *Cast:* Roger Livesey, Kay Walsh, Anthony Newley, James Robertson Justice, David Hutcheson, Petula Clark, Joan Young, Patricia Raine, Vida Hope, Vi Kaley, Ernest Jay, Kynaston Reeves, Harcourt Williams, Bill Shine, Robert Eddison, James Hayter, Alfie Bass, Hugh Dempster, Peter Jones, James Kenney, Cyril Smith

778. *La Vie Devant Soi (Madame Rosa)*

Rosa (Simone Signoret), an ex-prostitute and Auschwitz survivor, operates an unofficial daycare for her peers. Now aged and ill and with failing memory, she is cared for by her last remaining ward, Mohammed. A doctor and a friend want to move her but Mohammed does as she requests and hides her.

Lira Films. France. 1977. 105m. C. *Producer:* Jean Bolvary *Writer-Director:* Moshe Mizrahi *Cast:* Simone Signoret, Claude Dauphin, Samy Ben Youb, Michal Bat Adam, Costa-Gavras

779. *La Vie Est un Roman (Life Is a Bed of Roses)*

In the early 1920s at Count Forbe K's castle, the count tries to start a utopian society by drugging his guests into being reborn and forgetting their pasts. In 1982, the castle is now a progressive alternative school. During the summer it is used for an educational conference while some children remain to play knights and dragons. At the conference, Nora Winkle (Geraldine Chaplin) wagers that she can manipulate a love affair between sweet, naïve public schoolteacher Elisabeth Rousseau (Sabine Azéma) and oddball education researcher Robert Dufresne (Pierre Arditti). Walter Guarini (Vittorio Gassman), another attendee, is very interested in Elisabeth.

Soprofilms. France. 1983. 111m. C. *Producer:* Philippe Dussart *Director:* Alain Resnais *Writer:* Jean Gruault *Cast:* Vittorio Gassman, Ruggero Raimondi, Geraldine Chaplin, Fanny Ardant, Pierre Arditti, Sabine Azéma, Robert Manuel

780. *La Vie et Rien d'Autre (Life and Nothing But)*

Two years after the end of World War I, the French are still searching for their loved ones. Major Dellaplane (Philippe Noiret) is assigned to find amnesiac survivors. Irène (Sabine Azéma) is searching for her husband and schoolteacher Alice (Pascale Vignal) looks for her fiancé. Soon their paths will intertwine.

Orion Classics. France. 1989. 135m. C. *Producer:* René Cleitman *Director:* Bertrand Tavernier *Writers:* Jean Cosmos, Bertrand Tavernier *Cast:* Philippe Noiret, Sabine Azéma, Pascale Vignal, Maurice Barrier, François Perrot, Jean-Pol Dubois, Daniel Russo, Michel Duchaussoy, Arlette Gilbert, Louis Lyonnet, Charlotte Maury-Sentier, Frédérique Meininger, Pierre Trabaud, Jean-Roger Milo, Bruno Therasse, Gabriel Cattand, Michel Cassagne, Frédéric Pierrot, François Domange

781. The Village Chestnut

The amorous schoolmaster in a small town is in love with one student and is loved by another student. One day, members of the school board pay an unexpected visit.

Paramount Famous Lasky Corp. US. 1918. B&W. *Producer:* Mack Sennett *Directors:* Raymond Griffith, Walter Wright *Cast:* Chester Conklin, Louise Fazenda, Myrtle Lind, Paddy McGuire, Eva Thatcher, Al McKinnon, George Gray, Hughie Mack

Village in the Mist see Angemaeul

Village of Dreams see Eno nakano bokuno mura

782. Village of the Damned

One quiet morning in the small town of Midwich, every living thing abruptly falls asleep. Then, just as suddenly, everyone wakes up. Later, every woman in Midwich capable of childbirth is pregnant. Gordon Zellaby (George Sanders), a middle-aged scientist, and his much younger wife Anthea (Barbara Shelley) are overjoyed but not the unmarried girls or virgins. The fetuses develop at a fast rate. When born, the children all look alike with blond hair and strange eyes. When the children are a year old, they look like three-year-olds. George realizes that they have the powers to manipulate matter. When the children are five they look like nine-year-olds. The townspeople have become distrustful of the children. The children move to a house on the edge of town, where Gordon can continue teaching them, as he has for several years. The children can read minds and cause deaths and nothing gets in their way. They trust Gordon and tell him that their plan is to set up colonies. Gordon knows he must stop the children.

MGM. Great Britain. 1960. 78m. B&W. *Producer:* Ronald Kinnoch *Director:* Wolf Rilla *Writers:* Stirling Silliphant, Wolf Rilla, George Harley, John Wyndham (novel) *Cast:* George Sanders, Barbara Shelley, Michael Gwynn, Martin Stephens, Laurence Naismith, John Phillips, Richard Vernon, Jenny Laird, Richard Warner, Thomas Heathcote, Charlotte Mitchell, John Stuart, Bernard Archard

A Village Schoolteacher see Selskaa uchitelnitsa

The Village Teacher see Selskaya uchitelnitsa

Violet see Ljubica

783. The Virginian

The cowboy known as The Virginian has a pleasant personality and loves to play tricks on his friends. The town bully Trampas doesn't care at all for him. New schoolteacher Molly Wood attracts the attention of the Virginian, who proposes to her; she turns him down. The Virginian's old friend Steve joins Trampas and his gang of cattle thieves. Steve is sentenced to hang. Trampas escapes and hurts the Virginian but he is saved by Molly. Eventually the Virginian kills Trampas and marries Molly.

Paramount. US. 1914. B&W. *Producer:* Jesse L. Lasky *Director:* Cecil B. DeMille *Writer:* Owen Wister (novel) *Cast:* Dustin Farnum, J.W. Johnston, Sidney Deane, Billy Elmer, Winifred Kingston, James Griswold, H.B. Carpenter, Tex Driscoll, Cecilia De Mille

784. *The Virginian*

The Virginian, a beloved cowboy, is attracted to the new schoolteacher, Molly Wood fresh from New England. His childhood friend Steve decides to join Trampas, bully and rustler, and his gang. The Virginian makes sure that Steve is hanged. Molly is very upset by this. Molly saves the Virginian's life when he is confronted by Trampas. The Virginian and Molly fall in love.

Preferred Pictures. US. 1923. B&W. *Producer:* B.P. Schulberg *Director:* Tom Forman *Writers:* Hope Loring, Louis D. Lighton, Owen Wister (novel) *Cast:* Kenneth Harlan, Florence Vidor, Russell Simpson, Pat O'Malley, Raymond Hatton, Milton Ross, Sam Allen, Bert Hadley, Fred Gambold

785. *The Virginian*

The Virginian, a ranch foreman, meets Steve, an old friend, and gives him a job. The Virginian falls in love with the new schoolteacher, just arrived from Vermont. Steve joins a gang of rustlers led by Trampas. When Steve is caught, The Virginian must oversee his hanging. Molly is upset by his participation. However, when the Virginian is wounded, Molly nurses him. The Virginian and Trampas enter into a duel.

Paramount. US. 1929. 95m. B&W. *Director:* Victor Fleming *Writers:* Edward E. Paramore, Jr., Howard Estabrook, Owen Wister (novel) *Cast:* Gary Cooper, Walter Huston, Richard Arlen, Mary Brian, Chester Conklin, Eugene Pallette, E.H. Calvert, Helen Ware, Victor Potel, Tex Young, Charles Stevens

786. *The Virginian*

Ranch foreman The Virginian (Joel McCrea) sees his best friend hanged for rustling and defeats the local bad guy, all while falling in love with the new schoolteacher.

Paramount. US. 1946. 90m. C. *Producer:* Paul Jones *Director:* Stuart Gilmore *Writers:* Frances Goodrich, Albert Hackett, Owen Wister (novel) *Cast:* Joel McCrea, Brian Donlevy, Sonny Tufts, Barbara Britton, William Frawley, Henry O'Neill, Fay Bainter, Tom Tully, Bill Edwards, Paul Guilfoyle, Marc Lawrence, Vince Barnett

787. *La Vita È Bella (Life Is Beautiful)*

In 1930s Italy, cheerful Jewish Guido falls in love with schoolteacher Dora even though she is engaged to another. Guido wins Dora and they marry and are happy with a child until the occupation of Italy. Guido and the boy are shipped to a concentration camp with Dora following voluntarily. They are separated but Guido finds ways to communicate and convince his child it is all a game.

Miramax. Italy. 1997. 116m. C. *Producers:* Gianluigi Braschi, Elda Ferri *Director:* Roberto Benigni *Writers:* Vincenzo Cerami, Roberto Benigni *Cast:* Roberto Benigni, Nicoletta Braschi, Giorgio Cantarini, Giustino Durano, Sergio Bini Bustric, Marisa Paredes, Horst Buchholz, Lidia Alfonsi, Giulianna Lojodice, Amerigo Fontani, Pietro De Silva, Francesco Guzzo, Raffaella Lebboroni, Claudio Alfonsi, Gil Baroni

788. *Le Voile Bleu (The Blue Veil)*

A World War I widow, whose child dies at birth, becomes a governess and devotes her life to the care of other's children. She gives up a lover to be near her charges.

Leo Cohen. France. 1942. 90m. B&W. *Producer:* Raymond Artus *Director:* Jean Stelli *Writer:* François Camaux *Cast:* Gaby Morlay, Elvire Popesco, Marcelle Géniat, Charpin, Larquey

789. *The Volcano*

Ruth Carroll (Leah Baird), a schoolteacher on New York's Lower East Side, meets Bolshevist Alexis Minski (Jacob Kingsbury). When Ruth complains to her superintendent about malnourished schoolchildren, she is suspended. She now joins the Communist Party. Captain Nathan Levinson (Edward Langford) has been sent to investigate radicals in New York. Ruth's brother Davy Gibson, who once saved Levinson's life, arrives. Minski misleads Ruth into believing that Levinson must be killed. Davy breaks up all plots and Ruth and Levinson marry.

Pathé. US. 1919. B&W. *Director:* George Irving *Writer:* Augustus Thomas *Cast:* Leah Baird, Edward Langford, W.H. Gibson, Jacob Kingsbury, Harry Bartlett, William Fredericks, Becky Bruce

790. *Voskhozhdenie (The Ascent)*

In wartime Russia, idealistic young schoolteacher-soldier Sotniko and fellow soldier Rybak forage for food for their peasant friends, on the run from Germans. They are captured by Nazi sympathizers and tortured for useless information. One doesn't talk and the other betrays his friend and the peasants.

Mosfilm. Soviet Union. 1976. 105m. B&W. *Director:* Larisa Shepitko *Writers:* Yuri Klepikov, Larisa Shepitko *Cast:* Boris Plotnikov, Vladimir Gostiukhin, Anatoly Solonitsin, Sergei Yakovlev, Ludmilla Poliakova

791. *Vrema Cuda (Time of Miracles)*

In a small town in 1945 Yugoslavia, the school burns down, injuring its teacher, Nicodemus (Pedrag Miki Manojlovic). The local Communist teacher demands that the townspeople change the church into something else and paint over the religious symbols. No one helps him except the injured teacher. Mysteriously the religious icons reappear even though they were painted over. The leader is upset but it gets worse for him with the arrival of a stranger. This stranger restores life to the injured teacher who had died.

Singidunum/Television Belgrad/Channel 4/Metropolitan. Yugoslavia. 1989. 100m. C. *Producer-Director:* Goran Paskaljevic *Writers:* Borislav Pekic, Goran Paskaljevic *Cast:* Pedrag Miki Manojlovic, Dragan Maksimovic, Svetozar Cvetkovic, Mirjana Karanovic, Danilo Bata Stojkovic, Mirjana Jokovic, Ljuba Tadic

Vucjak see Horvatov izbor

792. *Waga koi wa moenu (My Love Has Been Burning)*

A feminist schoolteacher in 1884 Japan, Eiko (Kinuyo Tanaka) has her school closed because of her politics. She becomes very upset when a servant girl is sold into slavery. She goes to Tokyo, becomes involved in activism and is imprisoned. On her release she goes home to open another school for girls to help them understand their place in society.

New Yorker Films. Japan. 1949. 96m. B&W. *Producers:* Hisao Itova, Kiyoshi Shimazu *Director:* Kenji Mizoguchi *Writers:* Yoshikata Yoda, Kaneto Shindo, Kôgo Noda (novel) *Cast:* Kinuyo Tanaka, Mitsuko Mito, Kuniko Miyake, Ichirô Sugai, Shinobu Araki, Zeya Chida, Sadako Sawamura, Koreya Senda

793. *Wagahai wa Neko de Aru (I Am a Cat)*

A cat who lives with a poor schoolteacher observes and comments on what he sees around him. At the end, the cat commits suicide in despair.

Toho. Japan. 1975. 116m. C. *Producers:* Kiichi Ichi Kawa, Michi o Morioka, Ichirô Satô *Director:* Kon Ichikawa *Writer:* Toshio Yasumi *Cast:* Tatsuya Nakadai, Yoko Shimada, Mariko Okada, Juzo Itami, Kuriko Namino, Nobuto Okamoto, Hiroko Shino, Shinsuke Miname

794. *Wait Till I Catch You*

A teacher chases a dunce of a student.
Clarendon. Great Britain. 1910. B&W. *Director:* Percy Stow

Wake in Fright see Outback

Wake Up, Arezu! see Bidar show, Arezoo!

795. *Walk a Crooked Path*

At a posh boys' school, a tenured teacher is livid when he learns that the school board has again passed him over for headmaster. He pays a boy to claim that the headmaster molested him, creating a scandal. Then he and his mistress cause his wife to kill herself.

Hanover. Great Britain. 1969. 88m. C. *Producer-Director:* John Brason *Writer:* Barry Perowne *Cast:* Tenniel Evans, Faith Brook, Christopher Coll, Patricia Haines, Pat Endersby, Margery Mason, Peter Copley, George Simpson, Georgina Simpson, Georgina Cookson, Paul Dawkins, Barry Perowne

796. We Have Our Moments

Small town schoolteacher Mary Smith (Sally Eilers) is planning to marry Clem Porter (Grady Sutton), who wants to honeymoon in a nearby town so as not to interfere with his bowling schedule. Bored with her life, Mary books passage on a ship headed for Europe, promising Clem she will return in September. Posing as a sophisticate, Mary meets the Rutherfords, who are bank thieves; British Joe Gilling (David Niven), also a thief; and John Wade (James Dunn), an American detective posing as a schoolteacher. Mary ends up with the money. The thieves are arrested and John gets Mary.

Universal. US. 1937. 63m. B&W. *Producer:* Edmund Grainger *Director:* Alfred Werker *Writers:* Bruce Manning, Charles Grayson, Charles Belden, Frederick Stephani *Cast:* James Dunn, Sally Eilers, Mischa Auer, David Niven, Warren Hymer, Marjorie Gateson, Thurston Hall, Grady Sutton, Joyce Compton, Virginia Sale, Ray Brown

797. Web of Suspicion

A girls' school gym teacher is accused of murder. With the help of his girlfriend, an art teacher, they find the killer.

Danziger. Great Britain. 1959. 70m. B&W. *Producers:* Edward J. & Henry Lee Danziger *Director:* Max Varnel *Writers:* Brian Clemens, Eldon Howard *Cast:* Philip Friend, Susan Beaumont, John Martin, Peter Sinclair, Robert Raglan, Peter Elliot, Ian Fleming, Rolf Harris, Hal Osmond

798. The Webster Boy (Middle of Nowhere)

Back in England after serving time, American gambler Vance Miller (John Cassavetes) is looking for his long-lost love Margaret (Elizabeth Sellars). He finds her happily married to Paul Webster (David Farrar) and the mother of a 14-year-old boy Jimmy (Richard O'Sullivan). Vance causes turmoil trying to win Margaret away from Paul. Young Jimmy faces gossip and a sadistic headmaster (Niall MacGinnis) about his paternity.

RFI. Great Britain. 1961. 83m. B&W. *Producer:* Emmet Dalton *Director:* Don Chaffey *Writer:* Ted Allen *Cast:* Richard O'Sullivan, John Cassavetes, David Farrar, Elizabeth Sellars, Niall MacGinnis, Geoffrey Bayldon, Karl Lanchbury, John Bull, Norman Rodway, Seymour Cassel

A Week's Holiday see Une Semaine de vacances

799. Welcome Stranger

Old Doc McRory (Barry Fitzgerald) is planning his first vacation in 35 years. His replacement is a young, fancy-dressing, humming Jim Pearson (Bing Crosby).

Jim makes a play for pretty schoolteacher Trudy Mason (Joan Caulfield) at Doc's going-away party. Trudy is engaged to stuffy pharmacist Roy Chesley (Robert Shayne). Initially the old doc takes a dislike to Jim but changes his mind after Jim saves his life by performing an emergency appendectomy. Trudy breaks off her engagement with Roy but refuses to see Jim. McRory has competition from Dr. Ronnie Jenks for his dream position as the hospital's chief of surgery. McRory gets the job when Jenks misdiagnoses an epidemic and Jim wins over the girl.

Paramount. US. 1947. 106m. B&W. *Producer:* Sol C. Siegel *Director:* Elliott Nugent *Writer:* Arthur Sheekman *Cast:* Bing Crosby, Joan Caulfield, Barry Fitzgerald, Wanda Hendrix, Frank Faylen, Elizabeth Patterson, Robert Shayne, Larry Young, Percy Kilbride, Charles Dingle, Don Beddoe, Thurston Hall, Lillian Bronson, Paul Stanton, Pat McVey, John Westley, Edward Clark, Ethel Wales, Frank Ferguson, Elliott Nugent, Owen Tyree, Gertrude Hoffman, Douglas Wood, Charles Middleton, Fred Datig, Jr.

800. *Welcome to the Dollhouse*

In a sometimes brutal, often hilarious tale of seventh-grade hell, 11-year-old Dawn Wiener (Heather Matarazzo), called Wiener Dog and Dog-Face by her classmates, is the object of relentless cruelty by the class bully, the cheerleading squad. Her myopic seventh-grade teacher barely tolerates her. At home, she is either overlooked or unjustly punished. Her life seems to be falling apart.

Sony Pictures Classics. US. 1995. 88m. C. *Writer-Producer-Director:* Todd Solandz *Cast:* Heather Matarazzo, Victoria Davis, Christina Brucato, Christina Vidal, Siri Howard, Brendan Sexton III, Telly Pontidis, Herbie Duarte, Scott Coogan, Daria Kalinina, Mathew Faber, Josiah Trager, Ken Leung, Dimitri DeFresco, Rica Martens

We'll Live Till Monday see *Dozhivyom do Ponedilnika*

We'll Take Care of the Teachers see *Wir Hau'n die Pauker in die Pfanne*

801. *Wetherby*

One night a nervous young stranger shows up uninvited at a dinner party. Neither the guests nor the hostess knows who he is, but no one asks his name. The next day the stranger reappears at the home of the hostess Jean Travers (Vanessa Redgrave), a lonely middle-aged schoolteacher. After strained discussion, the stranger plays the ultimate practical joke by pointing a gun into his mouth and pulling the trigger. We learn about Jean's younger days.

MGM/UA. Great Britain. 1985. 102m. C. *Producer:* Simon Relph *Writer-Director:* David Hare *Cast:* Vanessa Redgrave, Ian Holm, Judi Dench, Marjorie Yates, Tom Wilkinson, Tim McInnery, Suzanna Hamilton, Stuart Wilson, Joely Richardson

802. What's the Matter with Helen?

In the 1930s, Adelle (Debbie Reynolds) and Helen (Shelley Winters), mothers of convicted murderers, move to Hollywood and open a school for would-be starlets. The school is a big success while Adelle finds love with the rich father of one of her pupils and Helen becomes obsessed with a radio evangelist and starts to go insane.

UA. US. 1971. 101m. C. *Producer:* George Edwards *Director:* Curtis Harrington *Writer:* Henry Farrell *Cast:* Debbie Reynolds, Shelley Winters, Dennis Weaver, Agnes Moorehead, Micheál MacLiammóir, Helene Winston, Peggy Rea, Logan Ramsey, Paulle Clark, Yvette Vickers, Molly Dodd, Samee Lee Jones, Robbi Morgan, Timothy Carey, Swen Swenson

803. When Brendan Met Trudy

Brendan Moore is a teacher, movie buff, and loner living in Dublin. He meets Trudy Fortune, a Montessori teacher, in a pub. Eventually they begin a relationship and for the first time in his adult life Brendan is having fun. First he fears that Trudy is a serial castrator, then learns that she is a burglar.

Shooting Gallery. Great Britain. 2000. 94m. C. *Producer:* Lynda Myles *Director:* Kieron J. Walsh *Writer:* Roddy Doyle *Cast:* Peter McDonald, Flora Montgomery, Marie Mullen, Pauline McLynn, Don Wycherley, Maynard Eziashi, Eileen Walsh, Barry Cassin, Niall O'Brien, Rynaugh O'Grady, Ali White, Robert O'Neill, Eoin Manley, George McMahon, Sean O'Flanagan, Luke Boyle, William O'Sullivan

804. Where Angels Go, Trouble Follows

In this sequel to the 1966 film *The Trouble With Angels,* Rosalind Russell is again cast as the conservative Mother Superior. The St. Francis Academy nuns and students are on a cross-country bus trip to an inter-faith youth rally in California. Mother Superior clashes with the younger and more progressive Sister George (Stella Stevens).

Columbia. US. 1968. 93m. C. *Producer:* William Frye *Director:* James Neilson *Writer:* Blanche Hanalis *Cast:* Rosalind Russell, Stella Stevens, Binnie Barnes, Mary Wickes, Dolores Sutton, Susan Saint James, Barbara Hunter, Milton Berle, Arthur Godfrey, Van Johnson, Robert Taylor, William Lundigan, Michael Christian, John Findlater, Alice Rawlings

805. Where the Lilies Bloom

A brave and stubborn Appalachian teenager (Julie Gholson) holds together her orphaned family and keeps them out of an institution. She also tries to deter her older sister's farmer suitor. Miss Fleetie (Sudie Bond) is a touching schoolteacher.

UA. US. 1974. 97m. C. *Producer:* Robert B. Radnitz *Director:* William A. Graham *Writers:* Earl Hammer, Jr., Vera and Bill Cleaver (book) *Cast:* Julie Gholson, Jan Smithers, Matthew Burrill, Helen Harmon, Harry Dean Stanton, Sudie Bond, Rance Howard, Tom Spratley, Helen Bragdon, Alice Beardsley

806. *Where There's a Will*

The headmaster of a school located near a prison and the Louvre is inadvertently involved in the theft of the Mona Lisa. It seems that one of his students is the son of an art thief, who has been planning the robbery for a long time. The father innocently asks to stay at the school. Unbeknownst to the headmaster, the thief draws him into the plot. Later, the boys help the headmaster return the painting.

Gainsborough. Great Britain. 1936. 81m. B&W. *Producers:* Edward Black, Sidney Gilliat *Director:* William Beaudine *Writers:* Will Hay, Robert Edmunds, Ralph Spence *Cast:* Will Hay, Hartley Power, Gibb McLaughlin, Graham Moffatt, Norma Varden, Gina Malo

Who Saw Him Die? see *Ole Dole Doff*

807. *The Whole Wide World*

In West Texas in the 1930s, young, down-to-earth schoolteacher Novalyne Price (Renee Zellweger) has a stormy relationship with pulp fiction writer Robert E. Howard (Vincent D'Onofrio), creator of Conan the Barbarian. He lives with a clingy ailing mother and an incommunicative father and writing is his escape.

Sony Pictures Classics. US. 1996. 105m. C. *Producers:* Carl-Jan Colpaert, Kevin Reidy, Dan Ireland, Vincent D'Onofrio *Director:* Dan Ireland *Writer:* Michael Scott Myers *Cast:* Vincent D'Onofrio, Renee Zellweger, Ann Wedgeworth

808. *Why Shoot the Teacher?*

Max Brown (Bud Cort) travels west across Canada in 1935 to take a teaching job in a one-room schoolhouse. He learns that he will be living under the schoolroom and that the farmers will have trouble paying the $45 they had promised for his teaching. He causes embarrassment to one poor family when he shares his lunch with the children. On the day the region's school inspector is coming to review Max's work, the children are covered with mud and gopher fur because they were out collecting gopher tails to sell for a penny each.

WSTT/Fraser Films. Canada. 1976. 99m. C. *Producer:* Lawrence Hertzog *Director:* Silvio Narizzano *Writers:* James DeFelice, Max Braithwaite (novel) *Cast:* Bud Cort, Samantha Eggar, Chris Wiggins, Gary Reineke, John Friesen, Michael J. Reynolds

809. *Wide Awake*

After his beloved grandfather dies, grief-stricken fifth grader Joshua Beal (Joseph Cross) goes in search of God. While attending the all-boy Waldron Academy, he runs into trouble. A sports-loving nun, Sister Terry (Rosie O'Donnell), befriends the boy and helps him in his quest for God.

Miramax. US. 1998. 88m. C. *Producers:* Cathy Konrad, Cary Woods *Writer-*

Director: M. Night Shyamalan *Cast:* Joseph Cross, Timothy Reifsnyder, Dana Delany, Denis Leary, Robert Loggia, Rosie O'Donnell, Camryn Manheim, Vicki Giunta, Heather Casler, Dan Lauria, Julia Stiles

810. *Widow Malone*

A rich widow fakes poverty to fool a schoolmaster and a councilor.
Film Company of Ireland. Great Britain. 1916. B&W. *Producer:* James Plant *Director:* J.M. Kerrigan

811. *Wild Beauty*

Schoolteachers Linda Gibson (Lois Collier) and Sissy (Jacqueline de Wit) arrive in Flagstaff to teach at the Native American reservation. Also arriving is Dr. David Morrow (Don Porter) who is asked by Johnny (Robert "Buzz" Henry), an orphaned Native American boy, to treat his injured wild colt "Wild Beauty." David gives advice to Linda about the need to understand the difficulties the Native Americans have on their reservation. When Johnny won't attend school, Linda has storekeeper Barney, Johnny's guardian, end his riding privileges. Johnny runs away but is found by David, who wants Linda to resign. Linda stays and apologizes to Johnny. Linda's old boyfriend Gordon Madison shows up wanting her to return East with him. Gordon makes plans to slaughter the herd of wild horses and use their hides in his shoe factory. Johnny senses that Wild Beauty is in trouble and disappears. The horses are saved but not before Johnny is shot and wounded. David and Linda are reunited, as are Johnny and Wild Beauty. David beats up Gordon and sends him back East.
Universal. US. 1946. 61m. B&W. *Producer-Director:* Wallace W. Fox *Writer:* Adele Buffington, Dorcas Cochran *Cast:* Don Porter, Lois Collier, Jacqueline de Wit, Robert Wilcox, George Cleveland, Dick Curtis, Robert "Buzz" Henry, Wild Beauty (horse), Eva Puig, Pierce Lyden, Roy Brent, Isabel Withers, Hank Patterson

The Wild Child see *L'Enfant Sauvage*

812. *Wild Geese*

Schoolteacher Lind Archer (Anita Stewart) moves in with the family of Minnesota farmer Caleb Gare (Russell Simpson), an evil and cruel man who has tolerance for no one. Lind becomes friends with Judith (Eve Southern), a highly spirited girl. She also falls in love with a worker on the farm of Mark Jordan (Jason Robards), who is the illegitimate son of Caleb's wife.
Tiffany-Stahl Productions, Inc. US. 1927. 70m. B&W. *Producer:* John Stahl *Director:* Phil Stone *Writer:* A. P. Younger *Cast:* Belle Bennett, Russell Simpson, Eve Southern, Donald Keith, Jason Robards, Anita Stewart, Wesley Barry, Rada Rae, Austin Jewel, Evelyn Selbie, D'Arcy Corrigan, Jack Gardner, James Mack, Bert Sprotte, Bodil Rosing, Bert Starkey

813. The Wildcats of St. Trinian's

The girls rebel against their educational responsibilities by organizing a union and going on strike. They also kidnap the daughter of an Arabian millionaire as a safety net.

Enterprise. Great Britain. 1980. 91m. C. *Producer:* E.M. Smedley-Aston *Writer-Director:* Frank Launder *Cast:* Sheila Hancock, Michael Hordern, Rodney Bewes, Maureen Kipman, Joe Melia, Thorley Walters, Julia McKenzie, Veronica Quilligan, Deborah Norton, Rose Hill, Luan Peters, Ambrosine Philpotts, Bernadette O'Farrell, Barbara Hicks, Diana King, Rosalind Knight, Patsy Smart, Jeremy Pearce, Ballard Berkeley, Frances Ruffell, Lisa Vanderpump

Winter Light see *Nattvardsgästerna*

814. Wir Hau'n die Pauker in die Pfanne (We'll Take Care of the Teachers)

A group of students play a practical joke on school director Dr. Taft (Theo Lingen). It seems that his twin brother went to Africa and got wealthy and they haven't seen each other in 40 years. The students fake a letter saying his brother has died and that he (Dr. Taft) will inherit a fortune if he complies with certain conditions such as caring for a chimpanzee and letting the students pass their tests. This is the fifth of a series named "The Boobies of the First Bench."

Constantin. West Germany. 1970. 84m. C. *Writer-Producer:* Fanz Seitz *Director:* Harald Reinl *Cast:* Hans Kraus, Uschi Glas, Fritz Wepper, Theo Lingen, Karl Schönböck, Rudolf Schündler, Ruth Stephan, Balduin Bass, Hans Terofal, Monika Dahlberg, Doris Kiesow, JosefMoosholzer, Kristina Nel, Axel von Ambesser, Jutta Speidel

815. Wizia Lokalna 1901 (Inspection of the Scene of a Crime)

The story centers on an incident in a schoolroom near the Prussian-Russian border of Poland in 1901. The teaching of religion, which draws protest from the Polish. A local priest starts a strike to support the children when they refuse to participate in the religious lessons.

Film Polski. Poland. 1980. 98m. C. *Writer-Director:* Falip Bajon *Cast:* Tadeusz Lomnicki, Zdzislaw Wardejn, Zygmunt Bielawsky, Jerzy Treta, Stanislaw Igar, Mieczysloaw Viot, Stanislaw Michalski, Janusz Michalowski, Hnryk Bista, Elzbieta Borysiak, Zbigniew Buczkowski, Grzegorz Dobrzycki, Marzena Frydryszak, Wirgiliusz Gryn, Tadeusz Gwiazdowski, Krzysztof Kozlowski, Michal Lesniak, Stanslaw Michalski, Wlodzimierz Musial, Daniel Olbrychski, Jack Recknitz, Renata Rózycka, Alfred Struwe, Jerzy Stuhr, Karl Sturm, Jerzy Trela Mieczyslaw Voit, Zdzislaw Wardejn, Andrzej Wasilewicz, Grazyna Witczak, Gabriela Wojtkowiak, Malgorzata Zaluska

816. Wo de fu qin mu qin (The Road Home)

When his father dies, a young engineer returns from the city to his village where he was born. His mother, crushed by grief, insists on a traditional funeral for his father. As the engineer remembers his father, we see his parents as youths. The mother (18 years old in the flashbacks) falls in love with the handsome 20-year-old schoolmaster who comes from the city. The villagers build the schoolhouse in which he will spend the rest of his life teaching primary school. She weaves the red cloth to be wound around the rafters. Every day she visits the school, listening to his voice as he drills the students. The courtship is interrupted when he is called to the city to face interrogation and she falls ill.

Columbia Tri-Star Home Entertainment. China. 1999. 100m. *Producer:* Zhao Yu *Director:* Zhang Yimou *Writer:* Bao Shi *Cast:* Zhang Ziyi, Sun Honglei, Zheng Hao, Zhao Yuelin, Li Bin

817. *Wo xin fei xiang (Rainbow)*

An art teacher has seen his students die during conflicts among warlords, and he himself has been injured and left a eunuch. Settling down in a small village, he marries a local girl, Rainbow, who is a mute and musically gifted. Rainbow is desired by the local schoolteacher and a violinist. Japanese forces are on their doorstep in the 1930s.

Syracuse International. China. 2005. 90m. C. *Writer-Director:* Xiaosong Gao *Cast:* Daoming Chen, Yongdai Ding, Lu Lu, Jun Zheng

818. *The Wolves of Willoughby Chase*

During the imaginary reign of King James III, in the snowbound and wolf-infested North Yorkshire countryside, children Bonnie (Emily Hudson) and Sylvia (Aleks Darowska) try to stop a sinister plan by their governess Letitia Slighcarp (Stephanie Beacham).

Entertainment/Subatomnic/Zenith. Great Britain. 1988. 93m. C. *Producer:* Mark Forstater *Director:* Stuart Orme *Writers:* William M. Akers, Joan Allen (novel) *Cast:* Stephanie Beacham, Mel Smith, Geraldine James, Richard O'Brien, Emily Hudson, Aleks Darowska, Jane Horrocks, Eleanor David, Jonathan Coy

819. *The Woman in White*

Tutor Walter Hartright encounters a mysterious woman dressed all in white on a moonlit road. She is confused and very distressed. He helps her back to London where she warns him about a certain baronet. A squire with two nieces, Marian and her half-sister Laura, hires Walter to be their tutor. Walter falls in love with Laura but she is promised to another, Sir Percival Gylde. Dark secrets abound about the families and the woman in white. There have been at least seven film and TV adaptations of this tale, the first in 1912. The Russian version is titled *Zhenshchina v belom*.

Warner. US. 1948. 109m. B&W. *Producer:* Henry Blanke *Director:* Peter Godfrey *Writers:* Stephen Morehouse Avery, Wilkie Collins (novel) *Cast:* Gig Young, Eleanor Parker, Sydney Greenstreet, Alexis Smith, Agnes Moorehead, John Emery, John Abbott, Curt Bois

820. *The Woman Who Was Forgotten*

Dedicated schoolteacher Miss Miller (Belle Bennett) is beloved by her students, but loses her job when she protects a favorite pupil, Richard Atwell. Years later a now-grownup Richard (LeRoy Mason) arranges a banquet to celebrate Miss Miller's years of inspirational teaching. At the event there is a confession from an embezzler, an apology from Mr. Riggs the banker, and also the promise of a position as principal of a new school for Miss Miller.

States Cinema Corp. US. 1930. B&W. *Producer:* Charles Goetz *Director:* Richard Thomas *Writer:* Bert Levino *Cast:* LeRoy Mason, Belle Bennett, Jack Mower, Gladys McConnell, William Walling, Jack Trent

A Woman's Law see *The Trap*

821. *Women in Love*

The characters in this story set in England circa World War I: Rupert Birkin (Alan Bates), an untidy, moody school inspector who strives for pure relationships with women and men; Ursula Brangwen (Jennie Linden), a sweet schoolmistress; sculptress Gudrun Brangwen (Glenda Jackson), Ursula's very liberated sister; and Gerald Crich (Oliver Reed), son of a wealthy mine owner and Rupert's best friend.

UA/Brandywine. Great Britain. 1969. 130m. C. *Producer:* Larry Kramer *Director:* Ken Russell *Writers:* Larry Kramer, D.H. Lawrence (novel) *Cast:* Glenda Jackson, Jennie Linden, Alan Bates, Oliver Reed, Michael Gough, Alan Webb

822. *X-Men*

Professor Charles Zavier (Patrick Stewart) has created a boarding school for children with an X factor in their genes that gives them special powers and makes them so different that there is no place for them in society. Besides teaching subjects such as philosophy, the faculty instructs the students on how to control their powers. The school is a haven for these misfit children. Charles, the teachers, and some of the students band together to fight the enemies of peace. This action movie was followed by two sequels.

TCF. US. 2000. 104m. C. *Producers:* Lauren Shuler Donner, Ralph Winter *Director:* Bryan Singer *Writers:* Tom DeSanto, Bryan Singer, David Hayter *Cast:* Hugh Jackman, Patrick Stewart, Ian McKellen, Famke Janssen, James Marsden, Halle Berry, Anna Paquin, Tyler Mane, Ray Park, Rebecca Romijn, Bruce Davison, Matthew Sharp, Rhona Shekter, Kenneth McGregor, Shawn Roberts

823. *Yi ge dou bu neng shao (Not one Less)*

An elderly schoolteacher painstakingly counts out 26 pieces of chalk, one for each day of the month he will be gone. His replacement is Wei (Wei Minzhi), a 13-year-old primary school graduate of the Shuiquan Primary School. She is only slightly taller than the kids. Her qualifications are: no one else wants the job, unsmiling bossiness, neat handwriting and her ability to perform one song about Chairman

Mao. Wei writes lessons on the blackboard and the children copy them into notebooks. The children try to humiliate her. (The impulse to abuse substitute teachers seems to transcend cultures.) When the class clown Zhang Huike is sent to the city to work off his parent's debts, Wei sets out to find him. She has been promised a bonus if she keeps the class intact. In the city, no one listens to her pleas until a local television reporter sympathizes and helps.

Sony Pictures Classics. China. 1999 106m.C, *Producer:* Zhao Yu *Director:* Zhang Yimou *Writer:* Shi Xiangsheng *Cast:* Wei Minzhi, Zhang Huike, Tian Zhenda, Gao Enman, Sun Zhimei, Feng Yuying, Li Fanfan

824. *Yijang Chunshui Xiang Dong Lir (Spring River Flows East)*

An idealistic schoolteacher leaves his family to join the Reds and the struggle against the Japanese in 1931. He is captured but escapes. He is then seduced by bourgeois life and marries another while his family lives in poverty.

LinHua Film Company. China. 1947. 188m. B&W. *Writer-Directors:* Cai Chusheng, Zheng Junli *Cast:* Tao Jin, Pai Yang, Wu Yin, Yan Gongshang, Shu Xiuwen

825. *You Can't Push the River*

Tony, a new boy in a city school, is trying to cope with his relocation. His teacher Joe Glass is an Irishman who has traveled extensively but desires to be a part of somewhere. Joe's lover Kohar, an Armenian raised in Australia, is trying to find her place. The film shows a bond of shared humanity between pupil and teacher.

Australia. 1993. 75m. C. *Producer:* Robert Alcock *Director:* Leslie Oliver *Writers:* Leslie Oliver, John Reddin *Cast:* Nollaig O'Flannabhra, Antonio Punturiero, Kathryn Chalker, Tony Punturiero, Eleanor Punturiero, Michael Lotito

Young Törless see Der Junge Törless

826. *You're Never Too Young*

At a posh hotel in Los Angeles, Bob Miles (Dean Martin), a girls' school instructor from Twin Falls, has a stolen diamond placed in his jacket by a thief-murderer. The diamond next ends up with Wilbur (Jerry Lewis), a young man whose dream is to become a real barber, now working as an assistant at the hotel's barber shop. Now unwittingly involved in the diamond heist, Wilbur is forced to disguise himself as a 12-year-old boy so that he can get away from the thieves. Still posing as a child, he gets unsuspecting Bob, who has come to say goodbye to his girlfriend, fellow teacher Nancy Collins (Diana Lynn), to purchase a half-price ticket for him. Wilbur takes refuge in Nancy's drawing room and convinces her that he is a scared boy traveling alone. The next morning, at Mrs. Brendan's School for Girls, Bob learns that Nancy's train is stuck outside town and drives to meet her, accompanied by Gretchen (Nina Foch), headmistress Elly Brendan's jealous daughter. In Nancy's drawing room, Gretchen discovers Wilbur and gleefully assumes the worst. After telling Bob, Gretchen rushes back to school to inform her mother and the board about Nancy's shocking behavior. As they are voting to fire Nancy, Bob arrives with Wilbur, still dressed in the sailor suit. Eventually the chaos is resolved.

Paramount. US. 1955. 102m. C. *Producer:* Paul Jones *Director:* Norman Taurog *Writer:* Sidney Sheldon *Cast:* Dean Martin, Jerry Lewis, Diana Lynn, Nina Foch, Raymond Burr, Mitzi McCall, Veda Ann Borg, Margery Maude

827. *Yours to Command*

Colleen O'Brien (Shirley Palmer), a schoolteacher, meets Robert Duane (George O'Hara) while he is driving through Oklahoma. He is posing as the Duanes' chauffeur. Soon after their meeting Colleen's father strikes, oil and comes to New York. The O'Briens decide to rent the Duanes' Long Island home. Robert continues to impersonate a chauffeur. Society crook Ted Hanson (Jack Luden) has Mr. O'Brien purchase a priceless tiara, which he plans to steal. Robert comes to the rescue and gets the girl.

Film Booking Offices of America. US. 1927. B&W. *Director:* David Kirkland *Writers:* Basil Dickey, Harry Haven *Cast:* George O'Hara, Shirley Palmer, William Burress, Dot Farley, Jack Luden, William Humphrey

828. *Zai moshengoe chengshi (In a Strange City)*

A Taipei schoolteacher becomes romantically involved with a corrupt (and married) politician after the death of her brother. She has her eyes opened when she learns that he is staging an assassination attempt on himself to look good. She must also deal with a suicidal student, a questionable business deal, and a possible new love.

Filmopolis Pictures. Taiwan. 1996. 107m. C. *Producer:* Li-Kong Hsu *Director:* Chi Yin *Writers:* Dai Wen-Tsai Dai, Chi Yin *Cast:* Yang Kuei-Mei, Winston Chao Wen-Hsuan, Chang Guo-chu, Ekin Cheng, Angela Chang, Gu Rong-gao

829. *Zbabelec (The Coward)*

In the closing days of World War II, in a remote Slovak village, schoolteacher Bodnarova (Ladislav Chudik) and his wife Frantiska (Daniela Smutná) discover a wounded Russian parachutist just as the Germans are arriving to occupy their village. Frantiska becomes involved with the resistance while the teacher collaborates with the Germans. The teacher finally finds the courage to save his honor and those innocent victims of the Nazis.

Facets. Czechoslovakia. 1961. 98m. B&W. *Director:* Jiří Weiss *Writers:* Ivan Bukovcan, Ota Ornest, Jiří Weiss *Cast:* Daniela Smutná, Ladislav Chudík, Oleg Strizhenov, Wilhelm Koch-Hooge, Jindrich Narenta, Frantisek Dibarbora

830. *Zéro de Conduite: Jeunes Diables au Collège*

At a dreadful boarding school in a Paris suburb, students are unhappy and plan an uprising. One teacher is a popular anarchist (Jean Dasté) who does Chaplin's imitations and plays games while asking nothing of his students. The headmaster (played by the long-bearded dwarf Delphin) is looked down upon by the boys. The film was banned until 1945 on political grounds.

Gaumont/Franko Film/Aubert. France. 1933. 45m. B&W. *Producer:* Jean Vigo *Writer-Director:* Jean Vigo *Cast:* Jean Dasté, Louis Lefébvre, Gilbert Pruchon, Le Flon, Delphin, Coco Goldstein

Zero for Conduct see *Zéro de Conduite: Jeunes Diables au Collège*

831. *Das Zweite Erwachen der Christa Klages (The Second Awakening of Christa Klages)*

Christa Klages is so committed to the progressive nursery school she opened three years ago, she robs a bank for money to keep it in business. She and her lover are now on the run.

Bioskop-Film/West Deutsches Rundfunk. West Germany. 1977. 93m. C. *Producer:* Gunther Witte *Director:* Margarethe Von Trotta *Writers:* Margarethe Von Trotta, Luise Francia *Cast:* Tina Engel, Sylvia Reize, Katharina Thalbach, Marius Müller-Westernhagen, Peter Schneider

BIBLIOGRAPHY

Bach, Jacqueline. "From Nerds to Napoleons: Thwarting Archetypical Expectations in High School Films." *Journal of Curriculum Theorizing* 22 no. 2 (2006): 73. Detailed discussion of Napoleon Dynamite and other nerdy characters in film.

Bauer, Dale M. "Indecent Proposals: Teachers in the Movies." *College English* 60 no. 3 (1998): 301. Delves into motion picture portrayals of college teachers.

Beyerbach, Barbara. "The Social Foundations Classrooms: Themes in Sixty Years of Teachers in Film." *Educational Studies* 37 no.3 (2005): 267. Analyzes how teachers and students are represented in films. The author examines over 50 popular movies and discusses how these films relate to the construction of race, class, and gender.

Bloom, Adi. "How Robin Williams Ruined Our Image." *Times Educational Supplement* (November 8, 2002): 2. Discussion of teachers becoming tired of being portrayed in film as too inspirational.

Bolotin, Joseph, and Pamela and Gail E. Burnaford. *Images of Schoolteachers in America.* New Jersey: Lawrence Erlbaum Associates, Publishers, 2001. Explores the images of schoolteachers in America from the beginning of the twentieth century to the present.

Brittenham, Rebecca. "Goodbye, Mr. Hip: Radical Teaching in 1960s Television." *College English* 68 no. 2 (2005): 149-67. The author uses the popular television series *Room 222* as a case study to open the debate about the meaning of radical teaching within television realism.

Cook, Ann. "Teachers as Team Players." *Education Week* 14 no. 24 (1995): 40. Commentary on the role of teachers in changing the educational system of a school.

Dalton, Mary M. *The Hollywood Curriculum.* New York: Peter Lang Publishing, 2004. This book analyzes 116 films distributed in the United States over the past 75 years to study curriculum in the movies.

Dollar, Steve. "Movies: A Core Subject in Hollywood; Movies about Inspiring Teachers Are Nothing New. Some Make the Grade, Many Graduate to Bigger Things." *Los Angeles Times* (January 9, 2004):E22. A summary of movies about inspiring teachers.

Duncan, Charles A. "A Content Analysis of Films: Images of Physical Education." *Research Quarterly for Exercise and Sport* 72 (2001):A-63. Exploratory study to determine how physical education and physical educators are portrayed in current popular film.

Duncan, Charles A., Joe Nolan, and Ralph Wood. "See You In the Movies? We Hope Not!" *The Journal of Physical Education, Recreation and Dance* 73 no. 8 (2002): 38. Perspective on the portrayal of physical education teachers in films.

Edelman, Roy. "Teachers in the Movies." *American Educator* 7 no. 3 (1983): 26-31. Examines various films produced since the mid-1930s for their portrayal of schoolteachers. Article highlights the stereotypical image of teachers.

Ellsmore, Susan. *Carry On Teachers!* Sterling: Trentham Books, 2005. This book looks at the charismatic teacher as portrayed in films.

Fallon, Jane. "Why Saintly Teachers Make Dull Television." *Times Educational Supplement* (March 30, 2001): 18. Discussion of a television drama that takes a more realistic approach to the portrayal of teachers.

Farhi, Adam. "Hollywood Goes to School: Recognizing the Super Teacher Myth in Film." *The Clearing House* 72 no.3 (1999): 57. Examines how motion pictures portray teachers as super-humans able to solve all problems. The author cites such movies as *To Sir With Love*, *Lean on Me* and *The Principal*.

Fine, Marshall. "Sticking to Basics; From *Mr. Chips* to *Mr. Holland*, Movies about Teachers Follow the Same Tried-and-True Lesson Plan." *Los Angeles Times* (December 23, 1999): 14. Teachers in films always have the same lesson to learn, that is, that teachers can learn as much from their students as their students learn from them.

Freeman, Miriam L., and Deborah P. Valentine. "Through the Eyes of Hollywood: Images of Social Workers in Film." *Social Work* 49 no. 2 (2004): 151. Reports on research that examined the images of social workers in film.

Goldman, David. "Go to the Head of the Class." *Biography* 2 no. 9 (n.d.): 58. This is a 25-question quiz testing the reader's knowledge on educators in movies and television.

Grant, Peggy A. "Using Popular Films to Challenge Preservice Teacher's Beliefs About Teaching in Urban Schools." *Urban Education* 37 no.1 (2002):77. *Dangerous Minds*, *Stand and Deliver* and *187* are the three films discussed in this article that reflect ideas that preservice teachers may have about teaching in urban school.

Hill, David. "Tinseltown Teacher." *Teacher Magazine* 6 no. 6 (1995): 40. A discussion of Hollywood movies concerning high school teaching in the United States.

Keroes, Jo. *Tales Out of School: Gender, Longing, and the Teacher in Fiction and Film*. Carbondale and Edwardsville: Southern Illinois University Press, 1999. A wide-scope examination of the representation of teachers in fiction and film from the twelfth century to contemporary works.

Krausz, Peter. "Does the Cinema Represent Teacher's Fairly?" *Australian Screen Education* 30 (Summer 2003): 62. Looks at the way popular cinema represents the teaching profession. Asks the question, "What we can learn about the career based on these depictions?"

Lasley II, Thomas J. "Paradigm Shifts in the Classroom (Movies about Teachers and Teaching)." *Phi Delta Kappan* 80 no. 1 (1998): 84. Claims that movies are an effective way to show how teaching can be made better by allowing the teacher to view the process from the outside.

McCormick, Patrick. "There's No Substitutes for Good Teachers." *U.S. Catholic* 61 no. 6 (1996): 46. Shows how good teachers are portrayed in movies as "loving, passionate, and knowledge-seeking people."

McCullick, Bryan, Don Belcher, Brent Hardin, and Marie Hardin. "Butches, Bullies and Buffoons: Images of Physical Education Teachers in the Movies." *Sport, Education and Society* 8 no. 1 (2003): 3. Studies the cinematic images of physical education teachers during the past decade.

Maloney, Henry B. "Films About Teachers: My '10 Best' List." *Education Week* 22 no. 24 (2003): 27. This article focuses on ten films about teachers, among them *Goodbye, Mr. Chips*, *The Miracle Worker* and *The Prime of Miss Jean Brodie*.

Mank, Gregory William. "The Hollywood Adventures of Pauline Moore." *Films in Review* 45 (July-August 1994): 23–32. Excerpts from an interview with actress Moore as she recalls her career from the 1930s to the 1950s. She was the teacher in the Shirley Temple version of *Heidi*.

Mourby, Adrian. "Conor MacMichael." *Times Educational Supplement* 4465 (2002):25. Interview with Glenda Jackson about the film *The Class of Miss MacMichael* and her

role as the teacher working with a group of maladjusted children in the slums of London.
Mourby, Adrian. "Dr. Smart Alec." *Times Educational Supplement* 4453 (November 2, 2001): 29. Examines the popularity of Will Hay in the 1930s based on his portrayal of the scowling schoolmaster in British movies.
Mourby, Adrian. "Fantasy Teacher." *Times Educational Supplement* 4469 (2002): 27. Reports on the characteristics of Elias Jones as a teacher in the film *How Green Was My Valley*.
Newman, Vicky. "Cinema, Women Teachers, and the 1950s and 1960s." *Educational Studies* 32 no. 4 (2001): 416. Discussion of women teachers in the cinema in the 1950s and 1960s.
"The Performing Teacher." *Wilson Quarterly* 15 no. 4 (1991): 132. Reviews the article "The Great Teacher Myth" by Robert B. Hellman.
Rubenstein, Gary. "Mixed Media." *Teacher Magazine* 15 no. 1 (2003): 46–47. Author concludes that if a film was made that all educators agreed with, that film would be unwatchable.
Seipp, April. "Action!" *Teacher Magazine* 18 no. 1 (2006): 20. Reviews several documentary films concerning education and teachers.
Swetnam, Leslie A. "Media Distortion of the Teacher Image." *The Clearing House* 66 no. 1 (1992): 30. Examines how the portrayal of teachers in television and film affects the public perception of the teaching profession.
Trier, James D. "The Cinematic Representation of the Personal and Professional Lives of Teachers." *Teacher Education Quarterly* (Summer 2001): 127–42. The purpose of this article was to explain how certain school films can be used to show preservice teachers the relationship between the personal and professional lives of teachers.
Vincendeau, Ginette. "Back to the Blackboard." *Sight and Sound* 9 no. 7 (1999): 12–15. A discussion of teachers in the films of Bertrand Tavernier.
Weber, Rebecca L. "Magic in a Rural French Classroom." *The Christian Science Monitor* (February 3, 2004): 12. Interview with Nicholas Philibert, who made the documentary film *To Be and To Have* about a classroom in rural France.
Willens, Michele. "Television; Showing their Credentials; Teachers Seem to Be the Heroes of the New TV Season. But Are These Portrayals at All Realistic?" *Los Angeles Times* (September 1, 1996): 4. Discusses the high number of television shows for the 1996 season that had teachers as their main characters.
Yakir, Dan. "Teacher, Teacher." *Boston Globe* (August 27, 1995): B27. An article discussing movies (*Dangerous Minds, Blackboard Jungle* and *Dead Poets Society*, to name a few) that look at the dynamics of the classroom and student-teacher relationships.

Websites

"Representations of Teachers in 60 Years of Films." *http://www.oswego.edu/~beyerbac/representations_of_teachers_in_6.html*, accessed September 8, 2006.

Other Sources

American Film Institute Database (online).
Connelly, Robert. *The Motion Picture Guide, Silent Films 1910–36*. Chicago: Cinebooks, 1986.
Gifford, Denis. *The British Film Catalogue, 1895–1985*. London: David and Charles, 1986.
Internet Movie Database. http://imdb.com.

Magill, Frank N. (ed). *Magill's Survey of Cinema: English Language Films, First Series.* Volume 1. Englewood Cliffs, New Jersey: Salem Press, 1980.
Magill, Frank N. (ed). *Magill's Survey of Cinema: English Language Films, Second Series.* Volume 2. Englewood Cliffs, New Jersey: Salem Press, 1981.
Magill, Frank N. (ed). *Magill's Survey of Cinema, Foreign Language Films.* Englewood Cliffs, New Jersey: Salem Press, 1985.
Marill, Alvin. H. *Movies Made for Television: The Telefeature and the Mini-Series 1964–1984.* New York: New York Zoetrope, 1984.
Nash, Jay Robert, and Stanley Ralph Ross. *The Motion Picture Guide (1927–1983).* Chicago: Cinebooks, 1986.
The New York Times Film Reviews (1913–1980). New York: New York Times and Arno Press, n.d.
Variety Film Reviews, 1907–1984. New York: Garland Publishing, Inc., 1984.

SUBJECT INDEX

References are to entry number.

abandonment 23, 56, 354, 448, 454, 474, 537
abuse, self 624
abuse, sexual and physical 6, 95, 96, 116, 147, 187, 202, 210, 217, 313, 333, 341, 367, 373, 382, 403, 415, 538, 588, 593, 641, 643, 766, 811
actors and actresses 371, 493, 578, 629, 700
addiction 294, 384, 419
adoption 29, 32, 155, 209, 318, 352, 355, 665, 676, 699
affairs, extramarital 44, 108, 109, 123, 191, 234, 239, 283, 388, 399, 436, 525, 533, 545, 574, 582, 593, 622, 626, 681, 714, 718, 724, 752, 779, 795
Africa 172, 186, 258, 268, 381, 410, 538, 671, 814
African-Americans 105, 268, 334, 615, 617, 662
AIDS and HIV 544
alcoholics and alcohol 313, 326, 367, 370, 558, 629, 656, 720, 724, 770
alternative school 43, 73, 779
amnesia 779, 780
apartheid 201, 285
apes and monkeys 814
aquarium 559
Argentina 118, 194, 318, 441, 479, 667, 772
arson 386, 418, 520
art and artists 104, 197, 269, 546, 628, 716
Ashton-Warner, Sylvia 709

Australia 33, 102, 187, 306, 345, 444, 548, 570, 589, 705, 706, 825
authors and poets 101, 121, 253, 337, 471

bandits and outlaws 64, 120, 204, 206, 549, 623, 767
baseball 243
basketball 55
bees and wasps 105, 131, 463
birds 76, 608
blacklisted and disgraced 74, 108, 109, 153, 205, 318, 397, 431, 435, 436, 460, 474, 532, 632, 634, 676, 725, 752, 811
blackmail 100, 204, 747
blindness 21, 476, 683, 687
boarding school 1, 20, 42, 59, 88, 134, 142, 151, 187, 196, 217, 225, 233, 276, 312, 350, 373, 395, 299, 300, 301, 302, 430, 431, 505, 542, 564, 570, 602, 618, 662, 736, 754, 755, 765, 822, 832
boxing 375, 407, 669
Boy Scouts 249
Bridges, Ruby 617
bullies 104, 298, 316, 327, 333, 337, 373, 382, 415, 458, 462, 488, 659, 696, 783, 784, 800

camp, summer 3, 5, 227, 414, 462, 530, 597, 735
Catholic schools *see* parochial schools
cats 294, 711, 793
censorship 231, 727

229

Subject Index

cerebral palsy 33
chess 302, 648
China 160, 190, 242, 390, 461, 586, 661, 816, 817, 823, 824
circuses 70, 468, 729
civil war 59, 113, 225, 329, 403, 595, 611
clairvoyants *see* psychics and clairvoyants
clergy 1, 20, 34, 40, 42, 56, 63, 67, 97, 118, 172, 173, 187, 229, 235, 240, 252, 261, 286, 309, 319, 333, 360, 401, 406, 466, 524, 526, 532, 552, 596, 619, 622, 626, 628, 669, 670, 676, 680, 714, 751, 775, 815
coach 9, 68, 673
comic books and cartoons 62, 93, 285, 493
competitions and tournaments 9, 93, 299, 300, 301, 302, 337, 423, 510, 607, 637, 646, 648
concentration and internment camps 55, 532, 787
concerts 414, 498, 729
conferences 149, 779
counseling and counselor 3, 462, 717
courtrooms and attorneys 98, 166, 296, 341, 344, 392, 516, 541, 619, 662, 732
cowboy 18, 163, 164, 204, 339, 488, 580, 783, 784, 785, 786
Crane, Ichabod 304, 402
criminal 2, 69, 99, 115, 122, 153, 178, 196, 263, 285, 286, 293, 328, 352, 439, 478, 598, 664, 679, 806, 827
curses 186, 188, 351
customs and traditions 24, 28, 67, 217, 368, 385, 427, 769

dancers and dancing 72, 92, 168, 227, 338, 516, 672, 725, 735, 774, 799
daycare and pre-school 116, 135, 171, 272, 341, 501, 604, 620, 698, 830
deafness and muteness 221, 335, 416, 419, 445, 447, 476
death, accidental 64, 225, 407, 466, 491, 495, 628, 670, 758
deception 191, 295, 632, 810
delusions *see* hallucinations and delusions
disgraced *see* blacklisted and disgraced
divorce 226, 272, 501, 504, 552, 698
doctors *see* physicians and psychiatrists
documentary 162, 233
dogs 32, 49, 50, 93, 316, 331, 466, 563, 634, 663, 664, 665, 677, 689, 699, 721
drowning 507, 514, 641

earthquakes 67
elementary schools and grammar schools 65, 87, 170, 203, 243, 266, 356, 371, 384, 394, 405, 506, 528, 535, 553, 572, 593, 609, 613, 614, 617, 637, 696, 716
elephant 111
epilepsy 396, 701
espionage and spying 47, 129, 264, 281, 348, 565, 695
explorer 8, 596, 770
Eyre, Jane 360, 361, 362, 363

factories and manufacturing 146, 275, 382, 436, 581, 604, 749, 811
false accusations 29, 100, 151, 154, 178, 327, 328, 341, 400, 412, 446, 484, 598, 615, 628, 664, 727
famine 40
farm life and farming 39, 55, 66, 70, 114, 166, 172, 185, 315, 316, 334, 369, 407, 409, 423, 449, 509, 682, 731, 775, 805, 808, 812
feuds 31, 140, 168
firefighter 231
fish 659
floods and flooding 433, 717
frontier and the west 48, 50, 137, 204, 209, 259, 422, 442, 488, 783, 784, 785, 786, 807

gambling 110, 256, 393, 457, 485, 517, 549, 598, 741, 747, 798
gay and lesbian 14, 20, 35, 139, 430, 431, 526, 544, 593, 685, 718
genius and prodigy 155, 408, 423, 464, 648, 817
ghosts *see* supernatural
governesses 4, 15, 22, 28, 58, 80, 87, 126, 127, 189, 283, 309, 346, 347, 360, 360, 361, 362, 363, 421, 479, 525, 633, 688, 726, 764, 788, 818

hallucinations and delusions 614
high school 39, 53, 404, 620
home schooling 217
honeymoon 496, 796
horses and horse racing 62, 175, 178,

240, 410, 495, 549, 594, 600, 725, 774, 811

imagination and creativity 6, 35, 72, 104, 144, 506, 659, 818
impostors and impersonations 78, 169, 232, 263, 281, 293, 314, 338, 348, 484, 573, 580, 618, 637, 708, 721, 741, 827
India 23, 36, 40, 46, 111, 119, 196, 202, 265, 366, 628, 707
inheritance 11, 80, 98, 155, 178, 426, 484, 502, 530, 555, 573, 576, 595, 814
Internet and video game 201, 501, 531
investigation and detective work 95, 171, 210, 232, 253, 264, 299, 300, 301, 302, 311, 348, 352, 384, 399, 411, 427, 487, 489, 495, 498, 497, 517, 559, 577, 588, 594, 597, 638, 676, 754, 758, 773, 789, 796
Iran 10, 67, 354, 364, 383, 592, 712, 717, 775
island life 11, 121, 152, 200, 227, 254, 286, 437, 478, 496, 510, 528, 695, 713

Japan 89, 134, 222, 238, 260, 292, 351, 388, 510, 528, 529, 531, 554, 641, 653, 711, 712, 737, 792, 793, 824
jungle 8, 254, 770
junior high *see* middle school and junior high

kidnapping 39, 45, 90, 107, 195, 196, 226, 314, 398, 440, 554, 600, 603, 702, 725, 761, 771, 813
kindergarten 36, 201, 263, 376, 384, 454, 459, 483, 715
Korea 24, 56, 303, 372, 483, 654, 655, 658, 766
Korean War 56, 534

Leonowens, Anna 27, 28, 385
leprosy 172

marathon 624
mental illness 186, 211, 239, 361, 535, 604, 661, 709, 770, 802
middle school and junior high 9, 264, 287, 294, 372, 458, 637, 661, 800
misfits and underdogs 6, 68, 142, 800, 802

monkeys *see* apes and monkeys
murder 1, 26, 50, 60, 66, 100, 107, 128, 147, 154, 166, 179, 180, 186, 188, 195, 204, 232, 233, 239, 251, 253, 262, 283, 287, 301, 338, 411, 444, 448, 466, 484, 488, 491, 495, 498, 497, 517, 525, 532, 547, 559, 561, 577, 588, 600, 619, 652, 673, 686, 733, 747, 763, 783, 797
music and singing *see* singers and musicians

nannies 5, 12, 52, 87, 211, 295, 453, 473, 480, 493, 507, 508, 550, 560, 563
native Americans and natives 25, 47, 73, 133, 154, 217, 254, 339, 405, 538, 589, 811
Nazis and German occupation 42, 78, 216, 224, 272, 475, 532, 535, 588, 688, 732, 790, 829
newspapers and reporters 14, 53, 69, 113, 228, 254, 264, 364, 407, 443, 502, 659
nuclear bomb 260, 394, 653, 711
nuns 63, 69, 77, 102, 143, 432, 486, 534, 583, 619, 671, 674, 755, 804, 809
nursery school *see* daycare and pre-school
nurses and nursing 52, 87, 685

orphanages and orphans 17, 32, 49, 55, 56, 84, 95, 97, 143, 145, 167, 209, 217, 225, 255, 309, 324, 328, 355, 360, 361, 362, 363, 409, 412, 474, 525, 589, 603, 699, 731, 746, 805, 811

pacifists 7, 73, 223
parochial schools 69, 552, 674, 768
physical education 271, 297, 471, 670, 797
physicians and psychiatrists 33, 40, 51, 52, 82, 107, 112, 145, 176, 186, 188, 209, 274, 275, 277, 324, 343, 368, 549, 583, 617, 628, 629, 665, 698, 775, 778
piano 246, 349, 417, 429, 567
poverty 36, 87, 116, 152, 167, 316, 368, 423, 528, 575, 592, 606, 810, 824
pregnancy 135, 155, 261, 265, 389, 536, 590, 628, 758, 782
prejudice and bias 118, 146, 210, 225, 258
pre-school *see* daycare and pre-school
priests *see* clergy

principals and vice principals 148, 152, 228, 277, 353, 371, 376, 394, 404, 430, 455, 458, 460, 498, 516
protest and reforms 33, 46, 55, 90, 102, 119, 213, 218, 283, 366, 375, 376, 378, 385, 408, 415, 423, 591, 622, 654, 673, 685, 813, 815, 817
psychics and clairvoyants 181, 299, 300, 301, 302, 675

Quakers 133, 392, 662

raccoon 596
radio and television 167, 231, 269, 319, 527, 625, 671, 721, 772, 802, 823
rape 25, 26, 35, 51, 73, 274, 296, 413, 615, 680, 685, 701
refugees 219, 460, 732
revenge and avenge 25, 42, 50, 66, 191, 296, 382, 393, 418, 438, 458, 733

sadism and cruelty 25, 29, 309, 313, 333, 375, 634, 733, 746, 798, 800, 812
serial killer 92
sex education 198, 490
singers and musicians 61, 63, 81, 117, 142, 246, 273, 320, 342, 357, 404, 414, 438, 464, 494, 625, 637, 671, 673, 674, 685, 700, 706, 707, 729, 735, 748, 761, 817
slavery 268, 578, 792
soccer 68, 173, 226
social class 12, 72, 146, 225, 318, 406, 479, 564, 581, 749, 760
special education and special needs 3, 14, 21, 33, 57, 114, 136, 138, 221, 396, 419, 447, 471, 702
spelling bee 9, 93
submarine 165, 695
substitute teacher 287, 354, 572, 637, 647, 661, 823
suicide 20, 26, 79, 230, 437, 510, 549, 560, 588, 633, 671, 725, 732, 733, 751, 758, 793, 795
superheroes 6, 470, 822
supernatural and séances 19, 177, 181, 188, 225, 267, 288, 299, 300, 301, 302, 347, 351, 437, 455, 614, 659, 675

teachers, retired 2, 121, 326, 345, 371, 428, 463, 656, 688
teachers, unemployed 3, 39, 117
time travel 48
trials *see* courtrooms
tutors 28, 236, 303, 356, 393, 446, 471, 554, 720, 724, 739, 743, 819

urban life 9, 129, 167, 205, 234, 287, 634, 661, 667, 693, 743, 816, 823, 825

vacation and travel 10, 11, 17, 18, 85, 97, 118, 129, 131, 135, 226, 284, 393, 426, 441, 478, 486, 487, 489, 498, 524, 578, 597, 650, 664, 694, 712, 713, 735, 737, 768, 772, 799, 804, 808, 826
vampires 103, 427, 603
Vietnam 734
village life 10, 24, 29, 35, 40, 66, 67, 77, 92, 121, 155, 156, 159, 169, 186, 213, 216, 222, 229, 235, 241, 261, 304, 307, 319, 351, 354, 366, 383, 389, 401, 403, 423, 433, 434, 494, 528, 532, 534, 537, 538, 562, 586, 591, 607, 608, 622, 625, 627, 628, 651, 654, 676, 697, 710, 717, 751, 775, 816, 817, 829
violin 303, 349, 414, 464, 498, 707, 729, 817
volleyball 510

widows and widowers 23, 28, 36, 87, 101, 123, 126, 134, 157, 219, 388, 428, 435, 484, 508, 511, 560, 564, 596, 620, 659, 696, 712, 726, 764, 788, 810
wild west *see* frontier and the west
witches and wizards 19, 186, 222, 299, 300, 301, 302
wolves 10, 448, 668
World War I 272, 523, 532, 582, 601, 695, 736, 780, 788, 821
World War II 17, 42, 47, 56, 165, 200, 202, 216, 219, 224, 238, 281, 334, 475, 528, 532, 582, 604, 683, 732, 829

www.ingramcontent.com/pod-product-compliance
Lightning Source LLC
Chambersburg PA
CBHW032049300426
44116CB00007B/669